New Dimensions in
Investor Relations

New Dimensions in Investor Relations

COMPETING FOR CAPITAL IN THE 21ST CENTURY

Bruce W. Marcus
Sherwood Lee Wallace

John Wiley & Sons, Inc.

New York • Chichester • Weinheim • Brisbane • Singapore • Toronto

Copyright © 1997 by Bruce W. Marcus and Sherwood Lee Wallace.
Published by John Wiley & Sons, Inc.

Library of Congress Cataloging-in-Publication Data:
Marcus, Bruce W., 1925–
    New dimensions in investor relations: competing for capital in the 21st
century / by Bruce W. Marcus and Sherwood Lee Wallace.
        p.   cm.
    Includes index.
    ISBN 0-471-14153-4 (cloth : alk. paper)
    1. Corporations—Investor relations.   I. Wallace, Sherwood Lee.
    II. Title.
    HD2744.M37 1997
    658.4—dc21   97-3288

Printed in the United States of America

10 9 8 7 6

To
Mana, Lucy, and Stefan
and
Lois, Adam, Corey, and David

Contents

Acknowledgments

It would take a very large room indeed to assemble all the people who helped put this book together. The subject keeps expanding, and the more experience we have in investor relations, the more we've come to know how much we need the help, knowledge, and input of others.

Our families, of course, helped, by being tremendously supportive in this arduous effort. Mana Marcus and Stefan Wolff did time at the computer keyboard, as well as a lot of the research. Jonathan Marcus, a genuine Silicon Valley wizard, helped bring perspective to the discussion of the computer industry.

The people at NIRI were particularly helpful, and we offer special thanks to Louis M. Thompson, Jr., William F. Mahoney, and Melissa Jones.

Special help came from Peter Horowitz, National Director of Communications at Price Waterhouse, and some of the accounting staff. Ellen Ringel of Deloitte & Touche contributed substantially. We couldn't have done the publication and public relations section without help from Jennifer Prosek of Jacobs and Prosek and Richard Weiner, and Deborah Brightman Farone and Stephen Friedman (partner and co-chairman of the corporate practice) of Debevoise & Plimpton helped with the SEC chapter. Patrick McKenna and Gerry Riskin of the Edge Group inevitably had much useful to contribute. Len Baker was our primary source of what's new in British and European investor relations. Sid Cato gave us great input. The public relations staffs of Lotus, Microsoft, Symantec, and others were terrific, too. Their puiblic relations firms, Waggener Edstrom and Lois Paul Partners were invaluable. Tami Hees of Lotus Tech support saved many a day. Annie Scully and Mark Haviland, who have handled press for PC Expo for many good years, were an excellent conduit to much of the computer material. Invaluable help came from Catherine Conroy of Donaldson Lufkin Jenrette.

Bernadette Baldino and the staff of the Easton Public Library patiently responded with the right answers to many last minute inquiries. Ken Hoffman of The Optima Group and Michelle Ward contributed useful technical advice and guidance. Ted Pincus graciously gave both time and the fruits of his experience. Debra Young, William Giles, and Theresa Hunter Owens of CompuServe were marvelously helpful. Lisa Slutsky of Bloomberg and Gwyn Summers of PR Newswire were terrific.

The list of investment professionals who helped is very long, but outstanding are Paul Ligon of Mesirow; Larry Udell of Cowen; Charley Potter and Fred Hoffman of Oppenheimer; Jim Kenney of San Jacinto Securities; Eddie Bloomfield of Rausher Pierce; John Doss of Dominick and Dominick; Larry Rader of LAR Management, Bill Witter of William D. Witter, and Jo Anne Barnes of Vestor Securities.

Special thanks to the IRC executives and staff, and especially Gale Strenger, Tom Laughran, Earle Brown, Myrna Dubow, and Senada Gromovic. And honor to Jerry Wallace and the late Paul Wallace.

And speaking of special thanks and honor, without the patience and support of Myles Thompson, Jacqueline Urinyi, Michael Detweiler, Jennifer Pincott, and Pamela van Geissen—all of John Wiley & Sons, you wouldn't be reading this.

Thanks to you all, and to the many more who are omitted only because of space limitations.

Bruce W. Marcus
Sherwood Lee Wallace
Easton, CT, June 1997

Introduction

Revisiting the history of the automobile in its hundredth year (1996), we see an extraordinary and almost magical change in the landscape and structure of our society. The automobile, in its first ten or twelve years, radically altered the way in which we lived.

This phenomenon—this radical change in our society and economy—happened again in this past decade. This time, the computer did it.

In our world, in our society, in our economy, things always change. But not like this. Bounding change. Avalanching change. Kaleidoscopic, massive change.

Never mind the past decade. Just look at what's happened in the past year or two. Significantly, the way we did business yesterday is not the way we'll do business tomorrow. The rate of change is so rapid and so chaotic that it's virtually impossible to adequately anticipate and describe the economic and commercial world in the next decade.

Obviously, investor relations—the process by which we inform and persuade investors of the values inherent in the securities we offer as a means to capitalize business—has also changed dramatically, driven by both technology and the context of the new business environment. So much of what's changing, after all, is in business, finance, and the capital markets, and what indeed is investors relations but a vehicle to the business, finance, and capital markets? And at the heart of investor relations is communications—the vehicle of marketing—which, with the advent of the computer, has also changed radically. That's why so much of this book is devoted to marketing and communications techniques—the contemporary technology, the techniques and skills of access to markets—that pervade all of business today.

This is radical evolution—things change and we respond accordingly.

But now, for many quite specific reasons, evolution has become revolution. The changes are profound, and substantially alter the way we function daily. And this is why we will not do business tomorrow the way we did business yesterday.

What has actually changed, beyond the lip service we pay to the concept of change as a matter of course? What is substantially different, by either evolution or revolution? At least these factors:

- Capital flows and financial instruments. Two factors have substantially changed the capital structure landscape—technology, and real economic expansion, which both requires and supplies more capital.
  - Normal expansion has, over the past decade, resulted in a larger economy, both domestically and internationally. This has required larger infusions of capital, which has also led to developing new investment instruments, from junk bonds to wrap accounts to hedging structures. This growth has, in turn, increased national wealth, feeding more dollars into the economy. Even in those recent years where growth has been slow, growth has been sufficient to change the capital climate and structure. More significantly, we've gone from an economy that focused on getting capital to one that focuses on using capital more productively.
  - The growth in institutional investment has been phenomenal. In 1995, a record $128 billion poured into mutual funds. In just the first four months of 1996, it was $99 billion, which puts it way ahead of the prior year. According to the economist David Hale of Zurich Kemper Investments, "The U.S. is in the midst of creating a whole new financial system in which the mutual fund sector is increasingly displacing commercial banks as the major repositories of wealth, as well as suppliers of capital." Between the 401(k) investment plans, and the aggressive marketing of financial institutions, the financial risk takers are no longer just the professionals. At the beginning of 1997, mutual funds held 13 percent of stock outstanding—up from 7 percent in 1990. Individuals, however, still own slightly more than 50 percent of total equity outstanding. It's the individual investor as well, taking money out of savings and investing in mutual funds and other investment vehicles.

    Technology has substantially changed the way in which we deal with capital and the financial markets. Neural networks and other forms of artificial intelligence, by processing and integrating information instantly, have made more information more useful than ever before by reducing the variables in assessing risk. Today, we invest smarter and more effectively, which further increases wealth and capital. Using contemporary technology, capital flows at electronic speed, crossing both domestic and international borders. Cash as a medium of doing business is becoming almost obsolete, replaced by electronics on every level, from the banks that deal with billions of dollars, to the ordinary consumer, who pays for groceries with a credit card.

- New businesses, based on new technologies, are proliferating at an astonishing rate. According to Richard Breedon, the former chairman of the Securities and Exchange Commission, it's not because our scientists are smarter, he says, ". . . it's because we're creating a system that provides capital more quickly to people willing to take big risks . . . and our economy is reaping the rewards." Venture capitalists add that there are more business opportunities than they can cope with. In 1996 there were a record $104.5 billion in new stock issued in public offerings. IPOs keep making new records. In October, 1996, a new monthly record of 106 IPOs was established, with total market capitalization of $6.3 billion.

- Consulting firms had record revenues in 1996, typical of which was Arthur Andersen with $5 billion.

- The emergence of the computer industry in just the past decade has created a major factor in the economy. This includes not only the many billions of dollars in software and hardware itself, but the ancillary services that supply every industry.

- As the business universe grows, configurations change. In 1995, there were a record $400 billion in merger and acquisition deals. In 1996, 170, 475 new businesses were formed, employing 15 percent more workers than in the prior year. In the prior year, 168,158 new businesses were started, employing fewer people per business (average 4.4) than in 1996 (5.0).

- The internationalization of business that everybody's been talking about for years is finally a reality. Markets for even small companies are increasingly international, and capital crosses borders instantly. In 1996 alone, the flow of U.S. capital abroad exceeded $105 billion. The company we used to call *multinational* is now truly global. For example, can you continue to call a domestically domiciled company that derives more of its revenues from abroad than it does domestically an American company? When Japanese and other Asian products are made here, either entirely or in part, are these American or foreign companies? When a small American manufacturer that doesn't even market outside its own state sells products to the Japanese car manufacturer in his own state, does that border on international commerce? At the same time, all world markets are refocussing, which at least demands new management skills in all companies that want to stay competitive. As third world and iron curtain countries emerge, so too do new markets. And where new markets emerge, so too does new competition arise.

- Investment in Eastern bloc, formerly communist, countries, particularly from the United States, begins to make an impact. While not without problems, whole new investment areas are opening up. And not just in Eastern Europe. In Africa and South America and Asia as well.

- Smarter, more competitive people are entering the workforce. Whether the business schools are turning out better and more skilled managers, or the competition in the workforce is forcing people to learn new skills, or the increase in population is increasing the number of smart people, there seem to be more smart people in business and government than ever before. This accounts for substantial innovation in the way business is done.

- These smart people, plus technological advances, are producing new industrial, professional, and commercial concepts and new levels of productivity. The influx of young people, raised in a computer environment, is invigorating management as never before. More and more, management skills seem to reside in younger people who grew up with the new technology, and with concepts that make traditional corporate cultures at least irrelevant, and probably obsolete. Add to this the influx of management theories from abroad, particularly from Japan, and we have emerging new concepts in management, and new corporate cultures, that are substantially different from their predecessors.

- The emergence of equal opportunity has brought an influx of very bright and competent women and representatives of minority groups. Their contribution has been to significantly expand the core of intelligence and capability within the business community.

- One result of this new intellectual elite in business is a new relationship between employee and employer. Traditional cultures of loyalty between employer and employee have long been eroding because they are counterproductive to both groups. The recent waves of downsizing, in the name of reengineering the corporation, have not only demonstrated this erosion, but have made erosion possible. Today's worker, particularly the knowledge worker, functions on virtually a contractual basis with his or her employer. The contract functions only as long as the agreement is mutually beneficial. Then the worker moves on and the company moves on. This emerging relationship has altered the trade union movement as well, tending to shift the trade union emphasis from increasing compensation to protecting individual rights and benefits in the workplace and making the benefits portable. The shift in emphasis from wages to health care and retirement benefits is a good example.

- The emergence of technology as a major factor in commerce has been profound. What this technology has done goes well beyond the mere electronification of a formerly mechanical process—it's added a new dimension to information processing. A profoundly valid definition of a company is that it's an organism for gathering and processing information to appreciate capital, labor, and raw materials—to convert information into profit. The new technology adds not only speed to the process, but dimension as well. Everything happens faster, which means information is gathered faster, acted on faster, and used more efficiently. This includes information about capital, about markets, about distribution— about every aspect of commerce. This process alone is probably responsible for more changes in the economic environment than any other factor. One example—the fact that the computer is now an executive tool, where the typewriter was a clerical tool. In the financial world, new computer-based techniques, such as investment models using neural networks and other artificial intelligence techniques, are increasingly changing the face of investment analysis. Annual reports now come on CD-ROM, investors learn about companies—including up-to-the-minute financial information—on the Internet, press releases are transmitted by e-mail. The rapid maturity of the computer has substantially altered the way information is transmitted, with changes coming at a breakneck pace.

- Regulatory shifts are not extraordinary, depending upon the political climate of the moment. As of the moment, the trend is strongly anti-regulatory. But more significant in the current trend is the *last straw syndrome*. The regulatory burden seems to be overwhelming, and is finally causing an anti-regulatory reaction that will have an impact for at least a generation. While different administrations will attack or support the regulatory structure one way or another, the overall trend seems to be away from burdensome regulation. For example, it looks as if the antiquated Glass Steagall Act of the 1930s, which kept banks out of the investment business, is finally likely to fall in the foreseeable future. That would be a landmark in regulatory change. There was hardly a raised eyebrow when, at the beginning of 1996, Bankers Trust acquired the brokerage firm, Alex Brown.

- A most profound change is in the erosion of the professional structure. Two major changes are evolving—the cross-pollination of the professions, and the twilight of the partnership as a form of professional firm governance.
  - Increasingly, accounting firms are performing traditional legal initiatives, and law firms are crossing into accounting territory in some practice areas. Both are heavily involved in management consulting. The discrete definitions of law and accounting—and consulting as well—are now blurred.
  - The partnership structure is in rapid decline for three major reasons—the need for professional management; the deleterious effects of partnership paths on firm management and ability to compete; and the need for far greater capital than can be supplied by a partnership. The current structure impedes a professional firm's ability to compete effectively in an increasingly competitive environment.
- And, as a measure of growth in the financial world, the National Investor Relations Institute (NIRI) passed the 3,000 member mark in 1996.

There are, of course, many other economic and cultural reasons why tomorrow's business environment will differ from yesterday's but these reasons are certainly central.

And now, managing change adds a new dimension to the total management process. Managing change has become, it would seem, an industry of its own.

And now, as well, the process we've come to know as investor relations must also change, to function successfully and competitively in this changing world. With a new context for investment information, and with new techniques to impart that information, the emphasis in investor relations changes. Where once the process was a communications function (called financial public relations), and then shifted to a financial function, it now changes again to include a new emphasis on marketing.

Such is the nature of the human condition that we defend the limits of our talents by excluding, and even attempting to diminish, the talents and occupations of others. Investor relations has, for a very long time, been cherished as a complex financial function. Finance is obviously more complex than mere marketing. After all, do marketers normally have to know how to read a balance sheet?

But the reality is that investor relations has *always* been a marketing function. It has *always* been a process of understanding the needs of the target audience, and of casting the information about a company in ways that persuade the investor or investment advisor that a dollar invested in *my* company will appreciate faster than a dollar invested in *somebody else's* company. Call it what you will, but any process that relates a company's product or services—or even cogent information about that company—to the needs of the buyer is *marketing*. And that, in one significant perspective, is what investor relations really is. To pretend otherwise is to put oneself in a poor competitive position.

Until now, the marketing process in investor relations hasn't been adequately dissected and explored. This, as well as utter denial of the realities of the marketing aspects of investor relations, is why marketing in investor relations has never been used with consummate effectiveness. And where the marketing process, under any name (it's not the name that counts—it's the process), has been used effectively, the results have been salutary. The measurement, as always, is in the value of the security by the market, relative to the security's real asset based value. In other words, when the marketing process is effective, and the underlying values are present, the price of the stock goes up—pure and simple.

A major purpose of this book, then, is to revisit the art, the craft, the process of investor relations, particularly as a marketing discipline. This approach becomes particularly cogent today, in view of the dynamic context in which business functions. This view is significant in that the new technology, and the advances in asset analysis, and the changing demands of the investor, and the new investment vehicles, are changing and evolving rapidly. To successfully compete for capital in this highly competitive marketplace requires far greater knowledge of many more disciplines than ever before.

To which must be added the fact that if the means of communication have changed, so too have the techniques of understanding and analyzing the value of a marketable asset changed.

It must be noted here that there is a peculiar phenomenon in information-based products—and securities are exactly that. That phenomenon is that as more information is known, the nature of the product changes to adjust to and accept that information. And then the commodity changes again, requiring more information. Information is light, and as light hits a phototropic object, the object changes, and attracts more light, which again changes the object. So it is with securities. Each new piece of information changes the value of the security, which then requires more and different information.

While this quality of responsiveness to information has always been inherent in a security, the computer, with its incredible ability to supply information at rapid speed, makes the changeability of value more meaningful; more valuable; more accessible. This accounts for the growing acceptance and success of the new theories of analysis, the upgrading of what we once called Modern Portfolio Theory, what we are now able to do with neural networks that supply usable information about a security and its market value in real time. In terms of security analysis, it's the difference between a Piper Cub and a supersonic jet. Not just more speed, but more maneuverability at a greater speed, and the ability to enter a new dimension that had not heretofore been available to ordinary mortals.

And that, too, is what the book is about. How to deal with information that is so fast, so powerful, so abundant, that it alters the nature of the security we are trying to persuade the target market to buy.

Once, the problem was that capital was scarce, and investor relations was a system to help a firm compete for that scarce capital. Today, capital is in great abundance—and lo and behold, the competition for it is still there. Only now, the competition comes from an overload of information, a competition for attention, and recognizing that the capital isn't scarce, but the allocators—the buyers and recommenders to the buyers—are disproportionately fewer than the sellers. The capital isn't scarce—the channels of distribution are overloaded. Investor relations, then, becomes a process of capturing attention by conveying information—faster, better, more clearly—than ever before.

Many of the techniques we describe in the following pages are not new. They are basic and will probably never change, as long as the market for securities stays essentially the same. But those techniques that are rooted in new technology, and the new environment, are very different, and must be learned and accepted if any security is to compete in the new capital market.

Ultimately, the techniques of investor relations are driven by two factors—marketing and the emerging techniques of security analysis and evaluation. Each requires as much artistry as skill. Each requires constant attention, because of the accelerated pace of change.

The goal of this book is to impart the skills, and to engender the artistry.

New Dimensions in
Investor Relations

Chapter 1

The Art and Craft of Investor Relations

It would be dangerously simple, in exploring the skills and techniques of investor relations, to lose sight of its ultimate purpose—to help companies compete in the capital markets. And never doubt that the capital markets are competitive. Each company with publicly traded stock is competing with other companies for the investor's dollar. That competition is won not just by the better company—that helps, of course—but by the company that's better known, better understood, and has done a better job of building investor confidence. The result is measured in increased market value, a stock price that's more relevant to the company's performance, and increased liquidity. Achieving that condition is the objective of the tools of investor relations.

This point can be made no better than it was in an article in *The Wall Street Journal* in October 1996, by Ted Pincus, chairman of The Financial Relations Board.

"When the history of the 20th century stock market is written," said Pincus, "scholars may well identify the openness and candor of modern-day corporate communications as a key factor in renewing and building investor confidence—ultimately leading to the amazingly sustainable buoyancy of the equity market in the '90s."

There is much evidence for this observation, such as the fact that more than 160 million Americans own stock today, compared to only 6 million in

1950. By recent measures, some 62 million investors actively trade securities, 25 million of whom became active in the market in just the four years ending in 1996. Individuals still hold a majority of the outstanding stock, but not by a very great margin. There is clearly a shift, though, from individual direct investment to individual investment in mutual funds, and mutual funds now hold almost twice as much stock as they did in 1990. The Dow Jones Average, which hovered around 1,000 in the mid-1970s, blithely hit 7000 in early 1997, and showed few signs of losing vigor.

Notes Pincus, "The upsurge in investor faith and confidence is due in large measure to the far greater predictability of corporate performance, thanks to the unprecedented flow of corporate communication."

The march toward the realm of ubiquitous stock ownership the past three or four decades has been as fraught with hardship as was Hannibal's drive across the Alps. The obstacles have been corporate ignorance ("we stand on our record"), an uneducated public, both complexity and oversimplification in financial and economic education, inept and naive communications skills, and regulatory lag. Success, for individual public companies, has been achieved where there is imagination and innovation, as well as a clearer understanding of the practices and nuances of the investing community. Investor relations, in its early days, had been primitive. It is not primitive today.

Where investor relations has been—its genesis—is relevant only in the context of the financial community it serves. And in the financial community, the changes have been profound. Where, in its early days, investor relations was a poor adaptation of the basic skills and promotional techniques of public relations, today investor relations is its own science, and its own art form. It's a highly sophisticated blend of technical skill, imaginative and active strategy, and art. Yes, art. It's the art, beyond the craft, of marketing.

What is emerging, as well, is a new role for investor relations—strategic planning. As investor relations professionals become more conversant with the art of share valuation, their input in managing for value becomes more significant. This is another giant step in appreciating the professionalism inherent in investor relations.

The organization that's arisen to serve investor relations professionals— The National Investor Relations Institute (NIRI)—is a model for all professional organizations. It serves its members with a level of technical information and generally appropriate news unmatched in sophistication and value.

Contemporary investor relations is now driven by three overwhelming forces—marketing and its disciplines, the dynamic changes in the financial world, and the communications avenues that serve it. This is a world, after all, in which electronics and the computer have brightened the night and lengthened the day. And in that bright light, everything we are and do looks very different than it did before.

We may not understand all of the dynamics of the current and recent market, nor all the ramifications of the underlying economy. But when so many of the traditional measures of the ebb and flow of the economy, and the stock market that reflects it, become virtually irrelevant, then we know that something new—something different—is happening.

For example, we now have the longest sustained growth in the economy on record, and without the inflation we might reasonably have expected to accompany that growth. Nothing seems to be on the horizon to change that. No dire predictions, and there have been many, seem to have come true. The economy remains vigorous. A battery of economists may whirl and cogitate and prophesy, but so far, no one seems to have come up with an explanation of why this economy is not behaving with historical patterns. Are cycles over? Have we found a way to transcend boom and bust? Is there a new kind of economy? No one seems to have a credible answer.

We do know a few things that are relevant here.

We know that a number of new economic elements have emerged. The switch from an industrial to a knowledge-based and service oriented society, for example, which seems less susceptible to traditional market forces. The increasing education of Americans, which generates new roles, new skills, new jobs, and, if you take a Keynesian view, new markets for goods and services. Have you ever wondered what became of that devoted, skilled secretary your father had? She's now a lawyer or a doctor or a computer programmer, making more money than your father made. And, by the way, she's investing it.

Investing in what? Judging from the statistics, mostly in mutual and pension funds. Or a 401(k). And all that money from those funds, and others, is going back into the economy. There is, indeed, a whole new world of not just investing, but money management. The blue collar worker who, a generation or two ago, had a savings account but no checking account, no debt other than a home or car, and who thought that investing was only for the rich, now has so much money in the market that he's virtually financing his own company and his own job. And a generation ago it was *just* a man, not a woman—yet another significant factor today. If this kind of configuration doesn't alter the nature of the economy, then nothing does. It's not—to paraphrase a popular ad—your father's economy.

In early 1997, the prestigious and aloof Wall Street investment banking firm, Morgan Stanley, merged with that down-to-earth stock flogger, Dean Witter, with its more than 8,000 brokers. The result was not just a large firm, but a new kind of competitive animal—the new kind of financial services firm of which Merrill Lynch was a forerunner. One-stop financial services—investing, banking, insurance, financial planning, and who knows what else. It's predicted that either Glass Steagall will finally fall, leaving banks free to move into investing, or the traditional bank will become redundant, to be superseded by this new kind of emerging financial services organization.

The shifting weight of the market to institutions is in itself a telling phenomenon. What it tells us is that the general investing public is now very much a part of the institution—the very one that was once available to only very private money. There are now more than 6,000 mutual funds, most of which are home to some very small investors. These funds, by the way, are also changing the face of corporate governance. Where once an institution would merely sell its stock in companies it no longer liked, today's institution is different. Recognizing the power of its holdings, the fund now uses that power to lean on management. It shifts, then, the emphasis of management from one that, in other times, paid little heed to shareholders to one that recognizes that the power lies not in the office suite, but in the mind of the shareholder. Shareholder democracy takes on new meaning.

The emerging power of institutions cannot long be expected to be ancillary to the market. One need only look at CalPers—the California Public Employees' Retirement Fund. With $108 billion under management, it produces a "report card" of underperforming corporations that strikes terror into the hearts of the world's largest corporations. It has forced such companies as Apple, Reebok, IBM, and Sears, Roebuck to do a better job for their shareholders. When institutions like CalPers—and their number and size are increasing—speak, it reverberates through the bones of corporate leaders.

It must be a great act, because everybody wants to get into it. Accounting firms, long proscribed from such activities, are now selling mutual funds, as part of their personal financial planning operations. They're forming alliances with brokerage firms and mutual fund managers.

With this new audience, and the increased competition for its attention—much less its investment dollar—sophisticated management now begins to see the efficacy of traditional marketing practices. Not just the traditional tools of investor relations, but thoughtful and original marketing programs.

The rule is simple—when everybody is doing the same things in the same way, nobody stands out, and nobody gets more attention than anybody else. That's hardly a competitive device. Only by doing it differently, by doing it better, can marketing succeed.

At the same time, today's marketer has available more tools, and more skills than ever before. There are better ways to understand the target market—the investor. There are better ways to get feedback from that investor, and to understand what he or she really wants or needs. There are better ways to communicate to that investor, or potential investor.

The data bases available today are astonishing. You can know your investor not only better, but faster. You can communicate with your investor faster, and get instant reaction and feedback. With the computer, it's a new game. The only problem is that technology and its uses are changing so quickly that what was avant-garde yesterday is obsolete today. You have to stay on top of it, because your competitor is.

Clearly, the financial landscape is changing. And so too are the roads to this new landscape changing.

In just the past decade, techniques of security analysis and evaluation have made profound advances. The stock market may still be an auction market, with all of the uncertainty and unpredictability of the auction market, but new mathematical skills and techniques, aided by computers, continue to diminish the variables that impede predictability. We are gaining on the secrets of chance and self-fulfilling prophecies, although the certainty we seek on stock market prognostication continues to elude us.

In just the past decade, perceptions of the investor have changed substantially, and so, therefore, have the skills needed to address the investor changed. If you were simply selling a stock, then all manners of persuasion might be useful. But in establishing a relationship between the ultimate investor and the company, which is what competition for capital has brought us to, the primitive skills of earlier investor relations practice are simply not enough. Today, the dynamics of even the smallest company preclude simplistic solutions.

The computer drives much of the change in the relationships between the seller of securities and the buyer of securities. No dynamic in history has accelerated at so great a pace, nor affected the world so profoundly so fast, one could safely wager, than has the computer. As a calculator, the computer has transcended everything we've always felt about or believed about the limits of calculation. It is not just fast, it brings a new dimension to understanding underlying facts.

As a communications device, making more information available to more people than ever before, the computer has changed the foundation for knowing and understanding. Not changed, really—transformed. The most casual investor today has access to more information than the most sophisticated investor had not much more than a decade ago. And faster, too.

When a company's financial data was recorded by hand, each financial statement was a point in time that froze the picture of the company. The balance sheet as of December 31 was not the balance sheet of January 2, but how could the change be recorded? By the time the information was written, printed, and disseminated, it was obsolete. Not so today, with the computer. Information can, if you like, be recorded and disseminated in real time. The days of the static view may well be over, which means new ways to look at companies.

One result of the force of the computer in this context is that where once information was a tool, now it can be a weapon as well. If information is the foundation of investment decisions, as has long been known, then how are investment decisions made when almost everybody has access to the same information at the same time? If information bombards us at so rapid a pace, doesn't it change the nature of the subject of the information as well, thereby requiring new and different information? It's a new paradigm—one that substantially alters the practice of investor relations. In one sense, computers have eroded cherished traditions. Off-board and 24 hour trading is increasing, both in the size and number of trades. There are now SEC guidelines that support online initial public offerings, which would have been unthinkable a few years ago.

Still, some basic simplicities are still relevant, even when they are cloaked in futuristic garb. For example, in considering the strategies of investor relations, it's extremely important to remember that the ultimate aim of the process is to use every legitimate means of communication to impart the values of a firm to the prospective investor. The techniques to achieve this aim may be infinitely more than a simple public relations process, although the tools of public relations—and certainly the communications skills—are an inherent part of achieving the aim, but the basic aim is the same.

At the same time, we are learning, in this new communications realm, that more is not better. Better is better.

And so the brave new world of computers and scientific financial analysis and sophisticated marketing may embrace and sometimes overwhelm the traditional principles and objectives of investor relations, but they go to the same objective—to impart the sense of real or potential shareholder value.

The role of marketing in investor relations has changed as well, as have the techniques of marketing. Where once the relationship between the company and its investors or potential investors was maintained almost entirely with basic tools—the analyst meeting, the shareholders meeting, the annual report, the press release—today the concepts of contemporary marketing, driven by the needs and desires of the market and not by the wishes of the company—alter the techniques used. More is known, and sought to be known, about the prospective investor, so that information can be more relevant to the investor's needs. Where once the pertinent information about a company was made available either reluctantly or using primitive communications devices, today the identified potential investor is pursued with a variety of devices, from Web pages to e-mail. Contemporary investor relations can mean an assiduous attempt to penetrate the consciousness of the investor. Electronic persuasion is not simple pleading for attention. It can be a driving attack on the mind and emotions. But where earlier attacks were rare and random, today they are targeted. We can know more about our target, and tailor our information to that target, and get the information out there—effectively and cost effectively.

And all this in the past few years.

How has this new paradigm affected and changed the stock buyer—the investor—and the seller—the company?

Competing for Capital

There is a basic reality that transcends the mere mechanics of investor relations.

Some years ago, James J. Needham, a former chairman of the New York Stock Exchange (NYSE), put it, "Even if the equities markets are called upon to supply no more than 10 to 15 percent of the total, we will be asking American investors to pony up an amount roughly equivalent to the entire present federal debt to keep U.S. business moving forward during the next ten years!" Ten years later, it's still true, particularly in this remarkably new thriving economy.

It's also true that the drive for capital for American and international business, most of which must come from equities, is at least a finite pool. Except for proportions—in recent years more than half of corporate capital comes from equity—that, too, hasn't changed. If no more than a portion of the total of American capital comes from equity, the major portion of the remainder of the capital needed to run even a moderate-sized company must come from either debt or retained earnings (real, not inflated). It must be noted that the profits from which come retained earnings are also the source of dividends. This distribution of earnings becomes an investor relations problem, incidentally, because shareholders must then be made to understand the balance between profits to be distributed and the need for profits to be reinvested. Thus, the case for more aggressive marketing as an investor relations discipline becomes even more compelling than ever before.

In earlier years, even in times when investor relations was simple communication, we knew that it contributed substantially by virtue of its ability to expose information and to focus attention on a company.

During the past three decades, we've had an opportunity to see investor relations function under a large number of conditions. We've had several business cycles. We've had recessions, profound inflation, and stagflation. We've had massive shifts of capital, new European economic configurations, and perfidy on Wall Street. We've seen virtually every possible event that could attack the market, other than another world war and another bone-crushing, 1929-style depression.

We've seen staggering inflation and remarkable stability. We've seen as well new industries emerge and overwhelm the economy, and once glamorous industries, such as steel, decline, or emerge as mini-industries. And through it all, the need for capital has relentlessly grown, and the role of investor relations has grown—its value proven again and again.

Equity Capital

While it's true that the equities market supplies only a portion of the total capital needed by corporations, its contribution to total capital formation is infinitely greater than just its dollar value. First of all, the contribution by equity represents a significant segment of the total capital formation in terms of the way it's used. It acts more often as a base for all of the financing. Equity capital most frequently represents the capital used for significant growth or expansion. At the time it's acquired (and aside from some of the ancillary reasons for going public, such as the personal needs of individual owners, capitalizing on personal assets in a rising stock market, etc.), it's usually used to move a company from one level of operation to another. While normal operational growth can frequently be financed from retained earnings, equity capital is used for the spurt; for the significant expansion of either operations or markets; for the acquisition program that sharply increases the size of a company. Moreover, equity capital belongs to the company. It's not subject to credit crunch, nor is it a drain on cash flow.

Second, a company moving from the private into the public market finds itself with a visibility that enhances its access to other sources of capital—banks, private investors, larger debt issues and so on.

Third, a public company is a regulated company, which implies that because its operations are publicly observed there must therefore be greater credibility in its financial reporting.

To the lender—banks, institutions and private investors—this implication of credibility also enhances the sense of stability about a company and makes it a more attractive investment vehicle.

It's assumed that the local bank extends its line of credit solely on the evaluation of financial statements. Unfortunately, and to the surprise of many a corporate executive, this is not universally and forever true. It becomes less true when the prime rate goes up and as the amount of money available from an institution goes down. Even granting the primacy of the balance sheet, the lending committee of any bank must make a final decision predicated upon an assessment of intangible factors—off-balance sheet factors that indicate a company's ultimate ability not simply to repay a loan but to maintain an ongoing strength. To more and more banks, the lessons of corporate decline and takeovers of recent years have become abundantly clear.

Foreign Capital

Capital from nondomestic sources, once an anomaly, is now a given. With the aid of electronics, capital travels around the world instantaneously and comfortably. It adds a capital pool that quickly and easily loses national identity—except that it must be wooed as if it were domestic. Another dimension for investor relations.

Without considering the argument of whether or not the Japanese or the Germans or the English own too much of America, the reality is that offshore money readily follows our market, including the tide of interest rates, the Dow Jones average, and real estate values. The last two decades have seen massive infusions of foreign capital into U.S. business, including substantial changes of corporate ownership. For the company seeking capital, this may be perceived as an opportunity, just as for the susceptible company it's seen as a danger.

And so the mere size of the contribution of equity to the total capital structure belies its actual effectiveness. A corporation's position in the equity market is of far greater importance to the financial community's total view of the company than may be surmised from the proportion of equity to other financing. It is for this, as much as any other reason, that the prime concern of an investor relations program never strays far from its focus on the equities market.

And the debt market, once able to be taken for granted because interest rates were generally stable, is now more susceptible to the ministrations of investor relations than ever before. Fluctuating interest rates have added a new dimension to the debt market, as have new debt instruments. Reliance on the rating service alone is no longer the rule, and while the nature of investor relations in the debt market tends to be different than in equities, more communication than ever is clearly prescribed.

As for the "current market," it is best viewed as the current in a river—always in motion.

The Stock Market

The market is always the current market. It doesn't matter that it was once better or worse, or even that it will ultimately be better or worse. The needs of the public corporation—immediate, near-term and far-term—must constantly be faced, regardless of the Dow Jones average at any given moment.

The stock market, for all its mystique, for all its implied wisdom by virtue of its self-imposed notion of fiduciary concern, is a vast, complex, and cumbersome structure. It is made even more so by the advent of technology, in which information and action flow and occur at a far greater rate than ever before. At best, it too often reflects not considered individual opinion predicated upon wise, conservative insights, but rather scantily masked emotional reaction. It is an auction market and functions like one. Stock market values rarely bear a one-to-one relationship to facts, so much as they reflect an over-reaction or an under-reaction to the news at any given moment, or to a dream of possibilities of the future. It has, in recent years, been so perverse that it falls on good news and rises on bad news, presumably out of fear that good economic news will fuel inflation.

This is made even more complex by the ongoing, and sometimes successful, attempts to fathom the underlying factors that control the way the market reacts to events and circumstances. New theories, again aided by the computer, proliferate daily, and some of them even contribute valid information. What it does, nevertheless, is complicate—not simplify—the relationship between the investor and the market; between the corporation and the investor. And as we shall see further on, the diverse theories add varying degrees of spice to investor relations.

In viewing the stock market in this context, one other observation must be made. There's a tendency to view the market not in the perspective of the individual companies that comprise it, but as a whole. Stock market movement is reported in terms of an average: the Dow Jones average, the Standard & Poor's index, the NASDAQ index, the New York Stock Exchange average price per share. It must be recognized, surely, that while these averages in a down market represent more stocks whose prices go down than up, there are stocks whose prices go up or remain stable. This is a significant point in considering the possibility of upside performance in a down market for a successful company.

For the individual corporation, viewing the possibility of improving the performance of its own stock in even the worst of the markets, certain basic facts must be recognized:

- Regardless of the price of a stock at any given moment, or the low to which the Dow Jones average—or any other average—may sink at any moment, there is still a market. It opens every morning and it closes every night. Granted, volume may diminish sharply, but liquidity—or at least the structure for liquidity—still exists.
- The number of firms in the securities industry fluctuates rapidly and wildly. But the industry doesn't cease to exist, even in the worst of times. Despite some severe economic downturns, and profound securities industry shakeups, the number of firms doing business in the securities industry went from 4,470 in 1970 to 9,021 by the end of the 1980s. The number of security analysts, those people responsible for analyzing a public corporation's potential for success in the stock market, went from as many as 15,000 in 1971 to 17,000 by the end of the 1980s. In 1997, with the increase in pension fund management and other institutional analysts, there are almost 23,000 analysts registered with the Financial Analysts Federation. By the end of the 1980s, there were 32,000 stock brokers. Today—reflecting the new economic environment—there are more than 74,000 brokers.

The structure of the securities industry in all aspects is now in its greatest state of flux since the stock market began in the 1700s under the Buttonwood tree on what is now Broad Street, but it still hasn't departed from its basic occupation of buying and selling securities. Institutions now seem to control the greatest thrust of stock trading—some 80 percent of daily trading is now institutional—with institutional assets, both pension assets and mutual funds, now in excess of $6 trillion. Pension funds alone hold about a quarter of all U.S. stocks, half of the stock traded on the New York Stock Exchange, and 65 percent of the Standard and Poor's (S & P) 500. Furthermore, it must be recognized that institutional decisions about a stock are theoretically predicated, to a large degree, upon the company's performance over years, plus the prognosis for that stock's ability to appreciate in market price. Not the same thing. In an auction market, liquidity—the ease with which a stock can be sold or purchased—is a major factor that greatly determines the increase in stock price. The institutions themselves must face the reality of destroying the liquidity of their own holdings. If their purchases go too far into the total number of shares available for trading, it's like killing the goose that lays the golden egg. The Securities and Exchange Commission (SEC) Rule 144a, which allows stock to be issued directly to institutions without being traded by the public, may ease the pressure on publicly traded stock, but probably not for a long time, if at all.

As the securities industry changes, internal structures for evaluating, buying, and selling securities change. The simple separation of power to analyze, recommend, buy, or sell a security is no longer simple, as will be shown in the next chapter. Now the research analyst, who went from lowly statistician to exalted status as a market prognostication superstar, is challenged by brokers, traders, money managers and others. Large firms like Merrill Lynch, which for years have had large research staffs that were relatively insulated from other segments of the securities industry, changed their operations by adding top-notch industry specialists, and analysts who can double as institutional salespeople. And as brokerage houses attempt to reduce costs by reducing research departments, a greater burden for research falls upon brokers and traders. The picture changes. The old ways and the old approaches no longer apply.

With computers to crunch facts faster than a speeding bullet; with databases regurgitating facts like the sorcerer's apprentice; with online trading tapes to input in real-time, information means different things than it once did. Analytic theories abound that would boggle the minds of Messrs. Graham and Dodd.

The focus of purchasing power continually shifts. When conditions in our capital markets—such as interest rates—warrant advantages to bankers abroad, capital flows from Europe and the Far East to the United States on computerized wings. The market never wants for massive blocks of capital, although the currency may be from strange presses.

What it comes down to is that the equities market is changing, shifting, and growing. And, so long as it merely exists, there is a necessity—as well as an opportunity—to represent and advocate the corporation to the market, not only to maintain that level of visibility necessary for success in all aspects of the capital market, but as a responsibility to shareholders as well.

The Rationale for Investor Relations

In view of the current structure of the capital markets—its changed configurations, its new sources and velocity of capital, what precisely is the rationale, and what are the techniques, for an investor relations program?

Both a bull market and a bear market have one thing in common. They are both markets, regardless of texture, regardless of the volume. Shares of stock are still bought and sold, and money from other sources is still being invested and lent. Under any circumstances, this capital must be competed for against hundreds—thousands—of other corporations.

If a corporation of any size has need for capital beyond its own cash flow, it must be prepared to compete for that capital.

In order to compete successfully for that capital, any corporation must be prepared to demonstrate—clearly, forcefully, honestly, and skillfully—those factors about itself that indicate that an investment in it is warranted.

Furthermore, the marketing effort in the capital markets is very much like a hoop—it keeps rolling only as long as you keep hitting it with a stick. The minute you stop, the hoop stops and falls over.

Nor can it be assumed that a company's record will speak for itself. True, there are rare occasions when a company's superior performance is discovered, recognized, and rewarded in the marketplace. But for each such company there are dozens of companies whose presidents moan in frustration that the price of their stock in no way reflects the company's performance. Under the best of circumstances nobody is watching. Under the worst of circumstances there is a lethargy and a suspicion that precludes the independent investigation that might turn up a corporate gem and follow it, quarter by quarter, through superior performance.

Moreover, the printed record is only half the story. It merely demonstrates where the company has been—not where it's going. Nor does it ever adequately expose the management team—the people who made the record possible and upon whom the investor must depend to sustain the record.

An extraordinary study done a few years ago showed a direct relationship between investor relations activity and coverage by the financial community. Using membership in the National Investor Relations Institute (NIRI) as a valid assumption of investor relations activity, the study discovered that companies with NIRI members on staff have more analysts following their stock than do companies without NIRI members (and therefore, it may be assumed, without formal investor relations programs). It was also discovered that the greater the number of analysts following a company, the higher its price/earnings ratio. According to a report of the study in the NIRI publication, *Investor Relations Update,* an attempt was made to determine through regression analysis whether other factors—profit margins, better returns on assets, superior growth, etc. might account for the results of the study. This analysis offered no other explanation than the investor relations program.

One of the most compelling reasons for an intensive financial relations program during a down market—as well as during an up market—lies in the basic nature of security analysis itself. The greatest part of analysis is based upon intangible and unmeasurable factors, such as management and the company's ability to plan and meet its objectives. The more precisely and clearly the elements that define these intangibles are projected, the more readily the company's ability to appreciate the invested dollar will be understood. The more readily this ability is understood, the more likely the acceptance—and investment—by a financial community that discounts for the unknown—the risk.

The Aims of Investor Relations

Essentially, the successful investor relations program seeks to demonstrate three basic things. It's true that security analysis and the attempts to judge a company's ability to succeed in the future depend upon an extraordinarily complex structure of characteristics, but still they all evolve to three basic points:

- Earnings and other measures of financial soundness
- Management
- Plans

Earnings, cash flow, and sound financial structure are, after all, what a corporation is all about. They represent the return on the investment. They signify the company's ability to succeed as a corporation. But at best, earnings, and even cash flow at any given moment, constitute only a small portion of the measure of a company's viability, and they demonstrate not the near future but the immediate past. If earnings and financial performance were the sole measure of a company's performance, there would be no auction market. It would all be done by computer. One could very well have bought the stock of a buggy whip manufacturer in its last great year before the invention of the automobile. What's more to the point is not just the earnings record of a company, nor even the consistency of its positive cash flow and earnings growth. It's the degree to which the pattern of financial performance demonstrates the ability of the company to continue to earn that must be projected. It's the degree to which financial performance and other factors contribute value to the company and its securities.

Second is management. A corporation may by definition have a perpetual life, but its ability to operate successfully is a function of its management during the tenure of the individual managers. This is as true of a $2 million company as it is of Microsoft, for all its vast size and greatness. If, during the next few years, Bill Gates, the president of Microsoft, makes a decision about the computer industry that differs from his predecessors, it will alter the entire structure of Microsoft—and perhaps the entire computer industry—for many generations to come. And what is it that must be projected about management? Not just the skill, intelligence, vigor, and clear-sightedness of its officers, but its ability to see the company, the industry, and the economy clearly. It's the ability of the management team to deal with the day-by-day problems of the company, and its ability to develop and implement realistic long-range plans. It's the ability to fathom all aspects of management—operations, administration, production, marketing, distribution, finance. It's the ability to deal with contingencies in changing situations. Is the management that brought the company from $10 to $50 million in volume capable of dealing with the same company when its volume reaches $100 million, and therefore with an entirely new set of problems?

Third is plans. Not just what the company is going to do tomorrow or five years from now, but rather its long range strategic programs. Where is it going? What are its objectives—long, medium, and short range? How does it mean to finance its plans? Are its plans realistic in terms of the industry, the market, the economy, management's abilities, and the company's financial condition?

When all of the elements about a corporation that can possibly be compiled in these three categories are projected and understood by the financial community, and when they are projected believably and consistently, then that company can expect to compete successfully in the capital markets. In fact, there is a premium that accrues to predictability.

Measuring Investor Relations Performance

And how is success in a financial relations program measured?

It is measured in a feedback of knowledge and understanding about a company and its management by those segments of the financial community that are most important to that corporation.

It is reflected in the relative ease with which a corporation can deal with the capital markets, ranging from banks to the equities market.

It is reflected in a realistic price/earnings (P/E) or price/cash flow ratio (P/CF), in relation to the overall average P/E or P/CF ratio of the stock market in any given time and, more significantly, a corporation's own industry.

It is reflected in increased liquidity—the comparative ease with which sellers find buyers and buyers find sellers, even in a sparse market, and in increased trading activity.

It is measured in the increased valuation of a company's securities in the market.

It is reflected in increased and enthusiastic sponsorship and more market makers and supporters, and, if appropriate, in geographic distribution of the issue.

Assuming a clear and honest reason to believe that the corporation's efforts are leading ultimately to success and greater profitability, there is no better way that a company can compete successfully in all aspects of the capital market other than through an intelligently designed and skillfully executed financial relations program. As any modern business person knows, the theory of the better mousetrap no longer functions in a complex competitive economy.

Not to be overlooked is the fact that investor relations has itself contributed to its own process.

Investor relations is now a mature practice, where once it was done tentatively by a handful of enlightened corporations. The investor relations practitioner, once a public relations person with enhanced and interesting responsibilities, is now a sophisticated and well-trained financial practitioner with skills in communication and marketing.

This was an almost inevitable change caused by a number of factors:

• The market itself became considerably more complex, requiring more financial training and skill than could be found even in the above average public relations practitioner. And while in earlier days there were indeed some retread security analysts brought into investor relations, early investor relations practice was still considered a slightly recast public relations person's domain.

• Competition for capital, and for the attention of the capital markets, increased tremendously. This meant that investor relations became a frank marketing function as much as a financial function. And so all of the elements of marketing came into play. Essentially these elements are:

    • *Know your market.* This means understanding who your best prospective buyers are, what they really want to know, and what they are looking for in terms of investment opportunities.

    • *Know your product.* This means knowing every aspect, and every perspective of that aspect, of what your corporation has to offer the investor.

    • *Know your tools.* These are the tools of marketing—including those of both communications and finance.

    • *Manage your tools.* This is the actual marketing effort, in which strategy is fulfilled by skillfully and imaginatively using the tools of marketing.

As in any competitive situation, the competition for attention bred new techniques and honed the old ones. Where once investor relations was a matter of press releases, shareholder reports and analyst meetings, it's now a much broader array of skills, techniques, and strategies, which is what this book is about.

At the same time the practice of investor relations has made its contribution to shaping the market.

Effective competition works that way. As more imagination is put into play to compete, more imagination is needed by other competitors. The result has been that in the past few years investor relations has helped to shape the market by:

• Popularizing higher standards on the kinds of information necessarily disseminated to the financial community. Better formats for shareholder reports; more informative press releases; better written and oral communication between investor relations specialists, their managements, and the financial community, and so forth.

• Making market research a standard tool in investor relations. Analysis of prospective markets for a company's securities has become intensive and sophisticated, going more deeply into motivation and investment needs than ever before. Today, the market functions on more knowledge about itself than it has ever had. Investment analysis by investors is virtually matched by analysis of the investors themselves

• Improving communications techniques, in which information is moved from the company to the investor, have not only improved but have become standardized. Today's investor lives by the computer, which means rapid input of information; rapid action in investing. Printed material is proliferating. Advertising is used more effectively. Shareholder lists are played like violins.

And so where once investor relations was a useful tool applied by some very bright company managers and their equally capable investor relations agents, it's now an integral part of the investment process itself—a primary pipeline of information that's at the very heart of the investment process.

There has been very little revolution—and much evolution—that bred this new world. Now, it behooves the company that must compete for capital to learn to navigate in its many new dimensions.

Chapter 2

The Marketing Approach

O f the many aspects of investor relations that contribute to its success, none is more central than the process behind the word *relations*. It is a function of one group—the purveyors of a concept—establishing a relationship with another group—the investors in the securities behind that concept. The process uses a number of specific strategies, devices, skills, and practices that communicate, educate, and ultimately persuade the investor that a dollar invested in one company will appreciate faster and better than a dollar invested in another company. This process—establishing a relationship between purveyor and investor—is called marketing, and its principles are too often ignored in the normal practice of investor relations.

The principles of marketing, especially in the context of investor relations, are simple to define. The art of marketing may be yet another matter.

But the art of marketing, perhaps like any other art, begins with the principles. If the principles of any art are not understood, then the road to artistry is especially tortuous.

Marketing is a terrible word. It's like a Rorschach ink blot. It means different things to different people. To some, it's selling or advertising, or direct mail, or any of the tools or devices of marketing, all of which are anathema to some people. To others, it's an arcane complex of activities that attempt to fathom the unconscious mind of the consumer. What marketing is *not* is any one of its tools.

In fact, marketing is a *process*, and if you recognize that, then you don't have to be concerned with what the process is called. The tools—selling, advertising, literature, press releases, and so forth—are simply the means to make the process work.

Marketing is the process that brings what you have to offer to the people who can most benefit from owning or using what you have to offer.

It's a process that's useful in investor relations because it most effectively helps you compete in the capital markets—and the competition for the investment dollar is fierce. That competition can be won only through careful use of marketing techniques.

It is a relationship between the seller and the potential buyer, whether you're marketing a vacuum cleaner or an investment. What you're marketing, however, colors the process—not the principles—of the marketing practice. The principles used in selling a vacuum cleaner differ from those used in selling an investment or a professional service.

There are three basic factors to consider.

The first and most immutable factor is that all marketing—product, service, investment—begins and ends with the market itself. No economic relationship between any two groups in which one group is trying to persuade another group to act, no matter what the purpose, exists without functioning under that fiat. The process always begins and ends with the market itself.

The second factor always to be kept in mind, is that people *buy* what they need. They are *sold* what they can be persuaded they need.

The third factor, perhaps more significant, is that when you sell a product, the product stays and you leave, which is why product selling techniques focus on the product, and why mass marketing techniques work so well for products. When you sell a service, on the other hand, you stay to perform that service.

And since an investment has more of the characteristics of the service than the product, the principles that guide service marketing are more relevant than those that guide product marketing.

Is an investment a service rather than a product? After all, the investor ultimately owns shares of stock (or any investment vehicle) in a company, and that's certainly as tangible as a product.

But a product stays the same. Go look in your closet. The vacuum cleaner you bought last year is still the same vacuum cleaner today. But is the stock you bought yesterday still the same today? Is the price the same? Is the company behind it the same? Are the underlying values of the company, its management, its markets, its inventories, all still the same? Of course not.

An investment, like a professional service, is constantly changing, and so, therefore, is the relationship between the provider and the consumer constantly changing.

And this is why the marketing practices in investor relations are specific to investor relations, and not to products.

What Is a Market?

The term *market* is used rather more broadly than is useful in devising a strategy to reach it. In fact, a market, in this context, is a group of people or organizations that:

- Can be defined by common or mutual characteristics, even allowing for variations
- Have in common a need or use for a particular product or service
- Can benefit from a particular product or service—or can be persuaded that such benefit exists
- Can be reached effectively and economically by comprehensive media

In investor relations, the broader market is, of course, the investor, or those who advise and guide investors. They are the ones who must be educated and persuaded of the advantages of a specific company and its securities.

But within that broad category are the subgroups—the *segments*—of people or institutions whose needs are rather more focused or specialized. The interest of each of these segments may differ sufficiently to warrant different kinds of information, and different kinds of appeals. Understanding this concept of markets is crucial to understanding the value of the marketing approach to investor relations.

In rather more specific terms, the target markets for an investor relations campaign might be buy or sell side analysts, mutual funds, money managers, high asset individuals, retail brokers, hedge funds, and various institutions defined by such preferences as market size requirements, portfolio turnover, investment time horizons, and so forth. In the age of the computer, these categories, as may be seen in Chapter 3, range from the obvious to the arcane. For example, an increasing number of analysts now use neural network computer models to determine portfolio composition. Each of these markets has specific requirements for the investments it purchases, the timing of the purchases, the length of time and criteria for holding, and so forth—all of which must be understood for successful targeting in investor relations marketing.

The Marketing Process

The marketing process itself consists of four basic elements:

- *Understand your market.* This means being able to define it not just in terms of its demographics or characteristics, but in terms of its needs and desires—its ability to benefit from what you have to offer.
- *Understand your product or service.* In investor relations, this means more than understanding the basic facts about your company and its asset values—it means understanding its value as an investment to a specific market or group of markets.
- *Understand your tools.* This is the craft of marketing. In investor relations, this is the spectrum of investor relations practices delineated in this book, from shareholder communications to knowing the practices and techniques of security analysis to dealing with the financial press. These are the tools of investor relations. They are, as well, the tools of marketing.
- *Manage your tools.* If you understand your markets and how your company and its securities relate to those markets, and you understand the tools of marketing available to you, then you must manage the process by using the tools of marketing effectively; by strategizing thoughtfully and executing the process assiduously.

Understanding Your Market

The strategy of the investor relations campaign, as you will see in the next chapter, depends to a large extent on being sufficiently flexible and adroit to react to changes in the securities market. Even for the smallest company, there is rarely a single large market for a security; rather, there are several target groups. Each of these groups is dynamic.

For example, during the glorious days of computer stocks, the early 1990s, an appropriate target for computer company stocks was the mutual fund specializing in high tech securities. But as the price of chips and other computer parts dropped sharply, and competition increased, margins began dropping. So too did the price of computer stocks decline. The market for sellers of computer stocks, then, shifted from the mutual funds to investors and funds who were willing to buy low and wait the long term for the category to change.

To try to sell a security to the wrong prospective buyer is expensive and wasteful, particularly when the range of tastes for securities covers virtually every kind of company and every kind of industry. The market options are unlimited, and it's certainly worth the effort to learn, to research, to explore, to be discerning. It pays off.

It pays, too, to be vigilant. Markets change constantly. Companies change constantly. Investor relations is no longer the passive game it might once have been.

For the vigilant investor relations practitioner, the sources of information about markets are multifarious. For example, they include:

• The stock market itself. As arcane as it may be, the stock market sends a message virtually every hour. It is at one and the same time reactive and predictive—a seeming paradox, but possible because of its size and the diversity of its participants. It reacts to the events of the day, both business and nonbusiness; both economic and political. It anticipates the future, however accurately or inaccurately—inflation that may come as a result of increasing jobs, the shortage of commodities generated by war or weather, the potential effect of political change on regulatory matters. It's responsive to psychological quirks and rumors. But it's the rare security that isn't responsive to some degree to the exigencies of the stock or bond market. Read the tape. It tells you a lot.

• Industry news, as seen in the general press and trade journals, will tell you a lot about the changes in each industry. This allows you to determine the market perceptions of stocks in your industry.

• The business press, which reports on institutional buying, as well as industry and market trends.

• Financial newsletters, which despite their unreliability as stock market forecasters, do have reliable information on what investors are buying, including institutions.

• Securities industry publications, such as *The Journal of the Financial Analysts Federation, Research Magazine, Registered Rep Magazine*, and *Buyside Magazine*.

• The market research organizations, such as Morningstar, Technimetrics, CDA Investment Technologies, and independent consultants such as T.R. Dawson in London

• Directories of analysts' societies, including industry splinter groups

- Your own lists, developed from your own contacts and experience, and from lists of current and former shareholders
- Databases available from the Internet, and from suppliers such as CompuServe, America Online, and The Microsoft Network
- Mailing lists purchased from mailing list houses

When a market is defined, it must be monitored. Markets change, fund objectives change, and investor needs change. To provide today's information to yesterday's market is expensive, wasteful, and ineffective.

Understand Your Product or Service

You may know a great deal about your company's products or services, and the market for them. But for effective investor relations, what you are offering to investors is the promise of return on investment. This promise is measured in those factors that project the values underlying the securities you're selling. It is defined by those factors, delineated in the following chapters, that demonstrate investment values, such as financial performance, quality of management, industry, economic projections, long range plans and their viability, and so forth.

But in a marketing context, this information must be packaged and presented in formats that are acceptable to, and understandable by, the target audiences. Which is not to say that the information can be exaggerated, or that it can misrepresent reality. The word *image*, which springs to mind at this point, should be as readily expunged. The word *image* implies that the perception of reality can be made rosier by manipulating symbols. This is a myth. The acoustics of Wall Street are too good, and what you are will speak so loudly that no one will hear what you say you are.

If you don't like the way in which your market perceives you, you can't change that perception by manipulating symbols. You have to change the reality.

You can, however, give yourself a competitive advantage in the way in which you present the reality—how you define your company, how you position it in the marketplace, how you project and deliver this information to shareholders and prospective shareholders.

Understanding your company, then, means understanding it in terms of the target market for your securities, not for your products or services.

Understand Your Tools

The tools of marketing in investor relations are those that define the values that underlie the security, and that project those values to the target audiences. In the following chapters, those tools are defined and detailed.

Manage Your Tools

The tools of investor relations, when used in a marketing context, must be managed both strategically and tactically.

Managing the elements of an investor relations program effectively is crucial to the success of the program, and to meeting its objectives. Subsequent chapters define both these aspects of investor relations in greater detail. We note here, though, that part of the success of any investor related program lies in defining objectives. What do you want the program to accomplish? With whom, and in what time frame?

Understanding these elements of marketing form the foundation for successfully marketing your securities to your target audiences. But important as well is how you focus and present your message—how you position yourself to your target audiences.

Positioning

There is no great mystique to the marketing concept of *positioning*. While it's not as simple as some would make it seem, nor as complex as others would have you believe, it's still very real.

Like so many words used in marketing, positioning has come to be shorthand for some ideas that have come a long way in the pursuit of sound marketing practice. It is a concept that took a basic advertising practice and codified it in a way that made it possible for other marketers to think differently about approaches to the market.

The idea is simple. Or at least, simple to state.

If you think of marketing as a process to move goods and services to the consumer, there are two ways to view that process—either you sell people what they want, or you try to persuade people to buy what you want to sell. The second is an almost inevitably fruitless exercise in egocentric behavior.

I can make you buy *anything because I'm a good salesman.* It's an uphill trudge, and yet, it seems to be the way to which most people gravitate.

Selling people what they want is obviously the better way, although it's not without its rigors. How do you know what they want? How do *they* know what they want?

We do know that people buy what they need. They are sold what they're persuaded they need. And if you have to persuade people that they need something, isn't that the same as selling what you want to sell?

Not quite—if you can cast your product or service in a context that addresses the consumer's needs or concerns. DuPont, when it first introduced a new product called nylon hosiery, solved the problem by asking, "Would you be interested in hose that were as sheer or beautiful as silk hose, but wore like iron, and didn't cost any more than silk?"

And that was positioning before the word was ever used. DuPont, and other good marketers of their day, did three things:

• They defined consumer expectations.
• They figured out how to meet those expectations with a product they had developed that nobody had ever heard of.
• They asked themselves, "What fact or value can we communicate to the market that would address those expectations and concerns?"

From these three points they developed the marketing campaign that sold nylons. That's positioning.

And these three points define the clearest approach to positioning that might be used today.

But articulating a position is hardly a total marketing plan. A number of elements must be addressed to turn a position into a marketing plan.

A caveat. There is a distinct difference, too often ignored, between a *position* and a *mission*.

A *mission* is a projection of objectives. It defines what the firm thinks its purpose is—where it would like to go in the business context . . . how it would like to serve its clients or customers . . . how it would like to be perceived by the community it serves. It is, essentially, a wish list and a blueprint for the company. But a mission is the company's business, not the consumer's. I say to you, "I would like you to be my friend and for you to love me." That's my mission. And you say to me, "That may be what you want, but what's that got to do with what I want? Why should I be your friend, and what have you done for me that's lovable?"

No, a mission statement is not a position.

A position says, "I understand what you want and need, and what concerns you most, and I'm going to give it to you."

In practical terms, how does it work? More caveats.

• The position must stem from the best possible understanding of the needs, aspirations, and expectations of the prospective buyer. There should be a perception of what your market most wants of a firm like yours—and that perception comes ideally from research. If you don't have money for extensive research—or the commitment—do your own survey. Ask your existing shareholders, your friends, their friends—anybody. But don't guess. Know.

• The position must be based on reality. You may take the position—and advertise—that you have the fastest growing company in your industry. But if you can't prove it, or it just isn't so, you're ultimately going to lose more than you gain. Don't promise what you can't deliver. The acoustics of the marketplace are magnificent, and if your promise is not deliverable, you'll get caught and hung.

• The position you choose must spring from—and be driven by—your own business strategy. You've got to look at your firm . . . see who you are and what you want to be . . . consider management aspirations . . . weigh skills, strengths and weaknesses. If you ignore this step, you stand in danger of not only selling stock in a mythical firm, but of being unable to deliver what you sell as investment value.

• There are at least two ways in which a position can be determined. The first is a perception of the market needs, however that perception is arrived at. The second is to choose market opportunity. The first is a careful analysis of what the market wants and needs, and that you can supply. The second sees an opportunity that may not have existed before. Either way, the position must be reinforced in a proper marketing campaign.

• Choose a single position point. Diverse positions are impossible to sell effectively, and each position, instead of reinforcing the others, dilutes them all. One point, one thrust. An investor's or a consumer's overall impression of a company is one-dimensional. Pepsi, for example, is associated with youth. Volvo with safety, Burger King with flame-broiled food. An airline stressing comfort and leg room in its planes. "Only when a market has fully accepted the unique position," says one expert, "should a company attempt to build positioning extensions. Now that BMW is fully associated with full performance, it can begin to extend its positioning to luxury as well."

• Emphasis, in positioning, must always be on how the public will perceive the firm, and not on how the firm perceives itself, or would like to be perceived. The position must stem from the reality of the firm and the market, and not from an arbitrary notion of what will sell, regardless of the reality of what the firm is. Reality counts, not image. The danger in the concept of image is that it implies that symbols can be manipulated to control any image—even one that's not rooted in reality. It simply isn't true. If you don't like the perception that the public has of your reality, change your firm, not the symbols. As the old man said, what you are speaks so loud I can't hear what you say you are.

• When the position is determined, it must be communicated internally, even before it's communicated externally. Simply, if you're going to tell the world who you are, don't you think you should tell your own staff and colleagues first? After all, they're the ones who have to breath life into the position, aren't they?

Given the defined position, three things must be kept in mind:

• Positions are dynamic. They should be rethought periodically, in every aspect, to be sure that they still apply. The market may change, or you may change.

• No position will work if it doesn't, in some way, differentiate your firm from others.

• The position is ultimately nothing more than a platform to project your firm's ability to meet the needs and expectations of a prospective investor. The marketing program, in all its aspects, must be used to make that position live and viable as a marketing device.

The marketing values of the investor relations program may be as elaborate or as simple as your budget and marketing objectives will allow, but if the position you select is to be effective, the program must spring from that platform.

The tools of marketing are used to project that platform—that singular reason for people to want to invest in your company—in an integrated and concerted effort. Advertising, even when millions are spent on it, and even if the ads perfectly reflect and project the position, won't produce a single investor if there isn't a well-rounded support program that includes some projection of specific capability.

A position, as with any aspect of marketing, or reputation in marketing, is only as good as the way in which it's used. If it isn't constantly reinforced, it's useless. It's like a hoop. As long as you keep beating it with a stick, it keeps rolling. When you stop, the hoop falls over, and the distance it's gone is lost.

Can you market without a position? Of course. But it's like cutting thick steak with a dull fork. It may work eventually, but it isn't worth the effort.

Targeted Marketing

Targeted marketing differs from mass marketing in one substantial way. In mass marketing, you sell to an entire market or market segment at one time, with one major appeal. The larger the mass market, the broader—more generally defined—is the message.

In targeted marketing, you hand-pick your customers—your prospective investors—and you direct your message to that individual, group of individuals, or institution. The group may be a carefully defined segment, but it's the smallest possible umbrella.

The advantage of targeted marketing is that you can better define your offering in terms of a market need that's itself clearly defined.

Taking it step by step:

1. Define the investor you want. A lot of ways to do this. Location. Size. Industry. Specialized need. Price. Risk profile. Investment turnover rate. An industry configuration that requires a specific delineation. Your definition, but do it in great detail.

2. Identify the prospects that fit your prospect profile. There are several ways to do this. It begins, of course, by defining your company's investment advantages. Then you identify the investors or analysts in your universe that you think would best profit from investment in your company. You find these prospects by

• Scouring your own lists of existing investors and prospects. There's more gold there than you think.

• Doing some simple secondary research. Use your research sources listed earlier. Check all those on-line data bases you've been reading about.

• Prospecting through direct contact with investors and those analysts and brokers and institutions that are generally likely to invest in your company, given a better understanding of the values underlying your company's securities.

• Buying a targeting service that specializes in finding prospects.

3. Devise your campaign strategy, using the definitions of your target market and your company, using positioning, considering the various tools of marketing and how they work in conjunction with one another.

- Identify the key people who make or advise about buying decisions. This is your target.
- Deal directly with that person to establish a relationship. Write. Phone. Use all the tools of marketing, aimed at the individual target

4. Do it. Strategy is a wonderful word. It rolls nicely on the tongue. But to make strategy more than a buzz word, you've got to:

- Have a plan that's realistic. No wishful thinking. Know what's doable, and who's going to do it. Don't identify and market to 500 investors or institutions if you can't cover more than 50 in one crack.
- Be precise in your profile of your prospective investor. Start with the investors you have, as a guide to what you do for them and what you can't do.
- Be professional in your marketing and investor relations tools.
- Be organized. Get it down on paper. Who does what, and by when. More good plans slip away undone for lack of drive and organization and a good manager.
- Be accountable. Work hard to know whether or not you're accomplishing anything.

Target marketing—choosing your prospective investors and then going after them with whatever it takes to win them—defines your competitive position in the investment community. It focuses the precise message to the precise target. That's why target marketing in an investor relations program is better than mass marketing for even the smallest or the largest firm.

Is professional marketing a valid concept in investor relations? If you consider again the meaning of the word *relations* and the competitive nature of getting capital on your terms to grow your company, then there is no more valid concept than marketing.

Chapter 3

The Cast of Characters

The primary commodity of Wall Street, even before money, is information. And all the world of Wall Street information, no matter how you slice it, and even allowing for overlap and dual roles, is divided into three parts—the buyers, the sellers, and the enablers.

The *buyers* of information—the brokers, analysts, money managers, portfolio managers, traders, stock specialists—translate the information into investment advice and investment action. They are the ones who can turn information into capital.

The *sellers* of the information, on the first level, are the executives of public companies. Their ability to sell information, and its quality, is what leads to (or away from, unfortunately) increased stock trading, increased stock value, and a stronger position in the capital markets. A growing group of information sellers are specialized research companies—analysts who produce and sell research to the group of buyers of information.

The *enablers*—the lawyers, investment bankers, accountants, investor relations practitioners, and random stock promoters—facilitate the process, each in his or her own way. While the process of capital investment is a function of the buyers and sellers of information, the enablers create the instruments of the process, and smooth the way for those instruments to do their work.

Today, vast amounts of information about most public companies—particularly the several thousand largest—are available, and are even thrust upon investors. The traditional sources—Standard & Poor's, Moody's, etc.—are loaded with facts and figures, and the on-line computer databases have much more. The on-line databases are not only instantaneously accessible, they are updated almost minute by minute, often round the clock. An increasing number of companies have their own Internet Web sites, affording access to more news about a company than can normally be found in traditional news sources. Release distributors, such as *The Business Wire* and *PR Newswire*, are available to anyone with a computer, as are the range of Dow Jones, Bloomberg, and Reuters news services. The volume of news is greater than had ever been imagined possible, and the speed at which this information is available is overwhelming—a constant input from the companies themselves, either directly or with the help of investor relations professionals, compounded by the vast array of Wall Street characters.

For some investors, the computer's ability to search by predefined parameters brings yet another dimension to information. The investor can build a paradigm of factors for chosen stocks, and search databases to find those stocks. No more arduous searches in directory services and heavy tomes for stocks with a specified price/earnings ratio, or dividend record; just define it and the computer will give you the stocks.

Today's investment professional not only absorbs information as fast as it can be generated, and manipulates it with awesome speed, but also subjects it to a dazzling array of analytical techniques that range from regression analysis and Modern Portfolio Theory to the classic hemline index, which somehow relates the rise and fall of the market to the rise and fall of the hemlines on women's skirts. There are, as well, a plethora of economic theories, such as the Kontradief Wave Theory, and other cyclical theories about the economy. Those who would fathom the stock market don't lack for theories. More on this in Chapter 5.

And since the stock market is an auction market, and stock market prices don't increase in a one-to-one relationship to earnings, what the professional investor is really doing is not simply determining those companies in which the invested dollar will appreciate at a reasonable rate. The aggressive investor is really trying to fathom which companies *the market* will bet on to increase stock price.

In other words, the professional investor or investment advisor, in whatever role, must try to grasp, in a very practical context, a great deal of emotional reaction that's tempered by facts, half-facts, half-truths, rumors, guesses and in a few cases, shrewd judgment.

The Analytic Process

The analytic process itself, however, as practiced by security analysts, falls into two broad general categories—fundamental analysis and technical analysis.

The *fundamental* analyst deals primarily with the facts and figures of a company, to which is added an assessment of how management will contribute to that company's success or failure. The factors that concern the fundamental analyst are dealt with in Chapter 4.

The *technician*, or *chartist*, as he or she is sometimes called, is concerned not with the company, but with the stock itself, almost as an abstraction. The technician believes that stocks behave in a particular pattern that reflects what is known about a company, and that the pattern may be charted to project their future behavior. The concern is with such elements as the history of a stock's movement, a statistical analysis of the market's behavior, volume, and so forth. By charting a stock's historical pattern, technicians believe they can project the pattern for the stock's future.

Naturally, there's a great deal of controversy among analysts and other observers of analysis about this approach.

There is, in fact, a great deal of peripheral viewing of fundamentals by technical analysts, deny it as they will, just as they tend to be persuaded by economic news.

The computer has given us yet another kind of analysis—modeling. Its practitioners are quantitative analysts—or *quants*, as they're known on the Street. They function by building a computer model that relates every factor they think can affect a stock price, and then using the model to predict a stock performance. They frequently rely to a degree on classic fundamentals, but are more concerned with configurations and relationships of data.

Analysts, whatever cloak they wear, whatever theory they cherish, are people too. They are frequently moved as easily by emotional reaction to the events of the day as are the most rank novices. Perhaps that's a good thing. If there were no diversity of opinion, there'd be no auction in the stock market.

Whatever the means of analysis used by the professional investor or investment advisor there are two considerations. Today, he or she has more information to use in analysis than ever before, and that analysis, aided by the computer, will be done faster and with more complex configurations and permutations than ever before.

These two factors have substantially changed the nature of analysis and who does it in just the past few years. It's also, incidentally, changed the nature of investor relations. If the way information is gathered and used has changed, so must change the way in which information is delivered.

While the security analyst is the prime practitioner of corporate analysis, he or she is not, however, the sole font of information to the capital markets. There are many others.

Until relatively recently, analysis was primarily the concern of the research analyst—the descendent of the statistician whose job it was to analyze information, to come to a conclusion about a stock or the market itself, and to supply it to brokers, money managers, and others. There were perhaps a few diligent and seasoned brokers who did their own research, but only a few.

Today, fewer analysts function solely in that capacity. Aided by computers and other sources of information, people with many other roles to play in the market, including analysts, are all participating in massaging information to make investment decisions. This includes brokers, money managers, individual investors, traders, institutional investors, investment and commercial bankers, and even venture capitalists. Venture capitalists, for example, tend to work closely with groups of investors for whom they supply a broad spectrum of investment ideas, primarily about early stage companies.

Where once the analyst analyzed and the broker sold, today many of both do both, and for a growing segment, the difference in their roles is represented more in shading than in distinct coloration.

At the same time, no matter how immersed the analyst or investment professional may be in the esoterica of the stock market, it's important to remember that this sophisticated technician and financial wizard is part of a sales effort. He or she is either directly involved in selling stock (a broker, for example), or is indirectly involved in the process as an analyst or advisor. Most people in the investment business are also investors, so almost everybody selling stocks is also buying them. The broker, whose primary job it was to buy and sell stock, is today involved in buying and selling stock for himself as well as others, and frequently, in analyzing the market as intensely as was once the sole province of the securities analyst. It is, after all, a market. In a market, people buy and people sell.

It's an auction market. In fact, a special situations analyst at A.G. Edwards was once asked, "What's the worst thing that could happen to an analyst who issues a research report? That nobody would buy the stock?"

He said, "No, the worst thing is that the stock goes down." What's the second worst thing that could happen? "That we recommend the stock and nobody buys it—and then it goes up."

It's important to understand this concept, as later chapters unfold the process, because it then becomes clear that the investor relations professional is part of the dynamic; is part of the marketing effort.

To the degree that we can separate each of the characters on Wall Street from his or her classic protective coloration, this essentially is what we find in each camp.

The Security Analyst

It's difficult to view analysts as a group, and to draw too many generalizations about them. In 1971 there were 11,500 analysts. The exigencies of the stock market sharply diminished that number in 1974 to 10,000. It is almost reasonable—*almost* reasonable— to assume that those who survived the valleys of the business cycles of the past decade are all superb at their task. This is hardly so.

There are now more than 23,000 analysts practicing in the United States. They do continuing research on more than 2,000 companies, with intense focus on only a basic 600—the group that comprises the majority of traded stock. As an example, in 1996, analysts at Smith Barney regularly covered 1,382 U.S. companies: Merrill Lynch regularly covered 1,140 companies; Salomon Brothers covered 1,147 companies; and Goldman, Sachs covered 1,081 companies. Bear Stearns covered 1,000 companies. Robert Fleming led the list, covering 4,122 companies.

Most analysts have a business school background and many have come up through the ranks of the securities industry. There was a time, during the bull market of the 1960s, when the need for analysts was so desperate that some of the larger brokerage houses were taking bright college graduates with degrees in other areas and training them in-house. That practice seems to have abated, and many of today's analysts are considerably more sophisticated than were their earlier counterparts. Good analysts are in short supply, and there is a great deal of inter-firm raiding, with substantial salaries for the more successful analysts.

Ideally, the analyst has trained for the job in a context of new analytic techniques, and the new information vehicles. With the speed of information flows, and the growth and increasing complexity of the financial environment, today's analyst is to his predecessor as the jet pilot is to the World War I flying ace.

Analysts, like most people, tend to gravitate toward specialties, and in some cases, those specialties have become institutionalized. The specialists tend to form splinter groups and separate organizations.

In fact, specialization tends to be a bit murky. For example, some analysts call themselves *special situations analysts.* This implies that they follow only companies that don't fit in other categories, and that portend vast improvement in both performance and the stock market. On the other hand, the growth in recent years of the entrepreneurial company has created a new and parallel category, called emerging growth companies. These are companies that are relatively immature, and yet give reason to believe—by virtue of their industries, their management and markets, or other prospects—that they are going to grow at least 15 to 20 percent a year in revenues, and comparably in earnings. Sometimes, but not always, the price/earnings (p/e) ratio makes the difference, with the lower p/e companies addressed by the special situations analysts. At the same time, an emerging growth analyst might not follow a turnaround company, while a special situations analyst would. In many cases, it's more useful to think of special situation or emerging growth analysts as having preferences, instead of rigid categories.

Which is not to say, as well, that *generalists,* who follow any company they think will appreciate in value, would not involve themselves in either special situations or emerging growth companies. They may, individually, have other criteria. Some, for example, will not follow firms in a specific (and probably more complex) industry, such as energy or insurance. Sometimes, by the nature of the firm, the generalists follow everything. In the larger firm, with larger research departments, there may be greater segmentation and specialization. Beyond size and interest, there's also the question of talent and instinct. Analysts, remember, are people. They have idiosyncrasies and proclivities and instincts.

Not to be overlooked are the *industry analysts,* who specialize in one industry or another. Here, the guiding factor for the analyst may be that each industry is so specific that specialization is the best way to become immersed in its characteristics, which makes it possible to better understand the performance and potential of companies in that industry. Some analysts are particularly versatile, and specialize in more than one industry. And some industries may be related, such as oil and gas and mining.

Analysts are often characterized by the companies they work for. An analyst for a firm with a large retail business, for example, might look at companies that are potential investments for the individual investor. This may be defined by size, float, trading reach, and so forth. An analyst at a firm that serves institutions, on the other hand, is less likely to be concerned with companies with smaller floats. Not a hard and fast rule, but a general approach. However, because of the nature of the market today, with its heavy institutional involvement, the lines begin to blur. It's difficult to find a retail analyst, for example, whose work doesn't go to some institutions. More significantly, because the market is now heavily institutional, obviously the greatest volume of research is done for the institutional market, and most firms with strong research departments sell their research to institutions.

The point to be remembered is that analysts, even in groups, are individuals, and must be dealt with as such. To try to sell a camel to a horse trader is not worth the effort, unless there are no camel traders around. Pick your target thoughtfully.

The Broker

The broker is usually the direct contact between the customer—the investor—and the company whose stock is being sold. In that context, the stock broker, or registered representative, is primarily a middleman and a salesperson. He or she has passed a relatively uncomplicated examination that determines an ability to understand the fundamentals of the securities industry. The broker's education beyond that need not be extensive, although some are highly sophisticated and skilled beyond their basic education.

Brokers work either on commission or, in some cases, on a salary predicated upon a sales quota. It is perhaps this one fact that opens the spectrum of brokers' range of skills, motivations, and performance. More than any other group of financial or analytical specialist on Wall Street, the broker is the hardest to categorize.

Some brokers want nothing to do with investor relations professionals; some cherish the relationship. Some brokers follow and recommend only companies recommended by their own in-house research staff; some have full leeway. Some are required by their firms to get permission to recommend stocks not followed by their firms; others—particularly those with large clienteles—have greater latitude. Most brokers are scrupulously honest and deeply concerned about their clients' assets; some are mere telephone pitchmen, and churners for commissions. There are brokers who are opportunists, selling the latest stock idea and then moving on to the next one, and there are thoughtful and responsible brokers, genuinely interested in meeting the investment objectives of their customers.

For the responsible investor relations professional, the broker to be sought after is the one who is thoughtful, knowledgeable, understands research and how to do it, has a large and well established following, and is interested in good relations with good investor relations people not for the free lunch, but for the useful information. The others should be dealt with cautiously.

Traditionally, brokers rely upon their firm's research department for basic information about a company and for the intensive analysis necessary to make a sound judgment about a security, to which they frequently add information from other sources. More and more brokers are doing their own research, and some are getting very good at it. They are getting better at looking at the numbers, and they are more amenable to meeting with management.

There are a number of brokers' organizations that serve as platforms for companies to make presentations, as analysts' organizations once did exclusively. The quality of these organizations, though, varies substantially. The best of the organizations are those run by the brokers themselves, such as in Houston or Allentown, Pennsylvania, and not those run by promoters or public relations practitioners. The AMEX (American Stock Exchange) clubs can also be valuable for an AMEX company.

Naturally, with brokers as the focal point for the customer, it's almost as important that brokers understand a corporation as do analysts, regardless of the degree of sophistication involved in that understanding. A knowledgeable and enthusiastic broker with a large following can place a substantial amount of stock, and some brokers form informal networks throughout the country with other brokers whose opinions they respect. Thus brokers are as important a target audience for corporate information as are analysts, if building a retail following is a goal.

Some of the larger wire houses appear to be discouraging broker research. This may arise from the danger of a firm's liability as a result of independent recommendations by younger and inexperienced brokers. This has spawned another trend. Some more experienced brokers who want to follow companies that they select and discover now feel more frustrated by the larger houses. They are leaving to join smaller firms where they can follow their own ideas and receive a greater part of the commission they generate. In some cases, these brokers develop large followings, and the kind of practice that allows them to sell mutual funds, as well as to sell fee based advisory business—the so-called wrap account.

When fixed commission rates for stock sales were eliminated, a number of brokerage firms sprung up offering a "plain pipe rack" brokerage service—stock trading without any of the frills, such as research. They cut commission costs to a minimum, seeking profitability on high volume of low profit margin trades. They are, in effect, stock discount houses. An increasing number of people work with these brokers by computer, from home to the broker's office or floor position. Virtually all of the discount brokers have computer trading, which helps sales and volume, but reduces the cost of trades. Some, like Charles Schwab, have even begun twenty-four hour trading. This is facilitated by on-line brokerage, in which discount brokers do business round the clock on the Internet, with the trade completed the next business day.

More investors now make investment decisions based upon their own analysis. They then merely instruct the broker—usually a low fee, no-frills broker like Charles Schwab or Olde—to execute the order. They are more likely to come to the broker with the name of a stock they believe, for one reason or another, to be a good one. The low commission brokers usually don't give investment advice, but simply execute orders (although some of the discount brokers are beginning to offer some research or opinions). The full service broker may inquire of his or her research department or simply give their own reaction to the idea, based upon knowledge and feelings they've gleaned from their own research. They are less likely than their discount colleagues to just execute the order without some comment.

The broker's job is the most precarious in the securities industry. Regardless of the general condition of the stock market, his or her job—and certainly income level—depend upon their customers' buying and selling stock. If the market is down generally and if the small investor is not investing, the average broker obviously does very little business. If the stocks the broker recommends, based on whatever factors, do not go up, or the stocks they recommend to be sold do go up after the sale, they lose their customers. Since it's relatively easy to become a broker, and extraordinarily difficult for a broker to make a good living in anything but a bull market, the turnover in brokers is overwhelming. In 1971 there were 53,000 brokers functioning. In 1974, with the market down, there were 33,000 brokers. In 1980, there were 48,400—and not necessarily including a great proportion from the earlier group. At the beginning of the 1990s, there were 57,000 registered representatives in the United States. Of these, there are no statistics on longevity. By 1997, there were 72,000 brokers serving the greatest bull market in history.

The Trader

Changes in the configuration of the market have altered and somewhat diminished the trader's role in some respects. Traders are no longer the buying force they once were. However, the power surviving with the trader today is sufficient to allow us to look back upon his or her previous influence with nothing less than pure awe. That was before NASDAQ and the heavy reliance upon the computer network for trading.

In the past, most good traders had substantial house funds available to allow active trading by taking positions in a stock (going long). Those were the days when information was scarce, spreads were erratic, and big profits could be made from smart trading. Now, with the computer, everybody knows everything immediately. Spreads are too narrow to make much money on active stocks, so traders widen the gap on lightly traded stocks to try to make more money there and to compensate for the risks. The spreads, then, are too wide on inactive stocks. More brokerage houses, seeing diminishing chances to make money, are committing less money to over-the-counter (OTC) trading. OTC trading is being compacted into a business for some wholesalers who are growing, and may someday dominate the market. This may be compounded by the latest SEC reforms of over-the-counter trading, which can lead to a less competitive market with fewer participants. The OTC markets are growing because there are more OTC companies and more participants in trades, but other than wholesalers, each participant is gambling a lesser portion of his or her total capital in OTC. The brokerage firms themselves seem to be reluctant to bet their own money for their own accounts. Most of the trading now, and the reason for growth, is to service the growing demand by customers.

Are the traders the profit centers they used to be? It seems to be less likely than in the past, except for wholesale OTC houses that make virtually all of their money trading, primarily in such stocks as Apple Computer, Anheuser-Busch, Intel, and so forth, because of their volume, and in lesser known companies because of spreads.

At times, over-the-counter traders will still take positions in stocks they like in order to make an orderly market. However, these positions are not as strong as they were in the past. To the company involved, the size of the trader's long or short position can make a profound difference in the success or failure of the stock in the marketplace. A good company can have four to six market makers. A very popular stock may have fifteen market makers, but that's exceptional, and today, few stocks have that many.

Because of the losses that traders have sustained in the last few years, fewer traders will position stock these days. This reticence to take a position can make a mockery out of an orderly OTC market for the average small company. Short sellers can turn the mockery into shambles.

An over-the-counter trader who works with a lot of active smaller stocks can make or lose a million dollars in one trading day, which makes trading a tense job. One typical firm, M. H. Myerson, known principally as a wholesale trading firm even though it has a strong retail business, trades about $30 million in stock daily and makes markets in about 800 stocks. A trader's survival is almost on the line all the time, and the pressure and speed they work under are phenomenal. It takes a very special personality to do it. You can't have a long conversation with a trader during market hours—"long" being defined as more than fifteen seconds. If the trader is a close personal friend, you might get three minutes, and their spouses probably get even less.

The best kind of trader to have supporting you is one who has a retail brokerage staff or institutional sales people in the company, because he or she can get some stock out at retail or with institutions. Increasingly, at firms other than the wholesalers, the trader is there to serve just the retail operation, and so is subject to pressure from brokers as to what stocks should be traded.

If the trader is with a wholesale operation, then he or she is generally just trading with other traders, and that can go on just so long, and the stock can go just so high, before some of that stock has to get out into the retail channel. There is certainly little impetus for traders to bid a price up among themselves in most instances. The SEC has been taking a dim view of this practice, and is moving to correct it.

Traders don't care whether the stock is going up or down. They work off the action. They get paid on the volume and on the spread, unless surprises, such as sudden swings, catch them on the wrong side of the market and there are some really severe losses. The trader doesn't care so much, then, whether your company stock goes up or down as long as it provides them with volume. In volume is the trader's opportunity to make money. If they buy at $5 when the spread is $5 bid and $5.50 asked, they can sell at $5.50. If the stock goes to $4.75 to $5.25, they can still sell at $5.25 what they bought at $5. A sixteenth of a point is important to them. A quarter is a nice profit, on volume. If the market goes to $5, they might sell and break even, but that's a 10 percent move. And what if the stock rises?

These traders want to trade only on the numbers. They don't want to know anything about the stocks they're trading. They're going for just the small price changes, which is an art in itself, and they want to focus on that, and not concern themselves with what the company's actually doing. They're more concerned with who's trading what, and what positions they have, and making a profit on a very small price movement.

Their emphasis is on every minute that prices change, and where they put the spread, and how wide they make it, and when they mark the stock up an eighth or a quarter or sixteenth and when they don't over a specific period of time. Some of these decisions are based on the size and price of their positions. This is what creates a trading pattern and this is what makes the price go.

Frequently, the trader is armed with no more than the information required by securities regulation, which is little more than the company's most recent financial performance and filings. Most of the smaller trading firms don't maintain a research staff, and so the onus for keeping the trader informed must fall upon the corporation.

The younger, newer breed of traders are more likely to want to know about the companies whose stock they trade. They realize that it might help them to get a feel of where the stock might go, so that there's less chance for them to get caught on the wrong side. This is clearly a trend, and one on which investor relations professionals should capitalize. Get to know your market makers.

The Specialist

On the exchanges, the orderly market is maintained by the specialist, a member of the exchange dedicated to buying or selling stock for his or her own account to balance and offset extreme swings in prices. In the over-the-counter market, traders have no such responsibility.

The specialist is an extraordinary figure in the financial world. Specialists are responsible solely for specific stocks. They use their own money, which means they can either make or lose a great deal, depending upon their judgment and the swings of the market on any given day.

A specialist tries to end each day as close to even as possible, which can't always be done. Millions of dollars are involved each day, and being a specialist can be as intense as being an OTC stock trader, or a commodities or options trader. While the specialist's primary function is to smooth the market by matching customers' buy and sell orders, there are many occasions each day in most stocks where matching orders don't exist. Then the specialist must step in and buy or sell for his or her own account. However, the specialist can buy more than required and build some inventory, or sell more than required and go short, depending upon the company and the current market action. This requires experience and judgment, and the ability to make several decisions almost simultaneously. When does a price move up or down and by how much? What price should a stock open at, given the book orders prior to opening? When should the specialist build an inventory, at what price and how much? Much of the specialist's role is governed by rules and regulations of the Exchange, but there are many instances when the specialist must step in on either side of a trade, quickly and surely, and turn a bad decision to a brilliant one. Like any other buyer or seller of stocks, the more the specialist knows about a company the better the decision may be.

At the specialist firm of Einhorn & Co., for example, a market is made in Time-Warner, HFS, and CMI Corporation, among others. Each of these stocks has its special challenges. Two trade robustly and one sporadically. Yet Einhorn must give all three the same meticulous attention, particularly at critical trading moments.

Specialists should be kept as well informed of a company's activities as should be analysts. There is no reason for a specialist to be surprised by the action of one of the companies he or she represents and protects on the floor of an exchange.

The Institutional Salespeople

Institutional salespeople, while essentially like brokers except in who they represent and who they sell to, deal with an infinitely more sophisticated, knowledgeable, and larger customer. Many brokerage firms draw their institutional salespeople from the ranks of the analysts.

Institutional salespeople are being seriously affected by the very low commissions that institutions now pay, even on volume. It's possible, then, that during the next few years, either they will be assimilated into other aspects of the industry or they will become the point for selling other brokerage house services to institutions. This may include responsibility for selling the research function or the research reports, or for selling bonds, or block trading. But they're going to have to make commission money from other products that the brokerage house offers.

The Money Manager and Institutional Portfolio Manager

A money manager is a firm or an individual other than a mutual fund, retained by others to manage investments. Money managers have the broader responsibility of overseeing entire funds or segments of funds, irrespective of how those funds are to be invested.

The role of the money manager, in any category or specialty, has become increasingly important as the financial universe grows and becomes more complex. The vast influx of institutional funds, the growth of the 401(k), the increasing sophistication of investors and the influx of new investors, the proliferation of new analytic techniques, the increasing use of technology, and the internationalization of the capital markets—all have substantially altered the financial landscape in just the past few years alone. Also altered is the need for more advice and guidance for investors who are unskilled in managing their own investments, and the need for managers who can be trusted to invest to meet predetermined objectives. Thus, the burgeoning of the money manager, the portfolio manager, the mutual fund manager, the wrap account manager—in fact, more managers and experts per capita than ever before.

The money manager may be a portfolio manager, the head of a mutual fund, or a bank trust department, or a pension fund, or hedge fund, or a small pool of private investment capital, or a discretionary account for a brokerage firm. Some stock brokers manage money for individuals, IRAs, ESOPs, Keoghs, or even small institutions, such as non-profit organizations with small funds. More brokers are now listing themselves, even if without cachet, as "broker and portfolio manager."

With the rise of fee-based asset management—now called the *wrap account*—has come an increase in managers of managers. These are portfolio managers who develop portfolios of other managers, both stock and mutual fund. Their concern is not the stocks in a portfolio, but rather the investment and risk objectives of individual managers or funds. They are performance experts who manage large funds of money, usually from individuals, and who purchase the services of other funds or institutions. Some stockbrokers have developed clienteles for whom they perform this service, in addition to their classic brokerage activities.

Most money managers tend to use the basic research supplied by their own or other research departments, including research boutiques, to which they apply their own judgment. There has been a trend, recently, for more money managers to do more of their own research. Money managers of smaller funds can be in positions where they have to make decisions quickly. They may not have the time to research an individual investment situation as completely as might an analyst. They do, however, combine instincts and training with reading and computer screening, and more and more, they meet with company management. They also seem to consider market, industry and general economic factors more than do analysts.

Alan M. Feinstein, writing in *Valuation Issues*, describes the needs of quantitative money managers—managers who rely heavily on computerized models. "They care about information that can influence a decision, not general, nice-to-know news about the company," he says. "Most important is news that can affect their models."

"While most company actions don't have sector-wide impact," he says, "a large acquisition or divestiture certainly does. Some models depend upon yield, making a change in dividend policy important."

Like brokers and analysts, money managers function in many different categories, each of which has different investment criteria. Money managers handling different portfolio sizes—$50 million and under; $50 to 100 million; $100 to 250; $250 to $500 million; $500 million to $1 billion; and over $1 billion—will generally have some common characteristics. But beyond that, the investment criteria—objectives and risk parameters—for each group will change. This means, obviously, that the kinds of companies each category will attract differs. For example, a company with a market value of $100 million will certainly get a better hearing with money managers managing $250 million or less than it will from managers at the higher end of the spectrum.

Managing money, too, is a precarious job, since it is directly performance oriented, with very little margin for error. Thus the money manager tries to be as informed as possible in order to have a basis for judgment of the research factors. Increasingly, money management looks to objectives, particularly where the Employees Retirement Income Security Act (ERISA) is involved. Pension fund money is considered to have been managed prudently not simply when its asset value is increased, but when it meets predefined investment goals and criteria. This concept is becoming more ubiquitous in all money management. Thus, while the classic responsibility of the institutional portfolio manager—the person specifically responsible for the performance of all or part of the portfolio of securities for mutual funds, pension funds, banks, insurance companies, and so forth—is to choose securities that increase the value of the full portfolio, new criteria tend to mitigate performance measurements. And obviously, the more sophisticated hedge fund is a useful tool here, as well, for managing performance.

The parameters of each portfolio are very different from one portfolio to another. Some funds have portfolios that are passively managed, and drawn to match an index, such as the S&P 500 or Wilshire 2000. Some portfolios are actively managed and chosen for growth, some for rapid appreciation, some for income. Mutual fund portfolios are most often highly specialized, and can be defined by an extraordinary number of different characteristics, such as risk parameters, industry group, geographic region, size or age of the companies within the portfolio, and so forth.

Funds are managed by fundamentalists, chartists, and subscribers to virtually every market theory ever promulgated.

This growing thicket of money managers poses an interesting problem for the investor relations practitioner trying to advocate a client's stock. There are no sure answers, but there are some rational approaches. For example, examining a portfolio will give some clues to the kinds of securities the portfolio manager might accept, keeping in mind that investment styles and practices may change rapidly, in response to a rapidly moving market. Managers' interests change as well. Certainly, talking to the manager will help. For a mutual fund, the prospectus defines the fund's parameters, but not the techniques used by its manager to select stocks.

The best approach may be to use data from the myriad sources that have sprung up in recent years, as well as your own experience and contact list, to choose the fund that best suits the security, in terms of size, distribution, industry, etc. Then, by examining the portfolio, determine the best approach to the manager.

This is further complicated, of course, by the fact that most portfolio management is fairly dynamic, and parameters change as market conditions change. This means that to deal with any institutional portfolio manager, frequent reexamination of requirements is necessary. Constant attention must be paid, with the help of a contact management computer program such as Goldmine or Act, but to have your stock accepted by the right institution, the effort is worth it.

The Economist

A little known factor in corporate analysis is the economist for the major bank, the larger brokerage houses, research firms such as C.J.Lawrence-Morgan, Grenfell (now owned by Deutsche Bank), and the major corporation. While economists are primarily concerned with larger economic trends, they rely to a large extent on industry information, and the performance of companies within that industry, for major elements in making their projections. Their output then becomes an important framework for security analysis.

As the financial markets have moved from individual country markets to world markets, it's become more important for investors and their intermediaries to have some knowledge of economic conditions and currency and capital movements world-wide and in each country. As a result, the role of the economist has become more important in the last few years. A lot of the language of economists is now coming into the average financial person's daily diet, such as M1 and M2, and now Eurocurrency. And today, the front pages of the newspapers and the broadcast media are loaded with stories on gold, oil, the value of the currency, inflation, and how business is in Japan and Germany versus England and the United States.

The Corporate Portfolio Manager

Where once the corporate portfolio manager's responsibilities were limited to managing a corporation's investments of its surplus cash (other than the corporate financial officer's cash management responsibilities), the portfolio manager is now usually responsible for the firm's pension fund investments as well.

Most larger corporations, with cash surpluses, maintain extensive portfolios of stocks, bonds, and money market instruments as part of their cash management programs. Companies in the Fortune 500 are those in that category, for the most part. Some firms, such as General Electric, even use their surpluses as venture capital funds.

But today the corporate portfolio manager, under ERISA, has extraordinary fiduciary responsibilities. There are vast sums involved, even for smaller companies.

While most corporations depend on outside sources for advice, and even to manage the money in the pension fund itself, the corporate portfolio manager still participates in making final stock purchasing decisions.

These potential investors are not to be overlooked in your investor relations program. Companies such as Amoco, General Electric, EXXON, and Masco have excellent and receptive money managers who will look at appropriate and interesting situations.

Other Investment Officers

Two groups that have grown in importance in recent years, with greater responsibility for investment decisions, are bank trust officers and insurance company investment officers. For example, Northern Trust Bank in Chicago sent a security analyst to examine a local mid-cap company as a possible investment for some of the trust accounts for which it has discretionary authority.

Here, too, ERISA is largely responsible for these groups' increasing role in investment decisions. Prior to ERISA, trust investment, and much insurance investment, was limited to state-approved lists of investments. ERISA, which is the first federal trust law, does not limit investments by list. Rather, it responds to the Prudent Man Rule with much greater reliance on the investment officer to make decisions. The Prudent Man Rule, incidentally, says that fiduciaries must invest funds under trust "as would a prudent man with his own funds." Under ERISA, the concept of prudence is fulfilled by adherence to investment goals, rather than to approved lists of investments.

Other Analytical Targets

Those segments of the financial community that have been described thus far constitute the main body of specialists to whom the elements of a company's potential must be communicated. Naturally, nothing in this area is monolithic. While the bulk of investment decisions rest with analysts, brokers, money managers, and others, there are still fragments of the securities industry whose opinions and impressions are important. The role of such other means of communications as the financial press will be dealt with later. The concern here is with specific focal points of judgment within the securities industry.

There is, for example, value in having the heads of the corporate finance departments of brokerage or investment banking firms be aware of a company's profile, since they are frequently people who are sufficiently respected within their own company to have their judgment considered.

The role of the commercial bank in investing is growing rapidly, as banks test the eroding Glass-Steagall Act that has kept them out of investing since the 1930s. J. P. Morgan has been particularly successful at this. Moreover, these investment officers are becoming increasingly sophisticated, a fact which is recognized by a growing number of individuals and pension funds that put money under management with the banks.

The person in charge of mergers and acquisitions for an investment banking firm is frequently looked upon as a source of new investment ideas, since the nature of his or her work brings the M&A specialist into exploratory situations with a great many companies. Within this context the merger and acquisition specialist has another interesting potential value. A merger is a form of investment of corporate assets. The merger and acquisition specialists can frequently put corporate information to better use on behalf of a corporation than can many other people in the investment community. They must be particularly careful, though, not to trade on inside information—as anybody who reads the front pages should know very well.

Financial companies are branching into new areas. For example, American Express now has new money management capabilities.

Credit

While the largest amount of activity for the investor relations professional is on the equity side, the greatest source of capital in industry is debt—the bank loan, the debenture, commercial paper—the full range. Credit analysis will be dealt with in Chapter 4.

Those who deal with credit analysis, however, are essentially the same kind of analysts as those who deal with equity analysis. The exceptions are the bank lending officers and the analysts in the bond rating services.

The Overseas Market

Until relatively recently, the securities industry outside the United States wasn't attuned to investor relations as we know it here. The way for Americans to go into Europe, for example, was through U.S. investment bankers with branches or associates in Europe. Access was limited, and very few U.S. firms Europeanized themselves enough to really make a dent in the market. PaineWebber might have been an exception, at least in London and Paris, but Merrill Lynch and most others made comparatively little impact in Europe.

Investor relations professionals who went to Europe and worked through a few local firms, such as Leonard Baker in London, fared much better, and maybe even have a little edge today. Currently, there are about 30 U.S. brokerage firms with about 100 offices in Europe. Slowly, slowly the wheel turned toward bringing European investor relations to a par with the way it's practiced in the United States.

Now, tremendous strides have been made in investor relations in Europe and elsewhere in the world. It's no longer true that the rest of the world is still generally behind the United States, and in many countries abroad, investor relations is now considerably more sophisticated than it had been. The gradual breakup of old club attitudes in the financial community in the United States allowed investor relations to develop. In Europe, the old school ties existed to a much greater degree than in the United States, to the detriment of the professional investor relations practice. But in Europe, too, the financial community is changing extensively. Such investor relations firms as Leonard Baker, based in London (Baker trained in the United States, however), and Garry Wilson, have made the grade in comparable professionalism, and England, at least, has a thriving investor relations profession.

The investment arena is very different in each country abroad. For example, in most countries there is no retail market as such. There are no individual investors as we know them, except in Japan, which is a market very much controlled by the largest Japanese brokerage firms. England is just beginning to develop a retail market. You must work, primarily, with institutional investors or very large individual investors through intermediaries. In London private client brokers work with the investments of extremely wealthy individuals in Europe.

Since the deregulation of the British securities industry in 1986, it has undergone a vast readjustment. From the rush of the first days of deregulation—the *Big Bang,* as it was known—the industry moved to a high, then a low of disorganization, volume and business. It seems now to be stabilizing. The securities industries of all European countries are adjusting to a new context as the borders between European Community countries have fallen, allowing a new era in international trade.

For the U.S. company seeking to sell stock abroad, there are some major considerations, not the least of which is in the relationships that exist between the corporation and the different European financial markets. Different legal and regulatory frameworks also exist from country to country, although they almost universally subscribe to the same rule of disclosure that obtains here—that potentially price sensitive information be released as soon as possible. Accounting standards and principles differ from one country to another, making international analysis difficult, although this problem is slowly mitigating.

The financial press in Europe, for example, is truly national in each of the major markets, and is more influential, in most countries, than it is in the United States. According to European experts, a symbiotic relationship exists between the press, stock brokering, sell-side analysts, and investing institutions. The press and sell-side analysts trade stories with each other, and in turn, influence institutional investors. This is particularly evident, the experts say, during mergers and acquisitions, where the importance of the press is at its most obvious. There still tends to be some skepticism about investor relations, particularly among British institutional managers, but that seems to be mitigating as the results of effective investor relations efforts begin to emerge.

It's important, then, that U.S. companies and their investor relations counsels functioning in European and Asian markets fully understand the workings of the financial communities in each of the countries in which they may choose to operate.

Identifying target stockholders should be the starting point of any program, and working with local sources is mandatory. This can be difficult, because there's no legal requirement to disclose foreign shareholdings. Moreover, in countries such as Switzerland, Germany, and France, obsessive secrecy prevails, making shareholder identification doubly difficult. For larger American companies, for whom three to five percent of their stock is in foreign hands, the job becomes a bit simpler, since the shareholders abroad are usually on the company's lists.

It becomes clear that establishing relationships with overseas financial markets is a task that requires ongoing commitment. It's not a casual exercise. Nevertheless, it's important for the growing U.S. company, because Europe and the Orient are sources of capital that can't be ignored.

The Corporate Sell Side

Taking aim at the array of analysts, brokers, money managers, etc. is a battery of corporate officers, ideally supported by investor relations specialists. The investor relations viewpoint would hardly be complete without a look, however brief, at the mission of those on the sell side of corporate information.

The Chief Executive Officer

At the head of the team, of course, is the chief executive officer (CEO), who may have the title of president or chairman of the board.

While each CEO may have his or her own agenda and visions for the company, inherent in the CEO's role is the charge to sustain earnings at a high level, and to build the substance to keep the value of the company's equity high and, if possible, increasing.

This simple mission is not without difficulties. Presumably, the CEO's job is to keep the company strong, and to keep it capable of coping with the changing exigencies of the economy. This frequently means that earnings that might go to the bottom line to support the stock price are better used by reinvesting in plant, marketing, distribution, or acquisitions.

It's clearly a paradox, because despite the fact that the CEO's primary responsibility is to his or her employers, the shareholders, fulfilling that responsibility is a business decision that requires great moral fiber. Should the short-term route be taken, the candle of stock price may burn bright, but without reinvestment, it can burn out quickly. Should the long-term route of reinvestment be taken, but not clearly explained, the CEO's tenure may be foreshortened.

The measure of a successful CEO, then, is the ability to function within that paradox.

The Chief Financial Officer

The power of the chief financial officer (CFO) varies from company to company. In some, the CFO is little more than an accountant, functioning at the whim of the CEO. In others, the CFO is powerful, creative, and if not the copilot, at least sits at the pilot's right hand.

The CFO's title is not as important as the function itself. The title could be vice president-finance, or treasurer, or any of several other designations. The responsibility, however, is to watch the firm's money and financial structure. This includes overseeing all procedures regarding how money is taken in, used, preserved, and paid out; monitoring the levels of capital either in or needed by the firm; dealing with the capital markets, including banks and investment bankers; dealing with various taxing bodies; dealing with the outside independent auditors, and to a large extent, dealing with investors and Wall Street. The CFO is usually directly responsible for the investor relations effort.

While no corporate role is so clearly defined as to preclude crossing lines for any responsibility—a CEO, for example, may assume any of the CFO's responsibilities, if that's a personal need or personal talent—these job descriptions are a good general guide to responsibilities.

At the same time, any responsibility may be delegated by a corporate officer. Large corporations, for example, frequently have, under the CFO, treasurers, controllers, chief accountants, internal auditors, and so forth—any of which may be assigned responsibilities beyond the textbook definition of a title. One such job, frequently delegated in larger companies, is the investor relations function. In those companies that recognize the professionalism of investor relations, that function is usually assigned to an investor relations officer. That role is more fully described in Chapter 12.

In an entrepreneurial society such as ours, the corporate face to Wall Street may be an individual or a team, and the size of the company is not the basis for choice of either. Some CEOs are so entrepreneurial, so energetic, so charismatic, as to preclude any other voice dealing with the investment community. Others choose support from their financial experts, lawyers, and investor relations professionals. Some deal with Wall Street enthusiastically and some do it reluctantly; some skillfully and some painfully.

The important thing to realize in all this is that the personality, skills, and texture of management are the crucial elements to be assessed in analyzing a company. The competition for capital is not one of numbers; it's a battle of people.

The Enablers

Such is the nature of our society and economy that specialists are required to guide us through the dark woods of finance and regulation. The simpler times when entrepreneurs could raise sums of capital by themselves, beyond start-up, are perhaps centuries behind us. Today, virtually no one can deal effectively with the capital markets without the help of lawyers, investment bankers, and investor relations consultants.

The roles played by each of these enablers are not manufactured by the professionals themselves; they are mandated by the complexity of the system. Laws designed for the good and protection of the public have become so complex that they must be interpreted by lawyers. The sources of capital are so varied they must be accessed with the help of investment bankers and their various levels of skill and experience. The competition for capital has become so intense, and is fought in so many arenas, that only the skilled and professional investor relations consultant can be relied upon to lead the charge effectively.

The Lawyer

While corporate attorneys have many roles and responsibilities—a corporation is, after all, a legal entity and not a person—our concern here is the role of the lawyer in competing for capital.

For the public corporation, the largest part of the corporate lawyer's job that relates to investors is dealing with regulation and disclosure—subjects covered extensively in Chapter 9.

Lawyers, whether internal staff or outside counsel, prefer to command and dominate the areas of their expertise, which can sometimes pose problems for others who must function in the same arenas. Lawyers, then, will occasionally find themselves in conflict with CEOs who want to take risky or daring action, with auditors who want to disclose marginal data, with investment bankers who want to move stock aggressively, or with investor relations professionals, who want to disclose and inform effectively and in depth where lawyers tend to be reticent.

Some time ago, a company was in the midst of a lawsuit that threatened its credibility in the market. Every suggestion made by the investor relations consultant for dealing with the press or shareholders was vetoed by the attorneys. Finally, in exasperation, the investor relations consultant said, "Look—your job is to see that nothing is said in public that will come back to haunt our client in court. My job is to keep the client viable in the marketplace. I'll respect your job if you'll respect mine." In interdisciplinary relationships with lawyers, this may well be the best approach.

Which is not to say that competent lawyers are not invaluable members of any corporate team, if only to bring legal perspective, and to find routes through the legal jungle. Lawyers advise, but business people must make business decisions.

The Auditor

The role of the auditor, visible as auditors may be, is rarely understood by even the most learned observers of the business scene. This includes judges who want to know why the auditors didn't catch the embezzlement.

The auditor didn't catch the embezzlement because it's not part of the traditional audit, although that seems to be changing. In fact, the nature of the accounting profession is changing dramatically, as the financial horizon widens.

The auditor takes the financial information given by the company, reviews the procedures for managing that information, and determines whether the conclusions to be drawn from that information are accurate. Not whether the *information* is accurate, but whether the *conclusions* are accurate.

This is possible because the auditor simply tests the procedures for reporting financial information to be assured that they are consistent with Generally Accepted Accounting Principles (GAAP). The auditor can be lied to, given false figures, or have information hidden from him or her. But if the material the auditor is given is organized and formulated according to GAAP, the auditor has to give the firm a clean certificate.

There are exceptions, of course. In the course of testing to see whether GAAP is being used, the auditor samples information. This may include, for example, verifying the cash in bank accounts, verifying that random samples of accounts receivable are indeed accounts receivable, or that the physical inventory is actually on the shelves. If, while doing this, the auditor discovers something not quite right, the auditor is obliged to report it in the proper place in the audited statement. This may be a qualification in the certificate, or a footnote to the financial statements. But it is all part of the audit.

The auditor's independence—freedom from any taint of subjectivity or self-interest—is a crucial factor in the auditor's existence. Lacking this independence, the auditor's attestations are worthless. Auditors, then, will go to great lengths to preserve that independence and integrity, even to the point of resigning an account rather than be persuaded to represent as fact something they don't see as fact. This independence, this objectivity, is the major currency of the auditor.

The potential conflict comes when the investor relations professional is trying to produce the annual report, and the auditor has his or her own ideas about how the information is to be presented. In most cases, the auditor is merely concerned with presenting information fairly and accurately, by his or her own lights. But auditors are not necessarily communicators, and their concepts of fairly and accurately may not be the same as the lawyer's or the investor relations consultant's.

The answer to the problem is that there usually isn't an answer, other than the persuasiveness, experience, and expertise on either side. The only protection for the investor relations professional is to know securities law and accounting—and that's why so much of it is addressed in this book.

And again, the role of the investor relations professional is covered in Chapter 12.

The Investment Banker

It's impossible to function in the capital markets without a clear understanding of the investment banker and the role he or she plays in them.

The role of the investment banker, which changes drastically from era to era in response to the changing needs of business, is dealt with extensively in Chapter 10. Here, we must be concerned with the investment banker's role in competing for capital.

Investment Banking Services

What exactly should a corporation expect in the way of investment banking services?

Essentially, it adds up to not only the supply of capital, but the intelligence necessary to maximize the return on that capital. It's a total range of financial services that embraces every aspect of corporate operation as it relates to capital.

Currently, there are really relatively few investment banking firms that are qualified to meet the full spectrum of needs of the growing corporation, although the number may be increasing as competition and need increase. Mergers and dissolution of firms place the inventory of skills in different hands, if not fewer hands.

A typical example of one such full service firm is Donaldson, Lufkin & Jenrette, Inc., which in 1997 was the leading underwriter of high-yield bonds, the third largest underwriter of common stocks, and one of the five leading merger and acquisition specialists. DLJ sees its role in relation to its clients as one that begins with a thorough understanding of the corporation and its needs, to which it brings:

- Access to capital markets
- Business and industrial analysis
- Economic, equity, and credit research

- Knowledge of financial markets and timing
- Tax accounting and legal skills
- Investment judgments

Its list of services brings to bear on any of its clients' problems an extraordinary range of capabilities in the areas of capital raising and corporate strategy advisory services, investment management, professional advisory services, and market-timing. It delineates at least the following services in several areas:

Investment Banking

Capital Raising

Public offerings and private placements of equity and debt securities and limited partnership interests
Asset securitization
Project finance
Venture capital
Private equity investments

Strategic Advisory Services

Merger, acquisition, and divestitures
Corporate restructurings

Merchant Banking

Pools of private equity dedicated to investments in U.S. and international corporations, leveraged buy-outs and build-ups and real estate related situations.

Institutional Equity Research, Sales and Trading

Research coverage of more than 1,100 companies in 80 industry sectors
Trading capabilities in U.S. listed and over-the-counter securities
Extensive U.S. and international distribution capabilities

Institutional Fixed Income Research, Sales and Trading

Research coverage of more than 500 issuers, in-depth analysis of the U.S. and international economies, and comprehensive proprietary research products relating to mortgage-backed and other structured products

Powerful franchises in trading high-yield and investment grade corporate bonds, U.S. government securities, mortgage backed securities, and other structured products

Commercial and residential real estate finance

Emerging Markets

Research, sales, trading, and development of structured products

Correspondent Brokerage Services

Trade execution, clearing and information management systems

Investment Services

Portfolio management services and proprietary investments for affluent individuals, pension and profit sharing funds, endowments

Full service brokerage services for high-net-worth individuals and regional institutions

On-line discount brokerage services

Goldman, Sachs & Co., another major investment banking firm, offers essentially the same range of services, but with perhaps somewhat stronger capabilities in such specific areas as international financing and commercial paper. In 1996, for example, its $2 billion Eurobond offering for the UK was the largest in that year.

It should be clearly noted that the services of these two firms are described here as examples of the several outstanding firms in the field. Nor does size imply superiority. What's most important is intelligence and the ability to grasp the full range of a corporation's needs, and the investment banker's ability to serve that range of needs. There are several smaller investment banking firms in which the focus of talent is so intensified or so specialized that they serve the needs of the smaller corporation or the specialized needs of the larger corporation. One such small firm, Harlan Castle and Associates, for example, is unexcelled in knowledge and facility in real estate investment and financing, although it serves other industries as well. Its size has not precluded its contribution to the very largest corporations.

Some firms are emerging on the basis of particular strengths in one or two areas. For example, Hambrecht & Quist in high tech; Rauscher Pierce and San Jacinto Securities in Dallas specialize in energy; Morgan Keegan in restaurant companies; Wheat First Securities in furniture; the Pershing Division of Donaldson, Lufkin & Jenrette in retail; and Dominick & Dominick in very high potential small companies.

Obviously, this kind of service is not compensated for in the old way. The commission fee from an occasional underwriting cannot supply the investment banker the wherewithal to pay for the kind of talent, and to run the kind of integrated organization, necessary to serve today's corporation. More and more, then, investment banking firms are moving to a straight fee structure. More and more corporations, recognizing the value of a full range of services, are happily accepting the fee structure.

More and more investment bankers are coming to recognize that the recycling of stock is not the major function of investment banking, and that it must never again be allowed to overwhelm the role of investment banking in capitalizing industry.

Thus the emerging investment banking firm is just that—emerging. As of the moment there are all too few investment bankers who function—or who are capable of functioning—in ways that serve the needs of the corporation. A talent here—a capability there—but very little total capacity. The answer has not yet caught up with the need, and the need is proliferating.

For the emerging corporation in need of sophisticated investment banking services, the search for it becomes arduous. As the competition for capital becomes keener, the spectrum of expertise needed to find and intelligently use the capital has not kept pace. It behooves the corporation, then, to search it out assiduously. Corporate management can no longer afford to be cavalier in accepting an investment banker relationship on superficial criteria—such as the number of retail outlets or even the prestige of the names found in its syndicate structure. Every aspect of investment banking must be reviewed, in the judgment of capability, including those for which a need is not immediately foreseen. Circumstances change. The corporation not interested at the moment in an effective real estate capability may suddenly find itself, as a result of a merger, in possession of several million dollars worth of real estate. That's hardly the time to go looking for outside real estate expertise.

More than just a conduit to the capital markets, the investment banker is a primary factor in any corporation's operations. No company begins without capital, and no company functions without capital. Not to under-stand the investment banking structure and its relation to the capital markets is a weakness that no company can allow itself in today's economy.

The fascinating thing about Wall Street is that there is no rigid structure of occupations, in an academic sense. While there are titles and jobs and roles, it's become abundantly clear, in the dynamic of the financial world in recent years, that roles change as opportunities present themselves.

The roles played by the cast of characters are determined by one thing— go where the quality money is.

Chapter 4

The Changing Landscape of Analysis

S tanding between the investor and the company that's offering securities there is almost invariably the skill, the craft, the expertise, and sometimes the prejudices of the analyst. Rarely is an investment decision of any magnitude made without the interpretive hand of the analyst. Nor is the analyst always a dedicated analytical professional. He or she can serve in any capacity in the securities industry—broker, trader, money manager, and so forth—or can even be the investor, the end user of the process.

In the attempt to unlock the mysteries of the auction process of a securities market that's growing in size and at an accelerated pace, securities analysis has become increasingly complicated. Not surprising, simply because the dynamics of the stock market are so complex, with many diverse factors affecting the way the market values a stock. It's much like attempting to jump inside one's own shadow, when even the jump itself changes the shape and position of the shadow.

Once the principles of stock analysis were relatively simple and primitive—so much so that early analysts were simply called statisticians. Now, modern science, combined with the overwhelming size of the market itself, has made analysis complex, arcane, and mercurial. The search for new techniques to better understand how to anticipate the forces that cause the market, and the securities in that market, to behave as they do is ongoing. And while extraordinary inroads have been made in understanding the interplay of elements that dictate market value, the ultimate goal remains elusive. We come close, and continue to better understand how to tame the variables that affect market valuation, but we really have better control in weather forecasting than we do in predicting the future price of a stock.

In our society, in our economy, the meanings and values of a company are multifarious. A company is, of course, an economic unit. But a company that, for example, creates a hundred jobs in a community in which those jobs had not existed is creating social values. A company that does business using child labor is doing quite the opposite.

But within an economic context, it's not inaccurate to say that the role of a company is to generate economic values, and provide strategies that generate economic values for its shareholders—its investors. The investor relations professional may or may not have a part in devising those strategies, but he or she clearly has a major responsibility to define and communicate those strategies.

It would be unrealistic to suggest that investor relations practitioners can unduly influence a stock recommendation if there is no appropriate underlying economic value in that stock. But it's just as unrealistic to expect an analyst or investor to know and understand all of the factors that affect the underlying values in each stock in the market. The role of the investor relations practitioner, then, is to assure that all of the factors about a company are known, understood, and seen in proper configuration and context by those who make or influence investment decisions. It is through clarity of information, not the misinformation of the *spin*, that investors and those who advise them are persuaded.

If the investor relations practitioner, then, is to succeed in transmitting a company's values to this new breed of alchemists, then a great deal must be understood about the changing analytic process itself, so that the investor relations practitioner may better serve the client company. There are rules. And as in any game, there are skills in playing the game by those rules. But the rules and skills should be known and understood.

Three things make the new analytic environment different:

- The size of the market has increased many times in the past few decades. In the 1970's, for example, a 25 million share day on the New York Stock Exchange was considered a heavy trading day. Today, the average trading day will include more than 500 million shares.
- Scientific methods have been applied to attempt to fathom the mysteries of stock valuation. Modern Portfolio Theory (MPT), a sophisticated math-

ematical approach to delving into the secrets of stock valuation, is now almost routine. Other refinements and approaches move the science of MPT even further than ever before.

• The computer, with its ability to manipulate and correlate data faster than anything ever before imagined, has made possible even newer approaches, and techniques that couldn't be foreseen a decade ago. Neural networks, in which data is input so rapidly that it alters the nature of original structure, and then continues to integrate data to the amended structure, on a real time and constant basis, generates an awesome control of relevant information needed to make informed judgments. The art and science of modeling, based on the principles of neural networks and other forms of artificial intelligence, bring a new dimension to analysis. It is as the speed of the horse compared to the speed of the rocket, except that what's traveling so fast is *information*—correlated and integrated data that affects the valuation of a security.

This configuration of elements now defines the arena in which investor relations must function. Successful investor relations depends to the largest extent on the ability to fall in step with, and serve, those who analyze the investment values of a security, and who then communicate their findings to those who invest. It's almost impossible to practice effective investor relations without understanding how the analyst works, what kind of information is needed in analysis, and how to be assured that the analyst is not only informed, but understands the information in proper context.

Thus, a significant role of investor relations is to supply those elements of information that go beyond the bare facts—to produce a perceived wisdom that tells the prospective investor that this may be the stock to invest in; that this may be the stock that will cause his invested capital to grow.

The raw facts about any public company are readily available. This is so by law, which requires disclosure by all SEC-regulated reporting companies of specifically defined company activities and performance, results, or information related to past, current and future performance. But if all the most pertinent facts about a company were known and readily available, such as data that may be found in such services as Standard & Poor's or Holt Value Associates, or the on-line services of Dow Jones, you still wouldn't know enough about the company to invest in it wisely. The investor, or the investment analyst, must still understand considerably more before he or she can make a judgment about the potential success of the company. There is infinitely more to contemporary investment analysis than the numbers and the raw facts.

The analyst's job is to understand the *meaning* of the raw data, and how each configuration of data affects the meaning of each of other configurations of data. But that is still just the beginning. Other factors enter into the picture—factors that, as will be seen, are not so receptive to quantification. The investor relations professional's job is to facilitate that understanding.

Working With Analysts and Professional Investors

For the investor relations practitioner, working with analysts and investors evolves to two factors—formulating the essence and substance of a company, and devising the mechanics of communicating both that essence and the substance—the raw data—about the company. But in addition to being a communicator, the good investor relations professional is also an advocate for the company.

It's here that the role of the advocate is really defined. Within the boundaries of ethics and truthfulness, the CEO who understands investor relations, or the investor relations professional who understands the company, moves the facts forward in a forceful and persuasive way. Which is not to say that the facts are moved forward to tell a one-sided story. A story that's all good is too good to believe. Corporate problems, however, do offer opportunities for investor relations professionals to consider the best ways to present the information in ways that, when the analyst or investor makes an assessment, the decision falls your way.

The capital markets are, after all, a competitive arena. The artfulness in presenting the company to the prospective investor resides in the ability to project and communicate the future—those elements that foretell the ultimate success of the company in the market place.

Is that ability artfulness? Probably, in that the difference to the financial community of the stock prices of two companies with the same fundamentals is the degree to which it believes that one company can outperform the other. Because this is frequently a subjective view, the assessment is susceptible to persuasion. Persuasion, within the boundaries of credibility, can be an art.

But it's an art that must be energetically pursued, if a company is to succeed in the marketplace.

And significantly, since it takes two opinions to make a market—one that says the market or a stock are going one way and the other that says they're going another—what are the analytical theories that must be understood if the advocacy role of the investor relations practitioner is to be effective?

The Analyst's View

The analyst is taught to view a company in terms of some rather specific elements, some of which are measurable and some of which are judgmental. Among those factors that enter into the analysis of the company are:

- The financial structure and performance of the company
- The economic context in which the company operates
- The nature of the securities market in which the company must be evaluated
- The nature of the industry in which the company operates, and the market for its products and services
- The management of the company
- The company's own projection of its plan for growth

Valuable factors that define the character of the company include:

- Customer satisfaction
- Product or service quality
- Effectiveness of internal and external information systems
- Marketing prowess
- Market share
- Intellectual capital
- Employee training
- Employee morale
- On time deliveries

Perhaps the best delineation of the fundamental aspects of security analysis is found in the superb and sustaining work *Security Analysis,* by Benjamin Graham and David L. Dodd (fifth edition, by Sidney Cottle, Roger F. Murray and Frank E. Block). Benjamin Graham is considered to be the dean of analysts, not only for his success as an analyst, but by virtue of the fact that his book was one of the first, and certainly the most masterful, to set forth the basic elements of security analysis. It remains a standard today, and forms the precepts used by successful investors, such as Warren Buffet. Even if

Graham's precepts are honored in the breach, they are still a standard that guides all analysts.

Basically, Graham believed that no company should be considered as an investment vehicle unless:

- The company is prominent and conservatively financed. Current assets should be at least two times current liabilities, and debts should be not more than 110 percent of net current assets.
- The company has been a consistent dividend payer. The more conservative investor would want to see dividends going back twenty years.
- There has been no deficit in the last five years.
- The price/earnings multiple is low. In a soft market, and with high interest rates, he suggests a maximum price of eight times current earnings per share.
- The stock is selling at one half of its previous high.
- The stock is selling at a price that is no more than two thirds of net tangible assets.

Obviously, these are very stringent factors, developed in a different time, in a different market and economic environment. Under many conditions, these principles would eliminate all but the smallest segment of publicly traded companies. And while very little argument can be taken with any of the points he makes, it can certainly be argued that the spectrum of investment possibilities is much greater than companies that fall within his parameters. An example would be a company in an emerging industry with a current ratio of 1.8 but long term debt of 15 percent of net current assets, and strong earnings gain. Dodd and Graham's credit standards may be too tight for this company, but the company may still be a good investment prospect.

The realities of the stock market today, the range of reasons for investments, and new analytical concepts, all dictate some rather more flexible considerations in analyzing a company. In the arena of new companies, with initial public offerings, there are many that, based on fundamentals, are sound investments by any standards.

Another variable today is that with the growing number of investors, new ranges and parameters of risk substantially change security analysis. For example, the value of a stock to an investor with long-term, low-risk goals is different than it is for an investor willing to put investment capital at greater risk to achieve rapid, high returns. Looking at the changing spectrum of risk tolerance, we see new analytical guidelines.

Growing in popularity are new—or newly articulated—concepts of economic value added (EVA). It's an attempt to express two concepts—net profit and rate of return—in a single number. A similar program—market value added—uses the same approach but with different elements. Whether these programs—called metrics—have any merit will be determined only in the long run.

Varying Analytical Points Of View

And so the person who does the analyzing often determines how it's done. Certainly, the analyst for the bank trust department, functioning in a fiduciary capacity, must be infinitely more conservative than the speculator who is going for high return and who is willing to take a greater risk for it. The analyst for the holdings of 401(k) funds might have very different investment objectives that the analyst for the large sector mutual fund.

The individual investor views a company rather differently than does the fund manager who will be held accountable to others for results. Today's individual investor is somewhat better informed than in the past. The tape watcher who looks to make his profit with every movement of the tape sees investment possibilities very differently than does the long-term investor who is willing to buy a stock at a very low multiple, but with long-term growth possibilities. The growth of 401(k) pension investment funds has brought in a whole new breed of investors—people who once didn't know a Dow from a Jones, but now watch the tape on cable television and the *Motley Fool* chats on the Internet, and the rapidly burgeoning world of mutual funds has moved investment involvement and interest to a larger stage.

The pension fund investment manager, concerned with ERISA's legal concepts of prudence and working within the confines of specific return goals, builds a different portfolio than does the hedge fund manager. All fund managers operate with investment goals, but today, the number of funds and managers has proliferated to a degree that specialization takes on a new meaning. Portfolios are now balanced not just with stocks, but with funds, and funds of funds. One fund will aim at emerging companies, another at mid-capitalization companies, another at blue chips, another at industry sectors or high risk companies, and so forth. This wide array of specialized funds allows portfolios to be fine tuned to meet the specific objectives of each investor. In fact, the growth of the wrap account, in which an investor pays a fee (rather than transaction costs) to a fund manager is made possible only because the fund manager can pick and choose investment funds and investment vehicles to meet the investor's own objectives. What is significant here is that the vast segmentation of the investment community affords opportunity for the investor. For the investor relations practitioner, it means that greater attention must be paid to target audiences, and greater opportunity exists to aim information to the right analytical context.

In this new configuration, analysts in each segment face the problem differently. The analyst for a bank trust department tends to consider investments rather more in terms of preserving capital than does the analyst for the hedge fund, who can invest more aggressively. The analyst for the mutual fund functions in terms of his fund's charter and objectives. The hedge fund analyst is looking for companies that he thinks the market will become enamored with, and whose stock the market would drive up rapidly. The analyst for the growth fund is looking for substantial growth with long-term staying power. The analyst for the pension fund is looking for companies that will not only grow steadily and appreciate over the longer period of time, but have a measure of safety within the fund's definition of needed return. The bank or institutional analyst may have another problem, in that bank and institutional portfolios are often so large that the ability to liquidate in volume is strictly limited. The analysts in the research department of the large retail house must deal with the broader spectrum of companies, because the retail customers have different portfolio needs.

With the magnitude of the market today, retail analysts tend to shy away from smaller public companies, particularly those with less than $200 million in market value. This keeps the analyst's universe more manageable— and certainly more profitable to the parent brokerage firm—because only the largest companies have the volume of shares that can be traded profitably.

Requirements of Analysis

The requirements of analysis of a corporation fall into three categories:

- Financial data
- Management
- Plans

Financial Data

Financial data—the financial information about a company—is, of course, the simplest to define. Basic financial data is embodied in the company's audited and non-audited financial statements, its government filings, including its unaudited "Management Discussion and Analysis" of the financial statements, and supplemental schedules. It's made available to shareholders in annual and interim reports, and is increasingly found on the Internet, and for larger companies, in the business and financial media. The proxy statement also answers some financial questions, and reporting services, such as Standard & Poor's, also supply the information.

The SEC has been increasing the depth of financial data it demands in these documents and some companies themselves have volunteered it. Although there are still important areas of operating information that many companies seem reluctant to disclose—quarterly segment reporting is one example—for a public company there is relatively little financial information to which an interested observer cannot become privy. The corporation that tells less deludes itself if it feels that bad news can be hidden from interested parties. More significantly, the reluctant corporation deprives itself of the opportunity to present the company favorably. It leaves itself open to a serious credibility problem, because most analysts feel that if a company is reluctant to disclose and broadcast information of any nature that's relevant to understanding performance, the reasons for doing so must be negative. And since most analysts tend to recoil at the least bit of negative information, any attempt to hide anything causes an almost immediate overreaction.

Furthermore, the SEC has been absolutely assiduous in its efforts to increase disclosure despite the damage done to disclosure by the courts serving the claimants' lawyers in shareholder litigation. Overzealous litigation has indeed amounted to a serious assault on increased disclosure and, as such, those attorneys, plaintiffs and courts are running counter to the interests of the vast majority of investors. Actual management abuses, which should be policed, pale next to the number of managements getting crushed by so unwieldy a weapon as expensive threats or more expensive litigation. Congress seemed to agree by passing the Private Securities Litigation Reform Act of 1995, the so-called Safe Harbor Bill, late in 1995, which offers protection against litigation for making appropriately qualified projections that are not met.

Despite these attacks on disclosure regulations and policies, one overriding factor remains—the more that is known about a sound company the more readily it will be understood, believed, and favorably viewed.

In analyzing a company's fundamentals, using virtually any process of fundamental analysis, at least the following financial information is essential:

The Earnings Record

Since earnings, and the ability to project a company's earnings potential, are a significant aim of most analysis, earnings history is a basic tool. It should be clearly understood, however, that the numbers for earnings never stand alone, and even the traditional view of earnings is now being reevaluated. For example the Financial Accounting Standards Board's mandatory accounting standard SFAS121 (called the *impaired assets rule*), sets standards on when the value of on-going assets should be written down. It allows companies considerable latitude to estimate future cash flows and the discount rate they use to arrive at their write-offs. By lowering the declared value of the assets, a company also reduces its depreciation in future periods. This non-cash item certainly muddies reported earnings and prior year comparisons. How can assets then be valued on a comparable historic basis? How can today's earnings, if they're based on non-comparable asset values, be made comparable to the earnings reported two years ago? Thus, earnings are relative to many other factors, all of which must be transmitted to analysts. Certainly, earnings are meaningless except in relation to revenues, as a percentage of revenues. They are meaningless if the role of inflation isn't clear. What is significant in analysis, then, is not just the earnings figure, even when there is a steady increase over the years. It's more important, for example, to note the degree of consistency and growth in earnings and margins. And even this doesn't stand alone, since a growing corporation is affected by many different factors during the course of a year. A sharp growth in earnings may be the result of astute management and a marvelously improved production, distribution, or marketing structure. It may also reflect a merger or acquisition, or a change in accounting practices.

The *quality of earnings*—an analysis of earnings predicated upon factors that are not immediately discernible, such as accounting changes that can alter the measure of earnings in ways that don't accurately reflect the company's actual performance—means more than the numbers themselves. Prime examples are changes in depreciation method or the basis for depreciation—here again SFAS121 can serve admirably as a current example affecting the amount of depreciation taken—or capitalizing versus expensing certain expenditures, or the treatment of foreign currency. For example, the measure of loss or gain from the sale of a segment of a corporation's operation is a function of the reserve set up for the disposal of those operations—and there is virtually no way to determine from most financial statements the basis used for establishing the size of that reserve. Historical earnings in the pure sense are themselves of limited value in gauging the ability of a company to continue to earn at a consistent rate.

With inflation or the broad fluctuation of raw material costs, the historical cost, for example, of raw material or finished products in inventory moves a great distance from current or replacement cost. How, then, can assets be valued on a comparable historic basis? How can today's earnings, if they're based on inflated costs and prices, be made comparable to the earnings reported two years ago? In fact, how can earnings comparisons be made unless there is a comparable basis for accounting for added risk taken on by the corporation to produce continued gains? The fact is that without some significant changes in accounting practices, they can't be made comparable.

While analytical methods that emphasize earnings growth have been important in recent years, and are still the most widely used, their shortcomings have become increasingly clear. The complexity alone of some methods almost automatically produces controversy. For example, the prestigious Boston Consulting Group offers a formula to define sustainable growth as a measure of created value. Alfred Rappaport, in his excellent book, *Creating Shareholder Value* (New York: Free Press, 1986), labels the formula "an unreliable indicator of value creation."

Properly analyzed, however, the factors behind a consistent earnings history are a measure of elements that contribute to ongoing earnings growth, and are usually a good indicator of a company's success. The key is to expand the concept of the factors behind, and in addition to, earnings. And successful investor relations depends upon the ability to impart to analysts not only the dynamics of earnings, but those other factors that enhance the value of the company's securities.

Revenues

Revenues (not to be confused with sales) are a measure of the size of a company—a way of categorizing the economic sphere in which it functions. Revenues come from many sources—sales, services, and so forth. Obviously, it may be readily inferred that many factors about a company with $500 million in revenues are different from those of a $25 million company. The large company is more likely to be older and better established, except in certain emerging industries such as computers and communication technology, where growth has been explosive, and would seem to have an even greater potential for growth and survival. It probably has a better grasp of its markets. It probably has a larger number of shares outstanding and a greater market value and liquidity in the stock market. It probably has a greater ability to withstand broader economic difficulties. Yet it mustn't be taken for granted that a very large company has any greater ability to succeed, or for its growth to compound faster, than does a smaller one. The number of giants that have fallen on hard times in recent years is too large to take size alone as a measure of investment safety. Witness IBM, Apple Computer, K Mart, Federated Department Stores, Sears, Roebuck, Unisys, and Woolworth. There are, in fact, fairly reliable measures of growth. Rappaport, in *Creating Shareholder Value,* discusses techniques for measuring fundable rate of growth and affordable sales growth. He warns that growth rate should be an outgrowth of strategy, and not the other way around.

Cash Flow

Because of some of the problems associated with earnings-based analytical formulas, more analysts are now turning increasingly to cash flow analysis, which they believe gives a truer picture of how a business is being run. Cash flow, many analysts feel, levels all the accounting acrobatics that sometimes obfuscate the picture of a company. The concept is an old one in economics that says that the value of an investment is derived from its *cash flow*—the organization's basic cash-in, cash-out.

Basic cash flow is most simply defined as net income plus depreciation. But, depending upon their needs and personal concepts, many investors use other definitions and measures. For example, one group of investors prefers to look for *operating cash flow,* which is the money generated by the company before the cost of financing and taxes. According to analysts at one investment firm, Goldman, Sachs & Co., a portfolio of stocks with the best *price to operating cash flow* ratio would, in 1988 and part of 1989, have doubled the return of the Standard & Poor's 500 stock index.

Today, an increasing number of analysts and investors look to current and prospective cash flow before they analyze other factors. They believe that *discounted cash flow*—estimated future cash flows discounted back to present value—has more potential for judging company and stock market success than earnings-based analyses. Cash flows are discounted by the cost of capital or an average of debt and equity.

Probably the best of these kinds of measures is *free cash flow*, which is earnings plus noncash charges, less the capital investment needed to maintain the business (there are other definitions). It's a measure of discretionary funds—money that can be taken from the company without jeopardizing it.

In 1995, Holt Value Associates, one of the leading security analysis services, introduced its Value Focus service, based on economic cash flow (CFROI) performance, and not reported accounting information. This is an example of the increasing acceptance of cash flow-based concepts today.

Margins

Normally, *net margin*—the percentage of net income to revenues—is relatively simple to measure. It's a major factor in determining both the efficiency of a company and its ability to cope with costs and expenses—both of which constantly change. Margins are affected by increasing competition in an industry in which product pricing becomes a significant competitive factor. Margins become even more significant in a period of unstable prices or raging inflation, when gross margins might reflect vast swings in the cost of raw material and labor. Under those conditions, the margins can be severely hit if the company is not able to pass on to its own customers the high cost of any basic materials. Margins affect the quality of earnings, when many companies must sell from inventories that had been built up at lower costs, and were reported at inflated prices. In many cases, this results in a distorted picture of the company's realistic margin, since it's difficult to discern the consistent level of future costs for the same items. When this happened in the past, many companies changed their method of depreciation to reflect accelerated deflation. Today, that inflationary factor is built into many corporations' financial structures, further distorting margins as well as earnings. Too, the computer's ability to recalculate on a real time basis keeps the report of margins current, usually enabling adjustments without broad swings in pricing.

Return on Equity

This is the earnings per share divided by the *book value* (the difference between a company's assets and its liabilities). Return on average equity gives a more accurate picture than return on beginning equity because it accounts for the equity added during the year and, therefore, presents a more complete picture. Many companies, such as Sharper Image, now use average equity in their calculations. For investors, this is a most significant measure of a company's success. It is, after all, what investment is all about. If the return on any investment in one company isn't as high as it is in another—and assuming that the difference isn't offset by dividend yield, or that the achieving company isn't so highly leveraged that it's threatened by high interest rates—then what's the point in investing in the company with the low return?

Balance Sheet

The balance sheet still offers the best picture of a company's financial position—as of the date of the balance sheet. If the balance sheet of Penn Central, which revealed an extraordinarily heavy debt, had been heeded, then its favorable earnings reports issued immediately prior to its bankruptcy might have been viewed with a bit more skepticism. The balance sheet does—or should—tell the analyst a great many things. It also poses a great many questions. And it behooves the corporation to anticipate these questions in order to prevent misunderstanding or misinterpretations, as well as to clarify the position of the company. There may very well be justification for a very high inventory or a substantial increase in inventory from one year to the next. For example, a major customer under a multi-year contract may have deferred deliveries from the fourth quarter to the first quarter of the following year. The balance sheet alone will merely indicate the size of the inventory. It will not explain it. A reduction of cash from the prior year against a reduction of debt implies that the cash was used to reduce the debt. Without explanation it is merely an implication. Certainly a disparity from one year to the next in accounts receivable or accounts payable warrants an explanation, even if it's an unfavorable one. The growth of pension fund assets poses an increasing balance sheet problem particularly under current accounting treatment, because the unfunded pension liability portion can be larger than it should be—a great worry to investors.

While the notes to financial statements usually clarify the debt structure, questions about debt—both long and short term—go beyond the balance sheet. The balance sheet, it must be remembered, is as of a particular date. Debt can be increased or decreased the day after the closing of a balance sheet, as can any element of the assets or liabilities. This is a prime example of why a balance sheet never speaks for itself in describing a company; the analyst wants to know more that it can show. And with accounting standards rapidly changing, the company must be prepared to defend its accounting methods.

The computer's ability to update information rapidly and easily makes it possible to have a running balance sheet. But for comparison, the dates must be consistent.

Ratios

The analysts, with their computers or electronic calculators, can compute a head spinning number of ratios, many of which, like astrological symbols, can assume meanings of varying import for different people. Ratios without explanation frequently imply a picture that, in view of changing conditions and other factors, may not be accurate in terms of the corporation's actual operations. Ratios, like any statistics, are a still picture of a corporation frozen at the moment the picture was taken, while the corporation continues to move on. It's extremely important that any ratio that differs from the industry norm, either up or down, is a signal for the need for elucidation and explanation.

The array of ratios is imposing. The ratio of *current assets to current liabilities*, if it is less than 2-to-1, sends a red flag flying. If the *debt to equity* ratio is too high, the analyst immediately wonders about the drain on future earnings by debt payments. The ratio of *return on total capital.* The ratio of *depreciation and depletion to sales.* The ratio of *earnings paid out in dividends to earnings.* The *price to sales ratio* for smaller, high technology companies. And this is exclusive of ratios of various factors such as earnings, dividends, assets, and sales to the market price of the stock. Graham, in his book, *Security Analysis,* leans very heavily on ratios as a measure of company performance.

Theodore H. Pincus, chairman of the investor relations consulting firm, The Financial Relations Board, believes that the ratio of the *price-earnings ratio to the company's average growth rate* over a specified period—the *PEG* ratio—is very useful to analysts. An average growth rate of 15 percent during the period studied, and a P/E ratio of 30, would give a company a *PEG* ratio of 2-to-1. Using *PEG* ratios for various companies, analysts can get a good sense of whether a stock is too high or attractively low. This is not the same, however, as the old adage about buying a stock selling for one-half its growth rate, and is infinitely more useful.

Cost of Capital

Some aspects of the cost of capital, such as the prime rate inflation, and taxes, are fairly evident. The company that must function heavily with short-term borrowing, such as a leasing company or an importer who depends upon revolving credit lines, will find itself in serious trouble when the prime rate starts to climb. The company that is fairly heavily leveraged—has a very high debt in proportion to its equity—is also in serious trouble. The expansion-minded company is always viewed in terms of its financial ability to expand either internally or externally. Even in an atmosphere that allows for additional capital through equity, the analyst must consider the cost of a company's equity capital in terms of its price/earnings ratio. This whole area then becomes a matter of major concern for analysts, and therefore of major concern for the corporation that wants to explain itself.

Increasingly, cost of capital and Capital Asset Pricing Models (CAPM) have become a focus of attention of analysts. In his publication, *Valuation Issues*, William F. Mahoney writes, "Corporate managements are focusing more on lowering their company's cost of capital, recognizing its importance to investors seeking to maximize returns of their portfolios." The goal, he says, is to achieve returns above the cost of capital. There is a great deal of controversy surrounding CAPMs as a valid measure of risk, but the models serve as a valuable tool for company financial officers in measuring company performance, and are therefore a valuable element to communicate to analysts.

In *Creating Shareholder Value*, Rappaport clearly explains that the cost of capital is a crucial factor in deciding whether shareholder value—the worth of the company—is being enhanced. He lists formulas to determine whether a company earns or will earn a return more than its cost of capital. If so, shareholder value is created. If not, no value may be created, or a company's value might actually go down.

A somewhat similar method of analysis is market value added or MVA. This is the cash investors put into the business over its lifetime, measured against the amount they could get out by selling their stock today. Then there's EVA—economic value added, which is net operating profit after tax, minus the weighted average cost of capital. Every analyst, it seems, has a preference among ratios. Some may be right. All must be served by the investor relations professional.

The Industry

Each industry has distinctive characteristics and requires analyzing additional elements, with a different emphasis on common elements. Sources and uses of funds and revenues differ. Accounting methods differ. Industry practices differ. Nevertheless the same rules of communication apply. All of these differing characteristics must be clarified to investors and analysts. Because the same ratios mean different things in different industries, ratios and changes require explanation, and nothing should be taken for granted.

For a company to represent its financial situation as independent of the industry in which it functions, or even of the larger economy, is to delude itself. Even the company that's out-performing its industry for one reason or another must still realize that in most cases it's being judged in terms of its industry. No company president functions successfully without intensive knowledge of his industry. But too often companies are presented to analysts without a clear explanation of comparable performances, common and uncommon problems and solutions, distinguishing industry characteristics, costs of raw materials and distribution, potential markets, and so forth.

Challenges of Industry Specialization

There is yet another challenge in that analyzing specific industry groups usually falls on a small segment of analysts who specialize in that industry. This poses two serious concerns. First, a company judged by industry specialists, no matter how well it is performing, is often given the same general value by the market as is the industry itself. If the industry is depressed, even a superior company within that industry faces serious stock market problems.

Second, the majority of analysts who fully understand the ramifications of a particular industry rarely change the relative rankings of major companies within that industry. If you are seen as number three in the industry, you are usually the number three forever, with that P/E seen as the norm for your company, unless there is a major company event or breakthrough of some kind. Moreover, these industry analysts don't always represent a sufficiently large number to warrant devoting a major portion of an investor relations effort to them. It therefore becomes necessary to deal with a larger group of analysts functioning in other contexts, and in other organizations, who are not as well versed in the ramifications of a particular industry as are the industry specialists, but who may nevertheless see other values. The communications effort then becomes more challenging. Not only must the company be explained and sold to analysts, but the complex specialized differences in dealing with the industry and the company and analyzing it must be made clear.

The problem of specialization also arises frequently in dealing with companies with large international operations. Even in today's international environment, where more companies than ever before have some degree of international activity, there are still a relatively small number of American analysts who feel they have the broader international economic background to properly assess a company with significant international activity. Too many others tend to ignore such companies and move on to those easier to understand. There are, after all, more companies in the broader economic sphere than any one analyst can follow.

These are the significant financial factors that must be communicated in judging a company. It should be clear, however, that in dealing with analysts and others who judge companies, numbers shouldn't be presumed to speak for themselves. They never do. They require elucidation and explanation. This is why financial statements have footnotes. It can't be repeated too often—a corporation's statistics freeze the picture as of the date of those statistics, and corporations are dynamic entities.

Prognostication for an entire industry is somewhat easier, at least within a limited range of time, than it is for any one company within that industry. The economic indicators of an industry are rather simple to define. If consumer spending is down as a result of inflation or higher interest rates, for example, or the economy is in a period of high consumer debt such as existed in late 1995 and into 1996, it's reasonable to assume that retail purchases in certain industries, such as appliances and apparel, will have trouble achieving earnings records. Competitive factors, such as catalog sales, adversely affected retail chains. If there are basic material shortages, with no relief in sight, it's reasonable to assume that those industries using those materials will have problems. In good economic times, the purchasing power increases, but selling labor gets scarcer.

When transistors were invented, transistor manufacturers enjoyed a boom in those products that used transistors, such as miniature portable radios and portable tape recorders. But then as the industry became saturated with transistor manufacturers, and technology reduced the cost of transistors, it became impossible for any company to compete successfully and with very high margins, and the transistor stocks fell on their faces. New technology helps, but is volatile. The advent of the Pentium chip caused Intel to soar—until Cyrix came up with a cheaper chip. Technology, analysts know, is a two-edged sword.

On the other hand, when a new industry emerges, such as computers, there are a new set of problems and opportunities. At first, there was a shortage of analysts and investors who fully understood the nature of the industry and where it might go. Then, as it began to grow and mature in the United States, new competitive forces came into play. No sooner did analysts and investors begin to grasp the basics of the new industry when both new technology and competition changed the scene. In the beginning, computer stocks, such as Compaq and Lotus, were at first undervalued, and then, as the companies broke growth records, moved into new competitive contexts that few analysts really understood. By the time the industry had matured, shares of market had shifted, markets became saturated, new technology changed and challenged leading companies, and there were new economic configurations that were unfamiliar to most investors. By the time the financial community began to understand Compaq, it was a mature company, revaluated its market, and redesigned its product line and marketing approach. By the time the financial community began to understand the pioneer Lotus, the company ran into marketing problems, and wound up being acquired by IBM. IBM, which had been overwhelmed by Compaq, Dell, Gateway, and other clones, and dropped from its leadership position, began its own comeback. At the same time, small companies get very big very fast—look at the giant Microsoft—and big names and former high fliers, like Borland, virtually disappeared. Now, with the emergence of the Internet, and the growth of communications technology (e.g. the cellular phone), things continue to change. As the popular industry writer, John C. Dvorak, puts it on his weekly radio show, "everything you learned this week will be obsolete by this time next week." This is how a new industry affects the financial community, in which technology moves faster than analysts can fully understand its nuances and ramifications.

Industry analysis is not without problems for the investor relations professional. Analysts tend to minimize, for example, the company that is outperforming its peers. They frequently fail to understand longer term industry trends, or the effects of new technology on the performance of a company, nor do they readily accept turnaround situations early in the turnaround performance. Despite all the warning signs, in 1981 analysts still expected $100 oil in the energy industry. IBM, not long ago, was considered dead. Chrysler had people saying it couldn't be turned around. Mini-mills saved a part of the steel industry. Perspective seems to be a foreign word to the finance industry.

Sometimes industry analysts find themselves susceptible to the same kind of short-term response to which the individual investor is victim. One of the groups to be hit when it was first announced that the plastic, polyvinyl chloride (PVC), was a factor in producing cancer in both the PVC industrial worker and the consumer was the plastics industry. Plastics analysts felt that most plastics manufacturers would be subject to regulation that would either curtail production or involve large capital investment in safety equipment. It took a considerable amount of time, during which plastic stocks were adversely affected, for the analysts to sort out those companies that were unaffected, or had already built safety factors into their production.

The problem of environmental pollution lends itself to a similar potential for overreaction. Many industries—paper, steel, chemical, utilities—are now subject to production strictures that will affect their processes, and attendant costs, to varying degrees. But there are relatively few facts available on how these strictures are to be defined or how to judge the costs for individual companies, much less specific industries, particularly with uncertainties as to the future of environmental regulation under each new administration. Very little research has been done in this area, and without facts, overreaction is found to be the rule.

In the arcane world of economic influences upon company analysis, the burden is on management—and by extension, the investor relations practitioner—to clarify, to explain, to define context. For example, when the price of the dollar on world markets changed abruptly a few years ago, it made it seem that companies with large overseas operations were losing revenues and profits. But given an understanding of foreign currency translations, those companies with better investor relations communications and marketing skills fared better in the stock market than did other companies in the same plight. More recently, when the dollar was falling, U.S. companies raced to do more business overseas and that message has helped the stocks of Coca-Cola, McDonald's, Caterpillar and others perform better in the stock market.

Analyzing Economic Conditions

In a growing economy, such as we've enjoyed for an extended period of time in the 1990s, even stranger things happen in the stock market than during a period of no growth or economic uncertainty. Bad times seem to make investors depressed, but good times seem to make them nervous. How else to explain that in the longest period of sustained growth in generations, every time there's good economic news, the market drops substantially.

One common explanation is that the history of double digit inflation is too fresh in people's minds. Good times mean inflation. Inflation is controlled by the Federal Reserve Bank's raising interest rates. Raising interest rates affects both the bond market and interest sensitive stocks.

And obviously, economic events affect the market.

Changes in health care law affect the insurance and health care industries, which affects the economy. The growth of HMOs has substantially altered the economics of health care, affecting not only the health care stocks, but the financial performance of all industries and all companies in which health benefits are a large portion of operating expenses.

In a sense, the economy is like an ecological structure, in which no event is isolated; every event affects all other tenets of the system, and does it with different timing in different segments of the economy. No economic leaf falls without affecting the entire environment.

Analyzing economic conditions is an arduous and sometimes frustrating task, and rarely do two economists agree on the meaning of any one event. But unless the company itself supplies the guidelines for evaluating the effect of these external economic factors on its own performance, the judgment by analysts as events unfold will almost invariably be an overreaction or underreaction. The responsibility for putting any economic news in perspective, even before its effect is felt by the company, resides with the management.

For all its apparent sophistication, economics is a most inexact science. Just when everybody thinks the arcane science has been tamed, some new and unforeseen element enters into it. A war. Currency devaluations. Inflation. Political uncertainty, such as the change from a Democrat to Republican-controlled Congress. A savings and loan crisis. A decision by the Federal Reserve Bank to tighten up the money supply. A beef shortage. A drought. A bankruptcy by a major company. And on and on and on.

Everyone knows where the economy has been and sometimes people even know where the economy is. But nobody ever really knows where it's going, despite computer models, economic indicators, or the ability to read the future in the entrails of sheep. Obviously this throws even the best analysis into a cocked hat. It moves it out of the realm of the economic certainty of a balance sheet, and the historical value of the earnings records, into a vast world of major uncertainty. It's not without its charm, however, in that it offers analysis the excitement of prognostication that one rarely gets with the electronic calculator or even the computer.

Projecting Management Capability

The two most important intangible factors of a company that must be judged by analysts are its management and its plans. There are in U.S. industry today many large companies that began as small companies. There are also many small companies—and many that no longer exist—that were started at the same time as companies that are currently large. One difference between two companies that started small, and of which only one thrived, is capitalization. The other and major difference is management, which, given management's role in raising capital, may in some measure be the same thing.

A study by the University of Iceland found that about 40 percent of the difference in the herring catch among the 200-boat fleet depended upon the captain. A look at hundreds of top companies in the United States and Canada showed that the personality of the CEO made as much as a 15 percent to 25 percent difference in profitability.

Management is less exact a science than long-range weather forecasting, and probably more arcane, mercurial, and convoluted. Judging management talent and skills can be difficult, not only because they're intangible, but because they're highly subjective. The elements of management may be definable, and with computer modeling, the science of divining those elements is undoubtedly improving. What is *not* definable is the way the configuration of those elements will function in terms of results. And as business grows in intricacy, so too do the demands on management become more complex, and so too does analyzing and assessing management become more speculative. Ultimately, and despite what they say in business schools and books, successful management is a function of skill, talent, personality, and luck.

Part of the problem of fathoming management, most analysts are finding, is that successful management can no longer be judged by traditional standards. The world moves more quickly than ever before, and using traditional methods of judging the skills of management is much like comparing the techniques of flying a single-engine prop plane to flying a jet in combat. The old skills are no longer any good in a world in which competition is international, the sources of capital are multifarious, technology changes the environment radically on a moment's notice, and the skills needed to run a company and to compete successfully include those that didn't exist a decade ago. And all this must be communicated to people who must make investment decisions based on information that travels with the speed of light. Success in investor relations, then, becomes more than a simple communications function—it becomes an art form.

The broad definition of management is the subject of a full library of theories, many of which conflict and none of which is definitive. What is important in investor relations is the ability to project to investors, believably, a corporate management's ability to manage its company, to cause it to thrive and to grow, and to survive, in both good and bad times. What's crucial to project is management's ability to create shareholder value.

Management theories abound, and continue to proliferate. But for the most part, complex management theories obfuscate, rather than help, security analysis. Essentially, the different theories are simply different routes to the same goal—increasing shareholder values. Whether the company is run from the top down, in the traditional model, or by a creative team, which seems to be the model in many high tech companies that require vast input from many people, the goal is still the same. And so too is the need to judge management's ability to meet that goal.

A person who invents a cure for the common cold may be a thoroughly bad manager in terms of marketing, production, or finance. The entrepreneur who invents a useful and valuable item in his garage may be capable of managing the company he develops with his invention until sales reach a level of $30 million a year. As his or her company continues to grow, the shape of the company alters, production needs change, and so, then, do administrative needs. Team strength should be developing. A company in transition is at its most vulnerable point. The entrepreneur who is capable of building it to $50 million may not have the capabilities to build it to $100 million. The management team of a one-product company that decides to expand its product line or to diversify suddenly faces new and generally unfamiliar problems and may not be able to cope. Again, team strength emerges, as a topic increasing in importance.

A good management team must have a grasp of a great many things—finance, marketing, administration, production, distribution, the economy in general and its industry in particular. And even within the context of these elements, abilities are limited and alter with changing conditions. And again, never underestimate the value of personality and luck.

Perception, in looking at a company, is often very different from reality. The problem is that too often, the facts don't count—it's what people perceive to be the facts on which they make judgments. This puts a particular burden on the company, and a profound responsibility on the investor relations practitioner.

In projecting management capability, three views must be defined:

- The chief executive officer's talents, personal characteristics and leadership
- The capabilities of each key member of the management group
- The team of managers itself . . . its interaction and effectiveness as a team

The CEO as Leader

Obviously, the chief executive officer, at the helm of the corporate vessel, is crucial to the success or failure of the enterprise and its voyage. Aided by the management team, guided, presumably, by the board of directors, the CEO has the key responsibility for vision of the firm, and for translating that vision into a reality that enhances return on investment. The CEO, while not necessarily capable of bringing full expertise and experience to every task in a company, must at least have a solid understanding of the full range of management skills, from marketing to finance to production and distribution. He or she must lead the planning and execution of the corporate operation, motivating others who must make the vision a reality. The concept of risk is always operative in the executive suite—risks to new markets, risks to new products or services, risks to capital expenditures, and the toughest risk of all—the risk of doing nothing. The successful CEO can see around corners, be able to turn the ship on a dime, repair it if it breaks down, and get all hands pulling in the same direction.

It is this capability that must be projected to prospective investors and analysts.

The mercurial personal qualities necessary for successful leadership are difficult to define, and the elements of success have long been the fixation of major articles in leading business magazines, books, and the academic world. What personal qualities might be successful? Brains, hard work, a talent for delegation, for choosing the right team members, a flair for marketing or production, creativity, honesty, articulateness, education, experience, charisma? What makes Gates and Allen and Welch tick? Is there some formula—some *seven habits*—that can be distilled and transmitted to CEOs of lesser talents?

Chief executive officers have been getting more scrutiny than ever before. Not all this attention is welcomed, particularly when it questions executive compensation, or an unusual acquisition or divestiture, or any other high risk decision. The CEO is always in a precarious position, and the degree to which he or she is willing to take risks, or manage risks, is an important measure of the CEO's effectiveness. As with today's top athletes and movie stars, large amounts of increasing remuneration beyond what the average investor makes brings increased public responsibilities. These large sums are being granted to senior officers, causing a measure of consternation among shareholders who earn considerably less. In fact, it could be argued that compensation is, in part, for the risk as well as the performance.

Still, the best guide to a company's potential for increasing shareholder value is the measure of the man or woman at the head of the firm. Projecting the elements that clarify and define those qualities is at the heart of successful investor relations.

The Senior Managers

While the company's vision emanates from the CEO, the job of making that vision a reality begins with the senior managers—and analysts and investors know it.

Analysts want to understand the talents of the key managers and even directors. What do they add to or take away from the management team? Who are they, what do they know, what do they contribute, and where do they come from?

Which of them is capable beyond his or her assignments? Who's next in line—the finance officer or the marketing director?

Which of them seems to work well with the CEO and which does not? Is there harmony or friction?

For the astute analyst, the answers to these questions is as significant as understanding the personality and skills of the CEO, and this should be a guide to the investor relations professional's communications plan.

The Management Team

A good management team must have, as a group, a grasp of a great many disciplines—finance, marketing, administration, production, distribution, the economy in general, and its industry in particular. And even within the context of these elements, abilities are limited and alter with changing conditions. How the team works together—its members' ability to cooperate with and support one another, their chemistry together—is significant information for analysts. It's a crucial measure of the potential success of a company.

When economic conditions are good and sales are coming easily, and the company is adequately financed and there are no production problems, a management team can be perfectly capable of showing profits. But how can an analyst judge how that same management will function when money becomes tight, when competitors start hitting the market, when a strike hits the plant, when there is a material shortage, when there is a takeover attempt by another company, when there are price controls, or when—as in the case of the transistor problem—the market becomes saturated with its product? Every management team of a high-powered company has potential problems predicated on both personality and the capabilities of the management team. The analyst must see the team for its cooperation, not its dissension.

When a company has the only water hole in the desert for 200 miles around, a manager doesn't need a degree from the Harvard Business School to know how to sell water. But most companies function in a competitive economy. The history of American business is laden with managers of major companies who made the wrong decision. A failure to move with the market quickly reduced companies like Borland and WordPerfect, once industry leaders, into such deep trouble that both are now in the hands of other companies. In fact, after two owners and a trip to the cellar, WordPerfect, under the Canadian-based Corel, has come back strong as a competitor to Microsoft in the word processing market. It's all done with management skill. Staples and Office Depot, two office supply chains that are competitive, would have changed course had their merger succeeded because the management of Staples was profoundly sound, and the management of Office Depot is less so. Had Staples acquired Office Depot, it would have expanded its operation, and reduced competition in key markets.

The managers of the large corporation are highly visible. Their efforts and activities and triumphs and failures are trumpeted regularly in the business press. It's the smaller company that needs to be better known by analysts and brokers and prospective investors. It's here that the art of investor relations has its greatest opportunity.

Credibility

It is absolutely imperative, for success in the capital markets, for a management team to build a record of consistent openness and truthfulness. Any misrepresentation will not only be readily found out, but will reverberate throughout the financial community like a lion's roar. Furthermore, the number of eyes on a public company are many and keen. A public company is under constant scrutiny. It can take only one disgruntled employee and one astute analyst to topple a corporate empire. It took one unsubstantiated *Wall Street Journal* article to begin the demise of Work Recovery's management team, and almost the entire company. Any corporate executive who thinks he can deal with the investing public by misrepresenting facts or by refusing to disclose pertinent material necessary for judging his company will not long succeed in the capital markets.

It's in the area of management analysis, particularly where credibility is involved, that the investor relations professional functions best as an advocate. Numbers can say a great deal in themselves, although they don't always say the same things to different people. The judgment of management, on the other hand, is subjective, and responds well to strong investor relations guidance and support. The investor relations professional should provide the appropriate information when it's appropriate, and not wait for the market to do it.

How, then, is credibility engendered and sustained? One can hardly stand before an audience and say, "This is what I want you to think about me." A company president can hardly stand in front of an audience of security analysts and boast of his or her abilities.

It's good form, on the other hand, for the president to describe, in speaking and writing, the company's management team as being excellent, forward-looking, and skilled. But why should he or she be believed? It's true that some corporate leaders are clean-cut, strong-jawed, and clear-eyed—obviously exciting and believable men and women—at least at the moment they are talking. Other extraordinarily competent corporate leaders are shy, reticent, introspective, and poor public speakers. Some of the most striking photos of chief executive officers appearing in annual reports show leaders of vision and forcefulness, obviously the kind of people in whom widows and orphans should invest their faith and savings. Training corporate executives in public speaking, dress, and television presence is now a big business.

In fact, credibility is a function of three things—corporate performance, consistent truth, and a willingness to deal forthrightly with the public and those who analyze securities in behalf of the public.

Projecting Management as Credible

The most tangible gauge of management is still track record. How successfully has management performed? What has it achieved in the growth of the company? How has it survived and dealt with problems? What opportunities has it seized upon and how did it capitalize on them? How has management restructured itself to meet changes in its corporation and its environment?

These and other elements of management capability are projected in real ways. The history of the company, however brief, can be told in terms of management decisions:

- "When we realized that the next decade would see a population growth in the number of women between the ages of twenty-eight and thirty-five, we decided to design a special line of sportswear and merchandise it to that group."
- "When we recognized that we were just a few years away from market saturation for our product, we began to explore feasible areas of diversification into products that, with our experience and existing capabilities, we could exploit."
- "As our company reached the $100 million mark, we recognized the need for broadening the management base, expanding middle management, and changing the nature of our management reporting systems. Three executives who couldn't comply had to be replaced by people who were better prepared to make appropriate changes."

• "As we recognized that the average age of our management team was approaching fifty, we began a recruiting and training program to develop the people who would ultimately be our successors. This has resulted in . . ."

Projecting the Facts

Yet another way in which management can project itself is to clearly and authoritatively present facts about its company. Consider the erudite company president, surrounded by his or her executive vice-president and vice-president of finance, who recites facts and figures about his or her company's operation, clearly delineates its present financial structure and its plans for future growth, and obviously has a grasp of the industry and the economy at large. He or she is much more likely to inspire confidence and credibility than the company president who merely recites, either by rote or from the printed page, material that has already appeared in the annual report, who never lets other members of the management team speak, and who limits the spotlight to himself or herself alone.

The company president who demonstrates the ways in which he or she has constantly broadened the management base to meet the growing needs of the company, and is constantly divesting responsibilities by delegating them to other able people, inspires infinitely more faith than the president of a company who is obviously a one-person band and keeps everything to him or herself, regardless of the number of underlings. The future of a one-person company is no greater than the length of the president's arm, and every analyst knows it.

Analyzing Plans

Yet another intangible in which corporate evaluation must be made is the company's own plans. Any analyst with twelve minutes experience has learned to make a distinction between plans and dreams, even though dreams occasionally come true. There are, after all, business people named Gates, Redstone, Thalheimer, and Eisner.

Fortunately, the experiences of the past decade have sharply diminished the number of corporate presidents who attempt to pass their dreams as valid projections or plans. It should be recognized by both management and investor relations professionals that the acoustics of Wall Street are magnificent, particularly for bad news or direct misrepresentations. Certainly, it behooves the investor relations professional to lead management to the path of clarity, cogency, and credibility.

What is specifically of the essence here are the legitimate and carefully formulated plans and projections of a company that express more than just its wishes for the future, but are rather the blueprint and road map of company policy for continued profitability, expansion, and growth. The future is, after all, what analysts are concerned with. They know what the present is and what the past was. They may find the management of a company to be charming, sincere, bright, intelligent, highly motivated, ambitious, and trustworthy. But as analysts, they must make an assessment of how these virtues are going to be applied to add shareholder value.

What Plans Mean

The CEO of a company with $1 million in sales may have dreams of heading a billion dollar multinational corporation, but may not have the foggiest idea of how to increase sales to $2 million. On the other hand, a CEO who recognizes the potential in certain aspects of telecommunications, is planning to expand existing marketing and production capabilities to meet that potential, who hopes to supplement that capability with an acquisition or two, and who recognizes the limitations of his ability to finance those plans, should clearly delineate his or her corporate ideas. The CEO should recognize publicly the dimensions of the potential market, the need to divest certain unprofitable operations, however painful and without emotional consideration, the ways he or she intends to finance the growth and how much it's expected to cost, the kind of management changes he or she is going to have to make, the kind of economic climate in which he or she expects to function, and the down-side risks.

In some cases the plans available for the analysts to consider are relatively simple and unsophisticated. "We are planning to grow through a program of acquisitions and our experience in the past has demonstrated that we can do this. This is the kind of acquisition we are planning to make, this is how we are going to buy the companies, this is the size company we are looking at." And so on and so on. Most of the factors, management is saying, are there for the analysis.

Or so it would seem. There are still many judgments to be made as to the validity of the program. One company in the office cleaning services business had a very simple concept and seemed to have the capabilities to fulfill that concept. It was in an industry made up of predominately smaller privately held companies. The company simply went around the country combining the smaller companies into the larger one. Cash flow was good up to a point. It was an industry that management knew and understood well and seemed capable of managing. The stock was selling at a reasonable multiple, and there was enough available at the right price to allow a considerable amount of it to be used as currency for making the acquisitions, and the banks and the institutions were in a mood to be generous. It worked very well for a while, and every analyst following the company could visualize the successful configuration of both tangibles and intangibles. But then the acquisition momentum outpaced both the ability to manage the rapidly growing company and to finance the continued growth. The company fell on its face. It had to sell off some of its properties in order to revitalize its balance sheet and make payments on its debt, and finally went bankrupt.

The Cautions of Corporate Planning

Corporate planning is itself a very complex business. At best, even supported by sophisticated thinking and computer models, it's precarious. Necessary, but still precarious. Today's commerce and industry move at so rapid a pace, and are interrelated with so many new factors, that traditional planning approaches become obsolete very quickly.

To distinguish the dream from the plan requires as much luck as skill, especially because so many unanticipated random events can substantially alter the best devised plans. New technology. New competitors. New regulatory controls and antitrust rulings. Some larger companies—IBM, Microsoft, Anheuser-Busch, Disney, Amgen, General Electric with its 400 strategic planners at headquarters, and Coca-Cola—have a far greater (but not absolute) capability to control their economic environment, and do plan more effectively than does the smaller company. As significant factors in their industries, companies like IBM, Coca-Cola, and General Electric receive little surprise from labor. Moreover, they have vast sources of input of economic information, not only domestically but worldwide. They have staff experts to both gather and interpret material, and relationships in every corner of the world. And yet, IBM, which once controlled a lion's share of its market, had the wherewithal to finance any reasonable plan, had the scope and diversity to offset and survive most economic swings, and had the marketing capability to expand and develop new markets, found itself swamped in its market by Compaq and other computer clone manufacturers that were little more than a decade old. The market changed abruptly, and IBM, with all its resources, didn't.

When Compaq entered the market, and attacked IBM on its own ground, IBM was overthrown as ruler of the personal computer business. Compaq, an upstart that went from inception to Fortune 500 in just a very few years, led IBM on technology and on reading the market. It addressed its market with a very different philosophy than IBM's, and was so right that IBM began to lose share of market to the newer company, and then, for the first time in memory, began to fail to meet profit projections. IBM is still a giant, and still has economic power, but has clearly shown limits to its ability to control its own destiny. No one, it seems, can take the marketplace for granted.

In other words, when General Electric, or any company of comparable size, develops a one-year or a five-year or a ten-year plan for its growth, it does it with infinitely more certainty than one applies to planning next Sunday's picnic.

The Smaller Company

If a vast and sophisticated corporate machine like General Motors could fail in its corporate planning, or an IBM, in the face of burgeoning computer technology, can be rocked back on its heels by newer and smaller companies, what can an analyst expect of a company a fraction of their size? A small company can blueprint, to a certain degree, its market opportunities and its plans to seize those opportunities, its capital expansion and the means for financing it, the normal growth patterns, and so on. Some of these plans may be perfectly valid, but not in an unforeseeable economic climate. Other plans may be reasonable, but perhaps not for the management as it is presently constituted. The projections may be unrealistic in terms of potential shortages of raw materials or foreseeable problems in distribution patterns and so on. The smaller company may at best have a fine grasp of its own operation and its industry, but its input in terms of the larger economic context or facilities for capitalization down the line are sharply limited, and the company is, of course, more likely to be buffeted in a rough economic sea than is the large corporation. This is the very element that gives a greater appearance of stability to the giant company—the so-called blue-chip stock. The same elements that portend stability and reliability for long-term performance for the larger company are the elements that make it easier for the larger company to plan for the longer range.

There is among analysts a skepticism that was ingrained following the glorious years of the sixties, the glorious late seventies, and for those following the energy industry, the glorious 1980 and 1981. Too many corporate leaders saw the world as a boundless cornucopia and were free in their declarations of a utopian future for their companies. They had, after all, achieved marvelous records so far. The names of a very large number of these people still come to the mind of too many analysts for them to believe any projection of glory that is not specifically documented in terms of how those plans are to be accomplished, predicated upon a record of achievement and comparable activities. Today, some analysts even want to see contingency plans as well.

It is precisely these elements that the analyst must assess as part of the job to determine the ability of the company to generate a profit on the invested dollar in the near-, medium-, and long-range future.

Communicating the Plan

Perhaps the most sensitive aspect of investor relations is communicating plans to the financial community. Credibility—projecting the plan believably—is only one part of the problem. The more significant aspect is the reticence of management to expose plans—even those that will redound to the credit of the CEO and the company.

There are two reasons for this, neither of them totally irrational. One is competitive. In a highly competitive environment, one doesn't give up the element of surprise, any more than would a general in warfare. The other is the fear of litigation in a highly litigious society.

The problem is that the management of a public company has to balance these risks against the risk of losing shareholder confidence. And even that problem is complex, if you consider that in recent years, company stock has generally dropped 10 percent on just the announcement of a shareholder suit. Of course, a 10 percent drop in stock price has also been known to trigger a shareholder suit.

There are tangible approaches:

• Plans can be specific to avenues, but general to specifics. You can say, "We are putting $10 million into research on a new formula we've developed that we think may offer a cure for the common cold." That is specific. What is general is that you've not identified the formula. You can say, "We intend to address the growing market for digital communication," which is a specific generality, without defining the product technology you're going to use. Or even the market segment you're going after. These are realistic and valid intentions, and without giving away competitive information, you've established a management definition of the company's future.

• You can realistically assess the company's market share. If your company has the lion's share of market, and a toehold into your future, then exposing more about your plans is less dangerous than it would be if you were a minor player, threatening to eat the lion's lunch.

• You can realistically assess the danger of exposing at least enough of your plans to give analysts and investors a sense of clear-headed direction. Too often, reticence is unwarranted. What competitors can do with your plans is sometimes like the man who read a book on tightrope walking. He knew everything about tightrope walking except how to do it.

• And ultimately, you can recognize the fact that what you're really after is not simply detailing your plans, but giving analysts and investors a sense of the directions in which the company is going; a reason to believe in its future as a vehicle for appreciating the investment dollar.

Much of these approaches are valid for anticipating and attempting to avoid litigation as well. There is an old legal maxim that it only takes a few dollars to file a lawsuit, but the best defense against a suit is to be able to go into court with clean hands.

There is also to be considered the natural friction between lawyers and those who must communicate. Lawyers tend to believe that the less you say in public, the less they can use against you in court, and so, they counsel, say nothing. The communicator believes that the more you say, the better you're known and understood.

Realistically, the balance must be between intelligent and rational caution, and the need to continue to be viable in the marketplace. If each side of the equation recognizes and accepts the needs of the other, there is usually mutual accommodation.

An example of how plans may be safely explained may be seen when Campbell Soup Co. announced to a group of analysts that, to accelerate slow sales growth, the company would take a one-time $160 million charge for a reorganization that included eliminating low-margin brands and cutting almost 700 jobs. This, said the company chairman, would lead to sales growth of about 8 percent a year, and earnings growth that would be somewhat higher than the company had achieved in recent years. Plants would be closed, advertising would be increased, and marginal operations would be divested. This kind of announcement may be construed to make these points about delineating plans:

- The company was showing that it was taking a bold step for the future.
- There was nothing in the details of the plan, as announced, to give advantage to competitors.
- It showed investors that it was not afraid to take bold steps to put the company on a new growth path.
- It showed investors a management firmly in control of its future and its destiny.

And besides, the plan may work.

Modern Portfolio Theory

No view of contemporary analysis can be complete without at least a passing acquaintance with *Modern Portfolio Theory*—MPT. MPT, simply, is a scientific approach to understanding the market value of a security.

While there is very little a company can do, beyond dealing with analytic fundamentals, to influence portfolio analysis using Modern Portfolio Theory, the increasing use of MPT warrants at least a minimal understanding of it.

Essentially, Modern Portfolio Theory is predicated on a concept that the degree of investment risk should be measured in terms of potential reward for that risk. But it also takes as its premise the concept that the greater the range of uncertainty about a stock, the greater the risk.

Portfolio diversification is not a new idea, nor is any form of spreading risk. The aim here, though, is not merely to diversify, but to do so with a balance of stocks with varying degrees of risk, and therefore varying likelihood of performance, so that the average uncertainty of the total portfolio—and therefore the average of the portfolio's risk—is diminished in relation to potential return.

For example, in a two-stock portfolio, if both stocks perform in the same way in response to the market itself, there is no real diversification. If, however, each responds differently to market forces, then you do have diversification. But not necessarily the best diversification, unless the potential performance of one effectively hedges, or acts opposite to and offsets, the potential performance of the other.

Measuring potential performance, and thereby potential risk-return, is done with a series of complex mathematical functions, but the basis is still a judgment of fundamental analysis of the elements of a company's potential. Beyond that, however, portfolio analysis becomes complex.

The aim is to build an *efficient* portfolio, one in which the balance of potential performance of all the stocks in the portfolio is one of minimum uncertainty. Taken into account are two major elements of risk—the risk in the individual stock and the risk inherent in the market itself, keeping in mind that not all stocks react or perform in the same way in response to the market at any given moment. Using the Standard & Poor's 500 Stock Price Index as a basis, price fluctuations—the measure of risk used—are broken down into the two risk elements (market and individual stock). The statistical technique, regression analysis, is used to measure the potential risk. A complex mathematical technique, it measures functional relationships between two or more variables, particularly where a variable (such as a price/earnings ratio) is measured against another variable (such as a market index).

Put simply, the term *beta* is used to indicate the measure of a stock's volatility, relative to the volatility of the market during the same period. The higher the beta, the higher the volatility; the lower the beta the more stable. A beta of one means that the stock performs exactly as the market does.

The term *alpha* is used to indicate the measure of average rate of return, in the same period, independent of the market return.

A portfolio that matches the alpha and beta of the S&P 500 should—and generally does—perform about the same as the S&P Index, and indeed many index funds (funds designed to match the Standard & Poor's 500) have been started based on the concept. However, there is a serious question in the minds of many professional investors, particularly institutional investors, whether indexed return, rather than one that outperforms the market, is sufficient.

In the several years since the theory was developed by the statistician Dr. Harry M. Markowitz, it has grown in popularity among analysts. But even its strongest advocates warn that it is a theory with a great deal yet to be developed and proven, and more significantly, that it is only one tool of many that should be used by analysts. It does not portend, in the foreseeable future, replacing all analysts with computers.

Analysis for Credit

At the beginning of this decade, the total value of publicly traded debt issues, both corporate and government, was about $2.5 trillion, and still growing. Most of it is traded institutionally, both by brokerage houses and individual investors.

There are about 4,500 analysts covering the bond market. They tend to specialize by type, industry or quality.

Analyzing a company for credit differs substantially from analyzing a company for equity investment. The equities investor is concerned with the ability of the company to increase the value of the investment. The creditor is concerned with the ability of the company to repay the loan within the prescribed period.

The fact that many debt issues are rated for quality by Moody's Investors Service, Standard & Poor's, or others doesn't mean the issues are automatically accepted or rejected by individual bond or commercial paper buyers, banks, or other institutions. The competition for capital via debt is no less keen than it is for equity. And certainly few banks automatically lend to any company, no matter how apparently sound, that applies for it. Investors in debt issues have choices to make, even between two bonds rated AAA.

While the approaches to analysis in each case are significantly different, there are many overlapping factors. Essential to both is a judgment of the viability of the company.

It is somewhat more difficult to know who bondholders are, as one does with shareholders, because there are no mandatory bond ownership reports. Most bonds are held in Street name, as well, which makes identification for investor relations purposes doubly difficult. This causes further problems in that bondholders, who can accumulate sizable positions without being identified, are participating more than ever in corporate management and other corporate activities, using their strength as major debt holders to force management positions favorable to debt holders.

With its own special investment parameters, bond analysis can be rather sophisticated, and therefore require a more concerted effort to impart information to analysts and investors. Obviously, cash flow is important, because the strength of a bond lies in the ability of its issuer to make payments as required. In an article in the March, 1990 issue of *Update*, the publication of the National Investor Relations Institute (NIRI), editor William F. Mahoney suggests that other concerns of debt analysts are:

- Historical trends in ratios and spreads
- Basis points of the issue compared with U.S. Treasury yield curve
- Terms of the indenture and where the company stands now in relationship with each term
- How the proceeds will be used
- Cash to be generated by the asset
- Breakout of reportable segments
- Overhead costs
- Depreciation schedule

At the same time, it should be remembered that corporate debt is not isolated from equity; telling the story to fixed income investors and analysts requires telling the equity story as well.

Thus the effort to reach debt investors must be as intensive as for equity investors. Virtually every element about a company that's of interest to an equities analyst is of interest to a debt issue analyst (with perhaps different points of emphasis), whether it's an individual, a bank lending officer, an analyst at a bond house, an institution, or a rating service. The company story must be just as carefully formulated, and as energetically presented, as for an equity issue. This holds true, incidentally, for a municipal bond as well as for an industrial or utility bond.

The rating services themselves are not infallible. They function predominantly from set formulas, but also consider subjective factors of judgment which can be just as valid a measure of a company's potential to repay debt as are objective factors. What this means, realistically, is that ratings can sometimes be upgraded by an intelligent presentation of facts to rating service analysts.

Living with the Analytical Process

There is no part of investor relations in which more is demanded of the investor relations professional than dealing with analysts. Truth is of the essence, as is vivid communications.

Advocacy is a major role as well. How, then, does the investor relations professional balance advocacy with truth, especially when the truth is not particularly favorable? The answer is that, as simplistic as it may sound, truth pays better dividends, sometimes in the long run, than does misdirection or deception. Once again, it must be recognized that the acoustics of Wall

Street are magnificent, and the truth will emerge sooner or later. If the truth doesn't square with the story being told, then the company loses more than if it had told the truth in the first place.

Even in advocacy, truth is the best weapon against adversity. The company, the shareholders, Wall Street, and the public are the winners.

Chapter 5

Working with the Financial Community

Information—the grist of the investor relations mill—is too dynamic to be limited to the simple mechanics of written or electronic communications. It can't all be done by mail, or in print, or electronically. People who make investment decisions have to *see* the principals; have to look in the eyes of management and make judgments about personality and credibility; have to hear the voice of leadership; have to ask questions and consider and explore the answers.

While all the tools of communications are the tools of investor relations, there are many invaluable vehicles for bringing management and the investor or investment advisor together. These vehicles have practices derived from necessity, from experience, and from expedience, and only the imagination limits the ways to do it.

Traditionally—and a vibrant tradition it is—these are the vehicles most often used, and the avenues most often traveled:

- Security analyst meetings, with either analyst societies or invited groups
- Meeting with or talking to individual analysts
- Meeting with stockbrokers, brokerage meetings and followup
- Money manager or institutional investor meetings
- Establishing relationships with portfolio managers

- Trader and specialist meetings and followup
- Issuing supporting material, such as a corporate profile
- Responding to unsolicited inquiries
- Electronic conferencing
- Talking to individual investors

And of course, all of these contacts are followed up and supported by a vast array of communications material, such as:

- Additional printed material, including annual and quarterly reports, to the financial community and shareholders
- Regular and periodic mailing of information about the company to the financial community, including copies of news releases
- News releases and features in the financial press
- Corporate advertising and other promotional devices
- Talking to individual investors

The guiding force behind all of these techniques is a singular objective—*to persuade investors and analysts that a dollar invested in your company will increase in value faster and more substantially than a dollar invested in another company.* These communications techniques, then, are more than an exercise in traditional investor relations practice. They are prime vehicles to establish intellectual and business relationships with investors and those who advise them.

Any meeting or contact that doesn't address that objective is a waste of time. If there is no education; no enhanced understanding; no persuasion—then the meeting or contact is an exercise in futility.

This is not to say that all analyst meetings are mere image sessions, in which symbols can be manipulated to present a picture of the company based upon fluff, and not reality. While the professional investor relations specialist can focus on the more cogent aspects of a company, no one can present a poorly run company as a paragon of management virtue.

All financial community contact, then, should begin with a clearly defined objective. That objective might well be the answer to the question, *What do we want them to know, think, or feel about our company after they've met with us.?*

With that objective defined, the rest is mechanics. But the mechanics are important to successful investor relations.

Given an investor relations strategy, the mechanics consist of:

- Defining the objective
- Defining the position—the focused message to be conveyed
- Selecting the target audiences (groups of analysts, brokers, individual investors, etc.) and the key individuals with each group
- Determining how the message is to be conveyed
- Preparing the appropriate materials (presentations, documents, kits, visuals, and so forth)
- Arranging for the meeting and running it
- Following up

Analyst and Broker Meetings

The most efficient way to get your story before the investment community is to hold meetings with groups of analysts and brokers.

Selecting the right analysts is a function, described more fully in Chapter 3. There are, however, some basic considerations that should be dealt with here.

In the early days of investor relations, luncheon and other group investor meetings could routinely include either buy-or-sell side analysts, brokers and money managers. Today, fewer analysts attend meetings that include brokers, and fewer money managers attend luncheons. Meetings are now more business and less social, with a focus on getting to the information quickly and wasting little time on frills. There are several reasons for this:

- Analysts and money managers have more options. More audio and video teleconferences, more broadcast information, more meetings for analysts only, more electronic input, including the Internet. They will come only if they feel they can gain insights not otherwise available.
- Analysts and money managers require more detail. Analysts have gotten better at their profession, and with Modern Portfolio Theory and other new techniques, they are more sophisticated. They understand their special needs better. A meeting including brokers is usually not sufficiently in-depth.
- Competition. Analysts have become very sensitive and don't ask their more searching questions in a large group. It tips off the competition to their investment strategies.
- Easier access. More companies are willing to see the analyst in his or her office or at a neutral site for private meetings. Both sides now see the greater benefits in a private meeting.

A luncheon meeting, which is the most common way to meet with analysts, should be held in a private place, preferably a luncheon club or restaurant with private rooms. The club or restaurant should have some measure of experience in dealing with meetings of this type, or else food service will extend well past the time to adjourn the meeting.

The number of attendees should be limited by your ability to serve their individual needs for information. If the meeting is to be held in a large city rarely visited by the management group, as many as twenty or twenty-five attendees are appropriate—and on rare occasions, fifty. (If you're announcing the cure for the common cold.) Otherwise, fifteen is a large number, certainly in terms of the ability of everyone present to ask intelligent questions and to allow time for questions to be answered. Any luncheon attended by more than twenty-five or thirty people can cause problems, such as not allowing an analyst to get important information. Moreover, most of the more sophisticated investment professionals won't attend a very large meeting.

Timing is important. While most analysts might attend a luncheon, particularly if it's for a company in which they are or might be especially interested, or even if they know it will be attended by other good analysts with whom they'll have the opportunity to talk shop, they are still away from their desks during the time that the market is functioning. The rule is very simple. Luncheon meetings, in most cities, should be called for either 11:45 or noon. Cocktails should be served until virtually all of the invited guests have arrived, and usually no later than 12:15 or 12:20. The presentation should begin a few minutes after the main course is begun, at about 12:25. West Coast meetings are held later, usually starting at 1:00 or 1:30 (after the East Coast market closing), otherwise they are about the same.

Lunch and the presentation should be over by 12:50, allowing those who must leave to do so, although management should stay to answer questions from the floor until 1:15 or longer, if necessary.

This may put pressure on the speakers, but professional investors want to be in and out in an hour to an hour and a quarter. Gone are the days of the leisurely meeting.

The current trend away from lunch time drinking allows for an alternative formula in which there is no pre-lunch cocktail service. Everyone is seated by 12:10 and wine, beer and soft drinks are served with the meal. That allows the main course to start earlier, at about 12:15, and the presentation to start sooner, by 12:20.

Occasionally, the analyst you invited will not show up and send an assistant instead. Some assistants are very good and impressive. Most are very junior and not able to handle discussions very well in a group with senior or experienced analysts. Too many junior analysts change the dynamics and complexion of the meeting, especially a small meeting, and management should be alerted to this contingency. It's useful to remember which analysts make a habit of sending an assistant at the last minute. Of course, it can be good practice to nurture a relationship with the assistant to build a relationship for the future. Good young analysts tend to grow up to be good senior analysts.

It's easier to get analysts than brokers to breakfast meetings. A breakfast with up to five analysts is a good vehicle. Be prepared, particularly in New York, to get up very early. Most want to be at their office for the market opening, so starting time for the meetings often is 7:00 or 7:30 A.M. EST (which for Californians is 4:00 or 4:30, a fact New Yorkers will cheerfully ignore and Californians will stoically bear).

Sometimes, two or three analysts might join management for dinner, particularly if the analysts know or know of each other, and each believes the others to be peers. A dinner or lunch for one analyst can be superb.

Analyst Society and Other Group Meetings

In major cities, local analysts' societies hold regular meetings to which companies are invited to make presentations. Usually these groups are only interested in the larger companies, unless they're splinter groups specializing in specific industries. The question almost invariably arises as to the value of the companies requesting an appearance before a city's entire society.

The problem with meetings of most analysts' societies is that they are attended by a number of analysts who don't follow any but a selected group of very large companies. This means that, except for the largest corporations, the overwhelming percentage of the audience is attending only out of curiosity. For the smaller OTC, NASDAQ, AMEX or NYSE company, most of the value in a meeting before New York, Chicago, Los Angeles or most other societies is the prestige and the usefulness of the reprint or video of the presentation. In most cases, those analysts who can best serve the company are readily identifiable, can be singled out, and can be better dealt with in other ways.

Splinter groups—segments of an analysts' society that specialize in covering a specific industry such as real estate, apparel, insurance, and so on—

are increasing in number. For the medium or smaller company, appearance before the splinter group makes infinitely more sense, because there's a greater likelihood of interest in the industry. For the larger company, its value is obvious.

There are also brokerage groups that exist in a number of cities, such as Houston, Allentown, and St. Louis. They hold luncheon meetings, paid for by the company and not the brokers, at which presentations similar to those given before other groups are made. Some of these groups are sound and useful, and well worth the money. The problem is that, unlike other investor meetings, some meetings are just a free lunch for many more brokers than can help a company. These groups should be considered with caution. Particularly beware those groups run by promoters for a profit, and not by the brokers themselves. As has been noted, brokers tend to be less detail oriented in analyzing a company than are analysts, a point to be remembered when meeting with their groups.

Individual Analyst Meeting

Depending upon your investor relations strategy, and the need to reach a specific group of investors, it can be worthwhile to target a specific individual analyst. Sometimes, an individual analyst will reach out to you, for reasons of his or her own.

When you target an analyst, do your homework beforehand, and send ahead as much information in print about your company as possible. The point is to take advantage of the occasion of a meeting by devoting the time to helping the analyst understand management, its plans, its skills and capabilities. Why waste that valuable time on information that can be sent ahead? The meeting could be about a double check of facts, new factors and developments, new directions and to get to know management personally. Be prepared to talk competition, industry outlook and your strategy.

It's also an opportunity to establish a relationship with an analyst with access to important groups of investors—to build relationships for the future. Better analysts tend to be cautious, and make few snap decisions.

While luncheons these days are wrapped up well within an hour and a quarter, a meeting in an analyst's office can impart much more information in one hour and, if the meeting goes well, it can last an hour-and-a-half. The opportunity for quality time is enhanced.

Stockbroker Meetings

Large group meetings with stockbrokers are not what they were once, and should be planned cautiously. It seems there are fewer brokers interested in doing their own research, and fewer willing to lunch if they're not actually interested in the company.

Those brokers who are still interested in selling stocks they research themselves are mostly older and more experienced, usually with large followings and with clients with large portfolios. They do their own due diligence, and live by their successes, their failures and their lawsuits. No other position in the sell side of the business does it all like those brokers who choose to sell their own researched situations. This group—the large producers—are among the best contacts. While they may occasionally come to a large lunch or dinner, smaller groups are more to their liking and meet their needs better. Minneapolis, St. Louis, and Milwaukee are three cities in which luncheon meetings with brokers are especially popular. Still, private meetings are best.

The structure and rules for running a brokerage meeting are essentially the same as for running an analysts luncheon meeting. While many brokers are delighted to attend a luncheon, particularly if it's for a company in which they are or might be especially interested, or even if they know it will be attended by other good investment pros with whom they will have the opportunity to talk shop, they are still away from their desks during the time that the market is functioning, and this should be considered in the timing.

The Post-Market-Close and Other Meetings

Not all analyst, broker, or money manager meetings need to be luncheons. For companies with an especially interesting story to tell, a post-market-close meeting can be useful. Brokers and analysts are selected and invited in the same way as for a luncheon meeting, but the meeting is held at 4:15 P.M. EST, after the market closes, as either a cocktail party or, if convenient, at the offices of the company itself. For an initial public offering due diligence meeting, or for those with a tight budget, a post-market-close meeting can be especially useful. Most investors will want to leave by 5:00 P.M. or a little before, although a few may stay on and chat for a half hour or so.

However, after-the-market meetings are difficult for analysts, because they tend to be much larger groups, and the presentations are too general and too long. They might work if the analyst is assured that this meeting is only for those who already know the basics of the company story, and that management will have some interesting material, hopefully on strategy, competition, direction, etc. Breaking news is not necessary, but meaningful additions to the mosaic would be appreciated.

Another variation is the single-firm broker meeting. Frequently, the sales manager or research director of a brokerage house can be persuaded to invite corporate management to the brokerage house's office after the close of the market, or during lunch or breakfast, to make a presentation to the staff of registered representatives. The rules of the presentation are the same as for the analyst meetings, except that it should be anticipated that the questions are likely to be somewhat less detail-oriented than those from the analysts, and will dwell more heavily on such market factors as the recent movement and volume of the stock, which is, after all, the broker's prime concern. Presentations are a little shorter, with ten or twenty minutes most useful, and thirty minutes at most. Questions will be light unless senior brokers attend, which doesn't normally happen. A special effort should be made to get some senior brokers to be there. Sales managers can only require the junior brokers to attend.

In some cities, there is an increasing tendency to hold both analyst and broker meetings at breakfast at a central location. Except for the tighter time constraints, this can be useful and effective.

Pre-Meeting Preparation

Organizing a meeting of analysts or brokers is a singular type of party planning. It's a balance between mechanics and strategy. Where and how you hold the meeting is a function of logistics. Who you invite and how you relate to them is a function of strategy.

The Mechanics

Once the list of invitees is determined and the date selected, simple but effective one-page invitations should be mailed out or faxed. There are always some analysts, brokers, and money managers, however, who are important enough to invite by telephone. Invitations should be sent three to five weeks before the meeting.

Two weeks after the invitations are sent, there should be a phone follow-up to develop a preliminary list of those who plan to attend. Those who have accepted the invitation should then be sent a kit of printed materials on the company. This should include the latest annual report, subsequent interim reports, the corporate profile, the Form 10-K and 10-Q (for analysts—brokers usually don't care about the 10-K or 10-Q), the last annual meeting proxy, releases issued since the annual report, reprints of material about the company that have appeared in the financial press or the trade press (or even articles from the consumer press if they demonstrate the company's claim to product superiority or widespread promotion), reprints of important and significant trade or consumer advertising campaigns, business biographies of top management, and, if pertinent, product material. Include a pad, or at least a few sheets of paper on which attendees can take notes. If you are using slides, you might want to supply reprints of the text of the slides, with room for notes. Lancaster Colony and other companies have used slide reprints effectively. Product samples can be effective, if they make an appropriate point. Companies like National Picture & Frame and Sharper Image have made product samples work effectively with the financial community.

It's rare that every one of the invitees attends, no matter how small or familiar the list is. The phone follow-up gives the first basic idea of what attendance is likely to be. There's usually a 10 to 20 percent drop-off of actual attendees from the list of those who accepted the day before. There can be a 50 percent fall off if the weather is bad or the brokers don't really know the company. Don't guarantee or set too many places. A lot of empty seats look bad.

The morning of the meeting, and perhaps even the afternoon before, everyone who has accepted the invitation should be phoned as a reminder. Convention style badges should be made for everyone who is to attend, including management. They allow the company officers to be readily identified and to be able to address investors by name. They allow the brokers or analysts to identify one another and to build valuable relationships, which is important in an industry in which interchange of information is extremely valuable. Attendance can be taken by noting which badges are used. A representative for the company should be responsible for checking people against invitation lists, and supplying badges to substitutes and uninvited guests. Uninvited guests can be refused admission if there's a good reason for it, but that should be done cautiously. The less reason they have for attending, the more vociferous will be their reaction to being refused admission. In some cities—New York, certainly—there is a network of luncheon guests who even the waiters know by their first name. If one of these attendees is invited, they sometimes bring ten friends. Have spare seats ready.

Including the press at professional investors' meetings has generally not been preferred, although opinion varies. Some investors believe they would need their firm's permission to be quoted, and might be inhibited from even asking questions if the press is present. Dow Jones frequently asks to attend, but unless the meeting is going to be used to impart important new information, the press should probably be refused. Societies and splinter groups should be specifically queried, particularly since some have strict rules about press attendance or how to go about it.

An attempt should be made to determine whether any other competing meetings for companies are scheduled that would draw away investment professionals you want. This is done by phoning a few key investment professionals you plan to invite and asking them if they know of any other company or any society group that's planning to have a meeting on that date and at the same time. There are also services that list investor meetings of various kinds. These services, while excellent in reporting on brokerage, analyst or industry conferences, are not always able to pick up smaller or independent meetings.

Meeting Strategy

Determining who is to be invited to group meetings and luncheons with investors is an art unto itself. And like in the world of fine arts, there are many different opinions, advocates and adherents to a myriad of different philosophies and styles.

You can, for example, chose a small group of the best and most interested individuals. This is useful for a company with an active and long-standing investor relations program and where the company has strong potential as an investment.

But sometimes, if there is no group of specifically dedicated investors, it can be more useful to cast a wider net. But if the company is not well known, or has an obscure advantage in the stock market, you may have to invite 300 people to get 30. In any event, there's no cut and dried rule—judgment must be exercised to function within the context of investor relations strategy.

Some pointers:

- The initial invitation list will expand to the extent you want to reach new investors. The smaller the company, or the less attractive an investment it appears to be, the larger the contact list. The less known the company is, even if it has $400 million in revenue, the larger the initial list must be.
- Lists will be longer for companies just initiating an investor relations program.
- The list will be longer if the company's management has never visited a city before, or if it did but hadn't met expectations.
- The list will be shorter if an outside investor relations consultant is used, and the consultant has a following in that city.
- The list will be shorter if the company has built a following in that city and it wants to speak primarily to those it already knows.

You may be placing yourself at a serious disadvantage if you eliminate any groups by categories such as brokers or analysts. You should, on the other hand, eliminate brokers—but not necessarily analysts—from houses that won't let their people sell stocks under $5.00 if your stock is selling for $2.50. If your stock is selling at $4.50, and if you're optimistic, let them come. If you have no bonds, and are not likely to, try to keep bond traders away.

The Presentation

Whether a prepared speech or an outline is used is the personal choice of the executive who is to make the presentation. Of the two, the outline is preferred, if for no other reason than that it seems to demonstrate more readily the executive's grasp of his company. It's too easy to assume that a speech was written by someone else. Some speakers use the slides as an outline, or as a guide to the oral presentation.

The organization of the presentation is extremely important.

Styles have changed in presentation. Once, presentations were rather formal, beginning with a very brief history of the company. Today's investment professional prefers not to waste time on preliminaries, but rather to get quickly to the heart of the matter.

Multimedia presentations, in which slides, videos, and audio are mixed dramatically with a live speaker, are being used increasingly. If they are professionally done, they make use of the best techniques of presentation. A caution, though. Too slick a presentation will put the emphasis on the presentation itself, and not the content.

The presentation should begin, then, with a brief statement of what management believes to be the most important factors about the company, including its strengths and competitive advantages. An important part of the presentation should be to focus on the core idea that epitomizes why the company is an especially good investment—the position, as described in Chapter 2. If no other point is made but that core idea, then the presentation must be deemed a success.

If appropriate, management can delineate those problems that the company has had or that the industry has faced in very recent history, certainly within the past year. This is followed by an explanation of the company's long range strategies—its plans to grow internally or by acquisition, or by developing new markets, its new product strategy, and so forth. It then briefly describes the company as it's presently constituted—what it is, what it makes, how it distributes, the size of its markets, why it is in those markets. This is followed by a discussion of the company's financial structure, based on the principles discussed in Chapter 4. This leads to a discussion of management and plans for the company in the short term—the current quarter and the balance of the year. The meeting is then opened for questions.

Strategy statements and information about the company's future are more important. There is no need to summarize key points, nor to go into financials in detail. Financial information should have been distributed before the meeting, and certainly before the presentation, and then the presentation can just touch necessary highlights. It can be useful to talk to a few of the key analysts ahead of time, to fathom what they believe is important, and then use their direction as a guide to the substance of the presentation. Knowing your audience is important.

It's absolutely essential that no company executive attend an investors' meeting without having anticipated as many questions as possible that might be asked by the investment professionals, and having prepared a thoughtful and considered answer. Preparing the questions and briefing management is a crucial role of the investor relations professional. If the speaker doesn't know the answer to a question, he or she may refer it to another executive, or even the investor relations officer. For questions for which there's no immediate answer, there should be a prepared response, such as, "Give me your name and we'll get back to you with an answer by this afternoon (or tomorrow)." The most impressive presentation can be destroyed in a moment by one important question that's badly or hesitantly answered.

The tone of the presentation should be honest, forthright, and positive. Negative factors should be expressed clearly and in no way avoided, but they need not be dwelt upon inordinately and out of proportion to their importance to the overall picture. Hostile questions should be handled patiently and forthrightly and, even if the answer is negative in terms of the total presentation, should be ended on a positive note.

Don't let one negative questioner dominate the question and answer session. When there is a negative line of questioning, suggest that it can be followed up after the meeting is adjourned, so as not to bore the others who don't have a great deal of interest in the subject. However, you'd better be right in your assessment. The last thing you need is for three other guests to say, "No, we want to hear the answer too."

It should be recognized that despite all care taken in developing the invitation list, a certain number of investors will invariably show up who really don't care about the company, even if they discover that during the course of the presentation. They will seem uninterested or ask cursory questions. It should also be recognized that not everyone present will see the company in the same way, nor with the same degree of sophistication. In any meeting of ten or more investors, there will almost invariably be three or four unimportant or irrelevant questions—questions asked because analysts feel they must say something to make their presence known or because they frankly doesn't understand something. These questions must be handled with the same patience as the more serious and delving ones.

The investor relations consultant or officer has a definite role, in the course of a meeting, to keep the meeting on track and to the point. That means shielding management from irrelevant questions by judiciously intercepting them before management answers, if possible; to help avoid confrontations by interceding as a mediator or clarifier; to deflect duplicate answers by gently interrupting; to avoid misunderstandings or direct attacks, and so forth. While the consultant or officer should not be obvious in a meeting, he or she should be an active participant, when it's appropriate and when rapport with management permits.

Using Visual Aids

A great many company stories are well told by visual presentations—a short film, video, or slide presentation. This can be useful and effective if it's carefully done. It works well if it is pertinent, tight, and to the point. It's useful in visualizing product and service, as well as in the graphic presentation of complex financial material.

The growing sophistication in technical equipment, including the computer, has fostered imaginative and dramatic visual presentations. Aptly called *multimedia*, the technique combines sight and sound to add a greater communications impact. In its most sophisticated mode, multimedia presentations combine voice, music, graphics, animation, video—the full technical gamut—to inform, to sustain interest, to focus on specific aspects of a company's virtues. In imaginative (and usually professional) hands, multimedia presentations can bring drama and excitement to even the most mundane company story, even as they communicate most effectively.

The visual presentation, however, should never preclude a personal presentation by the chief executive office, unless the CEO feels uncertain about public appearance. It should merely visualize that which is best visualized—the star performer should always be the corporate spokesperson. How else can those factors about management's capabilities be demonstrated than by a CEO's or other executive's own physical presence and participation?

Despite the fact that each person invited has been sent a kit of materials about the company, a duplicate kit should be placed on each seat before the luncheon. Many investors will have forgotten their kits, or there will have been substitutes to whom no kit was ever sent. Extra kits are usually welcomed. A potentially fatal mistake, incidentally, is to include a copy of the executive's presentation in the kit. There is nothing more distressing to a speaker than to look up and find ten or fifteen people following his words on the printed page, or reading ahead of him. It's good practice, on the other hand, to record the presentation and transcribe it for distribution to interested investors who didn't attend the meeting for one reason or another, or to pass it out or mail it after the meeting.

Electronic Meetings

Contemporary technology has opened some extraordinary avenues for communicating with large or selected groups of people at one time. And as with all technology, increasing use and technological advances have moved some of these techniques from science fiction to reasonably priced reality. It's now possible for an executive to hold a conference by phone, by video, by satellite, by Internet, with an unlimited number of people in an unlimited number of locations. And it is literally a conference, with the same give and take to be found in an on-site conference.

The advantages, as with all contemporary technology, proliferate only to the limits of imagination. We know that we can hold the meeting or discussion electronically. But we are just beginning to see that the imaginative options are awesome.

The obvious advantages, of course, are the effective savings in time and costs. If you can talk to a hundred analysts throughout the country—throughout the world, in fact—at one time and sometimes on very short notice, and not have to transport either the audience or yourself to a fixed site, then you have more than the electronification of a formerly mechanical process. You have a new dimension in communication. If you can impart news to a hundred analysts throughout the universe at one time, and have questions asked from different parts of that universe, and shared at the same time with all of those people, then the news itself takes on a new meaning. If you can reach a large but selected group of analysts at one time, and have them participate in a discussion with management, you've built a broader but selected following.

If you're able to hold several meetings during the course of the year with large or selected groups of analysts in different locations, instead of only once or twice a year, you can develop a rapport based on an intensive distribution of news. It can take the news release much farther and more urgently than can mail or even newswire, can give you virtual real time feedback, and can keep you constantly in touch with the market for your securities. And all within a fraction of the cost of doing it in person.

Which is not to say that management and the investor relations professional are absolved from having to prepare carefully and intensively. The medium, in this instant, is not the message, and the content of the message must be the same as one would impart using traditional vehicles. The medium does, on the other hand, introduce a new dimension in communication that can enhance the message by delivering it more quickly and universally than ever before, and by getting a broader base of response and feedback than could be found in a smaller, local, meeting. The impact is at least more urgent, and through the effect of a broader spectrum of feedback from many different participants, can perhaps change the texture of the message.

Ultimately, with increased use, the novelty of this medium will wear off, as it has with other technology. But by then, experience will have honed skills, and the medium will have come into its own.

To some extent, electronic conferencing is superseding some personal contact. Caution. Personal contact, in most cases, is still best.

The advantages of the new technology are very real, and will proliferate with time and experience. This is a technology, after all, that will breed its own practices and added values.

The Electronic Conference

The electronic conference, whether by audio, video, modem, or Internet, takes what has traditionally been a one-at-a-time event and turns it into a multi-faceted activity that can spread over several weeks with modest additional cost and much greater rewards.

Teleconferences are relatively simple to set up, and can be done by your own long distance carrier on very short notice. They are, in effect, simply conference calls. Telephone companies are very helpful in showing how to do it, and in helping to do it. Specialized teleconferencing companies are even better, and offer additional services as well.

The rapidly burgeoning Internet, which will be dealt with in greater detail in Chapter 6, allows quick access to vast numbers of people, either by e-mail or in a conversation mode (known as the *chat room*). Currently, most people in business are either online now, or will be soon. More and more companies now have active Web sites, and investors are increasingly taking it for granted that Web sites give instant access to new and constantly updated information. E-mail is rapidly becoming as ubiquitous as the telephone. Online discussions are also becoming popular, and a great deal of business is now done that way. It should be an industry standard well before the new century. No investor relations professional should be caught by surprise from an Internet rumor that affects the stock.

Video conferences, unlike teleconferencing and the Internet, require fairly extensive preparation, and are best done by professionals. There is a question of equipment on both ends, as well as the graphics one would normally use in any visual medium. Expertise is essential here, and fortunately, there are a growing number of companies that do it. Competition in this field is breeding more realistic costs.

As video teleconferencing comes down in price and gets easier to access and use it will more often be the medium of choice. It's already used regularly by very large companies like IBM. Video teleconferencing itself has changed. It used to refer to conferences set up for sight and sound communication by a third party supplier, such as AT&T. It's now making greater use of two-way communication, and using multimedia techniques. For example, it may not only be done live on video screens or a special teleconference terminal, but might be communicated over your personal computer. Firms leading the video broadcast industry are Medialink, NBC, Dow Jones, Bloomberg, and Reuters.

While video conferencing, whatever its form, might never completely replace the all-important face-to-face meetings that the financial industry relies on so heavily, it's likely to replace most of the routine, introductory and emergency meetings. Evidence of the seriousness of the industry's growth is that such a large company as Intel purchased a significant position in VTel, the third largest teleconferencing equipment maker. It has been reported that in 1993 the two companies agreed VTel would provide software to Intel, in exchange for a license to Intel's ProShare personal video conferencing technology. Vtel is said to be designing a family of video conferencing products ranging from desktop to large conference models. Intel reportedly provided $4 million for research and development early in the relationship. In 1996, Intel increased its stock ownership in VTel. This is serious business.

As with any activity, traditional or electronic, preparation must be meticulous. The planning should include at least the following steps as a guide, but not necessarily as fixed rules. Circumstances—and good imagination and skill—alter rules appropriately. The basics are:

- Determine the reason for the event, and its objective. The rules of the press conference (Chapter 8) apply. To hold an electronic event simply because it's possible to do it, or because it affords a broader audience, is scant reason. There should be a singular message, or at least a piece of news of magnitude, to impart; a realistic basis for urgency; a sound foundation for bringing a large group of investors together. The classic question to be addressed at this point is, again, *What do you want them to know, think or feel after the conference is over?*
- Determine the timing. Is each event discrete, and planned separately each time for a different audience? Is it a periodic event—quarterly, semi-annually or annually—to the same audience?
- Determine the target audience. Even though you can reach large groups at one time, you will still have a different message for analysts than for brokers; for retail analysts and for institutional money managers.
- Plan the invitation process. How will you invite people to participate?

What is the timing of the invitations? What is the best response mechanism? Fax? Mail? Phone?

- Detail and script the event. Who talks and says what? Who handles the questions from the audience? What material gets sent out beforehand, and what material afterward? What is the script to say and who is to write it? Do any of the speakers need training?
- Run the event. But rehearse, first. You're paying for the time, and the participants are paying with their time. Every moment should count.
- Follow up. How? With what? How often?

Determine the Objective

While it might be tempting to use a teleconference or a video conference to simply replicate the classic analyst meeting, it might be more useful to use the event as a means to impart something specific and something more appropriate to the new medium.

Obviously, differing factors dictate different approaches. A company that's new to a great many analysts and potential investors might want to hold and surpass the classic meeting, but the ultimate judgment lies in what could reasonably be expected as a result. If introducing an undervalued company to a great many potential investors is the objective, then the medium is used differently than it would be to tell a large group of analysts who have been following the company about the meaning of new products or new contracts.

One key to the success of an electronic conference is to recognize that, more than in the classic meeting, the level of focus and attention of participants can be exceptionally high. But that also means that the opportunity is best seized by focusing on a single message—a single position—for each conference. The answer to the question of what you want participants to know, think and feel afterward is a good starting point. While it's tempting to try to make more than a single point on your nickel, it just doesn't seem to work. One major point, reiterated and supported with facts, does work.

This assumes that you've done your homework in vetting the participants, and in sending ahead the kinds of facts and figures that participants can read and refer to at leisure, and that don't need to be reiterated in detail by management as part of the presentation. The facts and figures, remember, support the message. They should not be the message itself—unless, of course, the facts and figures are the point of the session.

Determine the Timing

If you're using the conference to supplement disclosure, then the timing is dictated by the Rules of Disclosure. (See Chapter 9) Teleconferences are useful on short notice, when special events require quick followup to disclosure of the kind of urgent news that you are also putting in a news release, like a major acquisition, an unfairly negative news story, a fire at a major plant, and so forth. The quarterly teleconference is becoming the standard for teleconferencing key investors and analysts in small groups, and in video conferencing larger groups.

A mid-quarter teleconference is an excellent vehicle for new or potential investors who might not fully understand the company. A call at the beginning of the third month of the quarter is opportune.

The time of day for a conference is dictated by the nature of the conference and the audience, remembering, again, that a video conference requires infinitely more preparation than does a teleconference, which can be set up on virtually a moment's notice. Obviously, as in all other communications to the investing public, it seems rational to release breaking news early—even before market opening (allowing for differing time zones). Negative news is sometimes held until after the market has closed, which can adversely affect credibility. A University of Chicago analysis suggests that releasing results and having the call after the market closes minimizes the unusual first few minutes of overreaction that sometimes occurs. In view of the increasing amount of after hours trading being done, these classic rules may now be irrelevant, but that, too, is a judgment call.

The conference call at the after-market close has two other advantages—it's backup if the disclosure wires don't print your release, and there are more investors available than when the market is open.

Determine the Target Audience

Because of the relative simplicity and lower cost in setting up a teleconference, there's more latitude in choosing a target audience, particularly in several cities at once. It can be new or current investors, analysts or brokers. The choice of the group is no different than it is for traditional meetings. For teleconferencing, the minimum useful group is probably about five to eight, although as many as twenty is manageable. More than 25 to 30 can be unwieldy, especially if questions will be accepted. It may even be feasible to hold several calls, back to back, with different groups with different invest-ment concerns.

For the videoconference, the number is limited only by budget and tech-nical considerations. In view of the original cost of equipment, larger groups are feasible, and for larger companies with larger followings, as many as a hundred people in one video conference is not unusual.

The Invitation

A one page letter or fax on corporate letterhead from the CEO or investor relations professional to investors briefly and directly states the purpose of the call—announcing quarterly results, current update, comment on a known acquisition, comment on a known management change, further explanation of an announced strategic change of direction, and so forth. The invitation shouldn't anticipate the key news, which would take the impact out of the conference, and might not be considered adequate legal disclosure. The letter tells the reader there will be a telephone, video, or Internet conversation with selected investment professionals or key investors and management, and that there will be the opportunity to ask questions. It should explain who else will be on the call, both management and participants, so that all invitees have a good sense of the company they'll be part of, and can prepare accord-ingly.

Depending upon the medium and the size and composition of the par-ticipating audience, letters may be varied for different groups.

The timing of the letter is a function of both the event and the content. For a conference on news that is closely linked to timely disclosure, the letter should be sent out urgently—perhaps even by overnight courier or fax. For larger events, a week or two beforehand might be appropriate. For Internet conferences, e-mail itself becomes the medium for invitation.

As with traditional conferences, some electronic events may require phone followup to invitees.

The Script

Preparation—and rehearsal—are necessary for a succinct, focused, and suc-cessful conference. Use professional speech trainers, if necessary. Hone the message to specifically address the point of the conference. Anticipate questions, and prepare answers beforehand. Surprises in front of a large group, even on a telephone conference call, can be embarrassing.

Careful preparation is also necessary because interest must be sustained—perhaps even more so than in a traditional presentation. A number of people in different locations are brought together not in a common room, where there is little choice but to focus on the speaker, but at their own desks, where they can be easily distracted. Dull, uninformative conference calls are a profound waste of money. Be interesting, be informative, or you're wasting your money and eroding your credibility.

For video and online conferences, prepare visuals that will supplement, not replace, the message.

The techniques and structure of electronic presentations are essentially the same as for traditional meetings. The difference is in the focus of the message, and in the time constraints.

The Event

The more people involved as participants, the more precise the timing must be. The conference should start on time, and end on time.

Even if key people on your staff are not participating, they should be present to supply information and help with questions.

In large conferences, such as videoconferencing with groups in a large hall, there must be staff at each participating location to help with microphones, and to direct and monitor microphones and cameras for questions. That assistant can also gather off line followup requests and information.

Follow-up

No contact of any potential value—not an analyst, an investor, a broker, a money manager—should be treated as a random participant. Until you have reason to believe otherwise, every contact is a potential investor or someone who will influence investors in your favor.

This means that every conference participant should be added to a mailing list for followup, and should get, at least:

- A thank you letter, and an invitation to make further inquiries
- A steady stream of company information at regular intervals

- An invitation to participate in future conferences
- An invitation to ask more questions
- If the individual is sufficiently important, an invitation to come visit, or to meet one-on-one
- An offer of additional sets of material for colleagues and clients

On telephone inquiries following a phone conference, shareholders can be told that if they call an 800 number for the twenty-four hour period immediately following the completion of the call, they can listen to the entire conference free of charge, possibly including the question and answer session. Shareholders get the first twenty-four hour period because they have made the financial commitment to the company and deserve it .

Tapes and transcriptions of these programs can be used as mailing pieces to both current and prospective investors. Certainly a transcription can be put on the Internet. It can be mailed to media. It can be used as a quarterly report to shareholders. These activities extend the value of the original event.

The Web Site

While the techniques and structures of online Web sites will be addressed in Chapter 6, it should be noted here that the online Web site is fast becoming standard for all public companies. Within a year of the publication of this book, virtually every public company will have a Web site. It allows the Internet user to log on to your site for a full array of information, from the latest financials to the latest company news to a discussion of management and a list of products. Even now, analysts are comfortable checking the Web sites of hundreds of companies in which they might invest or that they might recommend. Once a luxury and even an oddity, the Web site is now considered standard.

Earnings Projections

In speaking of meetings with analysts and investors, it's impossible not to address the question of earnings projections. Whether spoken or not, and despite the myriad new formulae for gauging stock value, earnings projections are very much in the thoughts of every investor—almost as an end product of analysis. There are many schools of thought about earnings projections.

An earnings projection by management that can be given any substance or validity is an analyst's dream. It gives the analyst something on which to focus. The assumption is that any well-managed company can make at least a short-term projection of how it's going to perform, give or take a few percentage points. Certainly, every company is likely to have a short term budget.

On the other hand, earnings projections have several inherent dangers. They may be viewed as an implied promise of performance that may well preclude factors beyond the company's control. They may place the company's credibility precariously on the line, and are frequently misjudged. A projection of $1.30 that comes out as $1.23 can cause the market to overreact irrationally. A projection of $1.30 that comes out to $1.40 can cause the market to overreact on the upside, or to not react because management apparently doesn't have proper feed-back programs.

An earnings projection also places an additional psychological burden on the management team by causing it to focus its energies on operations toward meeting that projection, which is not management's job.

Of course, properly handled, these concerns can evaporate. For the management willing to come forward and correct previous estimates as new data becomes available, projections can be a no-lose game.

What almost invariably happens, on the other hand, is that the analysts themselves will make a projection in the form of a question. If management chooses not to make a projection of its own, it can simply ratify the analysts' projection as *being in the ballpark* or otherwise too high or too low. Care should be taken that commenting on an analyst's projection doesn't give management ownership of that projection. Review the Safe Harbor law in Chapter 9. If management has decided to make no projection, it should in no way be bullied into it. There are sufficiently sound reasons to explain the refusal to do so if the remainder of the presentation has been forthright.

There is one important point regarding all investor meetings, and in fact, any form of financial communication. Although it will be dealt with in greater detail in Chapter 9, the Rules of Disclosure very clearly apply here. Any statement made in an analyst meeting, whether it be before one or many analysts, that is significant in judging the company, that may affect the trading or price of the stock, and that has never been made before, must be publicly and widely released as quickly as possible, according to rather stringent guidelines. If management intends to make such statements at a meeting, whether it be an earnings projection or a major diversification plan, a release should be prepared well beforehand for appropriate legal public disclosure at the time of the meeting. There should be no surprises or accidents. This is extremely important.

Meeting with Individual Investors

Investor relations has traditionally paid little attention to reaching individual investors directly. The primary means of individual investor contact has been through corporate printed reports and the press. Telephone and personal contact usually happens only if it's initiated by the investor. Emphasis on individual investors sunk even lower as more individuals invested only through mutual funds and corporate profit sharing and pension plans.

An exception has been the efforts by very small investor relations consulting firms, working for very small over-the-counter companies that targeted individuals directly through TV infomercials, other advertising, or mailings followed by phone calls or telemarketing. These efforts are not the norm, however, because smaller companies haven't had a great or positive overall impact on the market.

But in addition to meeting with investors in groups, it's frequently more valuable to meet with significant investors individually. A series of individual meetings may be more time consuming than group meetings to reach a large number of people, but the potential value to an investor relations program may be worth it. And the input from these investors can be valuable.

Simply because of the time involved, individual meetings should be limited to investors representing significant interests and funds. This includes analysts and investment professionals for retail houses, funds, or investment advisory services. The major criteria are the buying power and decision-making authority of the individual, and not the size of the institution.

There are distinct advantages in individual meetings for both the investors and management. Obviously, it represents a greater commitment for the investor giving time to the meeting, and because of the preparation that usually goes into such a meeting, the willingness to meet usually means greater than average interest in the company. In return, the investor usually gets a clearer and more intensive view of management. The questions tend to be more searching and wide-ranging and the executive may be more challenged. His or her answers are likely to be more detailed than they would be in response to questions from the floor of a larger meeting. Here, too, the company must be prepared to release publicly any information of consequence that had not heretofore been public knowledge. A record of the meeting—even on tape—should be kept so that it can be shown that no inside information was given, should it prove necessary to do so. (Beware. Some attorneys might recommend the opposite approach.) Of course, the new rules of the 1995 Safe Harbor Act should be followed. (See Chapter 9)

The meeting can be held at breakfast or lunch, or in the office of the chief executive, or in the office of the investment professional. Here the presentation, while almost as complete as for the larger investor meetings, and as well prepared, can be somewhat less formal, more direct and limited to key points. It's a discussion, rather than a speech.

The lack of enthusiasm for meeting with individual investors will change. Prompted by the excitement and growing participation in the Internet, the investor relations professionals and the individual investors increasingly meet each other on the World Wide Web, CompuServe, America Online, and the Microsoft Network. That means more direct interaction between public companies and their investor relations professionals and individuals.

The financial chat lines will remind a great number of investor relations professionals and companies that individual investors are out there. As the SEC's T3 ruling, under which all trades must be settled within three days, forces more investors into Street name holders, and companies lose track of more of their investors (more than 50 per cent in Street name holdings is now common), and brokers become less of a target as they turn more toward selling funds, there will be a growing need to aim efforts directly at more individuals.

Individual investors, most will find, are extremely accessible, and open to developing a relationship based on their share ownership. Should they hold their stock, or buy more, the investor relations professional's job gets easier.

Organized efforts to reach individual investors will help companies reach them cost effectively. They can always be found through organizations such as the well known National Association of Investment Clubs. Other ways to reach them must be developed. Investor relations professionals should keep lists of individual investors, and use them as part of a professionally developed marketing program. The lists, of course, have to be carefully managed, and frequently culled and updated.

It's a good idea to hold individual investor meetings where a company has shareholder concentrations. Teleconferences for individual investors will also prove valuable. The individual investors with substantial holdings can be invited to professional investor meetings.

Individual investors sometimes take, or can be cultivated to take, a very personal attitude toward the company and their investment in it. As such, they can provide some support in difficult times. They also give the investor relations professional a chance to test ideas (within the bounds of SEC rules) and hear directly what end users of investor relations services are thinking. When writing annual reports and interim shareholder reports, it's good to have first hand input about the thinking of some of your audience.

Individual investors hear rumors, which make them good sources for the size and nature of the rumor mill. This can help a company to decide whether to respond, or how to respond, to deleterious rumors, and to stem them before they are too widely spread.

In the current configuration of the stock market, the individual investor is emerging again as important, both as an investor and as a source of valuable information. Attention should be paid to them.

Money Manager Meetings

In the realm of important individuals whose needs should be addressed consider portfolio and money managers—the distinctive breed of individuals who manage huge pools of institutional funds, or the funds of high asset individuals. Their potential as prospective investors in any company can be overwhelming, as can be the size of the pools of funds they have to invest. This has been the most fertile area for targeting and segmenting, especially those institutions or capital pools managing more than $100 million.

Their needs for information about a company seem to be more intensive; more urgent. Their tastes and talents, as well as their individual investment theories, put them apart from most analysts. They ask highly technical questions, and demand substantial answers. They want access, and they want performance. They expect you to know about them and what they need before you contact them. As investors, they take large steps.

They are value or growth investors. They are theoretical. There are the *quants* who rely more on numbers than personal factors. There are technicians. There are fundamentalists. Money managers are more interested in macro trends than other investors. The world economy, the U.S. economy, monetary trends and policies, industry trends, momentum trading, new technologies, consumer spending, capital spending, wars, and so forth are all important fodder for them. Yet, like brokers, they are keenly interested in recent market action, in current stock positions—in the same things that concern any investor.

There is no doubt that the more you know about any of these investors the better off you are. Buying or building a file of them is mandatory. It must be computerized, to keep the list and the information current, including a contact history.

Investor Inquiries

Occasionally, a company (and especially those that for one reason or another prefer to remain obscure) will capture the eye of an individual analyst without any effort on the company's part. The analyst then calls the president and asks searching questions. Sometimes an individual investor will feel lonely and concerned and will take it upon himself to call the company president. Nothing inappropriate about it, but sometimes a surprise.

These inquiries should be anticipated by the management of every public company, and prepared for in much the same way as for the presentation for a full-scale analyst meeting. An individual analyst who surprises a company president and gets the wrong answers can do considerable damage to a company's stock, no matter how well the company is doing. There is no need for it. These questions should be anticipated.

All inquiries should be treated courteously and in detail. The company should follow up the inquiry by mailing the same material that it distributes at meetings. If the caller is an analyst who represents an important enough faction of the investment community, it's certainly appropriate to invite him to come in for a personal visit and a plant tour.

It's extremely important, in anticipating inquiries and preparing the presentation, that the company story be uniformly understood and told by any member of the management team who is likely to get such an inquiry or is designated as a spokesperson. In some cases it's appropriate for the chief executive officer to insist that all such calls be passed on to him or her, to the vice-president of finance, or to the investor relations officer. This approach may seem like a put-off, which in itself is an attack on credibility. It then behooves the chief executive officer to be sure that everyone who might receive such an inquiry is fully informed of the company's point of view, method of presentation, and proper answers to questions. This is now especially true under the new safe harbor rules passed by Congress in 1995. (See chapter 9)

When the company is some distance away from a major city, when there is a story of particular interest to tell, and when a tour of the company's operations can contribute to the analysts' knowledge, one or several analysts may be invited to visit with management at the company's plant. This is frequently done at the company's expense, although a large number of analysts' firms prefer that they pay their own way. Analysts also make field trips on their own, touring a particular area and some of the companies within that area.

Follow-up

Apart from conducting these formalized investor meetings, a properly run investor relations program, whether performed internally or with the aid of an investor relations consultant, must include a concerted marketing effort to build and service a following of investment professionals.

Merely to address a meeting of investment professionals is not, as will be seen in the chapter on strategy, to solve an investor relations problem, or to develop a marketing oriented investor relations program. The corporation is, after all, competing against hundreds and thousands of other companies, not only for capital, but for the investors' attention as well. This competition is a continuous effort. Simply because an analyst has met with management and heard its story once, and even if that analyst is impressed, there is no reason to believe that interest will be sustained or that the analyst will not be distracted by six other companies that command his or her attention. This interest is sustained by putting every analyst and investment professional who attends a meeting—or expresses any sort of interest—on an active mailing list. It calls for an aggressive effort to use every appropriate means to sustain relationships with investors.

The analyst must then be contacted periodically, updated on material, reminded of recent information that has been released, and to have any questions answered. It's an ongoing process that, to be effective, must be consistent with marketing principles in both structure and attention.

The mailing list you develop from any source, whether it be individuals who attended meetings or those who phoned with inquiries, or those who responded to any of your efforts, serves a double purpose. It contains the names of prospective investors, and it serves as a prime source for input, feedback and information.

An important consideration in keeping a mailing list is that a company changes, and the investor who was not interested in the company at one point may be interested in it at another. Sound marketing requires assiduous attention to changing needs.

At the same time, you have a marvelous source for learning a great deal about the market for your company's stock. You have the foundation for continuous informal telephone surveys that can arm you with significant competitive intelligence.

For example, a good survey should garner such information as:

- Whether your major positioning messages are being understood
- Individual investment goals, whether they match your positioning
- How many shares they own, how the shares are held, the name of the brokerage house and broker, and when they were bought
- How they decided to buy, and how they found out about your company
- What they think about your products, services, and management
- What they think about your recent performance, and strategies
- Are they thinking of adding to their position after calling?
- Did they buy or sell after calling, why or why not?
- Does this program help them to maintain interest in your company?
- Would they be interested in shareholder buying or dividend programs?
- Demographic information, such as income, geographical areas, schooling, product-service usage, age, sex, marital and family questions, etc. For an auto products company, for instance, you might also ask what kind of cars they drive, year, how many, etc.

Over time, these surveys can build a library of important intelligence.

Research Reports

A constant aim, in dealing with analysts, is to generate research reports by brokerage houses or research services. These are reports, issued periodically, for use by both brokers and investors. They may be either brief discussions of the company or intensive, detailed research studies. They almost invariably conclude with a purchase recommendation, or a recommendation to hold the stock for the longer term. A favorable recommendation by a major firm can be a virtual guarantee of increased buying, and frequently, a higher stock price.

A successful investor relations effort includes constantly developing new interest in the financial community for a company. A knowledgeable consultant will be aware, by virtue of consistent efforts in the field, of many analysts and what companies they're following, many of the changes among analysts and their affiliations, and the current basis for viewing companies. The consultant will spend a considerable number of hours every month talking to analysts and other investment professionals to determine those who are likely targets to hear the company's story. Earlier contacts will be followed up to keep them updated and to help maintain their interest. The consultant will develop a constantly expanding following for a company and eliminate those investment professionals no longer interested or no longer available to be interested. This also leads to developing sponsorship for a stock, as well as new market-makers.

Because of the intensive nature of this kind of outreach, many firms take advantage of the extensive facilities and breadth of contacts of outside investor relations consultants.

In many cases, and only with the permission of the issuing firm, a favorable report may be reprinted and distributed to the shareholders and others in the financial community. Good judgment suggests, however, that an analyst from one firm might be skeptical about a report from another, while some will welcome the input. Don't guess—inquire.

There is, as well, differing legal interpretation of the responsibility that accrues to the company that distributes the estimates in an external analyst's report. Some companies then, refuse to distribute analyst's reports. Others do so with a disclaimer.

Feedback

Feedback of market reaction to the company and its presentation is as much an element of the communication effort as is imparting information. By frequently speaking to investment professionals who follow the company, as well as those who decide not to follow it, the consultant or investor relations officer supplies an extraordinarily valuable view of how Wall Street sees the company. The investor relations professional will identify the problems to be anticipated in telling the company's story, and will be invaluable in determining strategy for meeting objections and for developing sustained interest. Although the general function of the investor relations consultant and investor relations officer is dealt with in another chapter, it should be noted here that the more effective consultants are those who have specialists not only in the techniques of dealing with the Street, but also those whose communication and marketing expertise dovetails with intensive involvement with the largest number of investment professionals and investment companies. This gives them the basis for a constant two-way flow of information and intelligence.

The effective consultant will also supply the company, on a regular basis, with reports of each significant Street contact made in the company's behalf. This includes a report of follow-up discussions with a representative sample of the investment professionals who attended any meeting. The report covers the date of the contact, the person who was contacted and his affiliation and position, what was said by the contact—including negatives—and the consultant's impression of the discussion. This kind of report gives the company an effective and continuous feedback of financial community reaction to both the company and its presentation.

The Overseas Markets

If investor relations in Europe and elsewhere abroad was once primitive, compared to the United States, the gap is closing quickly, according to Leonard Baker, Chairman of London-based Baker PR Associates, Limited and a leading European investor relations consultant.

"When the chairmen of France's three leading companies invoke the sacred mantra of shareholder values, you know the revolution has finally arrived," notes Baker quoting a Paris-based American broker. It sums up, he says, one of the most significant changes that has taken place not only in France but in the rest of continental Europe. "Five years ago, the French didn't know what the phrase meant and regarded shareholders and the investment community as nuisances hardly meriting benign neglect."

Baker further notes that with German management, until recently, the prevailing attitude seemed to be that shareholders were "stupid and impudent." Stupid because they bought shares in the first place, and impudent for expecting a return on their investment.

In the boardrooms of Paris, Frankfurt, Brussels, and Amsterdam this point of view is now regarded as old fashioned, if not downright dangerous. Where once disclosure was considered a dirty word, and investor relations was simply a mailing service for annual reports, a new transparency and professionalism has emerged in a race to understand and apply Anglo-American techniques of communication.

All of this, Baker reports, has been brought about by a number of factors:

- Savers recognized that long-term equities could produce superior returns, compared to other forms of investment
- A drive by underdeveloped continental stock exchanges to create real markets of sufficient liquidity to meet the awesome challenges of London and New York
- The growth of investment in continental securities by sophisticated international institutions, particularly American and British, demanding new standards of disclosure and performance
- The privatization of many state companies broadening share ownership
- The growth of cross-border trading
- The acceptance by an increasing number of continental senior managers that debt alone can no longer finance growth
- The desire of family-owned middle-sized companies to seize real opportunities to achieve wealth
- The pioneering efforts of such giants as Daimler Benz to cultivate the international investment community by listing their shares abroad and adapting their reporting procedures to Anglo-American requirements

London-based investor relations consultant Garry Wilson notes that cities such as Edinburgh and Amsterdam have long been recognized as receptive and significant investors in U.S. equities. And now even the traditionally smaller locations such as Dublin, Paris, and Stockholm hold larger amounts of funds.

Wilson also reports that smaller American companies should expect to see European investors own 5–7% of their shares; 5–6% of medium companies' shares; and about 5% of the shares of larger corporations.

Compared to America and Britain, investor relations on the continent is still relatively primitive. But all that is changing rapidly. One only need read the new, attractive, and sophisticated London-based magazine, *Investor Relations.*

Baker cites significant examples of the new climate. "In France and Germany, for example, there is an increasing demand for investor relations professionals, and specialist recruiting agencies have opened in both countries. New financial public relations firms boasting ex-fund managers, analysts, brokers and journalists have set up business. Where once road shows and analyst conferences at head office were virtually frowned upon, leading companies hold as many as twenty meetings a year, and their ranks are increasing daily."

Though much of Europe, including Britain, is still slower to embrace high technology, Baker says, no self-respecting investor relations professional would be caught dead without telling of his plans to use videotapes, CD-ROM's, teleconferencing, and Web sites in the near future.

Britain is the most progressive investor relations outpost in Europe for a variety of reasons. "Its equity markets dwarf continental competitors," Baker reports. "It has a long-standing tradition of international investment. It has an incomparable infrastructure of professional expertise and experience. It pioneered financial deregulation and privatization on this side of the Atlantic. It has introduced many financial concepts and products. It boasts Europe's most sophisticated, outward looking business media. Its language dominates business communications. And, in general, it has more contact and interaction with America."

Ten years ago, British financial public relations professionals stood in awe of their U.S. counterparts. This reverence no longer prevails, as the British rush to open offices in New York.

This presumed superiority by the British may be hubris, but one thing is certain. Business is booming, and U.K. professionals have attained a high level of respectability transforming them from messenger boys to boardroom advisors. The British Investor Relations Society now numbers more than 350 members, and runs frequent conferences, seminars and training programs. The people who have entered the field come from backgrounds in law, accounting, brokering, security analysis, journalism and even industrial management.

What has triggered this explosive growth has been booming equity markets, changes in the structure of the financial community, unprecedented merger and acquisition activity, the profusion of privatization and initial public offerings and the recognition by the managements of British companies that marketing their shares is not only respectable but critical to growth. Britain's entry into the European Monetary Union in 1999 is expected to enhance Britain's position as the financial capital of Europe.

The most exciting event in London in 1996, Baker reports, was the successful launch of the Alternative Investment Market (AIM). This is an equity market established to cater to the capital needs of young, small companies which heretofore lacked the means, size and track record to qualify for an official London Stock Exchange listing. In less than a year, more than 200 companies have listed on AIM, and the flow doesn't appear to be abating.

Though AIM is minuscule compared to NASDAQ, its success has required increased services of independent investor relations consultants. Much of what they do for these and larger clients is similar to work done in the United States. If there are differences, they are more a question of emphasis and style rather than substance. For example, British financial investor relations professionals generally spend more time cultivating the financial media and the tendency to use guarded leaks that the SEC might find questionable. On the other hand, U.K. operators are more reluctant than their U.S. brethren to approach fund managers directly, fearing to incur the jealousy of possessive institutional brokers. In the United States, investor relations practitioners and institutional salesmen frequently work closely together. Tom Stevens of Tucker Anthony and Dan Killian of Herzog, Heine, Geduld are just two institutional sales executives who have successfully worked with investor relations practitioners.

London is expected to maintain its pre-eminent position as the financial center of Europe. What is particularly exciting to investor relations practitioners in London is the prospect of continental business. More and more French, German, and Italian companies are coming to the City of London financial center to market their equity wares and to capitalize on the trend of increasing cross-border trading. The rush is on to establish networks throughout Europe and for once the impetus is coming from the Europeans rather than the Americans.

Corporate governance, Baker notes, has become an important hot-button concept on the east side of the Atlantic. As the U.S. institutional investors pour more of their money into European securities, the old practice of shielding certain management practices and financial data becomes increasingly untenable.

Even British fund managers, who traditionally voted with their feet when unhappy, have begun to exert their influence for better standards of management behavior. Just as in the United States, there has been a ground swell of outrage at those who reward themselves while underperforming. In France, where corporate governance is still vaguely understood, senior managers were shocked when at a recent bank shareholder meeting, a shareholder physically attacked management in a style reminiscent of the "Reign of Terror."

The subject of corporate governance has become so significant that no self-respecting European business school would be without a required course in it. And to crown this development, Cambridge University recently announced that it was contemplating establishing a college—the first in the world—devoted exclusively to the subject.

Corporate America still loves to woo the European capital markets. Says Baker, "There has been no let-up in the number of American companies crossing the ocean to attract European investors. With the exception of the month of August, a day doesn't go by without at least two or three U.S. companies making presentations in London."

Some people have suggested that the number of road shows will diminish because of the Internet and teleconferencing. But so far, American management appears to prefer the personal touch. Or, as one British fund manager put it, "Technology may shorten these companies' itineraries in the States, but they still find the European visit irresistible. After all, where would you rather go, Amsterdam or Akron?"

For aggressive, internationally-minded CEOs and CFOs, the news is both good and bad. The good news is that Europeans are far more inclined to invest in smaller-cap U.S. stocks, particularly in the information technology and bio-engineering sectors, than they were five years ago. The days of the Nifty Fifty—the top fifty stocks on a preferred list—are indeed past, and a company with a market capitalization of at least $100 million can expect a reasonable hearing if it has an interesting story to tell.

The bad news is that U.S. companies face much greater competition in the quest for European investment funds. A decade ago, the United States and Japan commanded the lion's share overseas equity investment, but that situation has altered with the rise in interest in other share markets, such as the Far East, continental Western and Eastern Europe, and Latin America. Though the United States and Japan still figure prominently in asset allocation terms, their relative positions have been somewhat diminished. Nevertheless, there are billions available. Companies should continue to take European investors very seriously.

Though some United States companies have been ardent and effective wooers in the past, there is still room for improvement. Baker suggests some key points to keep in mind when contemplating a more active program in Europe:

• Once a company commits to a program, it must stick to it. Coming when times are good and staying away when times are not so good just doesn't work. Europeans value consistency and respect companies who return each year through thick and thin. And they do remember those who didn't—Europe has a long memory. Try to understand the European financial marketplace and the audiences to be reached. This is essentially a job of education and targeting. Know what funds cover specific sectors; what their investment practices have been in the past; what are their market capital minimum requirements; and how active they are in trading their portfolios.

• Out of this study, develop a list of prime targets in each market and concentrate exclusively on these for future road shows and one-to-one meetings.

• The U.S. brokers who follow a company can be valuable allies, but don't rely on them too strongly at the expense of developing local supporters. In addition to organizing meetings with resources developed separately, seek the help of European practitioners in getting the right investors. When practical, relieve them of all local costs and offer to handle all the logistics through existing U.S. investor relations resources.

• Track the overseas ownership of stock consistently. Though this may be more difficult than it is in the States, information can be found provided one is diligent and seeks out the help of friendly brokers. The brokers have become far more effective in locating who owns what and how many and for how long.

• Go for quality, not quantity, at road show meetings. Having fifty to a hundred guests at a meeting may do wonders for the ego, but is not the most effective way to establish meaningful relationships. The best meetings usually have five to twenty invitees and this number creates a good atmosphere for informal, frank discussions.

• Be skeptical about the virtues of listing shares on foreign stock exchanges. With global and cross-border trading now increasingly in place such a listing will have little impact on share price. To be such a good corporate citizen will cost you dearly. It could run as high as a million dollars a year.

• European road shows might have a minimum schedule of at least five days to justify the expense of doing them. Must places to visit are London, Edinburgh, Geneva, and Zurich. The other key financial centers such as Frankfurt, Paris, and Amsterdam are also worth covering, but not as essential if time is a limiting factor. A two or three day trip to just London and Edinburgh can be worthwhile to establish a presence.

• Before each trip take time to be briefed on the organizations that will be attending the road shows. Europeans appreciate the courtesy, and will be impressed by the fact that a company does its homework.

• Constantly update European mailing lists by having the investor relations practitioner check to see if recipients still wish to receive material. This will save money and incur some good will.

• It isn't critical to have all financial material translated into local languages, but multilingual documents such as the annual report are appreciated.

- Capitalize on invitations to participate in sponsored investment conferences and seminars that cover a related industry sector. These meetings are becoming increasingly popular in Europe, and offer a good way to meet many new people and to get insight on how the opposition is faring on the other side of the Atlantic.
- Finally, time European visits to coincide with other business reasons for being there. It will save money.

Chapter 6

The Computer in Investor Relations

Most technology evolves, and enters our society and culture gingerly and over time. The computer, on the other hand, exploded into our lives, and infiltrated virtually every facet of our daily personal and business activities. And all within the lifetime of any adult living today.

The computer is infinitely more than an electronification of what we used to do mechanically. Word processing is not electronic typing, any more than a jet plane is simply a higher form of transportation than the horse. It's not simply an electronic version of mail, and the Internet is not a direct lineal descendant of the pony express.

These are important facts to recognize if one is to participate in contemporary business. The computer and its electronic auxiliaries are not just tools—they are a new dimension in human functioning. What computers do transcends almost every human endeavor that preceded them, and irretrievably alters those endeavors for now and forever.

When the first copy machines were invented, we marveled at the fact that we could eliminate carbon paper and expensive photo copying processes. Anybody could do it.

After a brief excursion into electronic transfers of text and graphics, primitive and cumbersome as they were, there came the modern fax machine. Simple, and so affordable that families could have one in the den for communicating to other family members elsewhere in the world. As a business tool it became so indispensable, even within the first months of its existence, that no one can remember how business was done without it.

And now comes the computer, with a word processing program that has taken the typewriter into the depths of museums, and given a new creative dimension to those who saw typing as a non-executive, nonprofessional function.

With a database function that puts a world of knowledge at the fingertips of the least technical of us—and then goes a step farther with a searching and sorting dimension that was almost impossible before. With e-mail that allows us to communicate around the world—as does the telephone—but with speed, terseness, and a lower cost than we could have imagined.

As for its role in investor relations . . .

Because of the computer, there is little done today as we did it five years ago. Or even one year ago, so rapidly is technology embracing us.

In a well run investor relations office:

- Executives communicate with one another, both internally and externally, with e-mail. More people know what's going on about more things than ever before.
- Intranet programs, such as Lotus Notes, allow groups of people to work together—literally—from different parts of the world, or the nation, or even the same office, and all on the same documents. Group efforts take on a new dimension, without expensive travel and long, burdensome meetings in airless offices or airport motel conference rooms
- Computerized financial data is available to all who need it instantly, on a real time basis. The financial picture of the company is now dynamic. It doesn't freeze as of a date certain.
- Through the computer, and the Internet, the entire financial community, including the financial press, is informed instantly, and the information is available to not only professional investors, but to the smallest individual shareholder at the same time.
- The analyst now has information that was once too cumbersome or arcane to capture. But the analyst also has computerized analytical tools that allow information to be massaged while it's timely—calculations that could never be done before within the time that the data was still current and useful. Analysis now takes on a new dimension as well.
- Through the Internet, every investor, every analyst, has access to government data, including SEC filings, that was possibly available, but rarely

accessible. Simply log on to EDGAR—The Electronic Data Gathering, Analysis, and Retrieval system, to retrieve any SEC filings since 1994. The address is www.sec.gov/edgarhp/.htm.

• Through the Internet, every investor has access to company Web sites that give more information about a company than was ever available in print, if for no other reason that the cost of printing it all was exorbitant.

• Through the Internet, conversations can be held with a company's executives, giving investors and analysts more access to the executive suite than was ever before possible.

• Using an emerging technology• called webcasting, users automatically receive, on their computers, ongoing broadcasts of financial news, data, and other information on an ongoing basis. It's a direct line to ever-changing data.

There are compelling reasons, then, why investor relations professionals must use technology as an integral part of their practices. The Lawrence Ragan Communications publication, *Interactive Investor Relations,* cites seven good ones:

• *Financial transactions are routinely being done electronically.* Many companies already distribute reports and proxy votes over the Internet, and technology exists to include video and audio in research reports. While Wall Street spends an estimated $500 million annually on printing, mailing, and producing investment research, this amount will drop dramatically in the next few years as more information becomes available faster and cheaper. And annual reports are now being produced on CD-ROM as well.

• *A substantial number of international and domestic corporations maintain dedicated investor relations pages on the World Wide Web.* These sites contain financial data, corporate organizational information, prospectuses, executive profiles, news releases, and sales figures.

• *Analysts are increasingly relying on the Internet to obtain and present financial information.* Today, primary source investment analyst firms maintain World Wide Web sites to provide electronic delivery to serve analysts who are working electronically. This could affect how firms rate their analysts.

• *Newsgroups—dedicated areas of online discussion about a specific topic— have discovered product flaws that can affect a company's stock price overnight.* This happened to Intel when a computer newsgroup discovered problems with the company's newly introduced Pentium chip.

- *Information is no longer being disseminated vertically.* Financial data used to move directly from corporations to analysts, without any intervening input. Today, new financial information—as well as rumor and analysis—comes from outside the established network. When IBM announced its tender offer for Lotus, it announced that it was holding a press conference at 1:30 P.M. on the day of the offer. But IBM provided more specifics on its WWW site at 9:30 A.M. From 9:30 A.M. until the 1:30 P.M. press conference, IBM's WWW site registered 4,000 hits (log-ons) from interested parties. (This raises, incidentally, some questions not yet answered. For example, are there now two tiers of information—the traditional press and wire, and the computer—which means that investors without a computer would get information later than those with a computer? How will that affect the Rules of Disclosure?)
- *A struggle is developing over who will control information.* Search engines and supersites (home pages in the World Wide Web listing a large number of companies) are making it easier for investors to find company information. These sites have the potential to organize companies by industry group, location, or financial ranking. The analysis appearing at these sources is being supplied independently of the issuing corporation.
- *Falling costs.* Almost all Internet costs—hookup, development, and maintenance—are falling. For example, institutions can save about $1,000 a month if they receive research materials through First Call workstations. Xerox investor relations manager, Charles Wessendorf, reports that the company saves $100,000 a year by delivering documents electronically.

Is this the investor relations of a decade ago? Or even five years ago?

At The Financial Relations Board, the nation's largest investor relations firm, an analyst, broker, or investor can log onto the FRB Web site, and through it, access the Web sites or data on every one of FRB's clients. FRB and others also use fax-on-demand, which allows users to fax requests by document number, and have the document faxed back automatically. It's an extraordinary request response service that disseminates information without tying up personnel for long periods of time.

Obviously, this new electronic structure changes the nature of investing, and therefore, the nature of investor relations.

- With this flow of information, more is known, and can be known, about a company than ever before.

• On the Internet, access is from anywhere in the world that has computers and phone lines, and so information is accessible throughout the world. The smallest company can reach out to the farthest reaches of the world.

• With database searches, an investor can find every public company with predefined parameters.

• With analytical computer programs, investors and analysts can use analytical techniques that allow greater predictability and probability of security performance than was ever before possible.

• The investor relations professional can search databases to find investors in any category; analysts with particular investment preferences; shareholders or potential investors by size of holding, preferences, geographic location.

• The investor relations professional can survey shareholders for preferences and reactions, and profile a company's shareholders quickly and accurately, without expensive and time consuming surveys.

• And under new SEC rules, a company can even have its own underwriting, with an on-line initial public offering.

And this is now. By the time you read this, the list of possibilities will be even longer.

Some statistics from recent surveys, all of which will be understated by the time you read this:

• A recent survey by the Columbia School of Journalism reports that a quarter of surveyed newspaper staffs access the Internet daily. That number is undoubtedly substantially higher now.

• A majority of the journalists indicated that they want all media relations submissions online within five years.

• A survey by Creamer Dickson Basford of 1,189 financial analysts found that 29 percent like to get annual reports by video or online. That was in early 1996. The number has risen substantially.

• A survey reported in Lawrence Ragan's *Interactive Investor Relations* indicated that 77 percent of U.S. companies will be on the Internet by 1997. It seems likely that the percentage has already surpassed that figure, and is rising rapidly.

• A survey by Computer Intelligence Infocorp, in mid-1996, reported that 57 percent of households with more than $40,000 income own computers.

• At the end of 1996, there were 1,569 newspapers online.

How to Do It

First, recognize that the inventory of software available to facilitate participation in computer and on-line services is vast. Some of the more useful programs are listed in the Appendix.

Aside from the basic computer setup—the computer, sufficient memory, a modem, and so forth—two things are necessary:

- *An on-line provider.* The choice is made by size and reputation of the provider, by cost, by accessibility, and by your actual needs. Many smaller businesses, for example, use CompuServe, Microsoft Network, or similar commercial services. The cost is reasonable, and they offer services beyond the Internet. For the larger business, a dedicated service, with national accessibility, is probably more practical.
- *A Web site.* A Web site is more than a location on the Internet. It's an interesting, even exciting, repository of information. It's dynamic, because the information can be changed and updated to serve your objectives. It offers value to whomever logs on to it. And most important, it's part of a total investor relations effort.

The On-line Provider

The on-line provider you choose for accessing the Web may not be adequate as a site for your own Web site, but can be fine for your own accessing needs. The major considerations in choosing a site for your own accessing are convenience, local access number, price, and services. The commercial services, such as CompuServe, Microsoft Network, and America Online (AOL), are simple to use, and in their latest versions, offer direct access to the net. They each also have a vast array of useful services, ranging from data to entertainment, including chatlines that allow you to hold scheduled conversations with celebrities and entertainers, as well as with people with like interests. They have either flat monthly fees, or flexible fees with a minimum number of hours for a flat fee, plus additional hourly charges for access beyond the minimum. They even have facilities for building modest Web pages. The problem is that Web pages built on their sites cannot be moved to another provider.

Dedicated providers, on the other hand, offer no services beyond Internet access. They charge either a flat rate, or an hourly charge. There are local providers with access only in a single region or area, and national providers with either 800 numbers or a variety of local access numbers throughout the country. For a fee, they will list, host, and in some cases, service your Web site.

While access to a provider is done with a regular phone line, supplied by your local telephone company, heavy users should consider an ISDN operation—a special phone line, using a special modem, that functions at extraordinarily high speed. Its cost is offset by the saving in on-line time, because data is downloaded so quickly. Check with your local phone company.

Building a Web Site

Operating a Web site consists of the following elements:

- Designing the site
- Choosing a provider
- Getting an appropriate Web address (a URL)
- Preparing the content
- Serving the site with updated content
- Promoting the existence of the site

There are two ways to design a Web site. One is to use a good Web site authoring program, of which there are several (see Appendix). Even if you lack graphics skill, these programs can take you through the process, and produce a fairly attractive site. The other is to have a professional Web site designer do it. If you plan to have a heavy duty site, that's the way to go. It pays off in the increased number of people who access your site.

Either way, design begins with a clearly defined objective. What do you want people to know, think, or feel when they log on to your site? What kind of content will you provide, and for whom? How often will it be updated, and by whom?

Some informal research by potential users will give you an idea of the kinds of information your audience will best use and appreciate. You should consider, too, the equipment on which your site will be viewed, and not make your graphics too elaborate for the computers generally in use.

It might be a good idea to think about a *webmaster*—someone in your organization who will take responsibility for seeing the process through and for keeping the content up-to-date.

Included in your design concept should be a consideration of the kind of visuals you want. Not just the site itself, but graphs, charts, and other illustrations as part of content. Whether you design it yourself or use a professional, these are questions only you can answer about your own site.

In planning content, build in as many key words as possible that can be used by search engines. A key word is one that is used in *hypertext*, in which clicking on the word brings up another Web site. Or search for a key word on a search engine, such as Yahoo or Excite, and it will bring up a reference to your site.

In considering content, think in terms of feedback. For example, you might have an e-mail option for questions to the CEO and other company officers. Texts of speeches and papers given at conferences should be downloadable.

Choose a provider who is capable of putting your site on-line and managing it, including keeping it refreshed with your content and readily accessible.

For certain kinds of information, you can use encryption, in which a password is needed to access the site. If you use the site for any purpose other than investor relations, you may want to charge for the data, which can be arranged by your provider.

You can use your site to build a database by having accessors register on-line before gaining access. This can be particularly effective as an investor relations tool.

Your site must be registered by submitting your address to the InterNIC, in Washington D.C. Your address will either be registered, or you will be advised that it's already in use by someone else, in which case you have to choose another address. Registration costs $100.

Your provider will also have a maintenance charge, which can range from $25 a month to several hundred dollars, depending on the provider, the site, and the usage.

You've got to let people know the site exists. There are any number of ways to do this:

- First is the key word. Be sure that all the search engines are aware of your existence, and that keyword and name searches will bring viewers to your site.
- Be sure to put your Website address—the URL—in all your literature and advertising, including stationary and press releases.
- Directly advise shareholders, analysts, money managers, and so on, by e-mail or letter.

A Web site that nobody knows about is as good as no Web site at all.

Who Should Do It

Ragan's *Interactive Investor Relations,* in exploring the options to set up and maintain a Web site in-house or to use a third-party provider, sees advantages and disadvantages in either choice.

Maintaining the site in-house commands the time and attention of at least one person—a webmaster—from at least a half day each day, to full time, depending upon the site and how it's used. Obviously, if the company is large, and the content is extensive, and the site is upgraded frequently, the webmaster has a full time job. Karen A. Wharton, vice president of investor relations for FTP Software, says that one person in their department maintains the site half-time, regularly inputting press releases, EDGAR data, and other investor relations information. The advantage is that the company maintains control of the site and its input. The disadvantage is the staff time (and cost) that must be dedicated to it.

Third-party providers, such as Vestnet, create and maintain a corporation's Internet address for a fee. They update regularly, and link directly by computer to the company. Fees are based on the kind of service needed, and the frequency of updating the page. The advantage is that the site is professionally managed. The disadvantage is that costs can run high.

E-mail

If there's any part of the computer generation that can be a mixed blessing, it's e-mail. It's terrific because of the ease of contact with others, and as more and more people get on-line, e-mail becomes almost as ubiquitous as the telephone. Another advantage is that you can read it at your leisure and convenience. You can't do that with a telephone.

The downside is that it's so easy to use that it can be overused. Some executives have complained that they could spend hours every day reading their e-mail, and that most of it is not important or urgent.

There are many approaches used to diminish e-mail. Some companies put a 1 to 5 priority system in place. Others mandate length limits, or access limits. The perfect approach seems not to have emerged, other than to recognize that the value of e-mail is greater than the downside.

The Intranet

In larger companies, particularly those with more than one office, Internet and Web technology is being applied internally. This is called *intranet*. The same kind of Web pages built and serviced for the outside world function well inside, by supplying needed information to staff elsewhere in the firm, anywhere in the world. It is growing into a major use of computer technology.

A structure that can be less elaborate, but just as useful, uses a program called Lotus Notes. Lotus Notes allows users on the same system to work on a document together, no matter where in the world they're located. Documents can be sent back and forth, can be written by several people working at their own screens. It can be used as an electronic conference, allowing people to develop concepts and ideas together. It has its own e-mail system as well, which can be used either internally or externally.

The automobile, they say, changed the face of the nation by giving us mobility that was cheap and convenient. The computer has changed the face of the world by making ideas and information accessible where they had been inaccessible before. It's the perfect definition of the true role of technology—to serve and advance civilization, society, and commerce.

Chapter 7

Corporate Communications

R eaching the professional investing community on a sustaining basis is a dynamic process. It works best in real-time, where action and reaction are constant and instantaneous. It means there must be a consistent flow of information to the analytic community and to shareholders. Face to face meetings with analysts and investors are crucial; but so is the sustained relationship that comes from the flow of printed and other forms of communication. It is, as well, a process framed in advocacy, as might well be expected in a competitive arena.

With the advent of the computer, and its total integration into the financial world, new opportunities arise to communicate, and to listen and learn. Reaction to events is accelerated, generating new techniques, new skills, and, for the most computer literate, new opportunities to compete more effectively in the financial markets.

It's all part of the marketing campaign; of focusing attention, and flowing information, to sustain an awareness, a concern and a consideration for the company and its stock. Sound and effective corporate communications is the best kind of support, as well, for management.

While there are traditional forms of corporate communications, ranging from the financial corporate profile to the annual and interim reports to the press release, there are really only two limiting factors to what can be done— the law and imagination. True, there are certain formats prescribed by tradition and trade custom, such as the form of the press release (which must function within the context of media—but which is being changed by electronic transmission techniques). But corporate communications devices are susceptible to whatever can be imagined that still accomplishes the objectives. An annual report, for example, can be on videotape, and even CD-ROM. It will ultimately be on full motion video on the reader's computer screen, as well as in other multi-media formats. You can, if you think it will work, wrap bonbons in financial statements and send them to brokers. This is, after all, a marketing function.

The basic documents inherent in virtually every investor relations program are the annual and interim reports to shareholders—the 10-K and 10-Q reports to the U.S. Securities and Exchanges Commission—and the annual meeting notice and proxy, all of which are also prime documents for analysts and other investment professionals; the financial corporate profile, a supplementary document designed to be useful primarily to investment professionals; and press releases. There are, of course, other printed documents that can be used (such as reprints and product literature), and there are other forms of corporate communication to the financial community (such as letters, videotape reports, faxes, e-mail, Web pages, and audio tapes).

The Annual Report

There is probably no investor relations device that's commanded more discussion than the annual report. Since every public company issues an annual report in one form or another, it's the one investor relations tool (other than 10-Ks and 10-Qs) that's universal, even for those companies that do nothing else in the field. Sid Cato, editor and publisher of the *Newsletter on Annual Reports*, noted in 1996 that more than 12,000 U.S. companies are required to produce an annual report. Millions of dollars are spent (and sometimes wasted) every year in the production of these documents. Millions more are spent in their distribution, and the dollar value of executive time is incalculable.

A great deal is written on the core issue of an annual report—what it really is and should be, and how it is to be used. An overwhelming number of annual reports are merely imitations of reports that have gone before, with the basic reasoning for the predecessor long since forgotten. A great many reports are issued that seem to be designed solely to fulfill an SEC or stock exchange requirement, and so lose the many great advantages of a thoughtful, well-planned and well-executed document and investor relations tool.

Even defining the basic audience for annual reports is controversial, most often predicated on irrelevant issues. One school of thought believes that the annual report should be written so that it can be understood by the least sophisticated shareholder. At the other extreme there is the notion that the annual report should be simply the company's Form 10-K—or at least as austere. Others think of the annual report in terms of a peculiar concept called the *corporate image*—a predetermined view of the company to be engendered and projected to the investing or general public, with almost total disregard for facts or realities. Even the elaborate regulations of the SEC, viewing the annual report and Form 10-K as a package, serve as a minimum document, in view of the potential value of the annual report.

There are moves, by the SEC and others, to abbreviate the annual report; to reduce and summarize its contents. The feeling is that in its current form, the information is so overwhelming that it inhibits communication. The feeling is that shareholders can then have the option to receive the fuller version. The argument about summary reports can be expected to rage for years.

Ultimately, there are two core realities that should be remembered in planning an annual report:

• An annual report is a financial document and a financial relations tool. It is not a graphics device. It is not primarily an advertising medium. It is the basic tool used by every segment of the investment community—the shareholder, the security analyst, the broker, the money manager, the bank, the institutional investor, the institutional lender, and so on—to help make the basic evaluation of the company as an investment or lending vehicle. Furthermore, it has an active life of at least one year—until the next annual report is issued. During that period it serves as the primary handbook for evaluating the company, regardless of what other documents or information are used to supplement the information in it.

• Each annual report should be approached virtually as if it were the first time in corporate history that any annual report has ever been written. This doesn't mean that the company should look as if it had been reinvented each year, but rather that a fresh view should be brought to the report every time it's done.

The legal requirements of an annual report under SEC and stock exchange rules, that it report certain prescribed facts about the company, can be met with a word processor and a photocopying machine. Therefore any decision to go beyond the bare bones must not only be predicated upon the needs of the company, but, as well, may take virtually any form, in any format, that serves to present a clear picture of the company without distorting the truth. Successful and communicative reports have been in the form of national business magazines, movie scripts, analyst meeting reports, children's picture books, videotapes, and CD-ROM. Annual reports now appear regularly on company Web pages on the Internet.

The greatest effort in developing an annual report should take place in the planning stage. A number of specific questions should be raised early, and examined very carefully in all aspects, before any work is done on the report. It's useful to put these questions, and their answers, in writing, as a form of prospectus for the report. The prospectus may even be longer and more detailed than the report itself, but the result makes the effort well worthwhile. It becomes a clear document and statement of policy for everyone who will have to work on the report. It can cut down the almost inevitable rewriting, and it eliminates time-consuming discussions over drafts that must ultimately be discarded because not everyone involved understood the same things about the directions in which the report was to go.

The prospectus should include:

- Outline of issues and unusual circumstances, and outstanding elements that form a context for this particular annual report. This should evolve into a single central theme for the report.
- The objectives of this specific report—what we want people to know, think and feel after they've read it.
- The target audiences—Shareholders? Analysts and brokers? Suppliers? Government? Special interest groups? Employees? If all, then which are priorities?
- The format. Size? Paper? Cover? Feel? Elaborate or stark?
- Special features. Industry? World economy? R&D? People? Corporate mission? Strategic changes?
- Graphics. Typefaces? Photos? Drawings or paintings? Bold? Colors? Institutional look? Classic or avant garde look?

Objectives

At the time a company prepares its annual report, it faces a specific set of circumstances and opportunities in regard to both its own operations and the capital markets—circumstances that are pertinent at that moment and no other. These circumstances and opportunities may be peculiar to the company, the economy, or the industry. They may pertain to changes within the company, its corporate structure, its products, the markets it serves, its people, or changes in financial structure. The company may be undergoing some unusual and highly visible litigation. The economy may have certain elements in it which particularly color a view of the company, such as the energy crisis, inflation, or devaluation. The industry may be undergoing significant changes or material shortages. The company may be appreciably out-performing its industry. The relevant context may be short-term, but it is the annual report that serves as the prime vehicle for management to address itself to the company's position relative to these factors. Or the situation may be long-range, such as a change in the direction of the company's operations or growth plans. For example, the stock market might find growth or cyclical companies particularly attractive for the coming year.

An example of how a change in corporate direction can be dealt with in an annual report is provided by a very successful company, National Picture & Frame Company. One year, this major producer of picture frames had as its annual report theme, "Framework for Growth," which was very successful. By the next year's annual report the company had determined it had the ability to be more than just a picture frame manufacturer, and actively broadened its product lines within related industry segments. The theme of the report that year, then, was changed to "Delivering Value and Fashion in Home Decor," maximizing several of the company's main messages at once, and indicating by the theme that the company was moving to be a broader sector competitor.

All of these varying factors serve as a context against which the company's story is to be told in its annual report. All planning for the report should be kept in this context, and the company's investor relations needs of the moment should be kept very much in the forefront. These considerations serve as the foundation for developing the objectives of the report. Obviously the primary objective is to inform and, ultimately, to sell stock. But beyond that, each report each year not only faces a different set of corporate situations, but a different set of objectives as well.

The objectives are determined as the answers to the question, "What is it we want our readers to know and think about our company after they have read this report?" Certain of the objectives are basic. For example:

- To define the essential nature of the company and its business within the context that augers well for the future

- To demonstrate that management has a firm grasp of all aspects of the company's business; that it not only understands but controls all aspects of the business. This includes a full understanding of the company's markets and market potential, both currently and in the foreseeable future
- To demonstrate that the company is internally sound and strong—both fiscally and in depth of management—or is aware of those areas in which this is not the case, and is taking steps to overcome these deficiencies as a foundation to engender further strength and growth
- To demonstrate that the avenues of the future for the company are to a large degree clearly identifiable; that the company understands them and is attempting to build the kind of flexibility that allows it to move readily into them
- To illustrate management's understanding of its cost of capital and how it plans to earn more than that cost over the next several years.

Beyond these general objectives, the company must develop additional goals predicated on specific opportunities or obstacles it faces at the time the report is to be prepared. This may include clarification of industry, economic, or specific corporate activities, or specific corporate opportunities peculiar to the company. This may include, as well, the opportunity to increase market share, or to move into new markets with new products, or to take advantage of the company's favorable relations with the capital markets by increasing debt or equity, and using the money to expand globally, or to increase R&D, or to restructure to cut unit costs. A recent Navistar annual report, for example, highlighted the need to cut unit cost production while growing the company.

The objectives should be carefully developed and clearly stated for the annual report, and should not be a broader statement of corporate philosophy or corporate objectives.

Target Audiences

The target audiences for an annual report must be clearly delineated. Without a firm understanding of who is to read the report, it's virtually impossible to determine intelligently how it's to be prepared. Each company must decide for itself the prime targets and their order of importance. For any public company there is no specific audience to the exclusion of the others.

Nor are the audience priorities the same from one company to the other. Ultimately, the target audience for any annual report is that which is most important to the company at the time the annual report is written, and this can, of course, change from year to year.

While there have been successful annual reports written with just a general idea of the target audience in mind, and without any formal review or analysis, this doesn't mean that increased knowledge of the audiences wouldn't have produced even better reports. Usually, the practitioners involved in writing the report had such broad experience, and possibly such broad first hand knowledge of the audience through day-to-day personal contact, that superior results were achieved with seemingly less structured effort. Don't underestimate the value of experience and intuition.

The distinctive audience segments can include:

• *The financial community.* This includes the analysts, brokers, money managers, and other institutional investors whose knowledge of the company must be maintained in as great detail as possible, and whose support the company must foster over both the short and long-range if the company is to compete successfully in the capital markets. Included are banks, insurance companies, and other lending institutions.

This target is particularly vital for smaller companies, whose access to other means of communications is limited. For them, the annual report takes on an even greater value as a source of information about a company. It is the annual report that's frequently the first point of contact between the financial community and the company—the first opportunity the prospective investor has to become acquainted with it. There is no question that for the annual report of most companies, the financial community is the primary target.

• *Shareholders.* The legal purpose of the annual report is to report the company's position to shareholders. Therefore, while they might not be deemed a primary investor relations target in some circumstances, shareholders are still an essential target. The objective in reaching shareholders, beyond the normal reporting requirements, is to demonstrate to them that their company is well managed, sound, and has growth potential. At the same time, management should tell what problems are being faced, and describe the programs to overcome them, the programs to get the company moving, and the vision for the company after the problems are mastered. Sometimes, the value in adversity is the opportunity to demonstrate strength.

- *The broader business community.* For many companies the report can be an annual demonstration to the business community of their structure, strength and capability. Companies do business with one another. The report demonstrates the soundness of the company to suppliers, customers, potential merger partners, and others with whom a relationship of one kind or another is valuable.

- *Prospective customers.* While an annual report is not a sales brochure, it's useful as a sales tool to demonstrate not only the range of services and products, but the substance of the company behind them. In the case of consumer companies, such as Sharper Image Corporation, the report has an advertising value, in that shareholders and prospective investors are also consumers.

- *Internal.* For some companies there's a value in considering internal staff or prospective employees as a target audience. The report offers an opportunity to enhance morale and engender pride. Not to be overlooked is the fact that employees are sometimes potential investors as well, or through their ESOP, actual investors.

- *Unions.* There occasionally arises a question of the place of the annual report in labor relations. Some companies feel that there's a danger in displaying profitability in ways that might incite trade unions to demand a greater portion of it. This is an unfortunate and negative view. It's unlikely that any labor union of consequence is not already keenly aware of the company's performance, virtually in as great detail as is the management. To consider labor relations as a reason for not fully reporting performance is not only a delusion, but uses a smaller negative factor to override a larger advantage. (The same is true in considering explanations for high margins to be dangerous, in that customers might look askance at prices in relation to profit margins, or that potential competitors might be attracted by highly profitable market opportunities.)

- *Civic and public interest groups.* Today's corporate audience, closely watching the operations of companies, includes local and national civic groups, and those with such special interests as the environment, international trade, medical, age-related, disability-related and race-related issues (e.g. South African segregation), abortion, HIV, gay rights, and political action.

- *Special government agencies.* More companies do business with the government today, not only in defense, but in labor, commerce and treasury. Included here are ERISA agencies.

- *The media.* Annual reports frequently go to media both for the news value and because media reporting can be influenced by annual reports. It's also wise to send a brief note or news release accompanying the report, pointing to any newsworthy material. This can lead to more extensive media coverage.

There are partisans for every point of view on the subject of audiences for annual reports. There are proponents for every target group, ranging from the unsophisticated holders of a hundred shares to the highly sophisticated analysts for a major institution. While no single statement can be expected to resolve that question once and for all, there are some basic principles.

For example, if an annual report is designed to achieve a number of complex objectives for one or more financially sophisticated audiences, the report will obviously address many more issues, with a clear delineation of significant aspects of the company's financial and other operations, than it would if the audience were just casual shareholders. But a report addressing complex issues shouldn't be more difficult to read and understand, if it's carefully written.

The report should be planned in a context of how investment decisions are made, which further defines an audience. The manager of a large fund makes his decision based not only on the contents of the annual report, but upon extensive analysis of other factors as well, such as actuarial projections. Individual investors rarely make investment decisions on their own. They may read the annual report, or any other document, and draw a conclusion. The number of such investors who will make investment decisions based on that conclusion, and without further consultation, is so small that this kind of investor must be excluded from any serious consideration as a target audience for an annual report. When the small investor who inherited a few hundred shares of stock reads a report and makes an investment decision, he or she is most likely going to consult a broker. The broker will then presumably contribute the knowledge and sophistication, backed by appropriate research reports, to enforce or amend that decision. Thus, as a practical matter, and legal requirements aside, the primary target audience is rarely the smaller individual investor.

This is not to say that individual investors don't constitute an important part of the audience for an annual report. The report is ostensibly a report to shareholders. Nor should this be construed to mean that any report should be obscure for the average investor. The point is that the target audiences are determined by more than a responsibility to keep shareholders informed. As the company's annual statement, it's a document that clarifies the company to a much broader financial and business community.

Theme

Developing and articulating a theme for an annual report, particularly for a successful and well-conceived company, or a company with a firm grip on where it's going and how to get there, readily enhances the ability to communicate the essence of the company to its target audiences. The theme is a track to reach the objectives—a way to tell the company's story in the context of the objective. Today, annual report themes tend to relate to corporate strategies for enhancing shareholder value.

The theme is often the platform to project the company's position, that key structure that distinguishes the company's potential to appreciate an investment. It should certainly be shaped by the company's marketing position.

Projecting the essence of a company's performance and substance is almost invariably enhanced by a unifying theme, which can also be carried forth from the annual report to the year's interim reports. There are several tangible advantages to articulating a theme:

- It helps to focus the essence of the company, both visually and in copy.
- It helps the designer visualize the company in the report, and the writer to write the text. The text and the design are then consistent.
- It serves as a benchmark against which to measure every element of the report.
- It provides quicker, simpler understanding of the essence of the company to the target audiences.
- It greatly increases what the reader absorbs from the annual report, adding impact to the report's messages.

A very large, but not nationally known, midwestern savings & loan holding company had a marvelous record of innovation in a number of areas, and of having avoided the classic industry problems. For its annual report, a few years ago, it chose (at its investor relations counselor's suggestion) as its theme, *selective growth*. In the cover, the text and the artwork, it carried out this theme to demonstrate its avoidance of industry problems, and its conscious choice to compete on its strengths. The theme said to the audience that management's ability to assess the company's strengths and weaknesses, and to choose where to compete, was an essential reason for the company's success.

This theme was carried out so effectively, and communicated its message to its audiences so well, that it won a *Financial World Magazine* award as the outstanding annual report for financial institutions with $1 billion to $10 billion in assets. The award cited "the power of its theme," and the effective use of the theme, as a major reason for the award.

Annual report themes work best when they try to make a single point that relates to corporate strategies for enhancing shareholder value. One year, Libbey's theme was "leadership." Sharper Image's "Growing Through Multiple Concepts" was more company specific. Sequent's "Big Open Systems That Work" is excellent.

A theme, remember, is not a slogan, or a wish, or even a position. It's a single thread that runs throughout a document, aimed at making one basic point in the reader's mind. It's the answer to the question, "What do we want the reader to know, think, or feel after reading the report?"

Format

The format of an annual report is a function of objectives and target audiences. The financials aside, several traditional practices have evolved for the front of the report that pervade an overwhelming number of reports. In some cases these formats are followed simply because they are traditional, and not because they bear any relation to the particular needs of a company.

Although the format is limited only by the imagination of the report author and designer, and can take any form that's consistent with sound investor relations principles, there is still the classic format used by most reports.

The inside front cover usually has a corporate profile that coincides with item one of the 10-K, and, for longer annuals, a table of contents. The corporate profile can say more than is in the 10-K, but it can't contradict what the 10-K says. Page 1 has financial highlights and a few graphs. Page 2 is usually reserved for the chairman's or CEO's letter to shareholders. The standard—and too often, clichéd—letter to shareholders starts out with either a statement of how good the year has been or an apologetic note for the company's poor performance. This opening is followed by several paragraphs recapping sales and earnings, or some brief cosmetic explanation of why earnings were not up to par, or a description of the several factors that resulted in superior performance. There will then be a few paragraphs describing some of the year's outstanding events, followed by a paragraph or two projecting the problems or opportunities that lie ahead, and a statement that the company intends to face the problems squarely or seize the opportunities effectively. The letter ends on an optimistic note for the future, with a bow of thanks to the loyal officers and employees without whom the company's success would not be possible.

The descriptive text, including pictures of the company's plant—which looks like every other plant—describes the company's products, processes, or services. Some reports discuss operations by divisional lines, or talk about products or services in terms of end users. Not to be ignored are the ancillary activities, such as merger and acquisition, and competitor intelligence (for which Wall Street is a prime source).

This format and approach to an annual report virtually guarantees that the report will not be read, nor will it be understood, nor will it be appreciated. Even if the company is performing magnificently and has great potential for the future, this performance or potential will be submerged and hidden in a deluge of dull words and clichés. The chances are that anybody in the investment community who reads one report will read many. It all begins to dissolve into one shapeless blur.

This need not be. Aside from reporting basic required information, the option of format lies entirely with the company. Hearken back to a point noted earlier—each report can and should be written as if it were the first time in corporate history that an annual report has ever been written. The number of legitimate and exciting variations is limited only by the imagination of the company or investor relations consultant who prepares the report. For two prime examples of excellent shareholder letters see Warren Buffet's Hathaway or Ralph Wanger's Acorn Fund reports, both of which are consistently informative and interesting, year after year.

For one annual report, a company's chief executive officer was put in a room with half a dozen leading security analysts and the interview recorded. The interview was then edited for style only, and printed in lieu of a traditional president's letter. In 1996, there were several reports with the traditional letter being replaced by an interview with the chief executive officer, but the interviewer is never identified. This is not as credible or effective as using an analyst or industry specialist.

Creative Management Associates, a publicly held theatrical talent agency, printed its report one year in the form of the publication, *Daily Variety*. All of the pertinent financial information was included, and the company's activities were reported as news or feature stories. State Farm, the insurance company, used a *Reader's Digest* format to tell its story in one annual report.

A company that was consistently a pioneer in health care information technology had a chief executive officer who is considered a visionary in the field. He had been virtually inventing an industry, and was seen as so far ahead of his industry that it was unseemly to have him do a standard report for his successful company. His letter was a projection of the industry, its opportunities, and where it was going. A second traditional letter was written, instead, by the company's president and chief operating officer. A third letter on financial results, usually included in the CEO's letter, was written and signed by the company's chief financial officer. The report, instead of having one traditional letter, had three separate letters, each uniquely appropriate to its author's subject.

A manufacturer of shoe lasts recognized that few of the people it wanted to reach would understand the shoe last industry, and devoted a full page to a discussion of the shoe last and its role in shoe manufacturing. It also recognized that the company could be judged properly only in the context of the total shoe industry, and devoted another full page to a discussion of the economics of the industry, its structure, and its current status.

Another company recognized that a description of its services in behalf of its leasing customers could be considered routine and mundane to those outside the industry. Its investor relations counsel suggested that these services be reported pictorially in the style used by *Life* magazine. The report pictorially followed a branch manager through a day of his activities—a fresh and effective approach to describing services that would otherwise have been of no interest to readers.

An excellent example of the use of technology is the 1996 report of the computer industry company, Cisco Systems. Included with the traditional printed report was a CD-ROM disk version of the report. The disk, which has room for considerably more material than does the printed version, included additional company and product information, in a vivid and graphic style, including sound.

Some larger companies have included articles discussing international economics written by prominent economists outside the company. Others, functioning in several countries, have printed their reports in several languages. Mattel included a section in the middle of its 1995 annual printed in six languages, including two Asian. That same report had a magnificent shot and reproduction on the cover of a child customer. That said it all.

Many companies include a discussion of end users of their products, and the benefits of their products to consumers. Sequent Computer did that effectively in 1995. A discussion of all a company's appliances used by consumers in a typical American community could tell more about a company than any other description of it.

In other words, the effectiveness of the report can be enhanced by shifting wherever possible from traditional approaches. No corporate annual report can or should be an imitation of any other corporate annual report, since no two corporations are the same.

In the mid-90s we are seeing a definite trend back toward foldout covers, gatefolds, to present more information in the front of the report. Wolverine World Wide and AMP used this technique effectively in 1996.

How Reports Are Read

From many surveys and interviews it's been determined that professionals who read annual reports tend to follow the same procedure. This is necessary because they read so many of them in the course of a year, and must determine very quickly whether the company offers any basis for further interest.

Most analysts and investment professionals turn to the first page for a quick look at the summary of revenues and earnings. They then turn to the back of the book to review the financials, beginning with the auditors' names and opinions, and then the income statement, balance sheet, cash flow analysis, management summary, and so forth. And if they are still interested in the company, they turn to the CEO's letter in the hope of finding an intelligent explanation of the financial condition of the company, its operating results, and key aspects of its strategy. And if they are still interested, they will go on to read the text describing the company's operations or industry.

No investment professional is ever overly impressed by the physical format of a report, although it seems unlikely that an attractive, and even an expensive-looking, report won't have at least a subliminal impact. Certainly, an attractively designed document is more inviting to read than one that's dull and mundane. At the same time, many investment professionals indicate a negative reaction to an expensive four-color report for any company that's not fairly large and doesn't show a significant earnings level. One of the most exquisite reports ever produced some years ago was for a multinational company. The graphics were extraordinary. The photography could have won prizes. It was obviously an expensive production. It reported an

$8 million loss for the company for that year. The reaction of shareholders upon receiving so expensive a booklet when the company lost $8 million was explosive.

Annual report producers now appear to be working to improve readability. One indication is that copy blocks on a subject are getting shorter. For those sections in front of the Management's Discussion and Analysis, more takeouts, more short sections and side bars, montages of copy, and many graphics techniques to break copy blocks to between 50 and 250 words are being used. There seems to be less long rambling copy. It appears that there is an awareness that brevity is better. More show, less tell. On the downside, the recent fad for smaller type faces may produce prettier reports, but less readable copy.

While expensive graphics seem designed for the shareholder, and not the professional, then, it's foolish to assume that professionals are inured to attractive packaging. Not to the point of being persuaded by well-packaged poor performance, perhaps, but certainly, an attractive document is more likely to get read seriously than an unattractive one. In fact, the objective of good design is to enhance readership, and to focus the eye on key elements of the document.

The purpose of an annual report is to impart information, and its format should be designed to do just that. Moreover, the SEC and the exchanges, despite considering summary reports, are insisting upon the disclosure of a greater number of factors, as well as more interpretation of those facts. But for the company competing for capital, the minimum requirements are rarely enough.

The Chief Executive Officer's Message

The CEO's message should be as complete and detailed a report as he or she might give in summary to his or her own board of directors. When one has read a chairman's or CEO's letter, one should have a clear picture of not only where the company has been and is now, but where it's going. There should be a good view, as well, of the kind of person who is leading it. The real choice in preparing the CEO's message is between a dry, bare bones narrative of the company's condition, and a thoughtful exposure of management's passion for success. Which is not to say that it can't be simple and even understated on the one hand, nor should it be overblown and hyperbolic on the other hand. Its limits are not what everybody else does, but the CEO's own distinctive imagination.

Nor should it be constrained in length. If the message can't be told in one page, then take three, as Gillette did in its excellent 1995 report, or even more if you need them. Should copy run longer than that, though, graphic techniques should be used to break it up.

Experienced and knowledgeable readers of annual reports look to the CEO's message for a rounded picture of the company's performance, strategy, and outlook. This doesn't mean a rehash of information that's delineated more succinctly in other parts of the report. Regardless of the format used, the chief executive's message should be simple, concise, free from clichés, and loaded with fresh information. It should not merely state financial data reported elsewhere. It should explain. It should point to significant changes in performance or financial factors and give sound reasons why those changes took place and what they mean. It should take note of critical variables—those elements in that particular business that are crucial to success or failure. It should dwell heavily on balance sheet factors, such as changes in inventory, accounts receivable, important ratios, return on investment, and so forth. It should deal realistically with inflation, as well as other economic concerns of the day. If employee turnover or absenteeism is down, compare that to the cost of securing new employees, hiring temps, and so forth. That gets back to the growing desirability of reporting soft information.

The CEO's message, in recent years, has become, on the one hand, a free-form, free-association outpouring, and on the other, a cliché-ridden apologia for bad performance. A famous example of the former is the Disney report, in which CEO Michael Eisner includes personal family details, and of the latter, in which the company's poor performance is described as, "we are well positioned for future growth."

Reports at either extreme serve no one—not the company, not the shareholders, not the CEO. Tell it straight out and simple. It pays off.

The CEO's message should outline the framework in which the business functions in terms of both the general economy and the industry, and should note any important trends, and should delineate a backup plan in case of recession.

It should describe the major changes in financial structure that have taken place in the prior year, not merely in keeping with formal requirements, but in a concerted effort to communicate. It should explain how the changes relate to corporate goals.

The Financial Text

The SEC has specifically indicated that annual reports be readable by non-professionals as well as professionals, and that annual report text not be in the same legalistic language as the 10-K. Other required information, whether it appears in the CEO's letter or elsewhere, includes changes in accounting principles, dividend history, product mix, relative profitability of lines of business, advertising, research and development plans and expenditures, acquisition or disposition of material assets, assumptions underlying deferred costs and plans for amortization of such costs, closing facilities, business interruption, and significant customers and new contracts. At one time, the SEC staff defined a material change as one in which any item of receivables or expenses changed by 10 percent and-or affects net income by more than two percent at any time during the prior three years. Now, however, they are much more realistic, and recognize that it's not just the numbers that count, it's the quality of the change as well. The numbers alone are no longer the sole focal point; the context, on the other hand, is considered very carefully.

This doesn't mean that the key financial factors shouldn't be spotlighted, as before. If a company's tax rate changes by more than one percent from one period to the next, separate disclosure should be seriously considered.

The SEC is quite clear that substantive material changes be included in the text, even though these items may be covered in notes to the financial statements. If a projection of the coming year's performance is to be made, it need not contain specific earnings projections, but it should certainly clarify specific reasons for optimism. It should clarify the debt picture as well as forthcoming plans for capital expenditures and how they are expected to contribute to the company's growth and future profitability. Potential returns in the light of the true cost of capital should be discussed. The SEC prefers that management comment not only on the year-end financial picture, but also on the company's current competitive position within its field.

It should clarify uncertainties that may affect future earnings. For example, will ratios, such as retained earnings being reinvested in the business to earnings held in reserve, change? It should clarify special problems such as international operations affected by foreign currency fluctuations, and special situations, such as an unusual tax structure.

Board of directors' committees are also being recognized to an increasing degree by many companies, and these committees are frequently described in reports. The Compensation Committee is coming under particularly close scrutiny, as is its philosophy and method of paying the top officers. Institutional investors and the public can now compare peer groups of similar companies, and more easily relate what the senior officers are being paid relative to their performance. Where once there might have been a question about who runs a large corporation today, the answer is that shareholders are increasingly taking control.

Corporate Responsibility

There is an increasing tendency to discuss various aspects of corporate responsibility in reports. Certainly, it's good for management to take responsibility for the financials and corporate good citizenship. In some cases, such as environmental control, this is an essential part of a company's business, and would naturally be included. However, some companies, as a matter of corporate philosophy, recognize a larger role of the corporation in the total society. Some companies, such as Gillette and Exxon (after the Alaska oil spill), have gone to great lengths to define what they see as an obligation to society, and devote a good deal of their corporate effort toward that end. The move toward recognizing corporate responsibility in society is, in many cases, a function of the individual consciousness of corporate officers. In other cases, like Exxon, companies are responding to criticism from consumer groups, including activists in civil rights, equal rights for women, and environmental considerations. On the one hand, it's argued that this kind of corporate activity is irrelevant to the corporation's profit-making function. On the other hand, it's argued that not only does this activity increase a company's favorable visibility, but it contributes to profitability in the long run, because by helping to guarantee quality of life in the future of the nation, a corporation also guarantees its profitability. Certainly, in those companies with a position or with activity in this area, reports of the activities are valid and preferred in the annual report, or a companion piece. Moreover, there is an immediately tangible aspect, in view of the costs and their effect upon earnings.

Many social issues directly affect the corporation to an increasing degree, and when appropriate, should be covered in the report. Issues such as maternity leave for employees, child care, the drug problem in the workplace, alcoholism, and so forth are very much a part of today's corporate responsibility, and are by no means ephemeral.

Of growing concern, during and following the 1996 presidential elections, is company financing of lobbying, and *corporate welfare*—legislation that gives specific benefits to business. While the annual report is not a political tract, nor an appropriate place for political polemic, a statement of participation in the political process may help explain a company's position. Political activity by a company, it's been argued, is done with the shareholder's money. Where there is company political activity, the shareholder is entitled to an explanation.

A word of caution . . .

While the social needs of the world are profound and legitimate, caution is very much the byword in corporate responsibility. Corporate responsibility certainly isn't a substitute for corporate performance. At the same time, there are fads and fashions in the area to which even the most dedicated and concerned citizen can fall prey. The problem with corporations taking up causes that are well on the way to being resolved in non-corporate areas is that it can redound negatively to an assessment of management judgment.

There is also a segment of the market that wants a corporate social audit, in which attempts are made to quantify the actual costs, commitments, and values of all facets of corporate responsibility, from environmental controls to minority training programs. For the company involved in this kind of activity, exploring techniques of reporting it on an economic basis should certainly be considered.

There is obviously a difference between social or corporate responsibility and corporate charity. Although linked, this may be an area, like dividends, where the shareholder might prefer to make his or her own decisions. In a recent survey on corporate philanthropy, IDPR Group, a Boston-based public relations firm, found that 67 percent of the nation's largest companies mentioned charitable giving in their annual reports. Gillette's report gave eight pages to the subject.

Management's Discussion and Analysis

A mandatory part of the annual report to shareholders, the MD&A—"Management's Discussion and Analysis of Financial Condition and Results of Operations"—is defined by SEC regulation. The most comprehensive discussion of these regulations, issued by the SEC in 1989, clearly defines what information should be included, and is periodically updated.

The purpose of the MD&A is to give dimension to the facts and figures to be found elsewhere in the report. It's intended, according to an earlier SEC release, ". . . to give the investor an opportunity to look at the company through the eyes of management by providing both a short- and long-term analysis of the business of the company. The item asks management to discuss the dynamics of the business and to analyze the financials."

In other words, to tell the shareholder what should have been told all along in at least the CEO's letter. This includes any information of a forward looking nature that might materially affect the future of the company's operations or financial status, an analysis of cash flows, material changes, segment analysis, and so forth.

It's the SEC's continued drive for exposure to shareholders of all information that may contribute to making an investment decision.

Noteworthy, at the same time, is what the SEC has not done since its original order. It has not told corporate executives exactly what to include. It seems to want managements to decide what information should be included. However, it reserves the right to prosecute those managements that are not forthright and honest.

The new Safe Harbor legislation doesn't affect the SEC's ability to prosecute. It protects only against private litigation. Nevertheless, companies are putting the appropriate Safe Harbor disclaimers into their MD&As for at least the private litigation value. See Chapter 9.

Financial Information

In the MD&A and financial statements of the report, the largest possible number of financial factors should be clearly presented, in addition to appropriate financial data. This includes:

*   Sales, earnings, and performance by product line and division, where possible, as well as foreign activity. The product line information has been a subject of considerable contention. It has long been felt that reporting this information gives away competitive information. But the fact remains that much of this information is available to competitors in other SEC-required filings, as well as from the marketplace. It's inconceivable that any competitor interested in the information will not have found it—or at least enough to make intelligent guesses. On the other hand, reporting by line gives a clearer picture of the company. And as with all financial disclosure, the greater the amount of information disclosed, the greater the credibility awarded to nonfinancial statements made by corporate executives.

- Financial statistics for eleven years or more. The SEC now requires at least a five-year summary of certain financial information, but ten years, when feasible, gives a better picture. (Keep in mind that you need eleven years of data to make a ten-year comparison, and six years of data to make a five-year comparison.) This is in addition to the two- and three-year summary given on the first page of the report (although smaller reports can use the five-year summary up front). The summarized information should cover as many factors as are relevant, including percentage changes and ratios. Granted that historical information contributes only partially to predicting the future growth of the company; it gives a rounded picture of progress over a reasonable period of time. It also demonstrates the effectiveness of management in moving the company through several financial periods and company business cycles. At least the following factors broken down by 10-K lines of business, where applicable, identical to the 10-K, should be included in the summary, with percentage increases over the prior year for each figure:
  - Revenues, broken down by lines
  - Costs and expenses, including cost of services, cost of raw materials, cost of sales
  - Gross margins, in both dollars and percentages
  - Income before provision for income taxes
  - Interest income and expense
  - Provisions for income taxes, both current and deferred
  - Net income
  - Net income per common share (pre- and post-dilution)
  - Number of shares outstanding, primary and fully diluted
  - Total assets
  - Stockholders' equity, including per share
  - Return on revenues
  - Return on assets
  - Return on stockholders' equity
  - Shareholders' equity as a percentage of total assets
  - Dividend history
  - Sales per employee
  - Key ratios, including current ratio, debt to equity, etc.
  - Plowback ratio (percent of net income paid out in dividends, and percentage plowed back into company each year)
  - Working capital amounts

- Annual Cash Flow comparison
- Long-term debt
- Effects of inflation
- Research and development expenditures
- Marketing, sales and advertising expenses, if relevant
- Frequency and amount of dividends during past two years and present and future dividend restrictions
- Inventory profits
- Compensating bank balances
- Effective tax rates
- Sales and earnings from foreign operations
- Breakdown of order backlogs
- New order amounts and rates
- Data on employee pension obligations
- Information on the exchange or market where the stock is traded, including market price ranges and dividends paid—for at least the most recent two years
- Unusual items, such as collection on insurance policy from executive

The purpose of the special section for Management Discussion and Analysis is to give a management interpretation of general performance and financial condition.

The SEC pays particular attention to this section, and has said that it will be quick to cite any company whose annual report is deficient in the discussion and analysis. The SEC has indicated its clear intention is to be tougher in this area than before, although follow-through hasn't matched the rhetoric. The section must include discussion of at least the following:

- *Liquidity,* including factors that will have a material favorable or unfavorable impact on it. Discuss, also, internal and external sources of liquidity and unused sources of liquid assets. The SEC says that if you see the beginning of a trend that would affect your liquidity, or any meaningful signs of potential change, you must comment on it.
- *Capital resources,* including material commitments for capital expenditures as of fiscal year-end. Discuss material trends in capital resources and changes between equity, debt and off-balance sheet financing arrangements.
- *Results of operations,* including:

- Unusual events impacting income. These should be quantified if appropriate.
- Other significant components of revenue necessary to understand results.
- A narrative discussion of the extent to which sales and revenue increases are attributable to increases in prices, volume increases, or new products or services.
- Impact of inflation on sales and revenues from continuing operations. Some companies are specifically required to do this by accounting regulation, but those not so required should consider doing so as well for clarity of results.

An increasing number of companies are reporting this kind of information in detail, and are going beyond the SEC's and the exchanges' mandatory disclosure requirements. The SEC now also requires brief biographical information about all officers and directors, including their outside affiliations.

As more managers get the SEC's point that more disclosure must be forthcoming in the future—that the goal is to have an investor truly understand what's important to measure a business—then the more will the competitive ante be raised for all companies. The information explosion begets additional information explosion, in order for a company to compete effectively.

In reporting financial information the rule should be greater rather than lesser exposure. The goal is to increase understanding. For any company competing in the capital markets, the need for full and prompt disclosure is overwhelming. Even for the company performing less than magnificently, the value of full and fast disclosure far exceeds the potential harm. The best relationships with investors are not built in the dark or murk, but in the bright sunlight of full disclosure.

Descriptive Company Text

The primary purpose of descriptive material in an annual report is not just to demonstrate the company's business or products, but to do so in a way that demonstrates the viability and potential of the company's business, as well as its competitive advantages. The objective here is to show where the company's money comes from—what generates the revenues and how it redounds to profits.

It must support representations of the company's potential for success made by the chief executive officer. Thus it becomes important to describe the company's business, people, plants, equipment, products or services, customers, in the context of potential profitability. Simply to describe the company's product is insufficient. It must be done in terms of the product's value to the public and industry, as well as its competition and market potential. It must be shown how that product or service contributes to overall corporate profitability. It's too simple for a company to take pride in its capital holdings—its magnificent new 500,000-square-foot plant, or its new process or equipment that produces four times as many widgets with half as many people. While this pride is justifiable within the corporate family, if it is not clear why the new plant will cut costs and improve product quality and productivity, facilitate distribution, and increase the ability to meet growing market needs, then the report becomes a hollow exercise in self-aggrandizement.

The technique used to describe a company's operations is not as important as that it be dictated by the overall format and theme of the report. The report can be broken down by divisions or product line, segmentation of subsidiary companies, markets, service, or user segmentation. Explaining operations can be a separate section or part of a long narrative included in the CEO's letter. The choice is a function of better communication and clarity. Whichever technique works best to communicate clearly, in keeping with the objectives of the report, is the technique to use.

In describing the company's operations, a careful and objective view should be taken to avoid reporting the commonplace as if it were unique. Every manufacturing company has plants and machines. It's expected that every annual report for every manufacturing company will report that its plants are the most efficient, its machinery more modern and productive, its service superior, and its employees the best trained, the most clean-cut and clear-eyed. But if no way can be found to demonstrate these things in terms of their competitive advantages; their genuine uniqueness and superiority, then there's a virtual guarantee that the space will be wasted and the report will be unread outside the industry. In describing a company's operations, every effort must be made to demonstrate uniqueness and clear-cut superiority. If any statement in the description of a company's operations doesn't clearly demonstrate a contribution to cost cutting or profitability, and increasing value, it probably serves no purpose and should be left out.

This sometimes requires imagination and thoughtfulness. Consider employees, for a relevant example. How do you say yours are better? Companies grappling with this difficult assignment have begun to turn more often to soft information that can be quantified to some extent but hasn't been until recently. For instance, the rate of employee turnover at various levels, the number of college graduates or Ph.D.s as a percent of the work force, percent of jobs filled by promotion from within, training programs by hours spent in them per employee per year, percent of employees owning stock, percent participation in an ESOP, sick day averages, sales, cash flow or profits per employee, outside awards, recognitions for or per employee, patents held, customer satisfaction indexes and trends in these over a period of years, and so forth.

Special Features

Every effort should be made to find special features that might be included to enhance the value of the report. Certainly, basic to every report should be a brief description of the company's operations on the very first page, or inside the front cover. It should be unnecessary for anyone to have to thumb through sixteen or twenty-four pages to find out what business a company is in. It's also an opportunity to sum up and clarify a description and perspective of a company as it sees itself and wants to be seen by others. This simple description is sometimes harder to do than it would appear at first glance, particularly if the company is a multiproduct operation or functions in some tangential area of an industry. This description, incidentally, must be consistent with Item One of the Form 10-K. But it should expand on it, as long as it doesn't contradict it. There is much greater opportunity for marketing-oriented copy here than might be expected. This section could also report three or five year compounded growth rates in sales and profits.

Special opportunities or problems should be dealt with in special sections. A company whose operation is complex should not hesitate to devote a section of the book, whether it's a few paragraphs boxed off or a full page, to describe itself. It shouldn't be necessary to read an entire report to fathom what the company is about. A company with special tax considerations should take a separate section of the book to describe its tax picture. A company that's ancillary to an industry and dependent upon it should take a section or page to describe the economics of the industry it serves. If your industry is one not generally understood, a special section to enhance understanding of that industry and how your company fits into it is clearly helpful to readers. Other special sections might deal with unusual aspects of competition or share of market. In some industries, glossaries can be helpful to understand the company better. An unusual educational program or retirement plan or public service program may also be useful in a special section. Research and development, marketing information, or user information may all be relevant and useful.

In fact, a context for any unusual aspect of the company should be included, and, where feasible, set apart from the body of the text.

A table of contents is sometimes warranted if the book is more than twenty pages and has sections. It certainly isn't necessary for a brief and concise report.

Graphics

The question of graphics shouldn't be confused by a conflict between reporting needs and aesthetics. As long as a report is complete, neat, and readable, its graphic presentation need not be elaborate. It should, however, contribute to making the report attractive and readable. There are several factors to consider:

• *Graphs.* The purpose of graphs is to give a quick and dynamic view of the direction in which a company is moving in several of its operational or financial functions. Graphs are helpful if they're well done. They are confusing if they're irrelevant and designed only for looks. The decision whether to use a bar graph of one form or another, a pie chart, or a line graph is a function of the information to be reported, not the aesthetics. The decision is predicated on the form that best demonstrates the information. The kind of material that should be graphed includes:

  • Revenues, net earnings and net earnings per share. If you are going to use graphs you must graph all three—or use no graphs at all. If you are not graphing any of these you must have a very good reason

  • Any other significant factor that shows historical progress or puts the company's situation in perspective, such as return on equity; divisional sales and earnings as a proportion of total sales and earnings (this is frequently useful to demonstrate the growth of one division or product line as an increasing portion of total revenues and earnings); sources of revenue; stockholders' equity; revenues from acquisitions made in the past ten years; and so on. Consider also capital expenditures, R&D, operating income, revenues per employee, sales per square foot, plant footage, units put out, inventory turns, and debt to equity.

The location of graphs in a report should be determined by where they are best related to the text. Sometimes it's useful to put the graphs on the same page as the ten-year summary. Sometimes it's even more useful to intersperse them with the president's letter, or in proximity to paragraphs describing the graphed information, such as the two or three year highlights up front, or, if the auditors approve, in the audited financial statements.

• *Executive Photographs.* There is frequently a battle between ego and value to the report in determining whose pictures are to be included in the book. It's very difficult to include the picture of one vice-president and not another, although the current trend seems to favor more rather than fewer executives. If the members of the executive team are attractive, clear-eyed, and exude charm and intelligence, by all means include their pictures. On the other hand, if it's known that there is a general feeling that the management team is considered too old and that there is no middle management being primed for succession, it seems rather foolhardy to lace the report with pictures of the management team. Often, a compromise must be found between reality and accommodation to personal executive wishes.

Obviously, the CEO's picture belongs in the report. People want to see the individual who has primary responsibility for the success of the investment. It should be a tasteful picture, and preferably an action photo and not just a two-dimensional portrait. Nor should it appear three or more times throughout the report, Sid Cato cautions, because that makes the company look like a one-man show. The directors' pictures should also be used, if there's space and if it's not inappropriate.

There is nothing duller than looking at pictures of people doing nothing, unless it's machinery doing nothing. If the executives are to be pictured in the report they should be shown working, and not just behind a desk. The vice-president of manufacturing should be shown in a plant. The vice-president of finance should be shown preparing his budget. Straightforward head shots, or posed pictures of people sitting at desks or talking on telephones, belong in college yearbooks—not in annual reports designed to demonstrate the excellence of a company's performance.

There is a trend to showing the CEO with one or more executives. This is a good idea. One of the best examples is the two-executive-shot in the 1995 Sequent Computer Systems annual report.

• *Illustrations.* Product illustrations that support the text are useful, but they must be adequately captioned. Pictures of plants and machines that look like other plants and machines are not helpful. Sometimes innovative ways can be found to illustrate a particular point. For example, one truck leasing company has a service that computerizes a broad spectrum of state and local fuel taxes to give the customer a single printed report, where there were many individual reports for each locality. The company wanted to demonstrate the wide variety of information that went into the single report. The photograph used to illustrate it showed thirty-five people, each holding a form, a phone, and a computer tape—all standing in a triangle at the apex of which was one person holding the single completed form. The caption read, "Behind the single piece of paper, on which is reduced an entire spectrum of details and services on fuel costs and state taxations, is FAST's large staff of experts."

The basic question of design of the report should be predicated on the contents of the report itself. First, the design of annual reports is a specialty that differs from the design of brochures or any other printed material. The designer should have at least a modicum of understanding of the financial nature of the report.

Second, an annual report is a financial marketing tool—it's not a graphics device. Too often the designer is asked to design the report before any other aspect is addressed, and that, of course, is a serious mistake. The designer should be made part of the planning team, but should not dominate it. And certainly, the designer should be made privy to the objectives and all other aspects of the report's prospectus.

This is not to say that the designer's contribution should be minimized—design is an integral part of the report. Moreover, the designer is an expert in his field, and should best understand how to translate concepts into graphic terms. As a professional, the designer's ideas should carry more weight than the personal tastes or vague feelings of a design non-professional. But still, the report is a financial and financial marketing tool first, and a graphics device second.

Too many novel graphics ideas can be distracting, Tissue inserts can be overkill for most reports. Too many kinds of paper stock in one report is counter-productive. Have a good reason for die cuts, certainly multiple ones, and be careful with embossing, which can be excellent when properly done.

The decision as to whether the report should be in one, two, or four colors, or simply black and white, also depends upon the objectives of the report, rather than on abstract design factors. It should be reiterated that no investment decision is ever made on the basis of color or graphic beauty, and, in fact, if the performance reported is not equal to the apparent cost of the report, the effect may be adverse.

There are times when color is clearly prescribed by the nature of the product or services illustrated (ladies' retail hair products, for example). There are times when crisp black and white is clearly dictated in order to give a dignified impression of the company. Retail companies such as Sharper Image Corporation use color effectively to better display the essence of the company and its products. To use color merely because it's colorful is wasteful if it doesn't enhance the content and improve the clarity of presentation. A mediocre color photograph may be more attractive than a mediocre black and white picture, but a fine black and white photo looks better than a mediocre color shot.

There are design trends and new colors. More pinks, reds and other such colors, used very sparingly in the past, came into greater use in the mid-90s. Still, judicious use of white space lends elegance to the report.

Many companies are separating the financial section from the text of the annual report and printing the financials as a separate supplement, or printing it on a different color stock. This is a useful technique in larger companies where the financial and statistical information is extensive. Another use of the separate textual and statistical sections is the flexibility it allows in giving the report additional uses. The textual section, for example, separated from the financial section, can be the basis for a valuable sales brochure.

The SEC regulations require that all financial statements and notes to financial statements be printed in a modern, legible type face. This means that no smaller than ten-point or equivalent type may be used for body text, with one-seventh of an inch, minimum, between lines. Eight-point type (72 points equal one inch) or equivalent, two-point leading, is acceptable in tables.

Some companies simply put a cover and very brief additional information on their Form 10-Ks and use that as an annual report. Certainly this is an extreme recognition of the annual report as a financial document. But at the same time, it's really a message to investors that the company has had a bad year, or else doesn't much care about its shareholders and communicating to them. While technically the 10-K fulfills every requirement of an annual report, it's very dull and difficult to read. Even the SEC has indicated it would like clearer language in 10-Ks. It's extremely difficult to achieve clarity of writing and improved readability in what is essentially a legal document written by attorneys with good reason to anticipate potential liabilities. To some management groups, a glorified 10-K may seem to say to shareholders that the company is being run tightly and sparely. What it really says is that the company doesn't want to communicate, or doesn't know how, which, to investors and shareholders, is saying more than any management wants to say. And the truth, here, doesn't matter, even if by some remote chance there's a valid reason to do it. The perception is what counts.

In the capital markets, this perception can be an expensive reaction to the company.

Timetable

The timing of the annual report is predominantly dictated by its juxtaposition to the annual meeting, because it's often mailed to shareholders with the proxy statement for the annual meeting. That brings it under the SEC proxy rules. Because brokerage firms insist on at least thirty days to mail to holders in Street name, time must also be allowed for them.

And a good schedule, incidentally, can save money in production and distribution.

The SEC requires that the Form 10-K, which is the legal annual report to that agency, be filed no later than ninety days from the closing of the fiscal year (although the first two-week extension for those who don't make the deadline is unusually easy to get). The annual report to shareholders must be mailed no later than fifteen days prior to the annual meeting. On the other hand, with the annual reports being mailed with the proxy material, the stockbrokers now say that if they don't receive your annual report at least thirty days before the annual meeting, they won't guarantee to get it out to holders in Street name in time for the meeting. At the same time, proxy material can't go out more than forty-five days before the meeting.

The NYSE requires that the report go out not more than one hundred twenty days after year end.

The best approach is to have the annual report deadline set thirty-two to forty days before the annual meeting. Sometimes, it's easier and cheaper to have the board vote to move the annual meeting, rather than to push through an unrealistic annual report schedule. Within reasonable limits, changing the annual meeting date is a ridiculously easy decision to make, as long as it's within six months of fiscal year end. There is rarely an unalterable reason why the annual meeting can't be set with a consideration of the timetable for the annual report in mind.

The problem is that there is almost invariably a tight squeeze because the auditors require a certain amount of time to do their work, and their report is an essential part of the annual report. Only when the annual meeting is set well ahead can an annual report be completed at a leisurely pace, without frantic last minute rushes and expensive overtime charges at the printers. It's here, by the way, that investor relations professionals and annual report specialists make some of the largest contributions.

The best time to begin planning an annual report is three to six months before the end of the fiscal year, depending upon the size of the company and the scope of the report. The very largest companies begin planning their annual reports a month or two after the prior one is completed, and it's frequently a full-time function for those responsible for it. The report is planned in much the same way as described earlier, and individuals within the corporation or the investor relations firm are assigned specific responsibilities. Considerable time must be allowed for researching the various elements of the report, and for photography and writing. Since most annual reports are carefully scrutinized by several officers of a company as well as attorneys and accountants, the best plan is for the first draft of every aspect of the report except the financials—the text, the photography, and the layout—to be completed by the end of the fiscal year. The next forty-five to sixty days will be consumed with the tremendous pressure of editing the text, including the president's letter, to coincide with the anticipated financial figures, as well as supervising the production of those sections of the book that can be moved forward, such as the cover.

Production Schedules

Production schedules should be carefully and realistically developed and adhered to. A timetable should be prepared—on paper—with a copy to every individual who has anything to do with the report. It should begin with deadline dates for research, photography, layout, and first draft. Approval dates for each aspect of the report should be scheduled. Deadlines should be set for initial planning and theme sessions, and for delivering the text to the art director, as well as delivering layouts, final mechanicals, printing, binding, and mailing. Arrangements should be made well beforehand with the transfer agent and others who are responsible for mailing.

It should be remembered that in the production of an annual report, if anything can go wrong it will. An attorney or an accountant will object to a statement on the grounds that it's potentially misleading. An attorney, accountant, or corporate officer will not be available on a crucial approval day. An operation will be altered, or a company will sell a division, after the text describing the operation is completed. There is a change in key officers or directors. A photograph will turn out to be inadequate. The first choice of paper may not be available in time at a reasonable cost. A failure to co-ordinate on annual report and mailing envelopes will cause a problem. And now, there are the complexities of coordinating a printed and CD-ROM report.

One potential danger is that when there is an unavoidable delay at the last minute, such as a printer running into high humidity and a drying or bindery problem, the delay will conflict with the date of the proxy. Obvi-ously, a delay in mailing a dated proxy is illegal (although twenty-four hours may be acceptable). The only solution, other than reprinting the proxy, is to ask the attorney to hold off dating the proxy until the last possible minute, and to deliver it two days before the date that will be put on it. It may help.

Defining the various production stages, and particularly changes in the text after the report has been set, is often a mystery to an uninitiated man-agement. It sometimes helps to buy understanding that this inscrutable production process does, perhaps, need a few more days. In the later stages, a tactful "this change of a word or two will cost $50 at this stage" sometimes helps prevent unnecessary changes. Computers have greatly speeded the production process and made some late-in-the-day changes cheaper and easier to execute, but demanding managements who do not understand the pro-cess can still manage to offset all time- and cost-saving improvements made in the past fifteen years.

The best answer to contingencies is to anticipate as many variables as possible, to plan as carefully as possible, and to try to include at least two extra days as a cushion for each major part of the schedule.

Interim Reports

Unlike annual reports, interim reports to shareholders are not a legal re-quirement of the SEC, although both the New York Stock Exchange and the American Stock Exchange prefer them for their listed companies. Some companies now promise them to shareholders in prospectuses when they go public. Part of what it means to be a 12-G reporting company is that the company will report quarterly. There is no question of the quarterly report's value in keeping the financial community informed of a company's opera-tions and performance on a regular basis, if it's well done.

Today, there is a raging controversy concerning the value of interim re-ports. But there's no question of the value in communicating financial performance information regularly. The question then becomes, "How do we inexpensively make reports available to investors who want them?" The question is understandable, in view of the information made increasingly available on the Internet. And perhaps, the time will come when on-line information will supersede all printed information. But that time isn't here yet.

One experiment is not sending interim reports to shareholders, or at least not to beneficial owners. A concurrent trend, and almost as bad, is forcing shareholders to call for reports, akin to asking them to ring a bell and salivate. The more roadblocks placed in the way, the lower the response from many people who should be reached. There was one person who owned shares of GTE in 1996 and was happy with the investment. Then he got an interim report that said this was to be the last one. There were few reasons given, other than emphasizing a tremendous cost savings and explaining how to get reports in the future. The shareholder immediately decided he wouldn't ever remember to call the 800 number or access the Web, so he immediately assumed he would not be up-to-date, and earmarked the shares for prompt sale. This one act changed a happy shareholder into an early seller.

It's argued that in today's communications world, the interim report is too little too late in delivering important information to shareholders. The position is that by the time the report is received, the information has already been delivered to those who want or need it. It comes on-line, or by press release, or by radio or television.

But this argument assumes that the investor relations process begins and ends with simply making information available. This belies the basic principles of marketing—of competing for the investor's dollar. It's rather like the man who defended himself in a divorce suit against a wife who claimed she was unloved. "I told you I loved you when I married you," he said. "It holds good till I revoke it."

In fact, the competition for the investor's dollar requires more, not less, financial communication. It requires more, not less, presence in the forefront of the prospective investor's mind. And when you realize that every other company is trying to woo and win your investor, then the need for every aspect of persuasive presence is a significant weapon in the armory.

The problem with all financial reporting is that it freezes an ongoing process as of the moment of the report; it seizes only one moment of an operation that is in vigorous motion. It's like a still picture taken at high noon of a crowded downtown square in a busy city. It's a photo of the instant. Minutes after the picture has been taken everyone in it has gone off in different directions, and the scene has entirely changed. So it is with annual reporting. The interim report, usually issued quarterly, updates the picture, and does so beyond the basic financial statement. It may be more valuable as an opportunity for management to keep its vision for the company before the investor than as a financial reporting document, but that doesn't diminish the report's value as a financial marketing tool.

The SEC, moreover, favors an auditor's review of the quarterly, even though the report itself is not audited. Management can cite the auditor's review without making it appear to be an audit.

The well-conceived interim report serves several purposes:

- It indicates the company's progress and financial performance since the end of the last reported quarter, and since the end of the last fiscal year. This includes updating significant changes in costs, such as the company's cost of capital.
- It compares the performance of the current interim period with that of the comparable periods in the prior year. This is valuable because very few businesses are level in their performance throughout a single year. Some quarters are traditionally stronger or weaker than others, and a comparison on a quarter-by-quarter basis with the same quarter in the prior year gives a valuable measure of a company's performance. For most companies it's a more valid measure of performance than comparison with the immediately prior quarter.
- It reports significant corporate activities since the annual report.
- It indicates the degree to which projections made or implied in the annual report are being fulfilled.
- It reports short-term changes in the company's direction.
- It can repeat, update, or emphasize long-term strategies.
- For the company attempting to compete in the capital markets, the notion of not issuing interim reports, in any form, is unthinkable. In at least one respect, the interim report is even more important than the annual report, because it shows a commitment to keep information flowing. In the competition for attention, success is a function of an ongoing effort. As in any form of marketing, competing in the capital markets is successful only as a cumulative effort.

As in the case of some annual reports, many interim reports have fallen prey to a kind of mindless repetition of everything that's gone before, without any consideration of whether the principles behind doing them in the first place still apply. And yet the interim report offers the opportunity for some of the most creative work to be done in financial relations.

Format

In its least complex (and least useful) form, the interim report can be little more than a copy of a release reporting the quarterly results. It can even be a reproduction of the SEC Form 10-Q. At the other extreme, it can be in an elaborate newspaper or magazine style, with interpretive articles covering virtually every aspect of the company's business, as well as the basic financial data and substantial financial analysis. The variety of formats between the two extremes seems endless.

As with the annual report, the format for the interim report is dictated by objectives (including marketing objectives). The shape and format of the report are determined in precisely the same way as for the annual report. The same questions about objectives and target audiences are asked, and, except where there is a significant change in the circumstances under which the company functions, the answers should be essentially the same as those for the annual. Naturally, in any fast-moving company these objectives will alter slightly from report to report as different problems arise. Nevertheless, there should be some measure of consistency springing from the last annual report, in both content and graphic look.

Considering that for most corporations the interim report represents one of the few opportunities during the year to demonstrate the company's condition in print, and to reach shareholders and prospective shareholders with current information, it seems sensible to include as much as is feasible. The report should include at least the following:

• The unaudited quarterly results. This includes not only sales and net earnings (broken out by lines of business), and net earnings per share, but any other financial information that is available at that point. This may include changes in cash position, changes in inventory, cost of sales, income before taxes, average number of shares outstanding—in fact, any pertinent financial information. Figures should be given both for the current quarter and the comparable quarter for the prior year. Percentage differences should be shown.

• Sales and earnings should be broken down by line, or division, where applicable consistent with the 10-K breakdown. Many companies show results by group, using a bar graph. Many also report backlog by group for the quarter.

- A cash flow statement and a sources and applications statement should also be included.

- Second- and third-quarter reports should include both the current quarter and the six- and nine-month totals, both current and previous year.

- An abbreviated—but not a sparse—unaudited balance sheet.

- The balance sheet as of the close of the quarter should be shown against the balance sheet for the fiscal year end.

- Because it's proving to be of such great value in analysis, and is also valuable to give a better picture of the company as dynamic, rather than static, an increasing number of companies are reporting, in addition to quarterly figures, figures for the trailing twelve months—the last four full quarters ending with the current quarter. This serves to put operations in proper and preferred perspective, instead of freezing the view of the company as just its last quarter of the current year. Many companies also include the figures for the last full fiscal year.

- The president's message to shareholders should be as well thought-out and almost as inclusive as it was in the annual report. In an active company, the events of any three-month period should be extensive and worthy of full reporting, including any update of goals and measures of performance against previously stated goals.

- It should also be remembered that the quarterly report should represent a full view of the company, without the necessity of having to refer back to the annual report, except for greater detail. It usually represents a shorter but still ample view of the company. The interim report will, for many of its readers, be the first document seen on the company. It should be sufficiently detailed and interesting to encourage readers to want to investigate further.

- The interim report can also be a useful vehicle for focusing on a single aspect of the company's operations with the kind of detail not normally found in the annual report. The R&D effort is frequently highlighted. Or new stores for retailers. Companies have devoted each issue to a biography of each of the key officers and operating divisional heads, with a description of responsibilities, and a report on performance since he or she assumed the position. CMI Corporation has highlighted its largest industry trade show and its leadership in participation. Other companies have used each issue of the interim report to describe a different product, its markets, its performance, and its potential. Each quarterly report can discuss the quarter in terms of the season and its effect on company performance.

• If the use of graphs is appropriate for the annual report, it is just as appropriate for the interim report.

In addition to favoring an auditor's review of the quarterly report, the SEC is pressing for more information, which may ultimately be mandatory. While the SEC's immediate concern is with the quarterly Form 10-Q, it seems reasonable to go beyond that to include the same information in the report to shareholders. They are also proposing that the annual 10-K and the quarterly 10-Qs reconcile significant differences between performance reported quarterly and annually. The trend seems to be to make the quarterly requirements much like those for the annual.

Typical of the problems these proposals seek to avoid is seen in the case of CNA Financial Corp. CNA reported, one year, that its first six months' earnings were the second highest in its history. It then showed a loss in the third quarter. At year end, it showed a twelve-month loss of $79 million. It seems that in the first half of the year they had neglected to report to shareholders that a subsidiary was in deep trouble.

Some reports include summaries of presentations before security analysts groups. Others include a summary of the presentation before the annual shareholders meeting, with significant questions and answers.

Some companies, to maintain consistency with the annual report, use the same cover photograph from the annual report—or at least, the same graphic family feel—for each of that year's interim reports. Many companies use a large number on the front page to indicate the quarter. Some companies also change the color of each quarterly, to help distinguish one from the other quickly. This clearly adds to the marketing aspects of the report.

One other interesting use of an interim report, particularly one filled with facts and reporting excellent results, is as a prospecting piece to broaden the base of interest in a company within the financial community. The interim report, which is infinitely less expensive than the annual report, can be mailed, with a self-addressed return postcard, to a larger, carefully selected list of analysts, brokers, money managers, and so on, than are normally included on the company's mailing list. This group can be all the analysts in a geographical area, or all the analysts covering a particular industry, or covering companies of a specific size, or other common financial specifications. The postcard indicates that the report is being mailed to them for their information, and the card should be returned if the recipient has any interest in receiving further material about the company. This invariably develops pockets of interest not formerly identified.

Physically, the interim report should be designed to fit in a standard letter-sized No. 10 envelope, unless it's a self-mailer, which is increasingly popular. Unusual shapes and formats are not only expensive to produce, but require specially designed and expensive envelopes. Self-mailers, of course, are freed from this limitation. Sometimes a little more paper, a five by eight inch size, for example, provides space for additional copy.

Advertising

Advertising—particularly corporate advertising—takes many forms, ranging from a full-page ad in *The Wall Street Journal* extolling the virtues of the company (*"Our company does great things"*) to participation in special editions of newspapers or magazines to advertise the availability of the annual report. Very large companies sometimes use television and radio as a corporate advertising medium, and now, advertising on the Internet is increasingly popular.

Advertising, thoughtfully done, can be effective, although there are as many negatives as positives for it.

Corporate Advertising

Corporate advertising is expensive, and its effectiveness as an investor relations tool should be considered very carefully. Just to put it in perspective, a major corporate advertising program aimed at the financial community can cost in the $2 million to $5 million range per program, with some campaigns costing as much as $15 million.

Research conducted by Rivel Research Group showed that among individual investors, 36 percent said corporate advertising is very effective, 43 percent said somewhat effective and 21 percent said it's not effective or worse. That same research said that after seeing corporate advertising, 61 percent of portfolio managers asked an analyst about the company, 58 percent asked for a research report, 47 percent asked for an annual report and 36 percent bought stock. The reported results were even better among retail stock brokers, noted *Investor Relations Business*, a publication by Securities Data Publishing, Inc. Eighty-two percent asked for research reports, 73 percent wanted annual reports, and 61 percent bought stock. Advertising can get attention, refocus attention, update, and remind investors. Corporate advertising can highlight competitive differences.

The overall effectiveness of any kind of advertising is not the question here, except that there are very few publications in which everyone who sees the ad is a prospective customer. In corporate advertising the same problem exists, particularly institutional advertising. If the purpose of corporate advertising is to engender a favorable attitude on the part of the shareholders or potential investors, a very narrow view of that purpose must prevail.

In advertising to the financial community it must be recognized that, first of all, there is a kind of inherent cynicism with which the company is viewed, predicated on some tangible facts about the company's performance. No company that's performing poorly is going to be loved by shareholders no matter how exciting the advertising program. In fact, there is likely to be a contrary effect, since shareholders can generally calculate how much advertising cost, and the claim that corporate advertising has a measurable effect on stock prices is a dubious assumption.

While it's true that the overall psychological effect of large-scale advertising will still serve to focus attention on the company, a judgment must be made as to whether the contribution the advertising makes is sufficient to warrant the cost. In some cases the answer is favorable. It's difficult to imagine, though, that a small or medium-sized company with stock that's not performing well, even if it is undervalued, will accomplish a great deal in proportion to the cost of advertising. The same amount of money put into other aspects of financial relations will be infinitely more effective.

Certainly there is one basic factor that may be overlooked in any advertising. Success is a function of repetition and a total marketing program. Rarely does any single ad make sufficient impact to stand alone without the support of additional advertising or other promotional efforts. It's one thing for a major corporation such as Disney or General Electric to take a full-page ad in *The Wall Street Journal* extolling its corporate virtues or to announce its latest financial results. These companies are already well known, and are supported by a consistent program that keeps their visibility high. It's yet another thing for a small company, with no consumer brand name franchise, to buy an ad one time. It will be overlooked and forgotten, even if it offers the cure for the common cold.

The use of advertising by a small company to sing the praises of its latest financial results is an expensive buckshot load. With very few exceptions, the number of people in the financial community who are concerned about a company to the point of doing anything effective about it is limited. Very few advertising media focus that intensively on an audience of individual investors (although that number is growing), and so even in the smaller financial publications the likelihood is that the ad will be seen by many more people than can possibly be interested. When the ad is priced on a dollar per reader basis, it turns out to be very expensive indeed.

It can be argued that this kind of advertising reaches individual investors. However, there is a very serious question as to the sources of information individual investors use to make investment decisions. Will an investor with $5,000 to invest in the stock market read an ad reporting the financial results of a company like, say, Diamond Home Services, or extolling the virtues of capitalism, and then, without considerable consultation with a broker, invest money in that stock? Will an investor reading an ad extolling the virtues of capitalism then, without considerable consultation with a broker, invest money in that stock?

This is not to say that some advertising can't be effective.

Advertising can be useful in a total marketing context in which it's one of several elements designed to reach an investing public. Some ads are better than others, particularly those that are intelligently thought out, that have clear objectives, that genuinely distinguish a company. Professional advertising people do know things that make one ad better than another. For example, an ad campaign that addresses a specific theme consistently will eventually portray an impression about the company. An ad that offers something, such as an annual report, and asks for a response, seems to make a better impression than one that doesn't.

Local response advertising, for example, is useful in getting leads to interested brokers. One company that appeared to be using corporate advertising effectively spent $5 million annually in corporate advertising, a prohibitive figure for many, but it did it well and got results. Using an 800 telephone number that appears only in its ads, the company calculated that by early 1996 it had received 30,000 phone inquiries about its stock. The company's investor relations director reported, "Research has proven it effective. It gets people to buy the stock or order an annual report."

But the true value of corporate advertising as an investor relations tool, except for the larger company that backs the advertising with a great many other activities, remains murky. There are times when a good local ad in the financial section of a newspaper, or in a financial journal, will develop leads from brokers and analysts, and that alone may warrant using advertising sparingly. But unfortunately there are many more opinions and myths about the validity of corporate advertising to the investment community than there are facts to sustain arguments in favor of it.

Annual Report Advertising

The same kind of judgment about advertising must be applied to annual report advertising. Sometimes it's useful for a larger company to summarize a favorable annual report in an ad. But again, the judgment must be made on the basis of cost versus results. Unfortunately, corporate advertising *seems* to be an easy way to tell the company's story. This is deceptive, because very little corporate advertising is effective on a one-time basis. Certainly no small or medium-sized company should expect miracles from a one-time ad without a specific offer.

Advertising the availability of an annual report, either alone or as part of a large cooperative arrangement in a special section of a publication, is sometimes useful in developing broader interest—if the medium is selected carefully. But there's a hidden cost in this kind of advertising, which advertising space salesmen frequently neglect to mention. That's the cost of the reports themselves in the quantity usually necessary for distribution in response to ads. Annual reports can cost as much as $3 to $5 per copy or more, plus mailing, although larger companies, printing in volume, may reduce the cost to as low as a dollar a copy. A successful ad in a major business publication can produce requests for thousands of annual reports. And if the people who make these requests are added to the mailing list, this can become tremendously expensive, since each name on a mailing list can cost the company as much as $25 to $50 a year in material, labor and postage.

Note that requests for 3,000 reports, which is common, would cause a company to spend another $9,000 to $15,000 printing reports to mail, and more if they have to be rerun. At $25, times 3,000 requests, it would cost $75,000 to service these names the first year. Certainly, any report mailed out in response to an advertising request should include a self-addressed, return postcard that attempts to ascertain the continuing interest of the inquirer.

Unfortunately, cooperative ads make it remarkably easy for the reader to request reports for a company in which one has only a casual interest.

Another word of caution. Listed companies that give sufficient copies to firms with holders in Street name to distribute to those holders are charged for that service. Scams have been uncovered in which payment was made, but reports weren't delivered. While not usually a problem when established firms are involved, payment shouldn't be made for a service regarding annual reports without very careful checking.

News Release Advertising

Advertising news releases, which some publications include in both full and summary form, can be an effective adjunct to an investor relations program. An element of their success resides in the prestige of the publications in which they appear. In highly specialized publications, such as *Barron's*, the readership is much more clearly identifiable than it is for the general business publications, and requests for information or reports are more likely to come from serious and qualified prospective investors. It's also useful, at times, for companies whose service is sold to other businesses. In this case, the release or annual report is being read not only by prospective investors but by prospective customers as well.

If it were possible to analyze the names of those who request information in response to an ad against transfer sheets, and to determine the number of inquirers who ultimately become shareholders, the likelihood is that the company will conclude that the cost is not equal to the result. And since so many shareholders make their purchase in Street name, particularly following the T3 ruling (in which all stock sales must be reconciled within three days), this kind of research is virtually impossible to do accurately without a substantial budget for it.

Only clearly identified serious investors should be kept on the list. Others are questionable. The list should be culled periodically to eliminate non-potential investors, such as investment bankers, librarians, suppliers, and so forth. On the other hand, keep individual investors and others you judge to be of direct value to the company. Today's computerized mailing lists make it easier to track individuals, and the technology continues to improve. More and more companies are communicating directly to end users—the individual stock buyers. After two years, if these individuals turn out not to have converted to shareholders, they can be removed from the list.

Advertising's place in investor relations seems to be growing, as the need to reach more investors increases. The rule in investor relations advertising is not to do it unless there is a clear and realistic picture of potential return on the advertising dollar. Make it pay its way.

The Financial Corporate Profile

An effective device for telling the company story to the financial community is the company-prepared financial profile—a succinct summary of the pertinent strategic operating, environmental, and financial information needed by analysts and other professional investors to understand and evaluate a company. While in many respects this background report is similar in form to the research report prepared by analysts, it is by no means the same thing, nor should it purport to be. It should be clearly identified on the front cover as having been prepared by or for the company. It should not render an opinion that might be construed as part of an offer to sell stock. This would be illegal.

The purpose of the profile is to summarize and focus, in professional form, most of that essential data that analysts and investors must search out before they can judge a company. It differs from the annual report in that its format is much more succinct and objective, and much more in the form preferred by investment professionals themselves. The annual report is a more elaborate document, and puts forth the company's subjective view of itself and its programs. The financial profile is a more balanced document, in that it presents, objectively, those aspects of the company that are specifically meaningful to prospective investors. It usually contains more competitive and industry information than does the annual report. It is cast to help the company better compete for the investor's dollar. It costs considerably less to produce than does the annual report, and is less widely distributed. It can be upgraded and amended frequently, as circumstances require. Size is not of the essence; content is. It can be as much as twenty-four to twenty-eight pages (most are twelve to sixteen pages), so long as it sustains interest and enthusiasm for the company and its future. Smaller brokerage houses find it particularly useful, because it cuts costs in research reports by reducing analysts' research time.

The genesis of the modern, dynamic financial profile is virtually the history of investor relations. In its earliest forms, it was a tentative (and even considered presumptuous, by some) attempt to present basic financial data to analysts. It eventually became the financial fact book—a dry compendium of facts and figures, mostly financial, about the company. It emerged in its current form as a competitive marketing tool, in large measure because smaller companies didn't have the breadth of impressive financial data to produce an elaborate fact book. It also became apparent that numbers don't speak for themselves to the contemporary analyst or professional investor, and so the smaller narrative form was developed to lend perspective to the numbers. Its value and success led to more elaborate and, ultimately, more useful documents. It is now, for many, the mainstay of the investor relations marketing effort, because when it's well done, it's the most intimate look at the company and its management. While this kind of information is increasingly available by video and computer, many World Wide Web sites are little more than electronic corporate profiles. The printed version is not readily superseded by the electronic version. In the future, undoubtedly, but not yet.

Primarily, in addition to the basic financial data, the report contains a brief summary of the company's position in its industry, a description of its business, a statement of management goals, an account of its recent performance in the market, a description of recent significant events, a description of some of the problems the company has faced and overcome—or is facing and how it is overcoming them—a discussion of competition, a list of market makers and available brokerage house research reports, (with attorney approval) and a brief description of management. The writing style must be sprightly, journalistic, and in active voice.

The message should be cast in the framework of the defined position, making the single most valid point about the value of the stock to the investor. And significantly, it's a dynamic document, presenting the essence of the company as a live, moving, growing and competitive entity.

Typically, a profile might note that "management's goal is to reach a 19 percent return on equity," and report that "return on equity has risen from 12 percent to 16 percent during the past three years," and that using an analyst's formulas, "the company plans to go from 16 percent to 19 percent in the next year or two by a combination of increasing sales, increasing gross margins, reduced expenses, and a little leveraging, while maintaining the same plow-back ratio on earnings." The profile might then use financial formulas to illustrate management's expectations about how these numbers might fit together in the future to produce the 19 percent. It would be noted that this statement is a hypothetical financial exercise illustrating how management might meet its target, and not a projection or a promise (Safe Harbor language). It's an active profile because it's written in active language about dynamic operations, and it involves both the investor and management in actively communicating through a dynamic discussion.

For the reader of the document to feel that the company is one that's clearly understood, and certainly well worth investing in, management must speak to investors about not only the company's current position (including the following year), but its longer-range future as well. What are the strategic plans for the next three to five years? What programs are in place to attain that goal? What are the contingency plans to deal with radical changes in the economy, or industry, or competition? How does management view its markets for products or services, both domestically and globally? How does management see—and relate to—the capital markets—both domestic and global? How does management interpret its own numbers? What are its financial targets, both near and long-term? The idea is to get beyond the facts to fathom management's thinking.

At the same time, the raw facts—the numbers and other company and industry information—must be presented in a format consistent with current needs of investment professionals. Remember, though, that many analysts are pioneering new ways to look at the numbers. Stay aware of developments in this area, and consider those new theories in presenting financial information.

The profile is used as part of the kit of materials given to investment professionals who attend meetings, or is mailed to investment professionals, both those who follow the company and those who can be persuaded to follow and invest in it. Because of its terse presentation of facts and management opinions, many investment professionals find it more useful than the annual report, not only as a research document and supplement to the annual report, but, in the case of those who have not been hitherto exposed to the company, as a primary tool in determining the degree to which they might ultimately become interested.

The classic fact books were frequently printed as a supplement to the annual report. Profiles are not. In fact, the profile usually updates the annual report by at least one quarter by including data and financial information developed since the annual report was published.

The danger inherent in a fact book (as compared to a profile) is the potential for overkill—for producing a booklet that's more elaborate than is warranted, and one that tells the reader more than he or she wants to know. The profile is a marketing document in the form of a reference tool, and like the fact book, must not be so elaborate or obtuse that it's difficult to get to the facts. The journalistic narrative in the profile, which is not found in a fact book, does much to prevent these problems. And profiles are now more frequently using charts, graphs and diagrams to explain the company's products, services, strategies, markets, distribution, financials, to a much greater extent, thereby increasing their understandability and usefulness.

Company Web pages may ultimately turn out to be one of the most effective investor relations tools of all. The mechanics and functions of Web pages are treated in Chapter 6. A well designed Web page makes a vast array of current information available graphically, interestingly, and instantaneously. And while having one's own Web page can be expensive, it's a small price to pay for the value received. In fact, the costs are coming down, so that it's becoming as feasible for a small company to have its own page as it is for a large one.

Printed Material

Printed material, including the annual and interim reports, reprints of significant press articles, reprints of speeches and information folders on significant new products, and reprints of conference calls, are useful to keep investment professionals informed of a company's progress. This material is not only distributed directly to analysts and brokers at meetings or in person, but most of it should be mailed to them at regular intervals, in keeping with a marketing plan.

Also to be mailed or faxed regularly to key investment professionals are copies of any financial news releases, as soon as possible after they are issued by the company. Analysts frequently ask that releases be sent to them quickly, either by fax, e-mail, or a commercial wire service. It shouldn't be assumed that any investment professional has seen or retained material about the company that's appeared on the Dow Jones, Reuters, Bloomberg, or any other news service. In many cases analysts will not have seen it at all on the wire. In other cases they will have seen it only fleetingly, when their minds were on something else. In some of the larger brokerage houses there may be several people interested in the company and only one easily available copy of the Dow Jones or Reuters tape. By mailing the investment professional a copy of the actual release, they can focus on it and retain it for their own files. Nor can you rely on computer access to this information to be seen by those you most want to reach. By mailing or faxing the investment professionals a copy of the actual release, you know they got it and can focus on it, and file it for future reference.

Multimedia Presentations

The rapid proliferation of electronic advances is changing the landscape of all communication, including financial communication. We now have videotape, closed circuit television meetings, and cable television business news programs. Multimedia presentations that can be shown on large computer screens, laptops, or projected for a larger audience, are increasingly popular. Annual meetings, annual reports, and discussions for investors particularly lend themselves to this kind of treatment, and have the advantage of giving dimensions to presentations. More companies are building in-house video capabilities, which they use for training and other purposes, including investor relations. If a company uses the facilities often enough, it can easily offset the initial cost. They are not inexpensive, however, and should be viewed in terms of the benefits, against cost, including duplication and distribution. As you might imagine, larger companies are becoming expert in these areas where smaller companies can't even afford to experiment. The costs are coming down, though, and a broader range of companies can be involved.

The value of multimedia presentations lies in the ability to dramatize information—to make it more dynamic and interesting. It can make dry figures exciting, and graphically demonstrate management's skills and character. The portability of multimedia presentations means that an elaborate presentation can be shown in many parts of the country—even shown simultaneously—without incurring vast travel costs.

There seems to be no question that, ultimately, the new technology will change the nature of investor relations. Just how that will happen, though, is now little more than pure speculation.

Mailing Lists

As marketing concepts become more firmly entrenched in investor relations, enhanced by computers, the classic mailing list becomes a *database*—an accessible list of prospective analysts or investors, defined by specific common characteristics. The difference is that the mailing list is a collection of names and addresses. The database contains considerably more information, such as ranges of size of companies an investor follows, investment interest, personal information, response record, and so forth. Moreover, the database can be accessed in many different ways—sorted by name or location or interest. This makes it possible to pinpoint a particular target group, narrowed down to surprisingly focused parameters. This makes it possible, using the computer, to bring niche or segmented marketing to investor relations. More and more companies are doing that now. Some are into database marketing, in which the database is used for market segmentation. As these techniques are refined, they should increase in popularity.

Nevertheless, the classic mailing list is still at the core of the database. And considering the amount of material that a corporation sends to each person on a mailing list in the course of a year—the annual report, quarterly reports, releases, and so on—the cost can easily mount drastically. For companies that accumulate names on mailing lists without ever reviewing the list, the cost can become exorbitant. It's essential, then, that mailing lists be reviewed at least annually, and preferably every six months. Changes must be made immediately as information comes in, such as in returned mail. Returned mail, incidentally, carries important notations that can help you update your list. Check the post office for translations. Unfortunately, not all undeliverable mail is returned.

Lists are built in several ways. The basic press list is easily derived from several directories, from experience, and from discussions with management. Financial community lists can be put together from directories, such as *The Red Book (Security Dealers Handbook), Nelson's,* and the membership list of the Financial Analysts Federation, from institutional fact books developed internally for the company, from analysts and brokers who have phoned or written in to inquire about the company, and from lists of people who have attended meetings. They can be purchased from a specialized financial mailing houses, such as CDA and Technimetrics. Other names are added as a result of random inquiries and requests for information about the company from shareholders and prospective investors. In some cases the company has advertised the availability of its annual report or run its news releases as paid advertising, and has added the names of those responding to the list.

Every major financial relations firm and every major financial mailing house maintains lists of the financial press and the financial community, usually with the financial community categorized by specialty of industry interest (apparel, energy, auto, construction, high technology, etc.). Computers speed the process, but computers must be fed correct information by people. There are a number of services specializing in selling this information to investor relations professionals.

There are serious concerns with mailing lists which, in view of the frequency of changes and the high cost of mailing, require considerable attention. Computer programs like Goldmine and Act are good aids for the process. Mailing lists are the bane of the investor relations industry. They are a basic tool that must be kept honed, and yet they require attention far out of proportion to the total role they play in a financial relations program. Some of the significant problems of mailing lists are:

- The turnover in the financial community is horrendous. A comparison between the Financial Analysts Federation directories from any one year to the next would show a startlingly high turnover of names and addresses. Analysts and brokers leave the business and change jobs with great frequency, and rarely a day passes without at least half a dozen changes.
- While turnover in the financial press is not as frequent, it still exists to a very large degree. Press people change jobs, leave or enter industry, or change assignment at a very high rate.
- In the past several years the number of brokerage houses that have merged or gone out of business completely is, as has been noted, startlingly high.
- Professional investors' interests change. An analyst who has been following electronics may switch to diversified companies. A broker may no longer be interested in following a particular company for any number of reasons, ranging from the cycle of the market, size of the company, to its listing, to his own impression that the company's performance no longer warrants his interest, and so on.
- Many individuals inquire about a company on a random basis or out of curiosity, and once their curiosity is satisfied they are no longer interested.
- Shareholders who are sufficiently interested in following a company closely will ask to be put on the mailing list for news releases not ordinarily sent to shareholders, and then sometimes sell their holdings and cease to be interested in the company.

The point is that it's very easy to add a name to a list and very difficult to find a basis for removing it. Computers help, but still need human input.

The standard practice in the industry, in periodically weeding out lists, is to take three steps:

1. Amend the list upon any indication of change, such as a returned envelope or a news announcement about an individual's reassignment.
2. Review the list frequently to eliminate those individuals known to be no longer interested or those firms known to have merged or gone out of business.
3. Periodically include in a mailing or fax a stamped self-addressed return postcard or fax back request. The return of these postcards is never more

than ten percent. Failure to return the card with any indication one way or the other, then, cannot be construed as a reason to remove a name from a list. Of those postcards returned, a small percentage will indicate that they are no longer interested in receiving material on the company. These names should be removed from the list, although they should be reviewed to determine whether any of the individuals are sufficiently important to the company to warrant a follow-up phone call to determine the reasons for the lack of interest, or to try to convince him or her to remain on the list. Another portion of the cards will indicate changes of address. And the largest portion of cards will simply reaffirm interest.

A question arises as to whether firms should be included on the list if there is no specific name. A sensible solution might be that if you believe that the firm you're mailing to is small enough so that the material will be seen by someone valuable to you, then by all means send it. Or you might call and ask. In larger companies, mailing to the company without a specific name is a waste. Considering the high cost of mailing, it pays to be selective. For example, should research departments or libraries of brokerage firms be included on lists? In most cases the answer is yes, since these files are central reference points for individual research people. On the other hand, should business school libraries be included on the list? Here the question of purpose comes into play. If there is any notion that the interest on the part of the school is for its own investment portfolio, then obviously the answer is yes. If the school librarian appears to be just building files for the sake of files, the answer is no. Or, if the decision is to add it to the list, at least put it on a public relations, not an investor relations, list and budget.

There is a scam you should be aware of. There are charlatans who request large quantities of materials, ostensibly for mailing to shareholders or other interested (but unspecified) investors. You then receive a bill for this re-delivery service, which probably never took place. These firms, usually just a mail drop, are careful to bill less than $100, the amount at which most corporations don't bother to check invoices. One warning sign is the invoice with no phone number. The Society of Corporate Secretaries has lists of known fakers, as do some investor relations professionals. Offshoots of these scams periodically arise. The message is that if a public company doesn't know who the firm requesting the material or its customers are, or whether the customers they claim to be sending to are really interested, call a few of them. Don't pay until sufficient documentation is in hand.

The Financial Media

The financial media, which is dealt with in detail in Chapter 8, is a significant means of communication with all segments of the financial community. It serves three purposes. The first is to impart up-to-date information. The second is to afford an independent editorial view of the company. The third and, in a way, most significant value of the financial press is that it's a powerful weapon in the competition for attention. Obviously a company that's written about in public print with some measure of frequency is better known, and an object of greater attention, than one which is not. Where appropriate, financial publicity should be sought in the most expert and assiduous way possible.

While many of the devices used to communicate to the professional investment community parallel those used to communicate to shareholders, the approach is generally more technical for the investment professional. Still, no marketing program to investment professionals is complete without a constant flow of printed or electronic information to those in a position to help a company compete in the capital markets.

Chapter 8

The Financial and Business Media

The financial and business media is a major conduit of news about companies. No view of the media and its role in investor relations can begin without an attempt to understand, first, what news is, and second, how news really affects the capital markets.

What Is News?

All news is relative. Every day the editor of even the smallest newspaper must review all reported events of that day and make a subjective judgment as to which of them will concern or interest his readers sufficiently to warrant the allocation of rare and precious space. On any given day the news of the bankruptcy of a company of, say, the proportions of a major airline will garner more editorial interest than will the news of a very large privately held company selling shares of its stock to the public. This in turn will preempt the decision of a company to build a $500 million plant. And this in turn will preempt the news of record earnings for a $50 million company (unless the company is the major industry of a small town in which its success or failure affects a great many local jobs). Lower down on the list is the appointment of a new vice-president.

Yet sometimes, if not very much has happened in town that day, the news of a joint venture between two relatively small companies may be the most exciting thing the newspaper has to report as business news.

Even feature material—background or general interest stories about a company or its individuals, and material that's not as time-sensitive as a media release—has its editorial stringencies. For all but the least consequential of the business publications, even the feature story must have its news hook— a fresh basis for writing it.

News and Target Audiences

Every segment of the media, financial and nonfinancial, has its own target audiences, and therefore its own point of view—its own definition of news. For example, *Fortune* magazine's audience is managers. It considers itself a service book for managers, telling them how trends in the economy and society will influence their businesses. Its goal, say its editors, is to deliver the stories that count to constructively influence the strategies and actions of its readers.

Business Week, on the other hand, is a news-oriented publication, although as a weekly it has the time to go beneath the news to get at the heart of the story, and to put it into context with both industry and the economy. It emphasizes analysis and interpretation, and includes stories on international business, science and technology, information processing, management trends, marketing, corporate strategies, financial markets, government, personal business, and important people.

Barron's is edited for private investors, money managers, and corporate executives. It prefers to update current knowledge and thinking about entire industries, new schools of thought about finance and the stock market based upon recent information or theories, or, in its occasional looks at individual companies, how the company relates to an industry and where the industry is going. Because of its stock market orientation (as opposed to *Business Week's* industrial and commercial news orientation), *Barron's* prefers to have a research report on any company it does an article about.

Financial World is edited to provide policy makers in the private and public sector, as well as the professional and personal investor, with insights into current management strategies within corporations with sales of over $1 billion in the United States and overseas. It also addresses major economic, government, and technology issues that are of interest to its management and investor audience.

Both *The New York Times* and *The Wall Street Journal* report general business news. But *The New York Times,* even with its expanded business news coverage and separate business section, must necessarily deal primarily with major economic news or very important stories about companies. This doesn't entirely preclude coverage of smaller companies, if space (or the nature of the story) permits on any given day. While *The New York Times* is considered to be the newspaper of record, it is not necessarily the newspaper of business record, since its limited coverage cannot possibly cover as much as *The Wall Street Journal.* In recent years, *The Times* has substantially increased its coverage of business and business-related subjects, and it is now undoubtedly the best in the country among general daily newspapers. *The Times,* incidentally, is spreading its distribution, and now considers itself a national, rather than just a New York, newspaper.

The Wall Street Journal on the other hand, covers reports of individual companies much more extensively. It, too, has limited space (although more, of course, than *The New York Times*), and neither *The New York Times* nor *The Wall Street Journal* are likely to run any but the most earthshaking stories on any domestic company whose stock is not quoted regularly in their stock tables. The *Journal,* like the *Times,* effectively covers broad economic news that it thinks will serve as a background for understanding the total economic picture at any given moment. The *Journal* now regularly reports material of a tangential nature to business that touches the economic news in ways that are somewhat mystical if interesting. It also covers general national news very briefly, and predominantly as its editors feel it serves as a background for understanding the economy. Its three-section breakdown allows it to broaden coverage, and to increase features, including more financial information.

The business news that makes the nonbusiness sections of the media is news of either a magnitude that affects the economy at large, such as IBM's acquisition of Lotus, America Online's overload, or scandal and crime, such as insider trading scandals. Another example is the merger of Disney and American Broadcasting Company (ABC), which made the front pages both for the size and importance of the transaction. Foreign acquisition of American companies and property, such as the Japanese acquisition of Rockefeller Center (and its ultimate failure) and the Rupert Murdoch ownership of large American media chains, are very much on the front pages of most newspapers today.

Part of the problem in reporting business news lies in the fact that so many business reporters—both good and bad—have very little business training. With exceptions, they come to business journalism from the general news side of the media, rather than from business. The increasing business coverage seems to be changing that practice to some extent, and more reporters with MBAs are being hired by major papers, such as *The New York Times*. While there are many good and astute business news reporters, and they are increasing in number, there are still a great many whose understanding of business and finance is shallow and superficial. There are, for example, few really good investigative reporters, although there is a trend toward increasing their number. Those who do exist function for just a few major newspapers and business and financial publications and cable companies.

To better understand business journalism, realize that few reporters have a vested interest in the stories they cover, nor the breadth of expertise in all but a few industries or companies. A reporter may cover a real estate story one day, and a medical economics story the next. The burden of supplying a reporter the background and context for any story, then, must be borne by the company or its investor relations professionals. When it's done effectively, reporters appreciate the help.

Generally, the state of reporting business news in the media—especially radio and television—is improving. In fact, business news coverage in the broadcast media now seems to be ubiquitous, even on local stations. There are now dedicated national and local business programs on cable and the networks, and both print and broadcast media are bolstering their news staffs with good business journalists. Increasing competition among business talk programs has sharply increased with the introduction of Cable News Network's financial network, and Fox TV's plans to cover business news. The cable station CNBC now runs the stock tape with only a slight delay, and has dawn-to-post-market-closing business news, including interviews with CEOs and analysts, on a continuous basis. Radio, on both news and regular broadcasting stations, has substantially increased its coverage of business news, and Bloomberg News now has its own radio station.

What has substantially changed the picture, in just a few years, is the growth of the Internet and on-line services. News that was once available on a timely basis to professionals only is now available to everybody. Anybody with a computer can log on to get Dow Jones, Reuters, AP, and Bloomberg news, and stock price quotes, on virtually a real-time basis. Company Web pages are updated regularly, with a full spectrum of company news. Access to the Business Wire and PR Newswire, which once went only into news-rooms, now comes into your living room by computer. And now comes

Webcasting, in which news is broadcast directly to your computer on a continuous basis. The average investor, today, knows more about any public company than the business editor of the local paper knew just a few years ago.

Considering all factors, then, a review of the total spectrum of all business publications would make it very difficult indeed to produce a definition of news that would be applicable across the board—that meets the criteria of all publications. But editors know it when they see it.

How News Affects the Stock Market

A second and perhaps more significant aspect of news is the way in which it affects the capital markets. The news that the chairman of the Federal Reserve suggested, in a public speech, that the stock market might be a little overoptimistic was enough to trigger a major drop in the market in one day. Every time the prime rate goes up, or drops a fraction, the market reacts. And the market seems to react to every election, regardless of which party wins.

One thing is certain. The market—the stock market as well as all other money markets—does respond to news.

In their excellent book on the subject, *News and the Market,* Frederick C. Klein and John A. Prestbo, two *Wall Street Journal* reporters, explored that relationship in great detail. They say, "It certainly makes sense to believe that the stock market responds to the news. Movements of the market as a whole and of the stocks that make it up spring from the decisions of thousands of investors. These people—be they steely-eyed fund managers on Wall Street or little old ladies in Dubuque—read the newspapers, watch television and so on, and presumably are affected by what they see and hear. If the United States economy seems to be functioning smoothly, it stands to reason that they will feel well disposed towards sharing in the bounty. If the opposite conditions obtain, a bank account or hole in the ground might seem more secure."

And *The Wall Street Journal* found itself having to recognize the effect of publicity on the market when it had to qualify the results of its popular feature, "The Investment Dartboard," when it found that results were skewed by publicity in its own column for the stocks picked by the experts. On publication days for the column, they found, stocks featured in "The Investment Dartboard" column rose an average of nearly 3.5 percentage points relative to the Big Board index. On the following days, the *Journal* reported, there was an after-effect as those stocks continued to rise slightly.

In his very popular and now classic book, *A Random Walk on Wall Street,* Princeton Professor Burton Malkiel covers many theories of stock market analysis and relates virtually all significant stock movement to news. Both books deal with time lag—the time between the reporting of news and the reaction to it in the stock market—an extremely important factor. The company issues a quarterly release that shows earnings lower than those of the same period for the prior year. The stock shows no motion or perhaps even advances a little. This frequently means that the market has anticipated the reduced earnings and sold off in proportion to them, or that the reduction is smaller than had been anticipated and that other events, or a new outlook, warrant stock purchase. The important thing is that all segments of the capital markets, from the individual investor to the manager of a major fund or trust department to the lending officer of a bank, are responsive to news.

Malkiel dealt with the *efficient market* theory, a basis of which is that the entire market is privy to the same information and so reacts accordingly as one. Critics point out, however, that the market isn't universally privy to the same news, particularly in smaller companies (which is why we frequently have a two-tier market), and not everybody interprets the same news in the same way.

How News Is Received by the Financial Community

What is harder to fathom is the way in which any news—and all news—will be received by the financial community.

First, it should be recognized that since news itself is relative, most news is viewed in a total context. Nothing is absolute. A report of an FTC decree to divest a division is bad news if the division is profitable, and not such bad news if the division isn't. (It can be argued that no order to divest is absolutely good news; if it takes an FTC decree to get a company to unload an unprofitable division, then certainly a closer look at the company's total operations is warranted.)

Second, it must be recognized that the nature of the capital markets is such that because of mass psychology, there is never a reaction to news (particularly if it's not anticipated)—there is only an overreaction. Again, the market is people, and the reaction is a human, not a mechanical, one. The market almost invariably recoils at bad news in anticipation of the worst possible consequences. It's just as likely to overreact, in a burst of optimism, in the other direction at the announcement of good news. The problem is that the overreaction is immediate, and the adjustment to reality, if it comes, is slower, sometimes barely perceptible in the short range, and frequently spread over time.

Beyond that, the reaction depends as much upon the type of news as the news itself. Some events, for example, are anticipated and then discounted by the market. While it can be tremendously frustrating to a company president to announce record earnings for a quarter or a year only to see virtually no reaction in the company's stock—or perhaps a reaction on the down side— the fact is that the earnings have probably been anticipated by those who follow the company. Then the announcement itself is not news at all, but merely an affirmation of what had been anticipated. This, incidentally, is part of the problem with projecting earnings. If analysts anticipate earnings of $1.50, they predicate their recommendations on that. When earnings of $1.50 are announced, the effect of the earnings on the price of the stock has already been taken into consideration, and, in effect, the good news is no news at all. If the analysts have anticipated and projected earnings of $1.50 and the actual figure comes out to be $1.45, this can be a disappointment, with an adverse effect on the stock price, even though the $1.45 may be a record. Nobody ever said the market was rational.

Even this is an oversimplification. Since the news of record earnings can be qualified by other factors, such as an understanding that the earnings are derived from inventory profits and not improved operations, analysts know that the high earnings are not always an accurate reflection of the company's performance.

Spin Control

News, then, is never quite pure and simple. It's always qualified by other factors. This, too, is a basic reason why news cannot and should not be manipulated by slanting, distorting, or withholding information—the infamous *spin control*. There tends to be further analysis and adjustment within a day or two, the truth emerges, and there is a loss of credibility, which adversely touches all company announcements for a considerable time to come. Credibility cannot be overemphasized as a major factor in all relations with the financial community.

The straightforward announcement of even the most favorable news, then, doesn't of itself always offer a clean-cut cause and effect in terms of the capital markets.

It must be recognized that, except for very large companies, or companies of any size that for one reason or another are constantly in the news, no single news announcement is going to make much of a dent on the financial community, other than with those individuals who are already interested in the company. While it's always possible that a single startling announcement about a company that's not widely known will attract someone's eye and engender an interest, it's merely the beginning of a process of investigation for this person. It's not likely that an investor of consequence will read a salutary piece of news about a company that he or she knows little of and make an investment decision on the basis of that announcement—even if it reports a cure for the common cold. It may cause the investor to investigate further. But between the announcement of the news and the investment decision, a considerable amount of investigation is done by the investor or investment advisor.

This is not the case with the better known company, to which each news announcement adds one more fact to what's already understood. And being better known and understood by investors and investment professionals is, of course, a major value of disseminating news about a company.

Categories of News

Seeing news and its relationship to the capital markets in this context is absolutely essential in formulating an approach to the news media. News generally breaks down as follows:

- *General news.* This may appear on the surface to have no relationship to buying and selling 100 shares of the stock of a small over-the-counter company, or of a bank's lending a small company $200,000 to buy a new machine, and yet it clearly sets a context for judging the ultimate economic reaction to that news. It's not difficult to see the signing of a peace treaty in the Middle East in terms of its meaning in international oil affairs. Obviously, the attempted assassination of a president or a prime minister has economic implications.
- *General economic news.* This more readily poses the background for judging general economic performance. Raging inflation or deflation. An increase or decrease in interest rates. The devaluation or appreciation of the

dollar. Or even more specifically, news of changes in the financial markets themselves, such as the attacks on program trading, or changes in banking regulations that permit banks greater latitude in selling securities. Mergers of financial institutions, such as the recent acquisition of Alex Brown by Bankers Trust, are clearly in this category. Or certainly, the activities in the control of supply of money by the Federal Reserve Bank.

But these are news events over which few business people have control. Affected as anyone might be by the nature of events that make this kind of news, few business people as individuals are in a position to influence vast sweeping activities, the results of which affect the overall course of commerce. There are exceptions, of course. A businessperson in a lawsuit, for example, may be awarded a decision that has consequences reaching farther than the company involved. And it's also true that it's usually just a few individuals that are behind events of such magnitude as insider trading, or the inroads of foreign owners into American media. But there are rare occasions when an individual corporation or executive can affect such events by design.

- *Specific business news.* This is news that pertains to the activities of a company or industry. It concerns the reader as a businessperson and investor, and interests the nonbusiness reader as background to generally understanding the economy.

Newsmaking Activities

There are a large number of newsmaking activities that come within the purview of the individual corporation:

- *The front-page news story.* When the savings and loan problem became a federal bailout, involving taxpayers' money, the consequences were of such magnitude as to warrant its being extensively reported in all media on other than just the business pages. Individual S&Ls were singled out, and the stories brought the S&Ls to the forefront as examples of both the best and the worst of an industry. This is news by any definition. A merger of such giants as Time, Inc. and Warner is consequential news. If a major company decides to close down a very large plant, this can be considered to have consequences that could affect a larger portion of the economic community than just the company or the plant's community. General Motors' search for a community in which to locate its plant for its new Saturn car held the front pages for an extended period of time. And this kind of news need not be generated by large companies alone. A smaller company announcing that it plans to compete with a larger and more established company in a particular field is sometimes of consequence. And certainly when a relatively small software company sued the giant Microsoft for patent infringement, it was front-page news.

• *Major corporate news.* This includes important business news regarding a company or an industry. The company can be of any size. The magnitude of the event is measured in terms of the effect upon the general financial community. An unusual merger, an exceptionally high record earnings report, the appointment of a well-known public figure, from government or otherwise, as head of a company. The attacks on Microsoft. McDonnell-Douglas merging with Boeing, or Apple Computer rapidly losing market share, are cases in point, as are Michael Ovitz' celebrated severance package from Disney, and the overload of America Online.

• *Routine financial news.* The rules of disclosure, which dictate the kinds of information that must be disseminated, and the timing, under the regulations of the SEC and the exchanges, are dealt with in another chapter. Essentially the basic news that's of consequence is financial data—reports on latest financial results—and news of any activity or trends the results of which could possibly be construed as affecting the economic future of a company. While this category of news is vital to investors, and is almost invariably reported on the Dow Jones, Bloomberg, and Reuters news tickers (for at least those companies whose stocks are quoted on the main tables of *The Wall Street Journal*), its importance to the media and its coverage is dictated first by the size of the company and ultimately by media space considerations. Nevertheless, under the rules of disclosure the news must be released whether it is printed or not.

• *Lesser company news.* This is a category of news that tends to be more important to the company, the trade, a local community, or an industry than it is to the business editors of most major media. Fewer and fewer minor executive appointments are announced in the financial pages. The *New York Times* has virtually eliminated such announcements of any officer lower than president unless the company is a giant or the individual is notable in some other capacity. This is not to say that these announcements—along with similar reports of new products, new plant, discontinued operations, union negotiations, backlogs, order rates, and so on—should not be reported. They are of interest in areas other than the major news media. But the decision of a $25 million company to open a $1 million plant in the Midwest is not going to throw the financial editor of *The New York Times* into paroxysms of excitement. Yet, when a $40 million AMEX-listed Chicago-based electronics company named a new president who was noteworthy in its industry it earned a two-column story in the *Times*. Extra effort sometimes breaks molds.

• *Feature material.* This is the descriptive article about the company, its management, and its activities that appears in the range of business and financial journals that go from *Fortune* magazine—read by industry leaders—to the *Equities Magazine*, whose coverage of small over-the-counter companies tends to make it a favorite of investors in smaller companies. It ranges from a broad-based, well-researched, and elaborately detailed company profile to a few simple paragraphs describing the company's recent performance, and perhaps quoting authoritative sources, inside or outside the company, on the directions in which the company is moving. It ranges from the brief, perceptive, and frequently skeptical searching of the short article in *Forbes* to the succinct page or page and a half review of a company's newsworthy activity in *Business Week*, to a company profile in *Financial World*, to a terse half column in *Time* or *Newsweek* reporting on a startling company event. Included in this category might be the *Dow Joneser*, a short feature article on a single company, usually an interview with its CEO, updating information.

It should be noted, though, that as the business media becomes more experienced and knowledgeable, it falls prey less often to the old-fashioned puff piece—the shallow handout that does a cosmetic job. Today, the feature story must not only be related in some way to a recent or current event—the news hook—but it must deal as well with some unique aspect of corporate strategy that offers information and guidance to the business world. Today's business editor is coming to realize, too, that most often the company story is really the story of management. "More and more," said one *Fortune* editor, "we find that a *General Motors* story is really a John Smith, Jr. story, and a *Microsoft* company story is really about Bill Gates."

The Salutary Effects of News

It's very easy to see that imparting news about any company can have several immediate salutary effects, even if the news is adverse.

• The news itself adds further information to help the investment decision.
• News that openly discusses the company adds credibility to all company reports.

- The appearance of the news keeps the company name prominent in the minds of those who make investment or lending decisions—certainly important in an arena in which the competition is keen not only for capital, but for attention. This is perhaps the most significant point, since in the competition for capital those companies that are best known and understood are those likeliest to succeed.

The Audiences for News

There are actually two major audiences for news. The first consists of those who already know the subject company, either as investors or potential investors, or as analysts or brokers following it for one reason or another. The second is the larger segment of the financial community. For this group, ordinary news falls on disinterested ears unless it's startling, or itself gives reason to warrant further investigation.

The feature material that appears in the vast range of business publications from *Fortune* magazine to the business section of the Sunday *New York Times* offers a distinctive point of view of a company. There's no question that frequent coverage makes a vast difference. With some 18,000 plus companies traded, obviously those that are better known get the greatest attention from the investment community. When two companies are performing equally well, the difference between the higher stock price or price/ earnings ratio of one company as compared to another is a function of its being better known and understood by a broader segment of the investment community. For the better known company, the simplest positive news announcement will have more beneficial results.

The broader reputation engendered by feature material can stem either from media recognition of the sheer brilliance or uniqueness of a company's performance, or it can just as validly be the result of an organized and carefully executed financial publicity program. In fact, the likelihood of the media discovering a superior company on its own, without the help of an investor relations or public relations professional, is slender. No media staff, in any medium, is large enough, nor are that many reporters experienced enough, to regularly discover companies serendipitously.

In any event, the result of media recognition is to draw attention to a company repeatedly. Repetition is absolutely essential. While a single media appearance of an announcement about a company may gladden the heart of its president, if it's isolated and the company has never been heard of before and is not heard of again, its effect on any segment of the financial community that's not directly involved with the company is fleeting.

There is another major distinction between the news announcement, such as the earnings report or the report of a merger, and the feature article in *Fortune*, *Forbes*, or *Business Week*. The news announcement may be required by the rules of disclosure of the SEC. As long as the company is large enough to be included in the stock tables of *The Wall Street Journal*, the likelihood is that the announcement will at least be carried over the Dow Jones and Reuters wire services and in the agate line listings in *The Wall Street Journal* and *The New York Times*. This should also be supplemented by fax, direct mail, and computer distribution from the company to investors, analysts, and prospective investors—not everybody you want to reach may be reading the paper that day—or by purchase arrangements for news releases to be published in the corporate reports sections of the several publications that carry them, such as *Barron's*, *Fortune*, *Investor's Daily*, *The Wall Street Transcript*, or the *Equities Magazine*.

In the case of publicity material, the fact of editorial judgment comes into play—and this remains the purview of the editor, not the subject of the news. The company may only beseech the editor. There is no effective external power beyond that, and the judgment of the editor who must serve the needs of his readers is paramount. We propose, but others dispose.

Aims of Financial Publicity

Nevertheless, the value of visibility through feature material is high and warrants the specific effort that must go into achieving it. Its ultimate aims are:

- To achieve and sustain visibility for the company, its products or brands, and its activities
- To project the company's capabilities in ways that demonstrate its ultimate ability to appreciate the invested dollar
- To demonstrate specific capabilities about the company—its abilities to earn, the capabilities of its management, its research and development, its future plans, its grasp of its industry and markets, its ability to control costs and ultimately increase its margin, and so forth
- To demonstrate the consistency of the company's performance, as well as the credibility of its management, as might be discerned in the veracity of all its management's representations of the company in the past

It's rare that a company, by virtue of its positive performance alone, will generate sufficient interest to warrant ongoing and continuous appearances in the financial media. A company in trouble, if the trouble is flagrant and the effect of the trouble is significant enough to a large segment of the financial community, has no problem in getting itself broadly covered by the financial media. Witness Mitsubishi and Apple. Since few companies purposely generate this kind of interest, professional efforts must be used to discern those elements about the company and its operation that are consistently newsworthy and valuable to these publications. This material must be presented to the publications in rather specific ways. Financial publicity on a consistent basis is at least a hard sell, best performed by experts, with full knowledge of not only the techniques of dealing with the media, but the individual requirements of each publication. There should also be a basis of experience that warrants credibility with the media for the financial relations practitioner, as well as for the company he or she represents.

Working with the Media

Dealing with the financial media breaks down into the following specific segments:

- News released under the rules of disclosure of the SEC and the exchanges
- Major news events beyond routine financial announcements
- Feature material
- Inquiries from, and stories originated by, the media

Disseminating Basic News

The general rules of disseminating basic material required to be disclosed are essentially simple and mechanical, yet if a professional approach is ignored, the effect will be sharply diminished.

Rules for Working with the Financial Media

In dealing with the financial media—or any media for that matter—some simple rules apply universally:

- The ultimate judgment of news value by the media is made by its editors. Even in those publications that cross the line that distinguishes news from advertising, the publisher knows that if his editorial content does not consistently interest readers, the number of readers will diminish, as will the credibility of the publication. This is invariably followed by a cutback in advertising revenue, which is inevitably followed by bankruptcy. A primary factor in any publication, then, is its editorial judgment.

- Each publication is predicated on a different editorial format—for example, *Fortune* magazine does not print routine earnings reports, *Barron's* rarely does personality pieces on corporate heads, and so on. The editorial point of view of every publication must be discerned and understood before any approach is made to it.

- Competition for news space is extraordinarily keen. Even though business news coverage is increasing in many newspapers, editors receive five and ten times as much news as they can possibly print. The avalanche of information is multiplied by technology, which increases the number of delivery systems (Internet, e-mail, and so forth). Therefore, the form of presentation of news to a publication is extremely important. It must attract attention for its essential news value in the shortest possible time—as short as five to ten seconds, according to a media trainer quoted in Ragen's Media Relations Report. It must be in a format traditionally acceptable to publications. Wherever possible, it must be written in a journalistic style acceptable to most editors.

The Rules of Disclosure dictate that certain material shall be released as rapidly as is mechanically feasible (see Chapter 9). Information most frequently considered in this category is operating results, significant board actions, or any news about activities that may materially affect stock prices. This may include merger announcements, dividends, consequential changes in a company's business, divestiture, an important change in management, a new director, change in accountants or accounting principles, the discovery of a new mine or oil well, and so forth. The Rules of Disclosure are considered satisfied when this information is released, as soon as possible after it is known to management, to the Dow Jones News Service, Bloomberg, and Reuters, plus the other major wires (AP and UPI), the company's major local newspapers, *The New York Times,* and the company's exchange or NASD and NASDAQ. What is essential is that the news is released through the broadest possible media spectrum reaching the largest number of investors or potential investors. And if the news is sure to affect the market, the exchanges and NASD want to be notified in advance as well.

This is best achieved by the following procedure:

- *Simultaneous release,* by a PR wire service, computer, fax, telephone, or hand, to Dow Jones, Bloomberg, and Reuters News Service, as well as other required outlets. This is necessary because the wire services are highly competitive and each is as important as the other. They don't like to lose the advantage of time to the others and each is quick to say so. Simultaneous release is the simplest and fairest way.

- *Distribution via PR Newswire or Business Wire.* PR Newswire Associates, Inc. and Business Wire are private organizations with direct wires into every major financial publication in the United States, as well as the general wire services, general publications, and major brokerage houses. Business Wire is the same kind of service, focusing primarily on business publications and brokerage firms. In most cases, Business Wire will also post releases on the Internet and on selected on-line services. Both cover more than 2,000 brokerage houses and similar firms. There are also regional private wire services. Most wire services interface with others around the country. It's the fastest and most efficient way to disseminate news. Distribution to Dow Jones, Bloomberg, and Reuters, as well as to all other appropriate publications, is covered by PR Newswire and Business Wire. The release may be sent to the commercial wires by fax, phone, or E-mail. It takes them under an hour to service the material and move it out on their wires. You may want to follow up with Dow Jones, Bloomberg, and Reuters, if the news is particularly sensitive, to explain any nuances or background. The commercial newswires will service local bureaus first. They usually service the Dow Jones, Bloomberg, and Reuters New York headquarters too, if you specify any New York distribution—which is important to know because it may conflict with direct distribution to those services.

- Dow Jones generally dislikes faxes, and prefers receiving information by either PR Newswire or Business Wire. Dow Jones also has its own proprietary electronic service, called DowSend.

- Depending upon the nature of the news, it's frequently a good idea to *fax or e-mail* a copy of the release to the business editor of the local newspaper. Notify the local editor that there's a Dow Jones, Bloomberg or Reuters release or feature on your company. While he or she may ultimately receive the news from one of the wires, it's a courtesy editors appreciate. It's important, then, to know how different editors prefer to receive information. *The New York Times*, for example, doesn't take faxes; a voice mail followup to a wire release is more appropriate.

•   An example of how that works in practice may have been seen when an investor relations consultant for a local Chicago company followed up a wire announcement by calling the assistant financial editor of the *Chicago Tribune* and discussing the release with him (the company's stock had risen 33 percent that day). The result of the followup was a major feature that included a color photo. A feature service saw it and followed it with a major feature of its own.

It's essential that news be distributed early enough in the day to warrant its being received by editors in the early morning for deadlines for the afternoon paper. The same is true of wire service distribution. Late releases may not make it through all the necessary distribution steps before market closing or by 5 p.m., after which readership by editors drops off considerably.

•   In some cases, if you're known to the local editor, and you have more than run-of-the-mill news, it's not a bad idea to call by phone and alert him or her to the fact that the news is coming by wire or by fax. Considering the amount of news the editor must deal with on any given day, this call focuses attention on your news and can sometimes make the difference between its being printed or not. Issuing unfavorable earnings reports very late in the day or managing not to be prepared to release them until Friday (for Saturday's paper) is bad practice. In the first place, it's illegal to hold any news of that nature for one minute longer than is absolutely necessary for the broadest possible dissemination. Secondly, it fools no one. Bad news reverberates as urgently and as loudly as a firecracker in St. Patrick's Cathedral at high mass. And there are, of course, editors who will happily give a story that arrives in those circumstances more play than it would normally receive. For companies in trouble there is no place to hide.

Beyond meeting the needs of disclosure, there are now myriad ways of reaching the financial community beyond the wire services. PR Newswire, Business Wire and others now serve the vast array of computer-accessed databases—CompuServe, DowPhone, NEXIS, Standard & Poor's and more. PR Newswire serves Bloomberg Financial Markets, which covers more than 5,000 brokerage firm terminals. First Call is doing an excellent job of maintaining an active database (material stays active for 90 days) of information for brokerage firms, including analysts' reports and estimates. Many fax services will take your release or report to brokerage houses and distribute your one copy to hundreds of outlets at one time. See the Appendix for a more complete list and description of these services. Electronic mail is fine— if the person you want to reach subscribes to the same service, and checks the electronic mailbox regularly, which is by now an almost universally accepted practice.

A word of caution about electronic distribution, particularly through computer or fax. The information in a computer-accessed database is useful only if it's accessed by a user, which is why information that must be in the hands of a particular publication or individual should be backed up by phone or fax. As computers become more ubiquitous, this becomes less of a problem. Fax poses a problem, in that many publications either don't make their fax numbers available, or change them every few weeks to avoid being inundated. Uninvited faxes are not always welcome—inquire before you send.

The Bulldog Reporter's publication, *Media Relations Insider*, suggests the following tips for pitching a story to the media by e-mail . . .

• Check first with the journalist to make sure he or she even has access to his or her individual e-mail account at hand, and how often it's checked for messages.
• Personalize the subject field of your message. Just as hand addressing an envelope often helps get it opened, a catchy subject field that speaks directly to the person you're contacting will increase the likelihood of getting it read. Unclear subject lines, on the other hand, annoy reporters.
• Keep it short.
• Use e-mail to foster a personal relationship with the reporter.
• Don't mass-e-mail press releases. It may be quicker and cheaper, but it will annoy reporters. "The greatest way to land on a scribe's bozo list," the publication says, " is to e-mail releases to long lists, revealed as cc:s in the header."
• Don't attach documents—or clip multiple releases—together in the same e-mail file.
• Don't duplicate releases you send via PR newswires, mail, or fax.
• Don't expect a higher rate of response just because you're using e-mail.
• Don't use e-mail as a substitute for the followup call. "Did you get my release?" is just as annoying on-line as it is on the phone.

An earnings estimate or some other news of urgency can sometimes be given in an exclusive interview to one of Dow Jones' reporters, such as for use as a Dow Joneser—an in-depth interview that appears on the wire and usually in the paper. The decision to do this is based upon circumstances. The "Heard on the Street" column, for example, usually uses material immediately and is very widely read. Frequently its news results in an almost immediate stock reaction. Not quite so immediate is a Dow Joneser, where the lead time can be three or four days before the confirming release of the quarter's final figures, although a few days in advance is preferred. Dow Jones usually prints these interviews within 24 to 48 hours, which means that it must be done more than that far ahead of the figures (or other news) being ready for public distribution. While this does not strictly follow the procedure for broadest possible dissemination, it is considered sufficient disclosure by the SEC.

Following the dissemination of the news to the wires and other appropriate media, the release should then be faxed or mailed to analysts, brokers, the trade media, shareholders (if appropriate), and any other interested parties. It's extremely important to distribute the release—by fax or hand for daily media and key market makers and investors, and by mail to others—even to those segments of the financial media and the financial community that might have received it over the Dow Jones, Bloomberg, or Reuters wires. First of all, it's unlikely that they will have carried the release in its entirety, even though the commercial newswires will have done so. Second, there is no way to guarantee that the individual at either the publication or the Wall Street house you are interested in reaching will have seen it on the wire or have it on a terminal. Third, it gives a file copy to those individuals in both the financial community and in the media that are following the company. And fourth, it is one more opportunity to make the company name visible.

News Release Form

The form of news releases is deceptively simple. Properly done, it looks easy. Nevertheless, it requires a substantial measure of expertise and experience.

The form should be that which is accepted and traditional in most newspaper city newsrooms. It should be remembered that most city newsrooms receive hundreds—sometimes thousands—of releases every day. The editors charged with poring over these releases grumble over the volume they receive, and invariably most of the releases end up in the wastebasket. They appreciate, however, those that are professionally prepared and that make their arduous job simpler. There are some basic rules:

The Printed News Release Letterhead

The subject of the printed release head versus the plain blank sheet is a matter of more debate in some quarters than one would find at an economists' convention. Obviously, there is an element of silliness in the printed head that trumpets "NEWS FROM XYZ COMPANY," and then reports that John Jones has been appointed assistant foreman of the third shift. "NEWS FROM IBM" or "NEWS FROM EXXON", on the other hand, is likely to warrant the editor's attention. The letterhead of a well-known investor relations firm that uses the words "NEWS RELEASE" is more likely to receive attention, since if it's a creditable firm, the editor knows that the release will at least have been professionally prepared. In the best formats (see Appendix), the name, address, and telephone number (including the home number) of the company contact appear in a conspicuous place right at the top, with the name, address, and phone number (including home phone) of the account person in the investor relations firm who is the point of contact. The name of the company contact is essential because Dow Jones, for one, frequently insists upon verifying most financial information with an officer of the company, regardless of the credibility of the company's financial relations firm. In other cases, an editor or an analyst might want some clarification or additional information. Having both names gives the recipient of the release an option. If the distributing investor relations firm has several offices, they should be listed, so that in appropriate cities a followup call is a local call. Each of those offices should, obviously, be advised of the release and appropriate backup information.

It's also useful to put the stock exchange or NASDAQ symbol conspicuously in the news release heading or lead paragraph. This allows the recipient to quickly check the current stock price.

The Headline

Newspapers write their own headlines. Furthermore, the headline is never written—except perhaps in the smallest newspapers—by the man who writes the story. Some of the commercial newswires eliminate the release's headline and replace it with their own. The purpose of the headline in a news release is to summarize the meat of the story and focus on the crucial point, so that the editor can quickly determine whether the story warrants his or her further attention. It should consist of no more than two lines stating briefly and succinctly what the release is about—for example, "FOURTH QUARTER SALES, EARNINGS, UP SHARPLY AT SHARPER IMAGE." It should be centered, all in caps, at the head of the release. If the story warrants it, and sound judgment dictates it, a subhead in lower case with initial caps describing a second important aspect of the story can be useful, particularly if it has additional news value, and can be intriguing. For example, *Higher Sales and Earnings Due to Strong Store Sales.*

Dateline

Following the format used by virtually all daily newspapers, the first words of the release should be the dateline. This means the city of origin of the story and the date it's issued: "Dallas, TX, July 10. . . ."

The Text

All releases should be double-spaced, with paragraphs indented. This makes it easier for the editor to read, to mark up, and to indicate notes in the margin. Newspapers have long since gotten away from the five W's—who, what, when, where, and why—as mandatory elements for the lead of the story.

Until recently, releases that didn't look like they were typed, with a typewriter face, were not acceptable. To some editors, a release printed on a laser printer in a printer's typeface looked like an ad. But that's all been changed by the universality of the computer and the laser printer. Today, the only people who use typewriters use them as planters or paperweights.

Successful Release Writing

Successful release writing—writing a release that gets published—is a function of capturing the exciting essence of the story in the very first line of the lead. After all, a release competes for the editor's attention against hundreds of others. It competes as well against the stories of every reporter on the staff, each of whom wants to see his or her story in the space or time you're soliciting for your story. If that first line doesn't clutch the editor, the rest of the release may describe the cure for the common cold, but the editor may not read that far, and it will still wind up in the wastebasket. The best education in release writing may be had by carefully reading a good newspaper, such as *The New York Times*. The lead tells the most salient facts—the essence—and tells it in a way that defies you not to read on. Subsequent paragraphs develop the story point by point, the most cogent first.

Editorial wastebaskets are filled daily with journalistic mythology, such as the five "W's", and the notion that editors still edit from the bottom up. Editors usually edit the entire story to meet their own journalistic and space requirements, which is done more easily now because of computers. Indeed, the last paragraph is frequently best used for a fuller description and identification of the company.

A typical company description for the last paragraph of a media release would be the following, used by Ace Cash Express, Inc.:

Ace Cash Express, Inc. is the nation's largest independent operator and franchiser of retail financial service stores. Headquartered in Irving, Texas, it offers convenient services including check cashing, money order sales, MoneyGram™ wire transfer services, small consumer loans, bill payment services, electronic tax filing, and refund anticipation loan services. The company has a total network of more than 690 locations in 40 markets, including more than 600 company owned stores.

The primary audience for a release, remember, is really the editor, not the public. Obviously, if the story doesn't appeal to the editor then the public never sees it. It might make the management feel better to send out a release that reads, "John P. Jones, president of XYZ Company, announced today that . . ." but unless Mr. Jones is a nationally known figure, that release goes straight to the round file.

On the other hand, "The first computer system that can speak was announced today by John P. Jones, president of XYZ Company (OTC) . . ." will be dismissed by only the most disaffected editor.

The first mention of the company's name, by the way, should be followed in parentheses by the company's listing and symbol—(AMEX—Ady), (OTC—Xdxy), (NYSE—Ge). This immediately tells the editor whether the company is listed or not, and on what exchange.

The text itself should be succinct and to the point. It should be written in simple English, grammatically correct, in the active—not passive—voice, and shouldn't read like a legal contract. There's no merit in dullness, nor in imitating every other release of its kind. It should focus on the unique, not the ordinary; on the original, not the mundane. Its job is to impart news, not merely to fulfill a legal commitment.

While the release should be written interestingly, it shouldn't be confused with a feature, or a proposal to an editor for a feature.

The text should not editorialize in any way. Adjectives should be kept to an absolute minimum. Opinions, projections, and other subjective points of view should not be reported as facts. They should either be put in quotes or attributed as indirect quotes to an officer of the company by name.

It's a good idea, if the release runs more than one page, to write MORE at the bottom of each page, and the company name and page number at the top of successive pages. In a busy newsroom, pages of a multipage release can get lost. This, too, is becoming obsolete because of electronic transmission.

The release is then ended with the traditional ending marks "###." The old telegrapher's ending mark—30—is quaint but has long since gone out of style.

Releases should be written by people who are experienced in release writing, or who otherwise have journalistic skill. Unfortunately, since most financial releases are issued under the rules of disclosure, they are too often written or heavily edited by lawyers. Lawyers—even the most literate—should not be allowed to write final drafts of releases. With rare exceptions, they tend to confuse releases with contracts, out of fear of being misinterpreted, misconstrued, or any of the other things lawyers worry about.

This is not to say that lawyers shouldn't assist in writing releases, if they understand the investor relations and media process, and will cooperate rather than attempt to dominate the release writing process. Certainly, releases should be cleared by lawyers when appropriate. Financial releases can have legal consequences, and it is this potential for trouble that should be reviewed by a lawyer. But the lawyer's purview is not literary style. It is fact and law, and the possibility of misinterpretation of facts as stated.

Releases sent to the financial media should usually be addressed to a specific editor by name only in those cases where it's known that the editor or reporter to whom the release is addressed is in fact the appropriate person to receive the release, is still employed at that publication in that capacity, and is in residence and at his or her desk the day the release will be received. A release specifically addressed to a reporter who is out that day sits on the desk until he or she shows up. If it's important that an earnings release get into the hands of a specific editor at, say, the *Los Angeles Times*, the release should not be mailed; it should be sent by fax or e-mail, and followed up with a phone call to make sure that it's not stalled at the financial department's reception desk. Otherwise, the release should be addressed to the Financial Editor or to the City Desk.

If a release isn't printed, it may still not be a wasted effort, according to some editors. They feel that some releases give them a sense of a company and its trends and perspective, and alert them to future events. Small consolation to the CEO and his or her representatives, but consolation nevertheless.

Except under extreme circumstances, it's bad form to call a newspaper to find out why your release was not printed. The chances are that it was not run because the editor didn't think it was important enough to print in the publication's limited space, in relation to other information received that day. No newspaper is legally required to print any news, no matter how important it is to the company, and pestering an editor will only incur animosity and risk that subsequent releases will find their way directly to the wastebasket. If you do have something special, it is, however, appropriate to phone ahead, talk to the particular editor, advise him or her that the release is on the way, and that it addresses some noteworthy points. In view of the large number of releases received every day, if the news is important enough the editor will appreciate it and watch for it. It will not guarantee that the editor will print it. There are times when it seems obvious that a release should have been printed and wasn't. It would be surprising, for example, if the earnings report of a major company in the apparel industry were not published by *Women's Wear Daily*. Under these circumstances, it's appropriate to phone the editor—not to ask why the release wasn't printed—but merely to confirm that the release was received. This is a subtle difference and frequently the publication will appreciate it if the editor has reason to believe that news that should have been received was not.

In this context, it should be noted that the media sometimes makes mistakes. Releases do get lost. A paper will print the wrong number, or the broadcaster will get a fact wrong. Corrections become a problem, particularly if the error is minor (and certainly if it's the fault of the issuer, and not the media).

When your story is one of hundreds received or dozens printed that day, a mistake is not likely to be of great concern to the publication unless it's a serious error, and you might be wasting your time—and risking the animus of the media—to make a fuss about it. If it's consequential, you're likely to get a rational response to a quiet (but not angry) presentation of the facts. The wire services particularly dislike taking up wire time with corrections, and Dow Jones can be made very happy by being told, "Look, don't worry about the wire, but get it straight in the paper." That's terrific—the record is in the paper, and the mail or faxes you send out to the data services will cover those records. But everybody's human, and everybody makes honest mistakes, and everybody does his or her best to correct them. Both Reuters and Dow Jones will correct mistakes if they think the correction is important, but the sooner after publication that the mistake is noted, the easier to get a correction.

Radio and Television

Many radio and TV stations carry some business news on their regular news programs, in addition to the growing number of dedicated business programs on both radio and television. As economic concerns generate more public interest in business news, and as cable networks demonstrate success in reporting it, business news coverage should increase. The measure used by broadcast media is the importance of the news to the largest number of viewers or listeners. The newspaper reader disinterested in business can turn the page; the listener cannot. This is why radio and television editors tend to choose only major or the most interesting business items for their newscasts. In most cases, it is pointless to send routine releases to radio or television stations, unless you know that they have expanded business news coverage. If there is reason to believe that something is particularly newsworthy, the station's news editor should be dealt with in exactly the same way as the newspaper editor. It should be noted that most broadcast media newsrooms receive Dow Jones, Bloomberg, Reuters and PR Newswire reports.

Major News Coverage

Major news can sometimes be treated somewhat differently than routine releases. If the news is of sufficient consequence to warrant greater attention than just routine dissemination, there are other techniques that can be used.

The News Conference

Newspeople are too busy to spend several hours away from their desks to attend a news conference. They get particularly disturbed—and appropriately so—if they are invited to a news conference and are led to believe that they will be given news of greater importance than it turns out to be. The fact that they are wined and dined is not of the essence. There is no law that says that a newspaperperson who accepts your hospitality has to print your story. Media people are further annoyed by being invited to a news conference to be given news that can just as easily be covered by a news release or even a telephone interview.

A news conference should be called only when:

- The news is monumental
- There is some clear reason, such as a demonstration of a new product or the need for an elaborate explanation, why the news cannot be covered in a media release
- Full understanding of the news requires questioning and elaborate answers

If a news conference is warranted there are some basic procedures to be followed.

The Invitation

The invitation should be sent out by mail or fax several weeks in advance of the event, if possible. It should state the purpose of the conference (focusing on the news value), the time, the place, and the speakers. If there are specific visual aspects to the story, this should be indicated and a separate invitation should be sent to the publication's photo desk. Broadcast people should be apprised of facilities and limitations. They should be told of arrangements for engineers, lighting outlets, etc. It is a good idea to telephone the invitees soon after the invitations have gone out to verify interest or to determine whether others in their organizations are interested, and on the afternoon before or the morning of the conference, to remind them and to verify their attendance.

The Place

The site should be appropriate for the event, and should be convenient to the media (particularly the broadcast media, which may have heavy equipment to transport). If it's convenient, the best place is always the office of the chief executive. Next best is a private room at a restaurant, hotel or club. Consideration should be given to having wide aisles for television cameras, although the equipment today is getting smaller and more portable. Obviously a public table in a restaurant is an inappropriate place to hold a media conference. The room should be large enough to hold everybody comfortably, but not so large that the crowd seems dwarfed and the room seems empty. It should be set up and prepared well beforehand to assure that all speakers are visible, can be clearly heard, and that all graphic material is easily presented.

The Time

The time for a news conference is determined by media deadlines. The best time for a news conference is late morning, lunch, or very early afternoon. A 10:00 A.M. news conference will make both the afternoon and the morning newspapers. If it's a major story the afternoon newspapers, which are getting to be scarce commodities, and are not as widely read as the morning newspapers, will preempt the story, which will not please the morning papers. On the other hand, it is better if a major story makes the financial wires while the market is still open. This means that time should be allowed for everybody not only to hear the news but to write it. Newspeople still go back to their offices and pound word processors. Only in the movies do they rush to the phones to call the city room.

Preparation

A complete media kit should be prepared for every newsperson attending. This should consist of a basic release, a background sheet on the company, any financial background material such as an annual or quarterly report, biographical material and photos of executives, and product data sheets. If product or plant photos are appropriate, they should be included. While the media kit should be as complete as possible, care should be taken not to overload it with so much material that a reporter can't find the facts for all the paper.

The Format

If cocktails or coffee are to be served, the length of time allocated should be just sufficient for everybody to arrive. Service should last no longer than twenty or thirty minutes. The media conference can begin while people are still drinking. Reporters' time, remember, is valuable. If a lunch seems in order, it should be treated essentially the same way as an analysts' luncheon—twenty minutes for cocktails, a rapidly served lunch, and the conference to begin over dessert or as the main course is cleared.

The presentation itself should be short, simple, and to the point. While there is a great temptation to dramatize, few newspapermen are impressed by this. The drama should come from the material. The material should be direct, and graphically illustrated. It should take no longer than thirty minutes to present. Time should be allowed for questioning. Immediately following the media conference, the officers of the company should be prepared to spend a few minutes to answer questions of any reporters that may linger behind the others. The chief executive officer should also be available in his office for the remainder of the day to answer any questions that may occur to a reporter back at his desk writing the story.

The Electronic Conference

Increasingly feasible and cost-effective are teleconferencing and video conferencing, in which the main conference is conducted by phone or is televised and sent to other cities by closed circuit television. This allows you to have interactive conferences in many cities at once, because the setup allows questioners from the audience in any city to talk directly to the main transmission point, as if everybody were in one place.

You can hook up with local media or trades, analysts and brokers, or anybody else you want to participate. Generally, the same techniques of the press conference apply.

The Individual Interview

There are times when the most effective way to break a major story is to give it to a single reporter in an exclusive interview. The strategy for this approach can be very subtle, such as an implied trade of major coverage in exchange for the exclusive, or when the reporter is important in his or her own right, as a columnist or well-known broadcaster might be. It's sometimes valuable, as well, when the story is somewhat technical, and requires a knowledgeable and concerned reporter for accurate coverage.

This may be effective, but it has an inherent danger. If there is any information imparted that comes under the rules of disclosure, that reporter's lead time and exclusivity may be lost, since the rules may require that the story be distributed to the general public within a reasonable period of time—and certainly the same day—as it is released to an individual. This is a matter to be discussed with the company's attorney. An exception is a *Wall Street Journal* or Reuters interview which, as has been stated before, is accepted by the SEC as having broad enough coverage to be considered adequate under the rules of disclosure.

Interview Guidelines

Here, too, the general guidelines for the interview are the same as for the media conference—careful preparation, no nonsense, to the point, and frank discussion.

In both the individual interview and the media conference there are two basic cautions to consider:

- *Be prepared for full disclosure.* Beware any question on a material matter a reporter might ask that you can't answer. If you can't answer because you don't know, say so—but be prepared to explain why you don't know. Promise to get the information and forward it on a timely basis. If a reporter feels you have anything to hide, the story based on the interview may nullify much or all of the positive effect that the story might otherwise have. Certainly, as in an analyst meeting, all possible questions should be anticipated and the answers prepared beforehand. Obviously, it's impossible to anticipate every question, and if an unanticipated question is asked, don't answer hastily, without considering how your words will look in type. And material questions should be anticipated. There should be no surprises, if they can be avoided.

  At the same time, no matter how open you're willing to be, there may be questions that you shouldn't answer, for competitive or strategic reasons. Decline to answer those questions, but again, state the reasons. Again, these are questions that should be anticipated, and for which responses should be rehearsed.
- *Absolutely nothing should be stated off the record,* unless its pertinence to the story is for background only. An off-the-record statement places an unwarranted burden on a reporter. The reporter's job is to print information—not to be a repository of facts. It is a burden that reporters rarely

appreciate. Furthermore, it almost invariably leads to the impression that something else is being hidden. If you don't want a reporter to report something, don't say it—on or off the record. On the other hand, don't confuse *off the record* with *not for attribution,* which means that the material can be used, but please, don't quote you on it. Know the difference, and follow the rules.

Feature Material

The approach to developing feature material in business and financial publications, as well as the general media, is considerably different than it is for the straight news announcement. In developing features, the attempt is to project a somewhat detailed and rounded picture of the company or some aspect of it, and to do so in a favorable way. The value of feature articles about a company lies not only in the general exposure of the company to the publication's readers, but in explaining the company with some measure of depth; to engender the impression that it's functioning well; and to increase the understanding of the company.

An article about a CEO featured his involvement in auto racing as a car owner, which told a great deal about the manager as an individual and personality. It humanized him. The feature article, then, may deal with the personality or idiosyncrasies of the company's managers, or the work of its research department, or its unique approach to using raw materials. It doesn't matter which approach is used—it tells more about the company than do the numbers.

Guidelines for Feature Articles

In approaching this kind of media coverage there are several basic rules and guidelines that are imperative. These rules apply whether the story is generated internally by the company or by the investor relations or public relations consultant.

• *The target publication must be clearly understood.* Several issues of the publication should be studied to determine the kind of material it seeks, its point of view, its style, its editorial viewpoint, and its apparent taboos. Any attempt to try to convince a publication to print a story that is not in keeping with its general editorial policy, or that is similar to one recently printed, is not only a waste of time, but could lead to adverse reaction by the editors to the company or the investor relations consultant.

• *Even a feature article must have a newsworthy point of view.* Sometimes this is a hook—an event or activity that serves as a focal point for the story; an indication that the timing for the story is appropriate. Or it can be an angle that is at least unusual and perhaps unique, such as a company's new approach to financing or a new production or distribution technique that should result in significantly altering the direction of the company. Or the reorganization of a management team to take into account the changing economic conditions under which the company must function.

• The story should delineate, in one aspect or another, a *significant change in the company's operation.* It is only under the rarest circumstances that a publication will publish a story about a company in which absolutely nothing significant has happened, or in which the company is shown to be no different than any other company in its field. An exception might be when lack of change is significant and salutary in itself, such as when every other company in the industry has made significant changes with unfavorable results and the subject company, by changing nothing, has outperformed the industry.

Developing Feature Material Angles

Developing feature material for publication usually requires a measure of skill, if not artfulness. Some time ago, as part of its investor relations program, it was deemed valuable to develop a feature article about a medium-sized insurance company. Basic investigation indicated that the company's operations seemed no different than comparable companies in its industry. Furthermore, an additional obstacle existed in that newspapers rarely find most stories of insurance companies of sufficient consequence to print. Every aspect of the company's business was carefully explored in the attempt to fathom some point that was unusual and newsworthy. Then there came to light the fact that the company's return on its investment portfolio was higher than most other insurance companies', including some of the giants. Further investigation showed that this was a function of the investment department's imagination and daring. It was company policy to seek out unusual situations, perhaps with somewhat more risk, and to be considerably more venturesome than is traditionally expected of the insurance industry. The company, for example, was one of the first to invest in the cable television industry in its early days.

This extraordinary success in portfolio management became the focal point of a proposal to *The New York Times,* which resulted in a large feature story on page one of the Sunday *New York Times* business section.

When a kid rescues another kid from drowning, it takes no public relations skill to get the kids' names in the paper. The skill is in fathoming the unusual but accurate in an otherwise usual story, and projecting it as the basis for a feature article.

Approaching a Publication

Approaching the publication requires some relatively simple procedures:

• Once a *target publication* has been selected and its editorial policies analyzed, develop the story specifically for that publication. The same general story may function for several different publications, but each approach must still be tailored.

• *The proper reporter or editor* is determined either by reading the masthead, reading the publication, or by calling the publication and inquiring. While the name can be found in directories, such as *Bacon's,* jobs change quickly and frequently, and names should be verified. In most major business publications, reporters can initiate stories, without assignment from an editor. In some publications, such as *Business Week* or *Fortune,* there are specific areas of specialty. In a smaller publication, the ranking editor on the masthead is the first point of contact. In larger magazines, such as *Fortune,* several people are given the specific responsibility for reviewing all story ideas. If there is a local bureau of the publication in or near your city, you will probably be better off working with it, rather than with the publication's national staff. (See Appendix for appropriate directories.) This is particularly true of *Business Week* and *The Wall Street Journal.* (However, being turned down by a local bureau doesn't preclude going to the head office of a publication, if you're sure that's the right publication for the story, and the local bureau is informed of what you're doing.) In some cases, if you know a staff reporter but want to pitch to an editor, you can call the reporter for advice about who to send the story to—but don't abuse this privilege.

• Write a letter to the editor or reporter describing the story. In some cases the letter may be preceded by a phone call or even a meeting with the editor. Experience will tell you who prefers letters and who will take phone calls first. Almost invariably, and with very few exceptions, the story will ultimately have to be presented to the publication in written form. Sometimes the letter can be prepared before the first contact. Sometimes, if a discussion with the editor beforehand is feasible, the letter should be written only after the meeting, and should be patterned on the guidelines set forth by the editor. If the phone call came first, the letter should follow within one day.

The letter should be concise and to the point. The editor is busy and businesslike, and even the fact that he or she has been bought a sumptuous lunch at an expensive restaurant is not going to preclude the necessity the reporter faces to maintain the level of his or her publication. The essence of the story should be stated in the first paragraph, with emphasis on the reasons why this story is newsworthy and warrants his or her consideration. The remainder of the brief letter should include facts to support the basic premise. It should indicate the availability of the people involved, and of graphic and visual material, if appropriate, that is available or can be made available to supplement the story.

If you feel that the story is too long and complicated to cover in one page, consider using an outline, as long as you can still make it sound interesting. The letter should rarely be more than two pages long.

The letter should not begin with the sentence, "John Jones, president of XYZ Corporation, is going to be in New York City at two o'clock next Wednesday afternoon and is available for an interview." If this is the case, then Mr. Jones' visit to New York should be stated further along in the letter—after the story idea has been clearly delineated.

• A few days after the letter has been sent it is appropriate to follow up with a phone call to determine the editor's interest, to answer questions, and to make arrangements for whatever interviews or further discussions are necessary. Because media people are so busy, it's a good idea to be sure not to call at deadline time (usually late afternoon, for morning papers), to say immediately who's calling (name and firm) and in regards to what, and to ask, "Do you have a minute?" If the answer is no, ask when you should call again. If the answer is yes, inquire, and tell your story quickly.

• The course of all interviews should take precisely the same form as interviews for major news events, and should follow the same rules described earlier in this chapter. The executives involved should be prepared to be frank and open. Nothing should be off the record except material that is necessary for background, but not necessarily newsworthy in itself. Questions should be anticipated and careful preparation made for each answer.

Sometimes, (but not always) an interviewee can control an interview to some extent. First, you should have a clear idea of what you want the results to be, in terms of tone and information imparted. Then, with careful rehearsal, you can ensure that the information comes out by being responsive to questions, and then going beyond the answer. For example:

Q. Do you think you'll make more acquisitions?

A. It's not in our immediate plans. However, we didn't plan to make the last acquisition, but the opportunity came up and we took it, because we always look at every opportunity in terms of our long-range needs. That, to us, is as much a part of our planning as a dedicated acquisition program, because the aim is growth and diversification—not acquisition. We do, however, have the financial resources to take advantage of such opportunities.

In the case of smaller newspapers, or papers in other than the ten largest cities in the United States, the letter may ultimately turn out to be unnecessary. Arrangements can be made by phone. If an executive is planning to be in Birmingham, Alabama, next Thursday and there is reason to believe that there is a newsworthy aspect to either the executive's presence in that city or to the company, it's perfectly appropriate to phone the financial editor of the *Birmingham News* a few days ahead, to indicate the fact that the executive will be in Birmingham next Thursday and to go on to delineate the basic points of the story in exactly the same way as is done in the letter. Be sure to point out a local angle to the company that might interest readers. Arrangements for the interview are then made by phone. Because unanticipated assignments may change plans, last minute confirmation is prudent. Obviously, more lead time than a few days affords a better chance for success, but that shouldn't preclude at least a try on a few days notice when that's all you've got.

In some cases an executive may be appearing in a city for purposes other than strictly company business. For example, the company president may be appearing in town to make a speech before a local organization. The procedure is to phone ahead to inform the editor of that fact. If the editor is not short-staffed and can afford time for coverage of the event, arrangements should be made. If possible, prepared material should be made available to the editor at the time of the interview. If the story is still considered newsworthy, but the editor is unable to assign a reporter to cover it, it is worth the effort to prepare a news release covering the event and to fax it to the editor on that morning.

Other Media Opportunities

Other media opportunities offer interesting possibilities.

An increasing number of publications, including *Barron's* and *Fortune, Investor's Business Daily, Equities Magazine,* and *The Security Trader's Handbook*, reprint media releases in a special section for a small fee. This is particularly useful for the smaller company that's not likely to get wide media coverage for its routine news. While this kind of service might well be construed as advertising, it can be useful in hitting a well-defined target audience.

Cable television has become a major outlet of business news. Aside from excellent business news coverage on such shows as the business news program on the CNN and CNBC, a number of local cable outlets offer special business and financial news shows. In some cities, such shows already exist on Ultra High Frequency (UHF) stations. In Chicago, for example, Channel 26 is particularly popular. In some cities, these programs charge a small fee for a 15 or 20 minute interview, although most are free. There seems no question that the growth of cable television will bring with it increased opportunities for disseminating business news.

Not to be overlooked is the trade media. Articles and interviews, as well as media releases with financial information, frequently find hospitality in the industry trade media for a company. Analysts read the trade papers of industries or companies they follow. People in an industry are investors as well as are readers of the daily media, and there are good marketing reasons for a company to be seen in its industry's media. The rules for dealing with the trade media, incidentally, are no different than they are for dealing with the financial media.

Increasing in popularity are new computer networks and forums serving brokers, analysts, money managers, and individual investors, to which companies can subscribe. Some of these services are listed in the Appendix.

Listing in Stock Tables

Extremely valuable to any company is its listing in the stock tables of newspapers. For the exchange-listed company, there's no problem in any paper that carries the complete listing. For over-the-counter companies the listing is supplied by the *National Association of Securities Dealers*. NASDAQ—the *National Association of Securities Dealers Automated Quotation* system—is now a major market, on a par with the AMEX and NYSE. While its criteria for listing in the tables in newspapers changes as its growth warrants, some 3,000 securities may be included, determined upon the basis of financial market standards. This is the list carried in most major newspapers, as well as *The Wall Street Journal*. There is also a National Market System National List.

NASD does supply the wire services with the quotations and volume on substantially all of the approximately 3,000 issues in the system. Nobody has printed this entire list except the late *Media General Financial Weekly*, a national financial publication whose recent metamorphosis signals the growing dominance of electronic databases that are readily available to all investors. It is useful, however, to local newspapers, which frequently print the bid and asked quotations of over-the-counter companies located in their area. About 250 papers carry either an abbreviated list or the stocks of local companies.

Occasionally a company may feel it is eligible to be included in the newspaper listings by virtue of changed circumstances, such as an increase in price or an increase in the number of shareholders. The company can make direct application to the NASD and ask to be included on the list by virtue of the changed circumstances.

There are two aspects of news coverage that are extremely important to businesspeople, even as they pose potential danger. The first is the story developed by the publication for reasons that might appear to be unfavorable to the company. The second is the routine media inquiry.

The Unfavorable Story

Forbes magazine is noted for ferreting out unfavorable stories about companies—or so it would appear. *Forbes* prides itself in anticipating danger points in industry or the economy, or potential disasters in companies. Their reporters are thoroughly professional and well-trained. *Forbes*, in dealing with a story on a company in trouble or potentially in trouble, has often been accused of doing a hatchet job. It isn't always the case.

A *Forbes* editor may hear of a potentially negative story about a company. In the course of investigation one of the first things the editor will do is call the company's chief executive officer. The chief executive officer, aware of *Forbes'* straightforward and irreverent attitude, becomes defensive. The CEO tries to hide facts or to sugarcoat them. He or she sometimes makes other executives unavailable. To the *Forbes* editor this is a red flag. It indicates that something is being hidden—that there is more to the story than meets the eye. The article will then be developed on the basis of *Forbes'* own research, without benefit of the company's side of the story. The result is a negative report written in *Forbes'* breezy style.

Unless the company truly has something to hide, the first reaction to an inquiry from an editor of *Forbes*—or any other publication—should be complete openness. If the company does indeed have something to be wary about, initial remarks should be restricted. For example, they called at the wrong time, or you don't have all the facts at your fingertips. In other words, without being defensive, buy the time to consult with your lawyer or investor relations professional. Rarely does a reporter call when there isn't fifteen minutes or more to wait for an answer. Experience with any major responsible publication, including *Forbes*, indicates that a publication is responsive to an open presentation of the facts—both positive and negative—by the company. No responsible publication ever refuses to hear the company's side of the story. This is not to say that the negative facts will not be printed. Very few publications will be deterred from printing pertinent facts, negative or positive. But at least the negative side of the story can be cushioned by the company's point of view.

It should be recognized that for the public company there is no place to hide—that's one of the things that being public is about. It is the most destructive form of self-deception to believe that there is any way in which a negative story, once it has been discovered by a publication, will not come out in its worst aspects. It should also be recognized that no company ever takes a consistently straight line to success. Not all decisions are correct, nor is any chief executive perfect. What's more important is that if the total story is told and told honestly, the resultant article may not read like a puff piece, but at least the company will come out ahead, with its credibility preserved, and possibly enhanced.

Does this always work? Of course not. Sometimes, despite all of the investor relations professionalism, and despite all the cooperation with the media, the story comes out badly.

The picture you so carefully and accurately painted is distorted, the wrong people are quoted and the right people are not, the facts are warped and bent beyond recognition, and the whole piece reads as if it were written by your most malicious competitor.

Beyond the first scream of outrage, what can you do?

The most useful course is to do nothing until you've recovered from your anger. Even doing the right thing in the wrong frame of mind can perpetuate, not cure, the damage. So:

- Don't act precipitously. Think of every action in terms of possible reaction. What seems like a good idea at the moment may backfire next week.
- After you've gotten over the emotional impact and the anger, don't think vindictively. You may have to live with that publication again someday, and vindictiveness in any event is not profitable.
- Assess real—not assumed or presumed—damage. That's where you've got to focus your attention. Much assumed damage at first light disappears when the sun comes up. What's left is damage you can deal with.

It's this last point that's crucial to successfully limiting the damage of bad media. Too often, the defense is predicated on imagined damage, in which case the reaction is an overreaction, and causes more damage than the original article.

Experts rarely concern themselves with *why* it happened. Unless libel is involved, or it's part of a bear raid, it doesn't really matter. The reporter could have functioned out of ignorance or laziness. Reporters are people, and are not immune to such foibles as preconceived notions that can subvert the professionalism of even the most experienced journalist. The reason for an adverse story is rarely an element that can be dealt with in damage control.

There are some specific questions to be addressed:

- What does the article *really* say? Is it bad because it's wrong—or because it's right?
- Is the article distorted because the facts are wrong, or because they are put in a wrong context that distorts the facts?
- What is the real damage? Is it libelous? Misleading enough to cause real business damage? Or just embarrassing?
- Consider the publication. Is it widely read, or will people you care about never see it? (Consider that under certain circumstances, your competitor may want to make a point by sending a reprint of the article, along with a favorable one about himself from the same publication). What's the publication's reputation for credibility?
- Is the potential damage internal as well as external? Sometimes an un-

favorable article can hurt internal morale more than it affects an external perception of the firm.

Staying power is an important consideration. How long after publication will the story, or at least its negative aura, linger? Depending upon the publication and the nature of the story, considerably less time than you think. As one experienced marketer put it, the impact fades quickly, but the impression can linger.

Assessing the damage accurately allows you to choose the appropriate response. There are, in fact, a number of inappropriate responses. You can:

- Sue, but only if there is real libel and real—and demonstrable—damage. There rarely is.
- Get on the phone and scream at the editor. Good for your spleen, lousy for your future with at least that segment of the media. And you'll never win.
- Write a nasty letter to the publisher. Only slightly better than screaming, but with the same results.
  On the other hand, there are some positive things that can be done:
- Avoid defensiveness. Plan positively.
- Warn people. If you know an article is going to appear that might be unfavorable, alert your own people, so that it doesn't come as a surprise.
- Have a plan and a policy, preferably before you need it. This should cover how to deal with the media, who does it and who doesn't, how to deal with customer reactions, how to deal with internal reactions. It should cover how calls are handled, who responds and who routes calls to whom, what to say to customers and who says it, and so forth.
- A letter to the editor is important, if only to go on record. But it should be positive, non-vitriolic, and deal only with the facts. It should not sound petulant or defensive.
- Deal with the real damage. If the real damage is in specific markets, mount a positive public relations campaign, and even an advertising program, aimed specifically at those markets. If the damage is internal, try to assess the root causes for the negative reaction. It would take a powerful article in a powerful journal to demoralize a firm that's otherwise sound and comfortable with itself.

No story is so bad that it should warrant extreme reaction. No publication that's still publishing is so devoid of credibility that some readers won't accept what they read. The role of the professional, trained and experienced marketer is to maintain perspective, to assess the damage appropriately, and to see that the response is equal to—but does not exceed—the damage.

If bad media meant nothing, then neither would good media, and we know that consistently good media means a great deal. But one story—good or bad—rarely has sufficient impact to seriously aid or damage a company (although a negative story is more titillating than a positive one). Most positive public relations is a consistent series of positive articles, interviews and news stories. If a negative media consists of more than one story, then the problem is usually not the media—it's the subject of the stories.

The perspective of the bad story, then, requires dealing with it as an anomaly. This means dealing with it as a calm and rational business decision. And no business decision, in any context, is ever a sound one if it isn't arrived at rationally and professionally.

It would be naive not to recognize the fact that not all reporters, editors, or even publications are honest. There are individual reporters on the take. There are hatchet jobs. There are publications that are unethical. There are publications that tie their editorial columns to their advertising sides. This is unfortunate and frequently illegal, particularly for a financial publication that purports to present honest investment advice. It's just as bad to tie advertising to favorable news without in some way making clear to the reader that the editorial material is not objective or that it has been paid for in some way.

There is nothing that can be done about unscrupulous publications except to assiduously resist all blandishments to tie advertising or any other revenue—including reprints, gifts and junkets (free media trips)—to editorial material. For the company in trouble, it is a short-term solution to a deeper problem. Since, on Wall Street, bad news reverberates loudly, there is no such thing—regardless of popular lore—as cosmetic public relations, particularly in business news. Other than protesting vigorously, which is usually a waste of time, the only recourse a company has to an unscrupulous publication that prints an unfavorable story is to deal more intensively with the honest publications in the attempt to disseminate the truth. Yes, it takes twice as much truth to counteract falsehood. But it's worth the effort.

Incidentally, the notion that newspeople can be bought is nonsense, despite the individual anomaly. It's true that a newsman who has friendly relations with either the company or the company's investor relations firm can in some way extend a minute measure of editorial favor to the company. This usually means listening to a story more patiently. But in the final analysis, the publication is almost invariably bigger than any of its editors or any story. In order to survive, the publication must be editorially consistent. True, there are exceptions. And occasionally, favor can be curried with a newspaperman or an editor resulting in a favorable story that might otherwise not have appeared. But no public relations program can ever be built, or sustained, on such a structure. In other words, don't depend upon it.

The Unexpected Inquiry

A reporter may hear a rumor, or have an intuitive thought, or otherwise draw a conclusion about a company—and call the CEO to follow it up. Whether the call is hostile or friendly, it's frequently unexpected.

The unexpected inquiry should also be dealt with in a straightforward manner. Remember, an officer of a public company has a fiduciary position. This means that public comment may have legal implications. This should be kept in mind in every aspect of dealing with the media, including the electronic media.

In responding to an inquiry, no attempt should be made to hide or dissemble—it will only make matters worse. The company president who is called by a newspaperman or an editor and asked to comment on an unfavorable rumor should react calmly and rationally. If the facts are clearly at hand, he should state them simply and straightforwardly, with no obvious attempt to influence the editorial stance. If he doesn't know the answer he should say so, take the reporter's name and phone number, get the information as soon as possible, and return the call with the facts. If warranted, he should invite the reporter to discuss the question in detail, and here too the same rules apply as for any other interview. It's absolutely imperative that every company have a basic news policy. Specific executives should be designated as spokesmen for the company. The corps of spokesmen can be broad, consisting of specialists in each field, but they should not be arbitrarily selected, and each should be capable of dealing with the media calmly and intelligently.

There should be a clear and simple directive from the chief executive officer to all executives and employees that spokespersons have been designated and that all inquiries should be referred to the appropriate spokesperson. Under no circumstances should an unauthorized person be allowed to supply vital information to the media, and this should be made clear not in terms of authority alone, but rather for the simple reason that only the spokesmen have all pertinent facts and policy at hand. It should be made clear that it is as unfair to an unauthorized person to be allowed to supply information as it is to the company, since it puts the unauthorized person in an untenable position. Unauthorized personnel should be advised to deal with all inquiries politely, to indicate that they are not sufficiently armed with the facts to answer the question, and then to indicate the name and phone number of the designated spokesman.

Designated spokespeople should be kept abreast at all times of company news policy and procedures. They should be briefed as well as possible on all potential inquiries and the appropriate answers. They should know company policy and the limits of the information they are authorized to divulge. They should be made to understand clearly the basic procedures for answering inquiries in terms of dealing with reporters politely, rationally, unemotionally, and openly. When a question exceeds the limits of a spokesperson's authority, the spokesperson should politely say so and refer the reporter to the proper executive to handle that inquiry. All inquiries and the answers given should be made known—preferably in writing—as soon as possible to the chief executive officer.

When to Say No

Are there ever times to tell the media to bug off, and leave you alone? Maybe.

If you're dealing with a hostile reporter or publication, and believe you're in a no-win situation, you may have more to gain than to lose by refusing to cooperate.

If you're dealing with a publication whose editor thinks the publication is more important than it really is, and you know you're not going to get a fair shake anyway, why waste your time?

If you're asked to comment about a competitor, or about a situation in your industry to which you're ancillary, and there's a good chance that your comment may be misinterpreted or even misreported, "no comment" is a great response.

If you know that you're going to take a beating no matter what you say or do, or if you know that the reporter is unlettered or unknowledgeable in the subject and is only passing through the beat, or if you know that commenting is going to get you involved in something that may turn out to be unprofitable to you, then tell the media, politely, that you choose not to participate.

If you know that a reporter is misrepresenting to you what he or she is writing, in order to get your participation in a story that you might otherwise be reticent about, or if that reporter has done that to you in the past, you're perfectly right to decline.

In fact, participating in a roundup story should be done cautiously anyway, with you asking the reporter as many questions as he or she asks you. And if you do consider participating, take notes of what you're being told about the nature of the story. You may want to complain later.

The media has an inalienable right to pursue. They don't have an inalienable right to catch. There's a difference between being firm in declining and being rude. Rudeness is somebody else's game. Declining firmly and politely may very well be the way for you to win your game.

Except in terms of their training, and the motivation of individuals to do their jobs as well as possible, newspapermen are no different from anybody else. The range of their capabilities, understanding, and limitations is about on a par with the total population. There are competent newspeople and there are incompetent newspeople. There are a great many reporters in the financial media who seem remarkably ignorant of business and finance. There are a greater number who are remarkably well versed in the field. Editors and newspaperpeople are no more exempt from hostilities, bad days, fights with their wives or husbands, and toothaches than anybody else. Nevertheless, if they are dealt with professionally they will normally function professionally.

The editor and the newsperson usually have no ax to grind. The realities of the world are that they react as humanly to a confrontation as does anyone else. Few newspaperpeople, however, will react unfavorably to an honest, simple, and straightforward presentation and to an unflinching response to even the most cutting questions.

The proper function of an investor relations consultant in dealing with the media is not to act as a spokesman for the company—unless he or she has been properly trained and specifically designated in this capacity by the chief executive officer—but to act as an intermediary, smoothing the way for direct relations between the company and the media. Nor should the investor relations consultant ever be used as a buffer—as a shield behind which the company can hide. The media resents this and rightfully so. Yet the major source of company news is still frequently the investor relations consultant or officer.

And it's clearly acceptable to the media that the investor relations professional can be an advocate for the company he or she represents. A senior *Fortune* editor once said that she understands that a public relations or investor relations professional is fulfilling an advocacy function when talking about a client or employer. A *Wall Street Journal* reporter who sometimes wrote the *Heard On The Street* column sees it from a different angle, saying, "I assume that everyone who gives me a positive story idea is long in the stock, and that everyone who gives me a negative idea is short." At least some reporters are aware of the sometimes unscrupulous use of the media by shorts.

Still, if there were no investor relations industry, every editorial body in the United States would have to treble its staff to ferret out the massive amount of news that is now brought to the attention of the media. Most newspaperpeople recognize this. Some, however, given reason to feel that the investor relations consultant is inserting himself or herself between the company and the media, will rightfully and vocally resent it.

The print and electronic media, when properly dealt with, are an important conduit to the financial community and the investing public. It's worth the effort of every corporate executive to learn to work with the media properly and effectively.

Chapter 9

Rules of Disclosure: The SEC and the Markets

H overing over all investor relations, like a great umbrella, is *disclosure*—who tells what to whom, and when. In the securities markets, the Rules of Disclosure are promulgated by governmental bodies—the U.S. Securities and Exchange Commission (SEC) and, in some cases, state authorities—and for those companies whose securities are traded on exchanges or NASDAQ, the governing bodies of those organizations. The purpose of disclosure regulation is to assure the public equal and timely access to all information that might affect the price of a security. The regulations attempt to preclude trading on inside information that might cause disadvantage to those not privy to that information at the same time.

But more significantly, the driving force for disclosure goes beyond regulation. In investor relations, telling more usually means getting more. Disclosing is not only a legal requirement, it's good investor relations.

There is a keen difference, in fact, between the *requirements* of disclosure under the regulations of the SEC and the stock exchanges and the *need* for disclosure for a public company seeking acceptance in the capital markets. The Rules of Disclosure are *requirements*, not electives. The *needs* for disclosure are dictated by the attempts by a public company to keep itself visible to the financial community, and at all times clearly understood. One does not preclude the other, and in fact, the values of disclosure far exceed the limitations of the Rules of Disclosure.

The SEC

All publicly traded securities are regulated by the U.S. Securities and Exchange Commission, a federal regulatory body established by Congress under the Securities Exchange Act of 1934. Its chairman and board members are appointed by the president of the United States. It has a very large and enthusiastic staff, with offices in major cities throughout the United States, as well as in Washington, D.C. Its major assignment is to regulate and monitor the offer to sell, the sale, and the trading of securities for virtually all public companies, stock exchanges, and securities dealers in the country. It does its job well and takes it seriously.

While the commission tends to take on the character of the administration it serves, as well as the commission's chairperson, in its emphasis on any particular aspect of securities regulation, it never strays from its basic purpose. Under the Reagan administration, for example, the drive to deregulate made it easier for some companies to go public, but didn't deregulate or ease enforcement. Under the Bush administration, deregulation was de-emphasized, while response to public reaction to insider trading, takeovers, the incursion of foreign capital, and concern for penny stock trading seemed to change the commission's regulatory focus. The assessment of the Bush administration was that it wanted fewer rules, but wanted those rules stringently enforced. The Clinton administration, in its first four years, tended to foster a wider variety of investment vehicles, but with controls that favored the company rather than the investor. Under that administration, for example, it has become more difficult to hold brokers accountable for misdeeds. But regardless of who heads it, or the leeway in enforcement, protecting the investor is still the SEC's primary role.

Each state also has its body of securities laws and regulations, most of which are enforced by the state attorney general. These laws are known as *blue sky laws*, since they were originally designed, many of them prior to the establishment of the SEC, to prevent unscrupulous securities dealers from promising and selling investors everything but the blue sky.

All companies selling securities to the public must conform to the laws and regulations of both the SEC and every state in which those securities are sold. A stock must be registered in every state—blue skyed—in which it is sold. Some states allow *manual exemption*—automatic clearance of stocks listed on national exchanges or on the NASDAQ National Market List, if the company is covered in the Standard & Poor's or Moody's Manuals.

All exchanges have rules and regulations governing disclosure practices of companies whose stock is listed—traded—on those exchanges. Naturally, these regulations are often developed to parallel, comply with, or function to complement SEC and state regulation. The exchanges, however, frequently define or expand the regulations for listed companies. Securities of companies not listed on exchanges, or listed on the NASDAQ system, are regulated by the National Association of Securities Dealers, an organization of member firms who trade on NASDAQ or otherwise in the over-the-counter market.

The vast body of regulations covers every aspect of security practices, particularly those that affect the value of that company's stock in the public market. The regulatory concern here is principally with the legal aspects of the dissemination of that information—the Rules of Disclosure.

Compliance with Securities Law

Primarily, the responsibility to ensure compliance with securities law remains within the purview of the attorney. Unfortunately, securities regulation is not only complex, it's not always completely clear. There are many areas in which judgment must be exercised, as for example, the moment at which prospective mergers become likely and must be disclosed. Since these judgments are invariably made within the framework of regulation, and are interpreted by a wide variety of regulatory and judicial decisions in different jurisdictions that sometimes disagree with one another, they need the professional assistance of a competent securities attorney.

The primary burden for complying with disclosure regulation, however, remains with the corporation's management, with the assistance of its attorneys (not the other way around). In the realm of disclosure communication, the responsibility resides with the investor relations counsel.

It may be useful to note here the difference in viewpoints that frequently arises between attorneys and investor relations consultants. The attorney, charged primarily with being able to defend his or her client to the point of walking into court "with clean hands", frequently takes positions that are extremely defensive. The investor relations consultant, on the other hand, is charged with keeping the client viable in the marketplace, which means outreach and communication. The points of view frequently conflict. It's well worth the effort, though, for management, its securities counsel and the investor relations professional to work together and respect one another's constraints. Each has a distinct point of view and experience to offer.

Disclosure Philosophy

Because the body of regulation regarding disclosure is so elaborate, and so much of it is a question of judgment, much of the direction necessary to make those judgments is not codified. Those covered by securities law have sometimes felt that in some cases, such as the classic *Pig 'n Whistle*, the SEC seems to be saying, in effect, "Do it first, and then we'll tell you whether you should have done it or not."

While the ultimate judgment may depend heavily on attorneys' advice, the corporation and its financial relations counsel should nevertheless adopt a basic philosophy that should pervade its disclosure program. This philosophy should should be grounded in two key points:

- *Full disclosure.* The company should be prepared to disclose any and all information that could conceivably affect a judgment of the company as an investment vehicle. If there is any question—disclose. Certainly, this includes any activity that warrants filing a Form 8-K with the SEC. The Form 8-K is used between formal reporting periods to report significant changes in corporate activity, policy or practice.
- *Disclosure timing.* Pertinent or disclosable material, such as earnings statements and dividends, should be processed for release no more than a few hours from the time the information is known by any officer of the corporation. The machinery for disclosure should be well established beforehand, whether it's done by the company itself or through the auspices of the investor relations counsel. It should then be a routine matter to prepare and disseminate any information.

For many corporations, this kind of policy may seem harsh and arduous. But the balance must be sought between the basic responsibility to investors and potential investors on the one hand, and the value of competing in the capital markets by disseminating every element of information that materially assists in the judgment of a company on the other. And while these two parallel goals may occasionally conflict, and there may be a temptation to hedge on the rules, it should be clearly understood that administration of the rules of disclosure can be rigid and assiduous. The SEC and the exchanges, it should be perfectly clear, mean exactly what they say. Furthermore, as understaffed as the SEC or any other regulatory body may be at any given moment, the agency is rarely lax in enforcing securities regulation.

And let us dispense immediately with any question of secrecy on the basis of competitive advantage. While the SEC has frequently said that it has no intention of putting any company at a competitive disadvantage, and will indeed allow competitive disadvantage as a defense in some cases, it still considers the dissemination of material information to be more important under the Rules of Disclosure. This can sometimes raise thorny points for a corporation asked to break down its performance by product line or by division, or for the corporation that feels that premature disclosure of merger negotiations might adversely affect those negotiations. Here, competent legal counsel is essential. But counsel notwithstanding, the SEC is quite clear. Disclose.

Furthermore, to the extent that individual and presumably unsophisticated investors are in the market, the SEC is increasingly concerned with protecting those investors. Purely and simply, the SEC wants no investor or prospective investor ever put in the position of buying, holding, or selling stock on the basis of incomplete or inaccurate information. The drive is toward greater and greater disclosure, however painful this may appear to be to corporations, or however time-consuming this may be to corporate officers.

Prior to the Securities Acts of 1933 and 1934, corporate disclosure was minimal. In 1926 all corporations whose stocks were listed on the New York Stock Exchange published balance sheets showing current assets and current liabilities. In these statements only 71 percent showed depreciation, 45 percent showed the cost of goods sold, and 55 percent showed sales. Today, it would be unthinkable for any published report of a public corporation not to include this and a great deal of other pertinent information. And even so, it's only within the past few years, with the growth of conglomerates and diversified companies, that corporate annual reports break down performance by lines of business, whether by division or product line or other business segmentation. Until the SEC made it mandatory to do so some years ago, there were still relatively few companies that included in their annual reports information that covers the range of material demanded by law in the Corporate Annual Report Form 10-K—despite the fact that the Form 10-K of any public corporation is available to the public.

To the company that recognizes that it must compete for capital over the long run, the problem of disclosure should be viewed not only as one of regulation, but as the opportunity to display every aspect of the company that can contribute to a rounded picture for the prospective investor or lender.

The Rules of Disclosure

As the economy has become more complex, SEC regulation has demanded more and more in terms of disclosure. Finally, in 1980, the SEC attempted to recodify and simplify some of its rules of disclosure. While the basic concepts remain the same, there have been significant changes in the mechanics.

Perhaps the primary change was based on a new understanding of the uses of the Form 10-K and the annual report to shareholders. Under the new regulations, the SEC attempted to unify the two in a comprehensive reporting system.

In the past, the SEC tended to see the two as separate documents, and added disclosure requirements to each independently of the other. Now, it sees the two as integrated. The current rules attempt to achieve a standardized reporting package that makes it possible to use the annual shareholders' report information in the Form 10-K and several other forms. In interim periods, the annual reporting financial package need only be updated by the condensed financial information in the quarterly Form 10-Q.

The required information is essentially in management's discussion and analysis of performance, and in audited uniform financial statements.

Two other forms about which the SEC is deeply concerned are the Form 3, which discloses when an insider (either an officer, director or 10 percent shareholder) takes a position in a stock; and a Form 4, which discloses when an insider buys or sells company stock. Deeply concerned means that the SEC monitors these situations, and may impose large fines for each day of non-compliance.

Disclosure Vehicles

The primary vehicles for disclosure and dissemination of information to shareholders and others are:

- The news release
- The prospectus
- The proxy statement

- The Form 8-K (significant changes and events)
- The annual and quarterly reports
- Personal presentations to investors
- The direct letter to shareholders
- The corporation's own profile and fact sheet
- The annual meeting
- Speech and article reprints
- The Dow Joneser or Reuters interview
- The Internet Web page
- The electronic bulletin board
- Teleconferencing
- Faxback services

The News Release

The news release to the financial press and broadcast media is the primary legal tool of timely disclosure. It is the first line of timely disclosure. Not only are news releases prescribed for routine reporting, such as earnings, but they are essential for announcing any event that might affect the evaluation of the company, whether it be a major contract, the development of a new product, the resignation or promotion of a senior officer, or a potential merger or acquisition.

In the amorphous area of timely disclosure, there is the pervasive question of when material news is considered officially public. At one time it might have been a simple matter—when Dow Jones or Reuters printed it, it was public. Then, with the advent of *PR Newswire* and *Business Wire*, it was assumed that the full text of the release would be in the hands of these key wire services within 15 minutes following release. Then came Bloomberg News Service, which became, with Dow Jones and Reuters, the third legally accepted full disclosure medium.

The rise of the computerized world has raised some new questions—and offered some new solutions. Internet. Web sites. Webcasting. News retrieval services. Simultaneous fax broadcast. Computer services, such as CompuServe, Microsoft Network, and America Online. All of these give investors instant access to financial news, and in most cases, do so on demand. No more waiting for Dow Jones or Reuters to run the news on their wires. No more waiting for the newspapers the next day. For the eager investor, and certainly for the investment professional, the news is available within minutes after release, and often minutes—sometimes hours—before the information is available through traditional sources.

And the problem is whether the investor who doesn't access the news on the Internet, and gets it well after the investor who does use the Internet, has a serious disadvantage. By the time the investor who must rely on only traditional news sources can act on the information, the electronically privileged may well have bought or sold, and thereby affected the market.

Suffice it to say this problem is being well debated, and is under advisement by the SEC. As of this writing, the SEC has indicated that posting material information on the Web does not absolve the company from the obligation to distribute the news in the traditional way. Posting on the Web alone, then, is not sufficient disclosure under SEC rules. This may change, though. The solution to the problem will be along in the foreseeable future—simply because the problem is too urgent to be mired in long bureaucratic discussion.

There is a trend to mail the quarterly earnings release to shareholders as well as to the press, instead of a quarterly report, or to make it available through electronic means, such as the company's Web site. As a communications device for shareholders, the news release is excellent. As a substitute for the quarterly report, it's a question of judgment, with the informed shareholder at the forefront of that judgment.

The Prospectus

The prospectus, issued when stock or a public debt offering is sold, is essentially a legal document. It's almost invariably written by attorneys, to legal prescription, and is written in legalistic terms. Therein lies the problem. In the attempt to fulfill every legal requirement of disclosure, prospectuses are meticulously prepared by lawyers, and therefore read like contracts. Unfortunately, it's virtually impossible for any but the most sophisticated nonlawyer to be expected to have the patience to read all of the information contained in a prospectus, much less to understand it. The SEC has recognized this in recent years, and as a result, it's encouraging companies to write prospectuses that are more readable and graphic. The change is coming, and increasingly, investor relations professionals are bringing to bear communications skills to generate documents that not only communicate clearly, but enhance the view of the company within the bounds of objectivity demanded by the SEC. The SEC wants a prospectus to be understood by the average prospective investor, and the company wants to be seen as positively as possible.

A prospectus can be concise without being obtuse. Furthermore, the SEC believes that while a prospectus should not be a marketing brochure, and should be objective, there is no reason why a prospectus can't be illustrated, especially if the illustrations increase the understanding of the company. Little by little, this feeling is having its effect, and more and more prospectuses now include illustrations, color, and a more narrative style. While the subject of prospectuses is primarily the province of attorneys, there is no reason why a company president should not recognize that the prospectus is the basic document for reaching into the public segment of the capital market, and therefore should be understandable and interesting to read.

Prospectuses and other documents filed with the SEC, it should be noted, are now available on the SEC's own Web page, called Edgar. The address is www.sec.gov1/edaux/wedgar.htm.

The Proxy Statement

The proxy statement is the legal document sent to shareholders prior to an annual meeting, so that they may understand and vote on the business to be presented at that meeting. While proxy statements contain the standard and routine agenda of items upon which the shareholders must vote, such as the election of the board of directors, the election of auditors, the approval of pension plans, and so forth, here, too, there is no reason why a proxy should not be readable and understandable.

More than just a simple legal document, the proxy is often a crucial means of communication to its shareholders for a company involved in an out-of-the-ordinary situation. For mergers requiring shareholder approval, for example, the proxy must contain considerable detail, sufficient to allow the shareholder to understand every aspect of the merger—not only the financial arrangements, but the reasons for it, a description of the other company, the structure of the company after the merger, and so on.

In proxy fights for control of a company, the proxy statement is a major document that management can use to present its point of view to shareholders whom management is trying to win to its side. By law in some states, it must also report any proposal put before the company by a predetermined percentage of outside shareholders.

There are times, then, when the proxy is much more than a routine document. And as in the case of prospectuses, new formats are emerging for clarity, including illustration and pictures of officers and directors. Clarity and readability need not subvert disclosure.

The Annual and Quarterly Reports

The annual report is the basic document in which the company attempts to tell its story to shareholders, the financial community, and the investing public. The annual report must be mailed to shareholders with or preceding the proxy statement.

An annual report is a financial document and not a graphics device. Historically, it was once used by an overwhelming number of companies as a cosmetic vehicle to show the company's good side, to make the company appear to be in better shape than it was. In recent years it's become a more balanced document. Each year, the SEC and the exchanges increase their demands for greater and greater disclosure in reports. While this has put an increasing burden on companies for more elaborate disclosure and inclusion of a greater number of facts, the ultimate result has been salutary. No company, even one performing badly at any given moment, has ever suffered as mightily from full disclosure in an annual report as it has from the confusion and uncertainty that arises from inadequate disclosure.

Letters to Shareholders

Individual letters to shareholders are sometimes a useful device to advise shareholders of major events that affect the company between reporting periods. They are prescribed in those circumstances where special action must be taken, such as a merger that will ultimately require the approval of shareholders, and for which a proxy for a special meeting is forthcoming. They are also useful to amplify a news report, to clarify a serious rumor, or to share news of special import, and should be used more frequently than in the past.

The Annual Meeting

The annual meeting is the official gathering of all shareholders to conduct the company's corporate business, and is the appropriate time and place to report on the past year's activities. It's also the time at which the annual "state of the company" address is given, and the year to come is examined.

As will be discussed in Chapter 10, it must be realistically recognized that the annual meeting is rarely attended by any but the smallest portion of shareholders. It cannot be assumed that any announcement made solely at the annual meeting is proper dissemination of information. Any announcement of timely material information should be followed immediately by a news release.

Professional Investor Meetings

Frequently, material information about a company is disclosed at meetings of analysts, brokers or other investors. Sometimes this is by design, but sometimes it happens inadvertently.

Should this happen, it's mandatory to issue a news release about the information as soon as possible, even by telephone from the meeting to the wire services.

Accounting Rules and Disclosure

In recent years, the increasing complexity of both domestic and international business, and the effects of the economy, have generated a number of issues that seriously affect disclosure. Problems of new financial instruments and derivatives, foreign currency translation and currency valuation, pension fund assets and their treatment on the balance sheet—all these and more have taken what was a simple reporting matter in other times and generated today a morass that requires legions of accountants and attorneys to penetrate. The changing nature of retirement policies, including both pension funds and other postretirement benefits (OPEB) continue to concern both the SEC and the accounting profession. It has become clear that the Financial Accounting Standards Board (FASB)—the accounting profession's rule-making body—concludes that OPEB represent a form of deferred compensation that should be recognized on an accrual basis.

One result of this growing complexity is that the SEC and the Financial Accounting Standards Board work more closely than ever in developing acceptable accounting principles designed to generate valid and useful information for investors, shareholders, lenders, and management itself.

Thus, regulations in financial reporting are constantly being developed, much of them concerning information never before required, to keep abreast of changing economic conditions and business practices. Most recently, this has included:

- FAS 105—Disclosure of information about financial instruments with off-balance-sheet risk and financial instruments with concentrations of credit risk.
- FAS 106—Employers' accounting for postretirement benefits other than pensions.
- FAS 107—Disclosures about fair value of financial instruments.
- FAS 109—Accounting for income taxes.
- FAS 114—Accounting by creditors for impairment of a loan.
- FAS 115—Accounting for certain investments in debt and equity securities.
- FAS 119—Disclosure about derivative financial instruments and fair value of financial instruments.
- FAS 121—Accounting for the impairment of long-lived assets and for long-lived assets to be disposed of.
- FAS 123—Accounting for certain investments held by not-for-profit organizations.

Continuing interpretive guidance in the requirements for the section in reports to shareholders known as "Management's Discussion and Analysis of Financial Condition and Results of Operation" (MD&A) are aimed at bringing operational perspective to the president's letter and financial reports. The aim is to include information that gives dimension to the business, such as trends, demands, commitments, events and uncertainties facing management; liquidity and capital resources; material changes; commentary of changes in operating results and financial condition; segment analysis; preliminary merger negotiations, if appropriate; participation in high yield financings or highly leveraged transactions; and the effects of federal financial assistance, if appropriate. Here too, it's expected that changes and amendments will be continuous, reflecting both the degree to which the reports effectively inform investors and shareholders, and changing business and economic conditions.

International Accounting Standards

Such is the nature of accounting that the accounting standards of one country are rarely the same as those for another. Thus, the financial statements of, say, a French company would tell an entirely different story to an Italian than they would to a French investor.

As long as most investment stayed within national borders, this was merely an academic problem. But the globalization of business, soon followed by the consolidation of the European Economic Community, made the promulgation of uniform international accounting standards somewhat more urgent than before.

Thus, a number of bodies, including the autonomous International Accounting Standards Committee (IASC), have been addressing the problem. IASC has more than 100 organizational members from 70 countries, for example. The U.S. representative to the IASC is the American Institute of Certified Public Accountants (AICPA), and FASB monitors IASC activities and is a member of its consultative group.

Substantial progress is being made, and uniform accounting standards are possible by the year 2000. This will be accomplished simply because the needs of international finance demand it.

Changing Role of the Auditor

In the past decade or so, there has been a radical change in the role of the auditor. At one time, the auditor had been limited to financial statements. Now, under pressure from both the SEC and the FASB, as well as other auditing and accounting bodies, the auditor is given other and nontraditional responsibilities, such as reviewing the president's letter in the annual report and other supplementary material outside of financial statements. Congress makes periodic sorties into the question of the auditor's role, usually following news of corporate fraud that a congressman or two thinks the auditor should have caught. There has long been a clear trend toward expanding the auditor's role, which portends, many believe, a substantial danger of bringing the auditor into areas beyond his training and expertise, and possibly, his authority.

Still, the accounting profession, bending to the demands of the public and pressures from legislators, now includes fraud detection as part of the audit—at least to the degree that it's possible for an outsider to detect it.

Yet another significant factor is that the accounting profession itself is changing. The services offered by accounting firms now move more substantially into consulting and all aspects of business management, and, to a certain degree, law. In fact, in Europe, the largest law firm is Arthur Andersen, the auditing firm. This is likely to be a pattern in the United States as well.

Material Information

The SEC uses as its definition of "material" the Supreme Court decision in the 1976 case of TSC Industries, Inc. v. Northway Industries, Inc. That decision said, "An omitted fact is material if there is a substantial likelihood that a reasonable investor would consider it important in making his or her investment decisions. Put another way, there must be a substantial likelihood that the disclosure of the omitted fact would have been viewed by the reasonable investor as having significantly altered the 'total mix' of information made available."

This definition may best be seen in a consent decree some time ago against Investors Diversified Service, Inc., containing the following language, "Material inside information is any information about a company, or the market for the company's securities, which has come directly or indirectly from the company, and which has not been disclosed generally to the marketplace, the dissemination of which is likely to affect the market price of any of the company's securities or is likely to be considered important by reasonable investors, including reasonable speculative investors, in determining whether to trade in such securities."

Any material information by that definition must be disclosed immediately, using the procedures described in the last chapter. While the kind of information that comes under that heading is impossible to list to the fullest extent, there are certainly some obvious activities that should always be reported:

- Financial results for a period
- Changes in corporate structure of any magnitude
- Mergers or acquisitions. Here, as in other areas of negotiation, timing becomes sensitive, since premature disclosure can sometimes adversely affect such negotiations. It is now generally accepted, however, that such negotiations should be announced at any point at which there is any feeling by both parties that the negotiations will reach a successful conclusion. This can be a verbal agreement or a letter of intent. Certainly, failure to disclose the negotiations at the time a letter of intent is signed is potentially dangerous. But the time to disclose prior to the letter of intent is still an educated guess.
- Earnings forecasts or estimates, with Safe Harbor (The Private Securities Litigation Reform Act of 1995) provisions
- Exchange offer or tender offer

- Stock split or stock dividend, or any other significant change in capitalization
- Decision to make a public offering
- A substantial loan or changes in terms of loans
- Listing on an exchange
- Changes in accounting
- Management change
- Major new product introduction
- Opening or closing a plant of considerable size
- Amendment of corporate charter or bylaws
- Any information that legally requires special filing with the SEC. In this context, include any consequential information filed in the 8-K report filed with the SEC.
- Significant environmental or civil rights matters
- Decisions of regulatory bodies other than the SEC, such as the Interstate Commerce Commission or the Federal Trade Commission
- Litigation
- Significant executive or board changes
- Rumors that may be damaging or too helpful

The list goes on and on, guided only by one's definition of material information for a particular company or industry.

Safe Harbor Legislation

In our litigious society, a popular target has been the corporation that announced an expected earnings per share in the foreseeable future, failed to meet that projection, and has been sued for that failure by disgruntled shareholders. The result of that growing tendency had been to inhibit corporate managers from forecasting legitimate and useful projections of performance.

Recognizing this inhibition, Congress passed The Private Securities Litigation Reform Act of 1995—the Safe Harbor Act. The new law was developed to address abusive practices committed in private securities legislation, including routine filing of class action suites when stock price dropped precipitously.

The Act puts a greater burden on the plaintiff to prove a case of negligence in making profit projections. But more significantly, it clearly defines a forward-looking statement that, properly delineated, protects management from liability. Under the law, both written and oral statements must be identified as forward-looking, and accompanied by meaningful cautionary statements identifying important factors that could cause actual results to differ materially from those projected in the statement.

The law defines a forward-looking statement as:

- A statement containing a projection of revenues, income (including income loss), earnings (including earnings loss) per share, capital expenditures, dividends, capital structure, or other financial items
- A statement of the plans and objectives of management for future operations, including plans or objectives relating to the products or services of the issuer
- A statement of future economic performance, including any such statement contained in a discussion and analysis of financial condition by management or in the results of operations included pursuant to the rules and regulations of the SED
- Any statement underlying or relating to any statement described in the foregoing paragraphs
- Any report issued by an outside reviewer retained by an issuer, to the extent that the report assess a forward looking statement by the issuer, or . . .
- A statement containing a projection or estimate of such other items as may be specified by rule or regulation of the SEC

While the new Safe Harbor law offers new and needed protection, NIRI points out to its members that the law makes more urgent the need for companies to establish written disclosure policies where they don't now exist.

The value of the Safe Harbor law is well assessed in a statement by The Financial Relations Board's Ted Pincus, who says, "The American investor can finally enjoy some far greater predictability of corporate performance, with less need to second-guess management's intentions and expectations."

Insider Information

Nor should the danger inherent in insider information be overlooked. This should be abundantly clear, in view of the events of the past two decades, which saw some of the most widely publicized insider trading scandals in American business history.

An *insider* is generally defined as anyone who has material information about a company that has not been publicly disclosed. It is assumed that any insider who trades on material information in buying or selling stock to his own advantage thereby functions to the disadvantage of other investors. Recent cases on both insider information and other categories of misuse of non-public material information have resulted in many a Saville Row suit being exchanged for prison garb.

All material information necessary to evaluate a company and its suitability as an investment vehicle must be made public and available to all interested parties on a timely basis. There is, however, an exemption for information for which confidentiality is based on a valid competitive business reason.

When material information about a company or its operations that could affect the evaluation of a company or its suitability as an investment vehicle, or that might influence the sale, purchase, or price of its stock, is known by only a limited number of people, they may not trade on that information, or misuse it for personal gain. This is defined as inside information. To protect against insider trading problems, all such information must be made available to as many segments of the financial community as possible, and especially the investing public. This must be done by those means most likely to broadcast it to the widest possible degree. It must be disseminated to the public before any insider trades on it. Timeliness is of the essence in specific cases, and is prescribed in specific cases, such as the board's firing the CEO. While some information may be withheld for valid business reasons, as long as no insider trades on it—information is sometimes not containable—in which case it must be fully disseminated immediately. In the case of earnings statements, it's the better part of wisdom to disclose as soon as possible, and certainly within 24 hours.

In any segment of securities regulation or public corporate activity (such as changing a board or an officer), these two basic points—concern for material and inside information—apply universally and without exception.

In 1964, the problem of inside information dramatically came to the public's attention with the classic Texas Gulf Sulphur case. Several engineers working for Texas Gulf Sulphur came upon a rich mineral body. This discovery was kept within a small group inside the company. Several members of that group, taking advantage of their inside information and with full knowledge that the value of the company stock would be greatly enhanced when that information was generally known, purchased Texas Gulf Sulphur stock for their own accounts. This resulted in civil charges against the offenders.

The court said that you must either disclose the information, or abstain from trading on it until it is available to all investors. It also strengthened and clarified the law regarding inside information.

Shortly thereafter, several Merrill Lynch staff members were given reason to believe that a forthcoming financial statement for the McDonnell Douglas Company would show a sharp decline in earnings. Before this information was made generally public, advice to sell their stock was given to selected institutional clients, at the same time that other Merrill Lynch customers were being given a buy recommendation. When the information was ultimately made public, the price of the stock declined sharply. The SEC took a dim view of the fact that there had been specific benefit from inside information to a selected few, and once again penalties were imposed.

Perhaps the major new category of misuse of information has arisen as a result of a 1980 Supreme Court decision dealing with a printer who, in 1977 and 1978, traded stock on information he got from a confidential financial document his company was printing.

The Justice Department case was that the printer (whose name was Chiarella), who had been entrusted by his employers to print confidential documents regarding a prospective takeover, had defrauded the shareholders of the target company (who weren't aware of a proposed tender offer) by trading on that information. The Supreme Court exonerated Chiarella, saying that he didn't have a duty to those shareholders, and that if you don't owe a duty, you can't breach that duty.

However, in a dissenting opinion, Chief Justice Warren Burger said that what Chiarella had done was to misappropriate—Burger used the word *stole*—the information from his boss, the printing company. Thus arose what is now known as the *misappropriation* theory. As subsequent events showed, had the government been able to apply that concept, the printer's conviction might have been sustained.

In 1982, in a case in which several investment bankers had traded on inside information obtained from their employer, Morgan Stanley, the government indicted on the misappropriation theory that had arisen from Burger's dissent. The investment bankers were convicted, and their conviction was upheld on appeal.

It was on the misappropriation theory that some of the most famous insider trading indictments were developed, including Winans, Levine, Boesky, and Milken.

Subsequently, other cases substantially emphasized the SEC's willingness to prosecute under insider trading statutes. In one case, Foster Winans, who wrote the important "Heard on The Street" column for *The Wall Street Journal*, was found to have fed information to selected brokers about material prior to its appearing in the column. Because "Heard on the Street" is the most popular column in the paper, and because many people trade on that information when the column appears, knowing what's to be in the column before it appears offers a great trading advantage. The court ruled that the information in the column, and the column itself, was proprietary— that it belonged to *The Wall Street Journal*. Winans was convicted for misappropriating the property of *The Wall Street Journal*.

In the most famous case of recent years, arbitrageur Ivan Boesky, highly regarded for his success in selecting companies about to be taken over in leveraged buyouts and other acquisition deals, was found to have been trading on inside information. Boesky and many of his associates, including some of the most respected names on Wall Street, were brought down by the revelation, and many were successfully indicted.

Probably nothing is so seductive to the investor as the idea of being privy to—and trading on—inside information. It seems so safe. But it's amazing how sophisticated are the regulatory agencies in seeking out and finding wrongdoing in trading practices. The jails are full of those who discovered too late the skills and enthusiasm of the SEC, in dealing with insider trading.

The SEC and Investor Relations Consultants

Significantly, the SEC doesn't automatically exempt from its regulations agents of the corporation. For many years it was the practice of companies to use external investor relations consultants and public relations firms as mere conduits of information. Historically, corporate presidents relied on investor relations consultants to simply take the information supplied to them by the company, cast it into its appropriate release form, and disseminate it. Investor relations consultants, since they are seldom accountants or lawyers, are often without the full means or facility to judge the validity of information supplied to them. They once relied on their clients to supply them with complete and accurate information. Unfortunately, they were frequently fooled. For many years this rankled the SEC, and quite appropriately. The particular anxiety was that investor relations practitioners were unwittingly being used to *condition the market*—to unduly influence the market. In 1969, the SEC decided to include investor relations consultants in its regulation of disclosure.

Now, if appropriate systems and procedures to verify information are duly established and followed, and properly documented in the agency's own files, an investor relations consultancy has fulfilled its public responsibility and is not compelled to insure the total validity of the information.

The SEC takes into consideration the fact that investor relations practitioners, particularly independent consultants, are not in the same position to verify information as are auditors and attorneys. However, the investor relations consultant is entitled, and should be encouraged, to ask for documentation on any information supplied by the client. Steps can be taken to assure, within the limits of any investor relations firm, the most feasible precautions against dissemination of misleading or inaccurate information. They may vary from company to company, but essentially they rely upon documentation of instructions from client to counsel, with approval in writing for all releases.

Compliance Procedure for Investor Relations Firms

A compliance procedure for practices by investor relations consultants in issuing information should be standard, and appropriate parts of the procedure should be disseminated to all clients. This protects both the company and the consultant, as well as the investing public. It assures that all issued information is carefully reviewed (and if necessary, questioned), and that all sources are clearly identified. And certainly, the consultant, for his or her own protection, should review carefully all available financial and corporate data and background on each of its prospective clients, to assure that it represents only reputable companies.

A primary factor in compliance procedures for investor relations consultants is that they know their clients. In a proper relationship, the consultant works closely with the chief executive and financial officers, and should come to know a great deal about them and the company. The consultant is well informed about the company's financial and corporate structures, as well as its day-to-day operations. This basic knowledge provides a framework in which to judge new financial and operational information, and should assure the consultant that he is not complicitous in disseminating false information. At the same time, the well-informed consultant may well be considered an insider, in that he or she has access to inside information. The consultant must function accordingly.

Proper compliance procedures for external consultants require that all issued material must be accompanied by an appropriate form, retained by the consultant, with a copy of the material, indicating the source of information, the time it was given for release, the time it is to be released, whether the copy has been or is to be amended, and by whom. Additional comments might indicate who prepared the original material, recommendations made by the consultant but not accepted or followed by the client, and how the information was transmitted for preparation for release. If additional approval is required or was given by attorneys, accountants, or others, it is indicated. The form is then signed by the company officer responsible, as well as by the consultant responsible. In the case of a release approved by telephone, or supplied by mail or fax, a variation of the form, designed for that purpose, is used, and signed by the consultant who received it.

Many consulting firms designate a senior firm member as compliance officer. His job is to oversee all procedures for compliance with SEC, exchange, NASD, blue sky regulations, and the firm's own policies, and should include a periodic review of all material and the ability to confer directly with the firm's securities attorney.

For the corporation intent upon disseminating false or misleading information, very little can be done by anybody to prevent it. Nevertheless, as has been noted before, the acoustics of Wall Street are magnificent. The value to any corporation of issuing false information is remarkably short-lived, and the penalty, in terms of at least investor reaction, if not the law as well, is swift and intense.

Current Reporting Requirements

It's in the attempt to address dynamic realities in business that new views of disclosure emerge. These disclosure regulations include both SEC and FASB requirements. Looking, then, at the basics of current reporting requirements we see mandated . . .

Audited financial statements. The balance sheet must cover both the current and prior year, and statements of income and cash flows must cover both the current and the prior two years. Under the regulations, minimum elements of disclosure, conforming to generally accepted accounting principles, must be included in all public documents. In addition, SEC Regulation S-X requires incremental discussion, including:

• Analysis of common stock and other shareholders' equity must be included in either a footnote or a separate statement.
• The balance sheet must disclose the amount of preference on involuntary liquidation of preferred stock, and a separate balance sheet presentation of the preferred stock subject to mandatory redemption provisions.
• Separate disclosure of current and deferred, and federal, state, and foreign, income tax expense; an analysis of the effects of income tax timing differences; and a reconciliation between the effective and statutory income tax rates. This will change as FASB statements evolve, and additional disclosure may be required.
• Significant amounts of material related party transactions and balances must be presented on the face of financial statements, rather than in footnotes.
• Significant restrictions on cash dividend payments by a subsidiary to a parent must now be disclosed.
• The excess of replacement or current cost over LIFO value of inventories.
• Details of receivables and inventories under long-term contracts.
• Disclosure of components of various balance sheet items, such as disaggregation of other current assets when an individual component exceeds 5 percent of all current assets (prepaid insurance, for example).

Selected financial data. A fluid summary that must include at least the following:

• Net sales or operating revenues
• Income from continuing operations
• Earnings per share from continuing operations
• Dividends per share
• Total assets
• Long-term obligations and redeemable preferred stock

Companies are expected to include, in this summary, any other material information of significance in understanding its operations, its trends, and so forth.

Management's discussion and analysis. Some years ago, the SEC mandated that annual reports include a discussion of operations, and this has become standard in annual reports to shareholders and the SEC. As indicated, the SEC constantly fine tunes the requirements for this section.

Essentially, the SEC requires management to present, in one section of the report, a coherent analysis of the company's financial condition, including the following areas:

- *Liquidity.* Full disclosure would require a lucid discussion of those elements that indicate the company's ability to generate cash as it's needed. This information would include trends and events that might affect liquidity; the structure of plans to meet liquidity requirements; internal and external sources of liquidity; unused potential sources of liquid assets; and of course, the outlook for future needs, including cash for taxes that exceed current tax expense.
- *Capital resources.* The aim here is to give a clear picture of the company's capital needs and resources. This would include commitments in the near and long term; sources and potential sources; relative costs of sources; and changes in debt, equity and off-balance sheet financing arrangements. Here, too, the SEC is particularly paying attention.
- *Results of operations.* Unusual or infrequent events that may have a significant impact; uncertainties that may affect the validity of information about potential results; the extent to which sales increases are attributable to price increases, volume increases, and the introduction of new products or services; and the effects of inflation and changing prices on revenues and income. And of course, under FAS 94, reporting that includes results of majority-owned subsidiaries is consolidated.

In addition, the SEC encourages management discussion that reveals a sense of where the company is going when such concepts can be reasonably drawn and are based upon sound information. In other words, as full a picture as is possible that would allow the reader to understand the company, its financial structure, its performance and its capabilities.

Market data. As noted, the annual report to shareholders should contain pertinent information about the market performance of the company's stock. This must include the principal markets for the stock; the high and low quarterly price for two years; the number of shareholders of record; a two-year dividend history; and a brief description of dividend policy and restrictions.

Form 10-K

The Form 10-K has four distinct parts:

• Part I. Disclosures pertaining to the company's business properties, legal proceedings and management ownership of company securities. The industry segment information required covers only three years, rather than five.
• Part II. Information required in annual reports to shareholders, particularly financial and operational material.
• Part III. Information about management and officers, including proxy material.
• Part IV. Significant supplementary financial information such as components and changes in certain balance sheet items, and, where appropriate, the separate financial statements of a parent company or unconsolidated subsidiaries.

The 10-K must be signed by the principal executive officer; the principal financial officer; the principal accounting officer; and a majority of the board of directors.

Form 10-Q

Form 10-Q information should be distributed to shareholders, although this is not legally required. Included should be condensed balance sheets at both the quarter end and the preceding year end; income statements for the most recent quarter, the corresponding quarter in the preceding year, and the year-to-date periods for both years; statements of cash flows for the year-to-date periods of the current and prior year; and management's discussion and analysis of financial condition and results of operations. While an audit of quarterly results is not required, a company may have a review, and include the auditor's report on his of her review of the figures if it chooses.

The significant factor in quarterly reports, as in annual reports, remains open, frank, and accurate disclosure of information that enhances the understanding of a company and its performance.

Exchanges and Disclosure

The exchanges, while they control only listed companies, have been no less lax or intensive in their own drives for disclosure regulation. The New York

Stock Exchange, recognizing the value of credibility in obtaining investor confidence, has a number of guidelines to increase corporate financial disclosure that parallel those promulgated by the SEC. The American Stock Exchange and NASDAQ have their own comparable disclosure regulations as well. In other words, every regulatory body concerned with the publicly held company is not only deadly earnest about fully disclosing information that's required to be disclosed, but is accelerating its drive to accomplish it and to increase those aspects of a company's operation to be disclosed.

Informing the Exchanges and NASDAQ

It's important that copies of all material—releases, proxies and so on—be filed with any exchange or market on which the company is listed as soon as possible, before and after they are issued. Afterward, add the company's listing representative on the exchange and its specialist. For the over-the-counter company, add the market makers, after distribution. At the same time, it's important that while specialists or market makers be kept up to date on the company's business and trading activities, they should never be made privy to any material information about the company before it's made public. The specialists' posture must always be one of objectivity, and they could be seriously compromised by any inside information. Only in extremely sensitive cases, where an announcement might have significant effect on the market and on trading, will the exchanges and the NASD want the material before it's released.

Registration for a Public Issue

One area of disclosure that can be difficult is the regulations that govern a company that has a public issue in registration. A company in registration is severely limited and prohibited from any activity that might be construed as offering, selling, or assisting in the sale of stock.

The basis for this regulation is the Securities Act of 1933, which prohibits offering or the sale of a security unless a registration statement has been filed with the SEC, or selling a security unless the registration statement has become effective. There are three periods of registration:

- There is the time before the registration statement has been filed.

- There is the period during which the registration statement is on file, but not yet effective.
- There is the period after the registration statement has become effective.

It's during the second period—when the company is in active registration review—that it's illegal to issue any material relating to the security, other than through the statutory prospectus. This is particularly true for an initial public offering. That second period is then clearly defined by the SEC as being "at least from the time an issuer reaches an understanding with a broker-dealer," and it ends with the completion of the dealer's prospectus delivery obligations. While the registration period is normally defined as 90 days for an initial public offering and 45 days for a secondary, completion may be considered by the SEC to be when the issue is completely sold by the underwriter, even if it's been only a few days, so long as the SEC has permitted the issue. This situation is interpreted differently by various attorneys, and there is no consensus. Not included are the initial discussions or negotiations between the company and the underwriter. It's only when there is some form of commitment by the underwriter that the period actually begins in which the company is considered to be "in registration."

With an initial public offering, it's during this registration period that the corporation may take no action, nor issue any publicity, that can be construed as an effort to sell the stock or enhance the ultimate sale of the stock. And here, in view of other aspects of disclosure regulation, lies the paradox between what can and cannot be publicized. However, if approval of the prospectus is delayed, and an earnings statement is ready, the statement can and must be released. If the prospectus is already approved and the issue is selling, the earnings are released and prospectus is *stickered* by adding the information to the prospectus. Other forms of information that might affect the company and be construed as selling the stock, however, remain questionable regarding release.

Acceptable Dissemination of Information

The SEC recognizes the problem, and further accepts the fact that it's impossible to define in absolute detail those activities that a company in registration may or may not pursue. Each set of circumstances must rest on its own facts. Nevertheless, the SEC has issued seven categories of information that it deems not only acceptable during an initial public offering, but which it in fact encourages:

- Continued advertising of products
- Continued distribution of customary reports to stockholders
- Continued publication of proxy statements
- Continued announcements to the press of "factual business and financial developments"
- Answering unsolicited inquiries from shareholders, the press, and others (if the answers are responsive to the questions and prudently do not go beyond the bounds previously described)
- Answering unsolicited inquiries from the financial community
- Continuing to hold stockholders' meetings and answering stockholders' inquiries at such meetings, without breaking new ground, unless information is disclosed in acceptable ways and added to the prospectus if necessary

Obviously, the information disseminated under these seven categories should not include predictions, projections, forecasts, or opinions with respect to value. Nor should it include any attempt to describe the company in ways that might be considered promotional and supportive of a securities sales effort. And so once again we come to the question of judgment. And once again we come into a potential conflict between attorneys and investor relations consultants. Here, too, attorneys and investor relations consultants must consider one another's positions in light of the company's needs and responsibilities.

Without attempting to skirt or stretch the seven categories of information approved by the SEC, it should be recognized that not only is there tremendous latitude in the amount and kind of information that can be disseminated by a company in registration, but that both the need for and the value of such continued dissemination does not diminish.

The Secondary Offering

The rules are perhaps more lenient during a secondary offering. Current shareholders must be kept informed, as in non-registration periods, and the company's stock must be supported in the marketplace. Subject to advice of legal counsel, it may be assumed that the same seven categories of dissemination apply, plus normal dissemination procedures. As with initial public offerings, projections of any kind that might be construed as selling the stock of the new issue must be avoided. This is a murky field, best navigated in conjunction with experienced securities lawyers.

There is also substantial value in an investor relations communications program begun well before the company goes into registration, in that such a preregistration program sets the tone for what may be deemed permissible while the company is actually in registration. On the other hand, there may be a problem if a company that has never communicated to the financial community suddenly begins such a program the minute it gets into registration. It's in this area that the experience of the investor relations consultant can be of exceptional value.

In the third stage, when the company is out of registration, all bounds are off for a financial communications program that's otherwise legal under any SEC regulations or sound business requirements.

In conforming to the disclosure regulations of the Securities and Exchange Commission and the Exchanges, it's important to be thoughtful and considered. Premature and untutored disclosure may be even more harmful than no disclosure. You can't disclose piecemeal.

To avoid piecemeal or inadequate disclosure, consider whether you have all the facts needed to make disclosure, and then, if you don't have all the facts, you must ask whether disclosure will have a worse effect on the company than non-disclosure. The concern should be with not only the timing, but with the content of what's disclosed.

Chapter 10

Going Public

In view of the health of the market for initial public offerings, and the competition for attention, good investor relations begins before the company goes public.

The company choosing to go public should know that there is a vast area of concern in terms of relations with the financial community. Investor relations activities begin well before the public stock offering, and continue well afterwards.

In addition to the process of introducing the company to investors, developing investor relations objectives, and helping to position the company for the investment community, investor relations addresses the selection of the underwriter, includes structuring and dispersing information about the company to the financial community, follows through the period of registration, and enters yet another phase with the sale of the issue and the after-market (the period following the initial sale of the issue). In view of SEC regulations regarding dissemination of information while a stock is in registration, an investor relations pattern must be established early so that it can't be construed as having been developed solely for the purpose of selling stock.

The Background

The process of going public is much more than a device for raising capital. It's a ritual that feeds on the dynamics of the stock market, and that has a mystique of its own. The initial public offering of a company—the IPO—

is fraught with an excitement that, to investors, seems to know no equal; that transcends rational investment principles. Perhaps more than any other aspect of investor relations, then, it's important to understand something of the context and background of going public.

There have been times in U.S. economic history when the simplest—if not necessarily the best—means of acquiring capital for a corporation was to go public. The late 1960s and a part of 1971 and 1972, for example, were periods of extraordinary economic growth in the United States, manifested by a flood of IPOs. In 1972, a record 568 companies went public. Corporate profits for most companies were high and the economic boom showed no signs of abating. The mid and late 1980s were another such period, in which the economic boom bred an overwhelming number of IPOs. In 1980, 237 companies went public, and by mid-1981 that number had already been surpassed. In 1989, in a very different market climate, there were 241 IPOs. By mid-1990, there were about 130, just as the notion of an economic downturn began to be perceived. But by the end of the 1990s, the surge in IPOs broke records, with more than 1,700 new issues in 1996 alone.

In the 1980s, however, there was a quality to the IPOs that was different from IPOs of earlier periods. First, this was the decade of the new technology. Companies such as Compaq and Lotus went from start-up to Fortune 500 in the blink of an eye. Genetic companies, such as Genentech, went from start-up and obscurity to lords of the stock market faster than it takes a home run king to circle the bases.

Second, the 1980s was a decade of rapid economic growth, new millionaires, precarious leveraging and other financial shenanigans the likes of which the nation hadn't seen since the turn of the century. It was the age, also, of leveraged buyouts, insider trading, and the glorification of greed—literally. Witness the success of the motion picture *Wall Street*. Even though the villainous takeover specialist got his comeuppance, he was still the hero of the movie.

It all came apart on a black Monday in October, 1987, when for complex reasons that go beyond the usual reaction to economic conditions, the stock market took its worst bath since the 1930s. That the market recovered within two years, and even brought back the market for IPOs, is one of the anomalies of economics.

Perhaps the parent of the new surge was the sudden growth of the high tech companies in communications, computers, software, and the Internet. In these areas, new companies were forming every day, predicated on the need for new technology to enhance not so new (but not so old) technology. A new era dawned, and spawned new companies to serve that new electronic era.

The newer companies had relatively little trouble getting financed. If the technology worked, the money was there—at least for a few years in the mid-1990s. And if the company gained any momentum toward success, the underwriter was there to take the company public. It was a flowing cornucopia. And naturally, the success of these IPOs, particularly in the sustained bull market, bred IPOs in other industries.

For the investor with access to an IPO, it was a heyday. For the company, it wasn't always an unalloyed blessing. Going public, many discovered, wasn't as easy as it looked.

The Psychology of the IPO

During periods that are so fertile for the newly public company, the psychology that fuels the stock market seems to be predicated on confident anticipation of consistent and sustained growth, which could only mean to the investor a consistent and sustained increase in the market value of stocks. Price/earnings ratios for some stocks reached astronomical multiples of 20, 30, and even 60 during the 1960s and early 1970s. The price/earnings ratio of the Dow Jones stocks reached an average as high as 17.3 (the more rational general average is about 13). Heaven only knows what the market and investors were anticipating in the way of corporate profits in the ensuing years to justify those multiples.

The recession of 1973–1974 put a quick halt to that period's breathless growth, as did the 1987 crash in its time. In both cases, the market quickly fell, brokerage firms (and particularly the quickie underwriters) disappeared by the score, and the individual investor returned to cultivating his and her own gardens. It would seem, in each case, that the Go-Go years were over.

But nothing is forever, not even good lessons learned. The ultimate return of the economy strengthens, as it should, the stock market, and the needs for capital see a steady growth in companies going public primarily because they needed equity capital. In the 1980s, this was enhanced by companies with new technology. The darlings of the 1990s are emerging. And the new configuration of the economy is a context of growth, and a new realm of IPOs.

Choosing an Underwriter

The choice of an underwriter is an investor relations concern because the underwriter will serve as a significant conduit to the financial community.

Choosing the wrong underwriter can be an investor relations disaster—one for which no investor relations program can offer quick relief.

An underwriter is an individual or a firm that acts as an agent for developing and distributing a public issue of stock. Usually (but not always) an investment banker as well, the underwriter quite literally underwrites the issue—supplies the money from the sale of the stock issue. In the real world, the money doesn't come from the underwriter's pocket, but from the sale of the stock. The underwriter takes a pre-determined percentage of the issue, in both cash and stock, as commission. When the lead underwriter guarantees the sale of the stock, it's called a *firm* underwriting. In some cases, however, the underwriter and the members of the syndicate merely indicate that they will sell what they can. This is known as a *best efforts* underwriting.

The underwriter sells stock both by distributing it to other brokerage firms and to its own customers. The other brokerage firms form a syndicate with the underwriter, in which each firm agrees to take a fixed amount of the stock for resale to its own customers.

The difference between an underwriter and an investment banker is really one of services performed, rather than a clearly defined professional distinction. The underwriter's primary responsibility is to underwrite and distribute a stock issue. The investment banker, on the other hand, has a broader role in guiding the company in its financial activities and in finding other sources of capital in addition to public sale of stock (see Chapter 3). Investment bankers may also sell securities, but their job is to understand the nature of all capital markets. The investment banker must help the client structure a company for the intelligent use of capital as well as to acquire it, to supply information on not only the capital markets and alternative sources of capital, but on the total economic picture as well. In an underwriting, the investment banker must guide the company through its many tortuous steps before, during, and after the underwriting. This is very different from merely putting out a public issue that serves as merchandise for the stockbroker to peddle.

The Wrong Underwriter

Most companies choose the wrong underwriter for the wrong reason. Before the Wall Street debacles of 1973–1974, there was a great proliferation of underwriters. These were predominately brokerage houses that did underwriting—who helped companies go public, not to capitalize the companies so much as to supply product to be sold by the brokerage end of their firms. They were not investment bankers.

Back in the halcyon days, when virtually any company could go public, underwriters were wooing privately held companies not only to solicit their underwriting business, but to convince them to go public even in cases where it wasn't warranted. Smaller unstable companies, eager to go public and take advantage of the rising stock market, frequently accepted the first offer to do an underwriting that came along, often with disastrous results. Frequently, an underwriter was selected simply because somebody knew somebody. Many smaller underwriters calculated that if only a small percentage of their underwritings succeeded, the profits would offset the many that didn't make it. Playing these kinds of odds, the trick was to do as many underwritings as possible, regardless of the quality of the companies being taken public. Another device, particularly with speculative ventures, was for the underwriter to take exceptionally large blocks of stock options as a kind of auxiliary fee for doing the underwriting. Here, too, the odds game was being played. If just a portion of the issues succeeded and the stock price went high enough, the underwriter made enough money to cover those issues that did not succeed. Forgotten in this whole procedure was the company—and certainly the shareholder. This wreaked particular havoc on the better companies that survived and thrived only to find themselves saddled with a poorly devised equities program that hurt the company in the long run. There are now hundreds of companies originally taken public by underwriting firms that are no longer in existence, or for which there is no longer a market at any price for their stock. The poor structure of the original issue left the company inadequately capitalized for its growth, which forced early demands of other sources of capital, such as banks. Many of these companies found themselves in the position of being unable to split their stock because the price was too low, unable to issue new stock because they gave away too large a percentage of the company in the original underwriting, and too highly leveraged because they had to go to banks to finance growth that should have been paid for by a proper equity issue.

Fortunately, most of the old-style and questionable underwriters are now gone from the scene. Those companies that survive are predominately investment bankers who predicate their own operations on long-range financial structures that serve companies in so many ways that they are able to withstand the assault of sustained bear markets.

Preparing to Go Public

Properly done, the company that feels it should consider going public must begin by doing a great deal of preparation. This should include taking a realistic view of its long-term capital needs, and assessing alternate sources of capital. A complete financial analysis should be done including pro forma operating statements and balance sheets for at least five years forward. This program should be done with the assistance of the company's own internal financial staff, and with the help of its accounting firm and attorneys.

The willingness of an underwriter to take a company public does not, of itself, mean that the company is doing the right thing in going public.

The company should review its decision to go public not only in the light of opportunities, but obstacles as well. The costs of going public are tremendous. Legal fees are astronomical. Printing costs for prospectuses are high. Most underwriters insist that a company going public use one of the larger accounting firms—one of the so-called Big Six—and this almost invariably means an increase in accounting fees. Furthermore, most company presidents don't discover until it's too late that when they go public they are suddenly in two full-time businesses—their own and the public corporation business. There is a tremendous difference between running one's own business and running a public corporation. There is a whole raft of new regulations and reporting requirements to conform to. Suddenly there are SEC reporting requirements, shareholders to deal with, annual meetings, annual reports, and so forth. These are all factors that somehow don't get calculated until it's too late.

Choosing an Investment Banker

In choosing an investment banker, there is always a subjective element in the judgment of intelligence, personality, and the evaluation of skills as they will be applied to the wide range of corporate problems.

The company should select and approach no more than three or four investment banking firms. With the aid of the accountant and the attorney, the firms can be readily identified on the basis of:

- The strength of reputation
- Limitations of the size of companies they will accept as clients

- The number of comparable client companies they have in terms of size, industry, and capitalization
- The history of the issues they have taken public

Even more significantly, the investment banking firms selected should be precisely that—investment banking firms. They should:

- Be at least reasonably large and well-established
- Offer a full range of services that include departments for acquisitions and mergers. fixed income securities, syndication, research, financial consulting, and all other aspects of the financial spectrum

The size of the retail operation is less important than would appear at first glance. Some of the most successful underwritings are achieved not by the firm's own retail operations, but by the ability to syndicate. The firms normally included in an investment banking syndicate are more important in the distribution of stock than the number of retail branches the underwriter has. The size and quality of its research department are better gauges of the investment banker's operation than is the number of registered representatives in the company's roster. The investment banker's trading operation is more important to the after-market than is the length of the list of underwritings it has done.

In other words, the measure of the investment banker's capabilities lies not in its obvious first capability to do an underwriting as much as in its ability to help the company over the long range.

Evaluating the Investment Banker

When the company has gone as far as it can go in identifying at least three good investment banking firms, it should then invite representatives of each of them to meet separately with its executives for discussions of a potential relationship. The evaluation should be based not on some ancillary issue, such as the pricing of the stock—that's a problem to be faced further down the line—but on the ability of the investment banking firm to serve the company's total financial and financial service needs. In fact, the investment banker doesn't price the stock—the market does. The banker simply assesses the price that the current market will accept.

Another value of these interviews is to further review the company's total capital needs, including its decision to go public. On the strength of these interviews the investment banker should be selected.

Basic Considerations

Within the context of these criteria, there are a few basic points that should also be considered:

• Get the best quality available. The smaller company need not feel it must settle for second best. Very few investment banking firms will refuse to discuss a relationship with any company of any size that can demonstrate real growth potential. Don't be put off by awe for the name of a Donaldson, Lufkin & Jenrette, a Goldman, Sachs, a Lazard, or a Morgan Stanley. An investment banker is interested in the future as well as the past or present. But don't be unduly flattered, either, by being approached by a name firm.

• On the other hand, don't be overly impressed by reputation. A lot of history has gone into building that reputation, but it may be just history. Or the reputation may have been built on elements irrelevant to a corporation's particular needs. A firm's present investment banking skills may not be sufficiently broad and innovative to deal effectively with today's capital markets and corporate needs.

• How important is your firm to the investment banker? If you're going to be a small fish in a large firm, you may have a problem getting the attention you need. On the other hand, don't assume that because you're small that you won't be important to the firm. Apple Computer was just beyond being a gleam in its founders' eyes when Morgan Stanley, who wanted to be strong in the computer field, took them public.

• Who in the firm will handle your account? Will it be a junior person— in which case, decline and walk rapidly? Or will it be one of the more experienced and seasoned people? Your company need not serve as the training ground for the investment banker.

• Where is the lead banker located? An underwriting requires a lot of hand holding. If the lead banker is 2,000 miles away, either a lot of hand holding won't get done or a lot of expensive and exhaustive traveling will. If there are co-managers, the lead banker does most of the work, and should be accessible on a consistent basis.

• Don't overlook the regional firms. There are some very good ones.

• The really superb firms will dazzle you not with their history or reputations or private dining rooms, but with their people. At the point of day-to-day contact, it is an individual with whom management must work, and not a firm's history. Nor are one or two superstars an indication of depth of capability and service.

- In this context, some newer and smaller firms have more capability to offer than do many of the older giants. Size and age are sparse measures of investment banking skill.
- The number and size of deals a firm has done are less a measure of capability then the *kinds* of deals they have put together, and the imagination with which they have been formulated in times when a more traditional approach to financing has not been possible. Aggregate amounts of private placements they have done will not help a corporation if it needs $2 million in a tight market, and the investment banker can only boast of $25 million placements for blue chip companies. The reverse is true as well.
- Ask questions. Lots of them. Simple and broad questions are the best, the better to gauge the investment banker's ability to grasp and understand a company, its industry, companies of comparable size, and the company's specific problems. See how thoughtful are the answers—or how glib and evasive.
- Ask to speak to their clients, especially those in comparable positions. Was performance as promised? Did the investment banker understand at all times the dimension and difficulties of all the problems? Was the range of service broad and intensive? Was the strategy functioning as planned? Did initiative come consistently from the investment banker, or was prodding necessary?
- Don't go to an investment banker for the wrong reasons. Don't hire an investment banker because he promises to support your ailing stock price with research reports you might not otherwise get from the Street, and certainly don't retain one that promises shallow short-term solutions when you have long-range problems.

And one more thing—don't be romanced by an investment banker. That's how so many companies got taken public in the 1960s—companies that are now either out of business, or undercapitalized or looking to go private again.

The best due diligence in choosing an investment banker, according to the noted venture capitalist Benjamin Rosen, of Sevin Rosen, is to interview five or ten institutional investors who are likely to buy into the deal. In today's institutional market, they are the ones who are best able to define for you the best investment bankers who do the best deals, and with whom they most prefer to work. If you can't depend upon reaching the market you most want because of your potential investment banker, you've got the wrong banker.

It's most important to remember, in choosing an investment banker, that times and the economy have changed. This is now the time of full service, the time for the broadest possible understanding of the full range of corporate needs and how to serve them, and the time for greater sophistication than ever before. The investment banking hero of the vast debt placement for the giant company is not necessarily the person capable of the hybrid deal so important today for the smaller or medium-sized company—nor is that individual always right to serve the full range of corporate needs for the emerging company. The investment banker of the past is clearly not the investment banker of the future.

A thorny point. Many companies have on their boards a representative of the underwriter who first did the public offering. Too often, this board member sees the investment banking function subjectively, in terms of the limitations of his or her own firm. The investment banker's presence on the board should not preclude objectivity in the search for sound investment banking relationships.

More significantly, there's an inherent danger in having on your board any service people, such as bankers or lawyers, when you may have to go outside for that service. The potential for conflict of interest is overwhelming. RCA had just such a problem, with its investment bankers on its board advising about acquisitions. The result was to load up with acquisitions of clients of their own board members. The ultimate divestiture of some of those acquisitions was expensive. In fact, you don't need anybody on your board whose objective advice you can buy when you need it.

The Syndicate

In any underwriting syndicate, as seen in the "tombstone" ad placed in a newspaper to announce the new issue, the firms in the listing are not in alphabetical order. They are in pecking order—the order of importance.

At the head of the list, standing apart, is the managing firm—or underwriting partners and co-managers if there are more than one. Next come the major firms, listed in order of the size of the portion of the issue each has agreed to market. This is followed by the secondary firms—smaller national firms each taking a smaller portion of the issue. Last come the regional houses and smallest firms.

While the tombstone ad is ostensibly for the company and its new issue, it's also an ad for the brokerage firms. This is why the tier in which a firm appears is important to that firm. And this is why the order of listing is a pecking order. The firms on the lower tiers are considered by Wall Street to be the lesser firms.

Regional Firms

In most major cities, there are investment banking and brokerage firms whose operations are generally limited to serving the geographic areas in which they are centered. Many of these regional firms are excellent, both in marketing securities in their areas and in serving investment banking needs for smaller companies in their territories. Properly structured and staffed, a regional firm can frequently offer the smaller company better service than can a major national banker. They are more likely to give attention to a small company in their area than will a New York–based national firm. A good regional firm that is generally included in a good syndicate also has access to that syndicate, which means that a regionally generated underwriting can be distributed as broadly as can a national underwriting.

There is a growing trend away from the traditional investment banking fee predicated on a portion of an underwriting, and toward the straight fee structure for investment bankers. A good relationship with an investment banker is extremely important for a growing company, and particularly a public one. To expect any kind of service from an investment banker whose total source of income from a company is the underwriting fee is a peculiar form of self-deception that almost invariably costs the company more in the long run.

The Nonpublic or Pre-Public Company

It's generally believed that the financial community will not concern itself with information about a privately held company. In an overwhelming number of cases, fortunately, this is not true—assuming that the program is properly handled. In skilled hands, a certain amount of premarket preparation can be done. An effective program has two advantages—it serves to notify and inform the financial community, as well as the general public, of the facts about a company and its industry, and second, it establishes a pattern of public relations activities which, if they don't flagrantly function to sell stock, serve as a pattern and precedent for an allowable level of public relations while a company is in registration.

Under skillful examination, any company can be found to have aspects about it that should be of interest to the general business press, even though the company is not public. It can be an unusual facet of the company, it can be an unusual relationship to its industry, or it can be an unusual approach to routine problems in an industry. Following the procedures outlined in Chapter 8, a nonpublic company can expect a measure of publicity in the financial and business press. Granted that it takes considerably more skill to develop newsworthy material for a nonpublic company than for a public company, but a review of the business press will show that it's done with regularity.

In many cases, and in selected industries, a nonpublic company can be a valuable source of general information about that industry to the financial community. Analysts specializing in any industry are always eager to receive fresh and pertinent information from any valid source. There's no reason why a nonpublic company can't take the initiative to supply the information to the very analysts they will ultimately be dealing with when they go public.

Certain kinds of product or service publicity in the nonfinancial press can also be useful to the financial community in contributing to its knowledge of a particular industry. There is nothing untoward in sending reprints of such publicity to selected analysts specializing in that industry.

The objective, of course, is to precede any public offering, much before registration, with a public relations program that engenders recognition of the company name and understanding of the company's activities and position in the field, even while it enhances the view of the industry in which the company serves.

The Pre-Public Pattern

As for establishing a pattern of public communications that will be acceptable while in registration, the basic rules of disclosure apply (see Chapter 9). Nothing is acceptable that can be construed as offering to sell stock or conditioning the market for the sale of stock. Nevertheless, the SEC says that, barring those specific exceptions, the company may continue its normal pattern of publicity. The point is to establish a normal pattern of publicity.

Prior to registration, and as part of putting the company's story together for presentation to prospective underwriters, the company should orient its material. This should not be done in the legalistic terms of a prospectus, but in ways that are acceptable to the financial community in general. One approach used with some measure of success is the financial annual report for the nonpublic company. The report need not be expensive or elaborate, but it can follow the same general procedure used for an annual report for a public company. This kind of report can also be used for customers, employees, suppliers, and, of course, the financial community, as part of a program to acquaint them with the company and its position in the industry. It can include full financials.

It may also be worth considering the preparation of a background report similar to that recommended for distribution to the financial community by a public company.

At all costs, in any pre-public publicity, or representations by a pre-public company to the financial community, all SEC regulations pertaining to a company in registration should be kept clearly in mind. Nothing will defeat an ultimate public issue so much as misrepresentation of the facts about a company even before it has gone public. And certainly, if the program is to succeed, it must be done in such a way that the pre-public material will be remembered well after the company has gone public. Any significant discrepancies in the information given in the two periods will seriously and adversely affect the financial community's view of the ultimate issue.

Registration

When a company is in registration for a public stock offering it enters a period of silence. That is, it may do nothing in the way of disseminating information about itself that can under any circumstances be construed as marketing the stock, promoting it, or conditioning the market for the sale of the stock.

This doesn't mean that the company must go into hiding from the public or the financial community.

First of all, the SEC requires that the normal Rules of Disclosure for a public company be maintained even for a company in registration. Any basic information about activities that alter the nature of the company, such as a merger, an acquisition, or a major contract, must be disclosed. The basic rule remains, however, that no activity should be undertaken, nor new public relations effort initiated, which can in any way be construed as selling stock or conditioning the market. This particularly includes any form of projections, any subjective material that implies growth potential for either the company or the industry, or any material that interprets any information being disseminated. The exception, perhaps, is product information which is consistent with an historical pattern of marketing established well before registration.

The New Issue

Once the company is out of registration it can begin to pursue the normal investor relations activities described throughout this book. The first step is a press release which simply announces the new issue, made available by prospectus. It should include the underwriter, the size and details of the issue, and a brief description of the company's business. This release and the tombstone ad in the financial press are usually taken care of by the underwriter, in conjunction with attorneys.

The Due Diligence Meeting

Immediately prior to the effective date of the registration, the underwriter holds a meeting for representatives of all the underwriting firms that might participate in the syndicate to distribute the stock. Legally, the purpose of the meeting is to demonstrate that due diligence has been exercised in the preparation of the issue and in the presentation and updating of facts about the company, and so it is referred to as the *due diligence meeting*. The more realistic purpose of this meeting is to assure that all participants understand the nature of the issue, to develop some enthusiasm on their part about the company, and to persuade some of the firms to sell the stock. Another purpose, however, is to assure the participants in the syndicate that they haven't made a mistake in their participation. There may be several such meetings in different cities—called the *road show*.

Due diligence meetings used to be cut-and-dried affairs, attended reluctantly by people who have already decided to help sell the issue. But times change, and the marketing opportunities at a due diligence meeting are now being better realized. For this reason, it's now the better part of wisdom to put on a thoroughly professional performance in explaining the company in order to engender the kind of enthusiasm necessary to make the issue a success.

The presentation should be carefully prepared so that the material is presented in an orderly fashion, and that it is succinct, precise, and to the point. The objective of the meeting is to have each participant understand the company's current financial structure and, for analysts, to demonstrate the company's ability to appreciate the invested dollar. And, as with analyst meetings, questions should be anticipated and the answers rehearsed. Management should appear confident, open, and willing to answer all questions.

In planning the investor relations activities, the syndicate is a key to developing the geographic aspect of the program. Since the location of the syndicate members is basis for the geographic distribution of the stock, there is a first inkling of those cities that might be targets for analyst meetings and press attention. Moreover, a representative of a syndicate member can usually be depended upon to assist in identifying the key people in the local financial community.

The After-market

The after-market is what happens to the stock after the public issue. In too many cases, a company is led to believe that the underwriter will take and maintain a proprietary interest in the stock issue after the company has gone public. This is rarely the case, even for companies that do well in the stock market following the original issue. There are several reasons for this.

Maintaining a sound after-market beyond the period legally required is arduous, time-consuming, and sometimes expensive. It demands skills and facilities that are frequently beyond the capabilities of even the larger underwriters. In order for the price of a stock—and particularly a new and untested one—to reflect consistently the company's earnings and earnings potential, there must not only be marketmakers, but quality sponsors. Presumably the underwriter will serve as both—but this is a presumption more often honored in the breach. Frequently, the underwriter will issue a research report, primarily to assist its own registered representatives in the sale of the stock, but the report is plainly qualified to indicate that the firm issuing the report maintains a position in the stock, or brought the stock public, and is therefore not entirely objective. Unfortunately, unless the company is growing at a consistent rate of 30 percent a year and expects to do so for the next five years, and its stock price reflects this growth, the underwriter has very little time to spend on any one stock—and that amount of time diminishes the farther away from the date of issue.

There is a realistic aspect to the problem, too, in that the underwriter has probably earned a fee from just the underwriting. Unless the stock really takes off and sharply increases in value, there is a limit to what the underwriter can profitably do.

He may continue to sponsor and make a market in a stock, but one sponsor and one marketmaker are not sufficient for an issue that is not performing superbly on its own. He may call upon friends and associates in other firms to help him, but there is a limit to the time he can profitably spend in pursuing this activity, and to the sustaining results he can achieve.

There is also the question of exposing a company to a broad spectrum of analysts and brokers. This, too, is beyond the capability of most underwriters, both in terms of time they can profitably spend and the overall perspective necessary for developing a strategy tailored to a particular company at any one time in the market's performance. Even the largest and soundest underwriting firm places a strict limit on what it can reasonably do in developing additional sponsors, marketmakers, research reports, and exposure to the financial community at large. Underwriters are not geared to support an issue to any degree that might enhance its long-range acceptance by the financial community. This is essentially the purpose of a separate and professionally performed investor relations program.

Be prepared for high volatility in the first days of the issue. There is now a common practice for investors with good relationships with underwriters or their syndicate members to buy the IPO, hold it for the first day or two of the runup in price that usually follows a new issue, and then to sell at a quick profit. The result is a drop in the stock's price, following which the market then values the stock more realistically. Be prepared for a roller coaster ride.

Internet Underwriting

It would seem inevitable, in today's technological context, that a firm would take itself public by offering to sell shares on the Internet. In 1995, Spring Street Brewing Co. did exactly that. After the first flush of turmoil, the SEC accepted the concept, but with modifications regarding disclosures and disclaimers. There are clear advantages for the smaller company, but inherent dangers as well. Consult a lawyer before, not after. It's safer.

The Employee Stock Ownership Trust (ESOT)

One way to raise capital, particularly for the private or closely held corporation, is the *employee stock ownership plan and trust* —the *ESOT*.

The company sells stock to a noncontributory trust fund it sets up for its employees. The trust uses the stock as collateral for a loan from a bank. The trust, in turn, gives the money to the company in payment for the stock. The company then pays an expensible maximum of 15 percent of its payroll annually to the trust. With ESOT, it is paid with pretax dollars. Furthermore, the plan is allowed to function with the margin requirements usually applicable in a stock pledge. Instead, the bank accepts the corporation's guarantee.

In a specific example, a company needs $1 million for five years. It has 300 employees with an annual gross payroll of $3 million and is in the 54 percent tax bracket. The ESOT borrows $1 million from the bank, which the company guarantees. ESOT then pays the $1 million to the company in exchange for $1 million in company stock. The company pays $300,000— or 10 percent of its payroll—annually to the trust. The trust pays the bank $254,976—principal and interest—annually on the debt, leaving it $45,024 for its reserve account. As the loan is paid off, the stock is allocated to the employees' account and is usually vested over a period of ten years.

The plan has several advantages:

- For the nonpublic company not in a position to go into the equities market, it allows the company to go public, in a limited sense, without registration.
- Because pretax dollars are used to finance the debt there is a substantial tax savings.
- Cash flow is increased substantially.
- Net worth is increased substantially.
- It creates liquidity at fair market value, comparable to that of a public company, without SEC registration or underwriting costs or time.
- It allows for capital gains sales by individual shareholders.
- The stockholder-employee accumulates values in the ESOT which are not subject to estate taxes.
- It establishes a definite valuation of shares for estate tax purposes of major shareholders.
- Buy/sell agreements for the stock of major shareholders may be funded by life insurance, with premiums deductible from pretax income by flowing it through the trust.
- For the employees, it builds unity and team spirit by allowing them to share in the capital growth of the company, to realize capital gains on income, and to accumulate values that are funded by employer contributions, with no diminution of employee take-home pay.

The ESOT is also for the closely held company, or for the company already public, but not in a position to issue additional shares due to existing stock market conditions. Experience has shown that the ESOT is not an unalloyed blessing, and so should be considered with a great deal of independent advice from accountants, lawyers and investment bankers.

The ESOT is sanctioned by the Internal Revenue Service. An ESOT is best established with the assistance of one of the several firms specializing in such programs.

The Private Placement

An increasing number of companies are going public, or are having a secondary offering, using the private placement. Most popular in this area are the private placements under SEC Regulation S, when the investors are all offshore; Regulation D, when the investors are either institutions or private investors qualified by high assets; Rule 144A, in which the investment may be made only directly by an institution, and where the institution may sell the stock only to another institution.

Most of these offerings use a preferred convertible stock. The danger is that after the legal holding period, usually forty days, the preferred is sold all at once, dumping the stock on the market, diluting the issue, and dampening the stock price. The investor benefits—the company loses. This is exactly what happened to a large number of Regulation S offerings in the late 1990s, putting a severe damper on this kind of placement. To offset the negative aspects of convertible preferred placements, several firms offered Regulation D placements, but with safeguards. Several firms offer Regulation D private placements with guaranteed managed conversion, so that only a very small portion of the preferred is converted each day. That process avoids rapid dilution and tends to protect the value of the underlying common stock issue.

Going Private

In the chastening cold light of changing economic conditions, an increasing number of companies sometimes come to feel that they are better off as private companies than as public companies. The procedures for going private are relatively—relatively—simple, so much so that the SEC tends to take a dim view of the process, as do many individual shareholders. When stock prices are very low and management feels the company is undervalued, and particularly when the stock price is considerably lower than book value, the decision to go private is very tempting. Unfortunately, the shareholder who bought stock at $20, now sees it at $3, and is being offered $5 for in a tender offer by a management that wants to go private and will obviously benefit from the transaction, is not likely to be overjoyed at the company's action. In some cases there have been stockholder suits, although considering the high cost to an individual for filing such a suit, these have not been abundant.

Globe Security Systems, Inc., a subsidiary of Walter Kidde & Company, Inc., is a typical example of a public company going private. It had 335,450 shares of its common stock in the hands of the public. It tendered for that stock at a cash price that was 38 percent higher than the last sale price on the American Stock Exchange. Globe had once traded as high as $31\frac{1}{2}$, but at the time of the tender it was trading at $3\frac{7}{8}$. As a result of the tender offer, Kidde's holdings in Globe went from 81 percent to 95 percent. With fewer than 300 shareholders, Globe was exempted from SEC regulations and was delisted by the exchange. It was, in effect, a private company. Those shareholders who did not tender their stock might just as well have done so, since there was virtually no further public market.

It doesn't always work that easily. Fuqua Industries tried it, and was slapped with eleven stockholder suits. For some time, the stock, at $14 a share, had been selling at a p/e of less than four, and had been consistently below a book value of $18.66 a share. It seemed to be a good idea. The firm tendered at $20 a share to acquire all outstanding stock. The offer failed, in large part because of shareholder objection to the plan.

Fuqua's response was interesting. While abandoning the plan to go private, it still decided to buy back a large number of its shares, at $20 a share. In recent years, corporate stock repurchases have become increasingly popular, as the market fails to reflect the value of a company. Some of the nation's largest companies have done it, including IBM, Sears, Roebuck, Ashland Oil, Texaco, PepsiCo, and many others. It is frequently a good corporate strategy that can at least represent a sound investment of the company's assets. Other advantages are to fine tune the balance sheet, to make shares available for acquisitions or stock options (within the limits of SEC regulations), or to increase earnings per share by reducing the number of shares outstanding. A typical success story in repurchasing is Mary Kay Cosmetics. At one point, more than 40 percent of its stock was held by institutions. When the institutions decided, at one point, to get out of the stock, the market couldn't absorb all of the institutional holdings. Mary Kay tendered for 800,000 shares at $13.25, thereby reducing the number of shares outstanding by 30 percent. Within a year or so, reflecting the reduced number of shares, the stock was selling at $39, with a p/e of 12. The strategy clearly worked.

Among those techniques for going private, there are several that are more commonly used in addition to the tender offer.

One of the most popular methods is to offer a new nonconvertible debenture in exchange for the common stock. Another technique is a merger or liquidation, usually using a dummy corporation. Management establishes a dummy corporation into which it merges the original company. The public shareholders don't get shares in the new company, but are instead offered a price for their stock in the original company. The merger is then voted by the shareholders, but invariably the buyers have enough votes to carry their proposal. Another technique is a reverse split, which sharply reduces the number of shares outstanding and leaves each share at a price so high that trading is precluded. The variations on the technique are myriad.

Among the dangers of going private, which are many, is the very strong barrier of antifraud and antimanipulative provisions of the Securities Exchange Act of 1934. This becomes particularly cogent in a deal in which the public shareholder is obviously going to lose out. A great measure of care must be taken in presenting any such arrangement so that there is no misrepresentation and that there is full disclosure of every aspect of it. Naturally, a company in the process of buying its own stock under any procedure must pay strict attention to SEC regulations.

There is also a question, the answer to which is difficult to anticipate, as to the future of any company going private. Perhaps it should not have gone public in the first place and going private is a proper amendment of that mistake. On the other hand, at some distant future date, the public company going private may need equity money to expand to meet changing conditions. How then will the market view that company, if, in going private, it had not done right by its shareholders?

For the company planning to go public, it's certainly a good exercise to view the experience and reasons of companies that have gone private.

Going public to find a source of capital that is appropriate to a company is fraught with pitfalls and expenses that somehow don't get readily talked about in discussions prior to an underwriting. While it's unlikely that these activities should reach a proportion to preclude a public issue where one is otherwise indicated, it would be foolhardy for any corporate management to plan to go public without being aware of the problems and expenses inherent in doing it.

The point has been made that the securities industry is in the greatest state of flux it has seen in the financial history of our country. The facts are too commonly known to review to here. However, one thing becomes crystal clear. In whatever form the industry ultimately evolves, it must be predicated on its primary purpose—to finance business, not merely to sell securities. No matter what else happens to alter the structure of the securities industry, that remains primary.

Chapter 11

Shareholder Relations

While the thrust of investor relations is to compete in the capital markets by getting more individuals and institutions to buy your stock—to invest in your company and its vigor and growth—too often overlooked is the existing stockholder. There is too easy a tendency to treat the sale of stock like the sale of a vacuum cleaner—once it's sold you can walk away from the buyer, unless you want to sell him or her another product. Yet, there's an axiom of marketing that wisely notes that it's easier and cheaper to keep a customer than to get a new one. It's easier and cheaper to keep a shareholder, and perhaps to get that shareholder to increase holdings, than to get a new one.

The Rationale

There is a sound rationale, then, aside from legal requirements, for painstakingly pursuing the loyalty of existing shareholders.

Presumably, an effective investor relations program will result in a warm feeling of loyalty to the company by its shareholders. But how many chief executive officers are now walking around with a glazed look in their eyes because, despite an intensive investor relations program, their loyal and intensively informed shareholders tendered their stock to the other side in a take-over attempt? How many loyal and informed shareholders, subjected to many years of a meticulous investor relations program, have sold their stock when it became apparent that the company was in for a rough year?

On the other hand, how do you gauge the degree to which shareholders held on to their stock when the company anticipated a bad year, because they fully understood that the company was inherently sound and would recover from any short-term problems? How many shareholders increased their holdings when it was made clear that the company was about to enter a particularly favorable period? A careful analysis of the stock transfer sheets, or continuing research and sampling, as well as market reaction, offers some measurable evidence, quantitatively, of a sound shareholder relations program. But not all evidence of value can be quantified, and certainly not at reasonable cost.

There is also the paradox of liquidity. In a company with a relatively small float—the number of shares outstanding that are available for public trading—satisfied shareholders who don't sell their stock can, in a measure, be self-defeating, because if there's no stock available, there's no auction market. And if there's no auction market, the price of a stock tends to stay static or decline. At the same time, investors who might want to buy the stock in any sizable amount leave quickly if they can get only small pieces of their orders.

And yet despite these questions, there is clear evidence that a carefully planned and effectively performed shareholder relations program is not only warranted, but almost mandatory. And the evidence is more than clear that a well-executed program makes a significant contribution to the company's capital goals. That evidence is in the increased market value of those companies with active and successful shareholder relations programs.

Certainly, beyond legal obligations, there's an inherent responsibility to keep investors informed of not only current operating data, but of both the general performance and outlook for the company.

Theoretically and legally, management is employed by the shareholders, and therefore the shareholders are entitled to an account of the way their company is being managed. Once little more than theory, the growing power of institutions makes this shareholder control a compelling factor in management. The control of most companies, traditionally held by either the management group or a relatively small group of investors close to the management, is shifting to the large institutional shareholders. Where once shareholder meetings were dominated by individuals such as the once famous Gilbert brothers, it is the voting power of such institutions as CalPers—the California Public Employees' Retirement System—which has $108 billion under management that prevails. This substantially changes the picture in the once theoretical concept of shareholder democracy. It is a more compelling reason than ever for a sustained shareholder relations program.

The Institutional Shareholder

Now the vast and overwhelming growth of institutional holdings in even smaller companies also poses the problem in corporate governance, which means, as well, a new problem in shareholder relations. It is becoming increasingly evident that many of the institutional holders, such as pension and mutual funds, are moving from passivity to aggressiveness. One has only to look at the increasing number of mutual funds buying into smaller companies to realize that IBM and Apple don't stand alone in the crosshairs of the institutional voter. The institutional holders now look increasingly at the potential power they can wield from holdings of 5 percent or more of a company's stock.

Where once institutional shareholders could be reasonably ignored, or at least catered to no differently than the ordinary shareholder, now attention must be paid. They must be kept as informed as is legally possible, and they must be wooed by management as never before.

Shareholders as a Source of Capital

Shareholders must be viewed for what they are—a source of capital, as well as a potential source of additional capital. And as such they must be as intensively cultivated as is any other group of potential investors. The fact that they are already shareholders is a twofold advantage. They have already made a decision favorable to the company, and management usually knows who they are. This doesn't mean that the selling aspect of financial relations is in any way diminished—a shareholder can become an ex-shareholder with relative ease. It merely means that the job of reaching him or her is simpler. It also means that, as a legal owner of the company, he or she has a claim to management's ear. Dissatisfied shareholders have a right to make their opinions known to management, and they have many ways to do it. They can ask embarrassing questions at an annual meeting, and be highly visible while doing it. They can write letters to management. They can telephone or call on management in person. Now they can legally talk to one another.

They can sue if they feel there's a basis for it. And then, of course, they have that ultimate weapon. They can become ex-shareholders.

If shareholders are satisfied they can use these weapons in management's behalf. The shareholder can get up at that same annual meeting and publicly praise management. He or she can write letters of praise. The shareholder can be an effective spokesperson for the company and its stock to friends and to brokers. And since shareholders are sometimes effective management people themselves, they can sometimes contribute useful ideas. As for the ultimate effective weapon, the shareholder can hold the stock during the company's trying periods, and buy more stock if the company's outlook is good, refuse to tender that stock to outsiders, and buy more stock in a secondary offering.

And so, on balance, an effective shareholder's program is warranted and has tremendous value, unquantifiable as the specific results of such a program might sometimes be.

It should be remembered, as well, that aside from keeping shareholders informed, the ultimate objective of an investor relations program is to engender understanding and a favorable attitude toward the company on the part of investors.

Tools of Shareholder Relations

While the normal functions of an investor relations program will ultimately reach and serve shareholders as well as prospective investors, there are some quite specific devices used as tools in a shareholder/investor relations program. These are:

- The annual report
- Interim reports
- The annual meeting
- Letters to shareholders, or a periodic newsletter
- Distribution of product literature or internal house organs
- Distribution of press reports
- Phone contact with shareholders
- 800 numbers to corporate headquarters
- Advertising and other promotional devices
- Speech reprints

- Dividend reinvestment plans
- Shareholder stock purchase programs
- Conference calls
- Fax on demand
- Web pages
- On-line bulletin boards

These are the tools—but the tools are not a program. Most of this list is dealt with elsewhere in this book. Certainly, every public company issues an annual report and many companies issue interim reports. All public companies hold annual meetings. Many companies frequently write letters to shareholders to inform them of special events or activities, and many even write welcoming letters to new shareholders or query letters to selling shareholders. But not only must each of these devices be looked at separately and used artfully, it must also be recognized that each functions best when it's part of an overall plan or program. They must not only interrelate and reinforce one another, but they are all judged in terms of specific objectives.

Shareholder Relations Policy

For a shareholder relations program to be effective, there must first be a clear-cut decision by management that commits the company to such a program. Internally, a specific officer must be charged with shareholder relations responsibility. If the program is considered important enough to do in the first place, it should be considered a serious responsibility. Too often, left-handed recognition of the need for such a program results in a half-hearted attempt from which the chief executive divorces himself, assigning the responsibility to a low-ranking officer, and allotting the performance of the program either to inexperienced personnel or to an advertising manager clearly not qualified to deal with it. In order for a shareholder relations program to succeed, it should ultimately fall under the personal aegis of the chief executive officer, no matter who is assigned to perform or oversee the actual task. Of course, for the company with internal or external investor relations counsel, the professionalism of the program is enhanced. But here, too, the investor relations counsel is thwarted unless the chief executive officer is not only dedicated to the success of the program, but understands the necessity of keeping the investor relations counsel keenly attuned to all aspects of the company's operation, as well as to current corporate policy. While the day-by-day activities of such a program—or any investor relations program for that matter—may be supervised by a designated executive (usually the CFO), there must be clear access to the chief executive officer.

The Program

The program itself must have clearly stated objectives. The ultimate objective is to keep shareholders informed, and to do so in ways that engender a favorable attitude toward the company. But aside from the basic rules and requirements of disclosure, how far does that go? The basic requirements of disclosure for even the largest company can be fulfilled with a copy machine. The degree to which the company goes beyond the rules in the elaborateness of its disclosure, as well as the graphic devices used as a medium, must be predetermined. What is the basic attitude of the company toward its shareholders? Are they the cherished group they should be, to be assiduously wooed and won, or are they to be considered as transitory, with the obligation to them minimal and limited only to basic information? Are they to be accepted merely as a necessary evil attendant to a public corporation, or is each new shareholder to be greeted with a personal letter from the president welcoming him to the family?

Are they to be seen as a distant group to be dealt with only as the occasion arises, or shall the program include a careful and regular analysis of transfer sheets and shareholder surveys to keep informed of changes in shareholders of record? This, incidentally, is a basic and important device in any investor relations program. It not only indicates changes in shareholders, but changes in geographical distribution, the entry or exit of participation by brokerage houses, unusual purchasing or selling patterns that might indicate the necessity for specific action or alterations in the investor relations program, or warn of prospective take-over attempts. Transfer sheets should be reviewed regularly, and each week a summary should be prepared for the chief executive officer indicating changes in shareholding of large blocks. Specific patterns should be watched for such factors as regular purchases of small or medium-sized lots by one buyer, or selling patterns in a particular geographic area.

CEDE

To some extent, the message of the transfer sheets must be seen in light of the fact that an increasing number of trades—perhaps half or more—are done in Street name now, and will be listed as being made through CEDE (The Depository Trust Company). This doesn't diminish the value of tracking, it simply qualifies it. The CEDE printouts should also be summarized often, and compared to prior periods to spot trends.

Today, more sophisticated techniques are used to poll shareholders to determine attitudes toward the company as an investment. Research is replacing guessing. Good research tells the company what the investor thinks about the company, and what's important and what isn't. But a word of caution. Attitudes change, and if an investor relations program is to be predicated on current investor attitudes, then these attitudes must be fathomed frequently.

Only when the investor relations program is carefully planned can specific decisions be made on such questions as how elaborate should the annual report be? Should an audiovisual or film presentation be developed for the annual meeting, or should it consist solely of a president's message? Without a clear-cut overall policy regarding investor relations, decisions and answers to these questions and myriad others are arbitrary.

As with much of investor relations, the tools used for dealing with shareholders are not as important as the ways in which they're used. Nor are the tools of shareholder relations immune from being used imaginatively. The devices of corporate communications—annual and interim reports, and so forth—although prescribed by law, are still susceptible to imaginative treatment. And still, there are other conduits to shareholders.

The Annual Meeting

The annual meeting of shareholders is a legal requirement rarely looked upon by corporate executives with pleasant anticipation. Even if a company is performing beautifully, and management expects that the event will be a display of unmitigated pride, it requires a great deal of preparation that seems to most corporate officers to be irrelevant to the specific business of running a company. They may be right, but they cannot avoid the annual chore.

In smaller companies, meetings are rarely well attended unless the company is facing some specific challenges. In even the largest companies, only the smallest portion of outstanding shares is represented in person, and most matters on the agenda have been predetermined by the mail proxy vote, combined with the votes of the shares held by management groups.

In companies with problems, the president anticipates being roasted by dissident shareholders who are more vocal and visible than usually seems warranted by the number of shares they represent. Some companies' meetings are sometimes besieged not only by legitimate representatives of minority shareholders, but by publicity seekers who seize the opportunity to be difficult in public; to use the meeting as a vehicle for their own personal publicity and aggrandizement.

The Meeting Date

The date of the meeting, usually prescribed by corporate charter but not difficult to change, further serves to put pressure on the production of the proxy material and (if it's to be mailed with the proxy) the annual report, which should be mailed thirty to forty days prior to the meeting, and certainly no later than ten days for unlisted companies.

And so it's not difficult to understand why few chief executive officers look forward to an annual meeting as anything but an unpleasant but necessary chore.

Yet, properly run, an annual meeting can go beyond its basic legal requirements to be a useful communications tool. It can be a focal point for presenting a company point of view not only to shareholders, but to the entire financial community. For listed or NASDAQ companies, it can be publicized. It can serve as a sounding board to allow management to fathom the reactions of its shareholders to its activities. And there is no question that shareholders have frequently come up with useful suggestions at annual meetings.

The secret of success of an annual meeting is in its preparation. Its basic elements are prescribed by state corporate law. The meeting is generally run under Roberts' Rules of Order, follows the agenda prepared well beforehand by the attorneys, and covers specific items which have been outlined in the proxy statement. Predetermined motions and seconding are usually assigned to executives and directors who own stock, so that the meeting runs smoothly. These usually cover the motion to dispense with the reading of the minutes, motions to cover the business of the agenda, such as elections of the board of directors and auditors, and any other business that must be legally covered. Proxies are collected and officers are appointed to tally both proxies and votes made in person. This formal part of the meeting is usually scripted by the attorneys to assure that the format protects the company under legal requirements.

These activities are formalized and cut and dried. The potential problems come in three areas—the CEO's message, the questions and answers, and new business.

Every meeting, even those where minimal attendance is anticipated, should be prepared meticulously and with every detail covered. The CEO's message should be either written, with ultimate publication in mind, or outlined in great detail.

Anticipating Questions

Every question that might be asked should be anticipated in writing and, in a rehearsal, the appropriate answer carefully worked out. It is important for the success of an annual meeting that every likelihood be anticipated. There should be no surprises.

The CEO's Message

The key to the meeting, of course, is the president's or CEO's message. The annual meeting is the management's report to shareholders—to their ultimate employers—usually delivered by the CEO. The CEO is expected to report on the condition of the company at that moment, its progress, and the directions in which it is going. It's easy to assume that the message will be essentially the same as the message in the annual report, which presumably all shareholders will have read. The fact is that most shareholders will not have read it, or if they have will still appreciate hearing the report in person, and that the speech will include more detail.

The message will differ from the report in several ways. The company will have several months' progress to report since the time the annual report was written. In all probability the first quarter figures will be available, and if the timing is right, the annual meeting may be used as the medium to report the quarter's results. Some companies release preliminary numbers at the meeting, but this is generally frowned upon as "milking the news." Safe

Harbor regulations apply, of course. Since the target audience is quite specifically the shareholders, the kinds of information and the format in which they are presented will be much more focused for them, even though it's anticipated that the speech will be reported by the financial press, or broadcast via closed circuit or videotaped, and will subsequently be mailed to shareholders and the financial community in a post-meeting report.

Furthermore, if the speech is well prepared, and addresses the key points of the moment, it should anticipate—and therefore forestall—some of the thornier questions that are likely to be raised in the question and answer period.

More and more companies, today, hold the CEO's message until after the formal meeting has been held and adjourned. The presentation, then, doesn't become part of the official minutes. This is particularly useful in today's litigious society. The speech is heard by those present, and copies of the speech, with answers to questions, can then be distributed to shareholders in an edited (but not distorted) version. Other companies feel that they would rather have the speech on the record to protect and prove what was said.

Contents of the CEO's Message

The message should be as short and concise as possible and still cover the material to be presented in 10 or 20 minutes. It should contain the following elements:

• A summary of the latest operating results, including, if appropriate, the first quarter's results, and general estimates for the coming year (but not necessarily the specific numbers). Again, *Safe Harbor* rules apply
• The operational condition of the company in terms of its products, services, markets, people, and finances
• Special events during the course of the prior year that are significant to the company's past, present, and future activities
• The economic climate in which the company is now operating, or expects to be operating during the coming year
• The near-term corporate strategy, longer-term strategy, and a general prognosis for the future. Here, great care must be taken to be realistic and cautious. Better to err on the side of caution. External economic events can alter the best laid plans, and it's better to do better by one percent than to

do worse by one percent. It's well to remember here, too, that any significant projections made for the first time must be reported immediately that day to the general public under the rules of disclosure. The process should be set up beforehand.

Questions and Answers

Following the president's message come the questions and answers. It's at this point that many meetings that might otherwise be successful turn into a shambles. The importance of anticipating questions cannot be overemphasized. And if the company is large enough for press coverage, it must be anticipated that questions and answers reported out of context can sometimes be distorted. Some years ago, the chairman of the board of a large company had anticipated announcing that since he was gradually withdrawing from active participation in the business, he was taking a reduction in salary. Prior to the meeting he was advised to include that statement in his presentation. He waited instead for what he deemed to be an appropriate moment during the question and answer period. As it turned out, questions were somewhat hostile. His announcement of a pay cut was reported in the context of the hostility, and appeared in the press to have been a decision forced by the attacks made during the course of the meeting. The report was wholly inaccurate, but arose naturally from a failure to anticipate the effect of bad timing upon the announcement.

The question of executive compensation is a typical example of the kind of problem the CEO must face from the podium—a problem that seems to absorb shareholders for generation after generation. During periods of economic downturn, and certainly in a company reporting lower earnings or slower earnings growth, it's almost certain to arise. Other questions, depending upon economic conditions, might address questions of company performance, corporate governance, social responsibilities, mergers and acquisitions, and so forth.

It's here that the value of anticipation and preparation is best proven. Questions can be anticipated by clearly understanding the issues facing your company, the economy, the world, and society.

Every possible question should be anticipated, and the facts marshaled to formulate a cogent, direct and documented response.

If the meeting is orderly, as it should be if the chief executive officer is calm and patient, the question and answer period should be allowed to last as long as is necessary for all shareholders to have a fair chance to participate. Any attempt to rush a meeting, or to cut off the questions, will only serve to inflame the shareholders and turn the meeting into a fracas. Which is not to say that, in the interests of fairness, each speaker can't be limited to three or five minutes. Or a generous period of time—a half hour or so—can be specified beforehand.

The chief executive officer should not allow himself to be goaded into anger, or to allow the meeting to get out of hand. There are some shareholders who make a practice of disrupting meetings, apparently for publicity purposes. Their questions are antagonistic and irrelevant. A meeting should be run strictly under Roberts' Rules of Order, and in some cases it may be necessary to advise a questioner politely that his or her question is out of order or irrelevant. Some questions, particularly thorny ones, can sometimes be deferred by suggesting that the topic is not of interest to the entire group, but will gladly be discussed after the meeting. There are even times when shareholders become unnecessarily abusive and may have to be physically ejected. The judgment resides with the meeting's chairman. A good rule of thumb, however, is to visualize tomorrow's headlines before taking any extreme action. In some cases where chairmen have had to physically eject obstreperous shareholders, it's been done so deftly as to garner sympathy for the chairman rather than for the ejected party.

In answering questions, the chairman of the meeting should call upon other executives to participate. The purpose is to demonstrate the depth of management; that the company is run by others besides the chief executive officer. Properly prepared, it can also be expected that the vice-president of finance will give a more detailed answer to financial questions, or that the vice-president of marketing will give a more specific explanation of marketing programs.

Shareholder Resolutions

Under clearly defined circumstances, shareholders of a corporation are allowed, under the Securities Act of 1934 and subsequent SEC regulations, to submit resolutions to be voted upon at annual meetings.

To do so, a shareholder must have owned at least one percent (or $1,000 in market value) of the stock for one year, and must submit the proposal to the corporation at least 120 days before the proxy statement is sent to shareholders. Each qualified shareholder is allowed to submit only one proposal a year.

At the same time, management may veto these proposals if they are substantially the same as other proposals submitted in the past five years; would require the company to violate the law; are submitted with false or misleading arguments; relate to a personal claim or grievance against the company; seek to require the company to pay a specific dividend; or cannot be put into action by the company.

Should a proposal be made that fully qualifies, it must be dealt with on the floor as would a management proposal, although there is ample opportunity for management to prepare and present arguments should it be deemed valuable to do so.

Under recent rulings shareholders are now permitted to communicate with one another regarding pertinent matters, a right once granted only to institutions.

Hostile Questions—the Dissident Shareholder

Even for a company in deep trouble, most questions are cursory and honest, reflecting the legitimate interest of shareholders in their company. Some questions, on the other hand, are flagrantly designed to attack and to antagonize management. Dissident shareholders, dissatisfied with anything from the stock's performance to the dividend policy to the company's environmental practices, come well prepared and armed with their own research data.

While individual investors rarely have the voting power to affect change in management policy, they sometimes win by the power of their ideas. Institutions, on the other hand, frequently do have the voting strength, as well as the sophistication, to make their positions viable.

Other special interest groups have also become prevalent in recent years. These include environmental and women's rights groups, and groups opposed to investment or doing business in undemocratic or segregated countries. The participation of these groups, and others that will undoubtedly emerge, become increasingly forceful, and must be recognized as a fact of corporate life.

The executive who doesn't allow any such dissident shareholder his or her full measure of public voice will almost invariably find himself in trouble, not only during the course of the meeting, but in the press. For the press, most annual meetings are dull and not particularly newsworthy. A dissident stockholder is the most exciting event, and therefore the most reportable event, at most meetings.

The dissident shareholder is best disarmed by being given the fullest and most polite audience possible. He or she must be recognized and his or her point of view given full consideration, even if the outcome is predetermined and the views are inconsistent with corporate realities. There is no better answer, in situations such as these, than "I want to thank you for your suggestion. We will certainly take it under advisement."

There are times when the complaints of the individual shareholders are particularly pertinent. For example, one group of individual shareholders had always defended the rights of a successful corporation to make legitimate charitable contributions. However, some time ago, a major airline made a $500,000 five-year pledge to pay for a new production of a Wagner opera by the Metropolitan Opera Company. Particularly in view of the company's profit picture at the time, a shareholder's statement at the annual meeting was quoted in *The New York Times* as follows: "I defy anyone to prove one extra benefit to the company from that gift. It is for the social benefit of one man so he can sit at the opera,' said Mr. Gilbert." Whether Gilbert—long a well-known shareholder activist, was right or wrong didn't matter quite so much as the fact that his highly damaging statement was widely broadcast in the public press.

The women's interest groups are functioning on a rising tide of favorable public sentiment. They deal with issues of national concern that quite naturally focus on many aspects of a corporation. This is particularly true of any corporation that functions in areas and in companies in which women are not represented as executives or members of the board of directors. Larger companies, such as AT&T, have been through some highly publicized and expensive problems in affording equal employment opportunities for women, and naturally the subject has been a matter of concern to shareholders. Increasing in public awareness, as well, is the serious problem of sexual harassment, a problem that quite rightly created havoc for the Mitsubishi Corporation.

Comparable action has come from consumer groups, a subject also very much in the realm of general public awareness. In fact, a most successful attack was made on General Motors in this area, with the annual meeting used as the focal point. Public interest groups even went beyond that to approach universities and other institutions that were holders of large blocks of General Motors stock, in an attempt to pressure them to vote their stock in behalf of specific measures proposed by the groups. Among the responses made by General Motors was agreement to include on the board of directors individuals who specifically represented public interest viewpoints.

For companies subject to shareholders' discussion on these topics, the questions can be anticipated by covering the subjects in the president's message.

Running the Meeting

In setting up a room for a shareholders' meeting, seating should be arranged for the convenience of shareholders and particularly for those who wish to ask questions. If the meeting is for a company large enough or sufficiently newsworthy to warrant television coverage, wide aisles to accommodate cameras may be important. A sufficient number of microphones should be strategically placed in the aisles, or should be of the hand-held type that can be passed to a shareholder at his or her seat.

It's a good idea to decorate the meeting room with a display of the company's products and services. There are times when meetings are further enhanced by supplementing the president's message with either a film or a slide presentation. Care must be taken that the audiovisual devices are supplements, and not a substitute, for the president's report. If the room is to be darkened for presentations, care should be taken to keep the speaker lit.

In some larger companies, where meetings may be expected to take several hours, lunch is sometimes in order. For shorter meetings, refreshments should be served. This can consist of coffee and pastry, or perhaps a light snack.

Meetings held on a plant's premises can usually be enhanced by a post-meeting plant tour. This, too, should be carefully planned.

Media Coverage

Media coverage for a meeting, aside from the company's own desire for it, depends on the size of the company, the prospective newsworthiness of the information to be imparted, and the availability of a reporter to cover the meeting. Certainly, the media should be invited beforehand by letter or fax, and phone. It's pointless to believe that the media can be excluded from a meeting that might prove to be unfavorable to management. If the company is important enough, any attempt to exclude the media will not only fail, but will result in hostility and a negative or erroneous report.

The presence of any representative of the media will, of course, be known, since all shareholders and guests check in at the door. If a member of the media does come to the meeting, a representative of the company, and preferably the investor relations counsel, should spend a few minutes with the reporter before the meeting, and then sit with him or her to answer questions as they occur to the reporter during the course of the meeting. Prior to the meeting, (assuming there is something newsworthy to say) a news release should be prepared for immediate distribution, either during its course or immediately following. Complete press kits, including the release, should be on hand for any member of the press who attends. The kit should contain not only the release but, if possible, a copy of the president's speech and material on the company including a background report, an annual report, product information, and any other printed material that may be available.

Analysts and Brokers

Frequently it's advisable to invite selected important analysts, brokers, money managers, and other representatives of the financial community. The meeting affords them a good opportunity to see management in action at first hand, as well as to gather more information about the company. Regardless of the number of this group who attend, each one will be qualified in terms of expressed interest. The same kind of material prepared for the press should be made available to any representative of the financial community who attends.

Immediately following the meeting, the officers of the company should make themselves available to meet shareholders, reporters, and analysts, and to accept or place phone calls to or from media, especially major wire services. This should be done even if a directors' meeting must be kept waiting for a few minutes. Frequently some have questions that they prefer not to ask from the floor. These are usually questions that are most important to the questioner, and should be answered in the same responsive, forthright manner as were questions from the floor.

It's sometimes appropriate to use the occasion of the annual meeting to arrange for a specific interview by the press with the company's officers. This can be done beforehand, with an opportunity to sit down in a separate room or a quiet corner where the interview can proceed undisturbed. Dow Jones, Reuters, and Bloomberg readily accept telephone interviews, provided that they're called immediately following the meeting, and the information is newsworthy.

The Post-Meeting Report

The post-meeting report is an extremely useful device to multiply the value of the annual meeting for the financial community at large, and particularly those shareholders who didn't attend the meeting. It can be a simple printed version of the president's message, including an edited selection of questions and answers from the floor. In a more elaborate report, photographs of the meeting can be included. This report is facilitated by taping the entire meeting, even though the president is speaking from a prepared text. Some companies include a summary of the meeting in their quarterly report, although this is not quite as effective as issuing a special post-meeting report. The timing of the quarterly may make combining the two not feasible. The post-meeting report is then mailed to both shareholders and segments of the financial community that have expressed interest in the company.

The report should include information about required actions resulting from the voting, new directors, new auditors, stock option plans, how many shares were eligible to vote and how many did vote for each item, and so forth. If this information is not reported in print, it's easily available later on when it's needed for other investor relations purposes.

Through careful planning, then, the annual meeting can be turned from a legal chore and unwanted responsibility into a favorable investor relations device.

Letters to Shareholders

There are times during the course of the year when special events warrant a letter to shareholders. For the company that issues interim reports, these occasions should arise infrequently. A letter is particularly useful in announcing an impending merger, or a major change in business direction, or to dispel a serious rumor. Some companies use a letter to shareholders to introduce a new product by making it available as a sample or at a discount.

A welcome letter to new shareholders is an effective investor relations marketing tool. It's a standard form, signed by the president, welcoming the new shareholder and describing the company, its products, and its aims in a few short paragraphs. Unfortunately, there seems to be little tangible research to provide evidence that the letter to new shareholders contributes to a sense of loyalty. It certainly won't overcome bad performance over the long term. There is no question that it contributes to the overall goodwill that's useful in shareholder relations. As to whether the expense is warranted by the results is open to some question. As part of a large and full-scale investor relations program it's certainly useful. As an isolated activity unsupported by other activities it's questionable.

The use of the publicity reprint as part of regular or special shareholder mailings, as well as for other marketing activities, is especially effective. It focuses attention on favorable articles that the shareholder isn't likely to have seen. With a little covering note attached, it puts the article in its proper context. Since press coverage is presumably objective, a news or feature article adds a kind of editorial third-person endorsement to the company's story, which has an effect of giving added credibility. The reprint takes on the aura of the publication in which it appeared. Also included in this category are reprints of favorable research reports by brokerage houses.

One word of caution in the use of reprints of either articles or research reports. Such material is copyrighted and may not be reproduced without written permission of the publisher. This is usually easy to obtain, and there is no excuse for distributing such material without prior permission.

Many companies publish internal house organs for employees or external house organs for customers. Shareholders, too, are interested in this information, unless the internal house organ is too completely taken with purely personal information such as bowling scores or engagement announcements. If the house organ contains useful information about the company, it should certainly be considered as part of a regular mailing to shareholders.

The Web Page

Suddenly—and perhaps, thankfully—ubiquitous is the Web page. Few large corporations are now without one, and an increasing number of smaller ones have them. To varying degrees, and depending upon their design and management, they are becoming a major source of communication to shareholders. The Internet is growing exponentially, and as more shareholders become aware of them, Web sites and the Internet are becoming the major source of investor communication.

On the Internet, today, there is virtually no corporate information or news not available, and almost momentarily. Company Web pages usually include company news, shareholder news, product information, management news—the full spectrum of company information.

Today, the company without a Web site is depriving itself of a major tool for investor and shareholder communication.

Inquiries from Shareholders

There is nothing more unnerving—although legitimate—than the unexpected phone call from a shareholder to the chief executive officer of the company. The shareholder may own fifty shares, but feels entitled to information, and that it should come directly from the president. When a chief executive officer does take the call, it should be dealt with in exactly the same way he or she would handle an inquiry from a security analyst or broker. The shareholder must be dealt with politely and given the information asked for, if possible. Perhaps the best way to handle these inquiries is to be simply responsive to the question and to volunteer no more information than is asked for. Going beyond that leads to more questions.

Naturally, a measure of judgment must be exercised. A shareholder with a block of 25,000 shares will certainly want more intensive information than a generalization of the company's progress. In any event, patience, courtesy, and being solicitous wins the day. A written record of such communications should be kept to offset any questions about inside information.

Shareholders frequently write the chief executive either to complain or to inquire. These letters should be answered politely and promptly. The answers should be specifically responsive to the question and should be brief.

As part of a full-scale investor relations program it is sometimes useful to plan plant tours and visits for shareholders. Plant tours, too, come under the category of shareholder activities that are meaningless as isolated practices. They work best only as part of a total program. Certainly it's out of the question if it means disrupting operations. A plant tour is also useful in dealing with environmental groups, to demonstrate at first hand the measures the company is taking to deal effectively with any problem.

Special Situations

There are special situations that sometimes arise in shareholder relations that require specific attention. There is the situation, for example, of the company that is potentially subject to a take-over attempt because management holds too few shares of stock outstanding. There is the problem of geographic distribution of stock where too many shares are concentrated in too few geographic areas. There is the concern of the company whose stock price is being buffeted by large block trading by institutions over which the company has no control. Sometimes deleterious rumors must be dealt with, using letters to shareholders, faxes, e-mail, news releases, advertising, or media contact, as appropriate. Here, too, the Web page can be a valuable tool.

These situations must be dealt with thoughtfully, and with as much planning and foresight as possible. Most of these situations are dealt with throughout this book.

Dealing with shareholders is frequently a function of looking inward rather than outward, as one does in dealing with the financial community at large. But if experience is any measure, no CEO has ever gotten into too much trouble, under the worst of circumstances, by dealing frankly, honestly and directly with the company's own shareholders.

Effective investor relations is a marketing function that relies on management and investor relations skill. Since it's so difficult to measure results on a day-to-day basis, the program must always be viewed with perspective, and constantly monitored. Research and surveys should be a part of every active shareholder relations program.

Shareholder relations rarely works if the process is treated as an isolated jumble of irrelevant activities. It almost invariably works if it's planned, programmed, and executed by sensitive management and experienced investor relations counsel.

Chapter 12

The Investor Relations Counsel

With all the changes in the competitive arena of the capital markets during the past five years, none has been more acute than has the role of the investor relations counsel.

Until about 1975, during the early days of this craft, investor relations was performed primarily by public relations people, usually with little understanding of the financial world. The greatest skill required of them was to send out a dividend or earnings release, and perhaps to set up a meeting with security analysts. Gradually, former investment professionals were hired, and that brought into the investor relations practice many more people who knew how to read a balance sheet. The concept of investor relations as a discipline to help companies compete in the capital markets was so new, a decade ago, that many company managers had to make a broad leap to get the connection between the world of finance and the practices of communication.

Today, the investor relations professional is someone with either a strong financial background, or with a profound understanding of both corporate finance and the capital markets. No longer the purview of general public relations, today's investor relations professional tends to be a financially trained individual with well-honed communications skills. One has merely to read the excellent publications of the 3,000 member National Investor Relations Institute (NIRI), the association of investor relations professionals, and the technical nature of its content, to grasp the current level of sophistication of the investor relations practice.

Marketing and Investor Relations

Now, the increasing competition for capital and the growing sophistication of the investing public has placed more urgent emphasis on another element of investor relations practice—marketing.

As the competition in the capital markets continues to increase and become more intense, classic marketing skills must be adapted to telling (and selling) the corporate story to the financial community—to investors, shareholders, and those who advise them. And the more that marketing skills are applied to investor relations, the keener the competition becomes. And the keener the competition becomes, the more marketing skills are needed.

Moreover, the arsenal of marketing skills, when aptly applied, frequently moves the investor relations practitioner into yet another nontraditional role—advocacy. Where the earlier practitioner was merely a messenger—a conduit of information from company to investor—today's competitive demands require the investor relations professional to frequently advocate the company's position, earnestly and forcefully, in order to gain the attention and confidence of those in the marketplace responsible for buying, or recommending that others buy, the clients' stock.

And so today, and certainly in the coming decade, investor relations will be successfully practiced by those who are skilled in not only the financial aspects of the process, but in the marketing aspects as well.

Like most marketing and financial skills, the techniques and mechanics are the relatively easy part. It's the artful practice of these skills that matter. While NIRI has fostered a large body of knowledge that qualifies the practitioner, as in law or accounting, there is no codification that can quantify the artfulness of it.

Many corporate executives have a natural talent and affinity for visibility, for example. Many companies are glamorous and deserve wide attention just by virtue of their own performance. When the cure for the common cold is found no news editor will have to be harangued by a public relations practitioner to report the event in detail.

But exposure for its own sake, without focus, purpose, support, and to serve clearly defined corporate goals, can never be more than partially effective. The truly effective investor relations program is one that is well-rounded, and includes at least several of the elements described in this book. Obviously it requires a measure of time and attention, as well as a broad spectrum of skill and experience. The question is, who is to do it?

Sources of Investor Relations Expertise

Setting aside for the moment those activities and aspects of a company's operations that attract attention by virtue of their own interest or excellence, a well-rounded program must be designed, developed, and performed. There are five possible sources of investor relations expertise and performance capability:

- The company's investment banker
- The internal investor relations executive
- The external investor relations counsel
- Stock promoters
- Shareholders, investors, and friends of management

Excluded from this discussion are those ancillary services that are sometimes called upon by virtue of their ability in one or another facets of communications, such as the nonfinancial public relations firm, or the advertising agency. Unless there's a specifically experienced and qualified person in either of these structures, neither type of firm is in any way qualified to function effectively in investor relations. Investor relations is not, after all, merely public relations directed to the financial community. It's a separate and distinct practice, and is as different from general public relations as it is from advertising. The two are not interchangeable.

The Investment Banker as Investor Relations Consultant

The company's investment banking firm would, on the face of it, seem to be a logical candidate to conduct an investor relations program, by virtue of its involvement with both the company and the financial community. Unfortunately, this rarely turns out to be true for several reasons:

- The investment banker, through his or her own research and brokerage structure, is sometimes equipped to deal with only one dimension of the investor relations program—limited Street contact. Rarely does an investment banking or brokerage firm have the capability to deal professionally with the financial press, or to prepare corporate shareholder literature, nor does it have the structure to direct an effective marketing-oriented investor relations program.

• No investment banking or brokerage firm is financially structured to supply a full-scale investor relations service, either mechanically or economically. Most investment banking firms are paid a fee earned by performing specific investment banking services, such as underwriting, or financial structuring. To allocate time and personnel to such a nonremunerative activity as investor relations, even though it helps support their clients' stock, is uneconomical, and they are not likely to give it their greatest attention, nor have their more experienced people involved.

• It's unfortunate but true that the perspective of most brokerage houses and investment bankers is limited to the scope of their own activity. Their view of overall market conditions tends to be pervaded by conditions at the moment, which invariably means undue optimism in an up market and undue pessimism in a down market. There is all too frequently lacking the perspective necessary to develop the kind of strategy, in its totality, described in previous chapters.

• The pursuit of an investor relations program requires an up-to-the-minute understanding of changes in both attitude and personnel throughout the entire financial community. Investment banking firms are not geared to do this, as much as they may be in touch with current conditions in their own world.

• The scope of the investment banker's contacts in the financial community is usually limited to his or her own circle of friends and business relationships. In some cases, this may be adequate to the needs of a program. In most cases it is not.

• There is a great potential for conflicts of interest, by advocating where they should be objective.

• Investment bankers simply don't understand the marketing function of investor relations. They're not in that business.

On the other hand, the good investment banker or broker does have a service to perform in behalf of his or her client, and can contribute in some measure to an effective total investor relations program.

The Investment Banker's Responsibility

The investment banker certainly has a responsibility to the client to support the after-market for a new issue, and indeed, any issue the banker has been responsible for underwriting. This includes, when appropriate, issuing a research report (qualified by the fact that the investment banker is the underwriter), sponsoring and making a market in the stock, and introducing the company to those houses and institutions he or she knows. Nor should any investor relations program, whether done internally or externally, be performed without the complete cooperation and participation of the investment banker, since the banker is not only a beneficiary of the underwriting, but is also a valuable source of information about both the company and the stock market.

Internal Investor Relations Capability

The size of a company, the nature of the program itself, and the budget available for the program, may dictate the feasibility of using internal counsel. The staff professional's skills and capabilities may be more than sufficient to perform a program for a company, either done or supported by an outside investor relations firm.

If the responsibility is assigned to a qualified person, there is a singular advantage in that the internal counsel knows the company, its management, and its activities, operations, objectives, and plans. The internal professional is on the scene, and has immediate access and a context for understanding meaning and, if necessary, nuance. If properly qualified, the internal professional can also function as a spokesperson for the company in ways that even the best qualified external counsel rarely can.

When there is both external and internal counsel, the internal person serves as a liaison, as coordinator, and as educator. In most cases, the internal person performs most aspects of the program, usually aided by a staff, as effectively as does the external counsel. Sometimes, the staff counsel is highly qualified in one or several—but not all—functions of investor relations. That individual is perhaps a former financial writer whose efforts in dealing with the financial press or in writing annual reports cannot be excelled, or perhaps a former analyst who superbly understands the needs of analysts and brokers, or a former executive of an investor relations firm, in which case the knowledge of the total investor relations function is available. An outside counsel may be retained to supplement efforts in those areas in which the internal practitioner's experience is not as strong as in others, or to supply additional manpower, or to supply the broader perspective and expertise that should be expected of the external counsel.

Today, most staff investor relations executives are former analysts, or financial or legal executives. This can be work. Indeed, some of the best work now being done in the field is being done by internal staff professionals.

To establish an effective internal capability, there are only two hard and fast rules. The first is that the person designated or hired be properly qualified. A public relations person with no financial background, or an advertising manager with a smattering of knowledge about public relations, is in no sense qualified to function effectively in investor relations for any company of consequence. A financial executive with no communications training or experience, or knowledge of Wall Street is also not qualified.

Second, it's next to useless to retain an internal investor relations counsel who doesn't have the ear, the respect, and direct access to the chief executive officer or chief financial officer. Without this, investor relations executive, no matter how well qualified, is merely a clerk. If there is no respect within the company for the investor relations professional's value and capabilities, the professional will quickly cause the company to lose respect in the financial community and with the financial media. The financial world and media are very quick to discern the degree of authority a spokesperson has. To attempt to deal with the financial community with even the most highly qualified internal investor relations executive who doesn't have access to the inner councils of management is foolhardy and wasteful.

External Investor Relations Counsel

The properly qualified investor relations counsel has several distinct advantages in serving the company competing in the capital markets. The external counsel is:

- A specialist. The professional's total concentration and effort are in the practice of investor relations.
- With a firm that's structured to deal with all aspects of an investor relations program. The firm is equipped for quick dissemination of releases, as well as for direct personal contact with the financial community, both mechanically and electronically. It's geared to maintain up-to-the-minute mailing lists and lists of appropriate personnel in both the financial community and the financial press, which change constantly. Some firms have the capability and structure for financial community research, investor surveys, and proxy solicitation.

- With a firm that's up-to-the-minute on the Internet, e-mail, the Web, and all other contemporary electronic media. In today's fast moving financial world, instant access and instant dissemination are crucial.
- In constant liaison with the financial community and the financial media, which should make the counsel aware of shifts in attitudes and personnel, and which allows the professional to supply an extraordinarily valuable perspective of changing needs and changing attitudes in the media.
- Able to bring to each investor relations program the breadth of experience in serving many companies and industries with a wide variety of problems, and a broad experience in solutions.
- Objective. Any investor relations counsel must serve two roles—objectivity and advocacy. One is useless without the other. Advocacy that's not based on objectivity is weak, frequently irrelevant, and often borders dangerously close to creating problems of credibility.
- A marketing expert. Today, investor relations is as much a marketing function as a financial one. The skills, talent and artistry of marketing are necessary to help companies compete successfully in the capital markets.
- A reliable source of broad economic and financial information not directly related to investor relations, such as shifting sources of capital, as a result of ongoing relations with the financial community. In fact, for the company seeking new investment banking relationships, the experienced and qualified investor relations consultant is an excellent source of information about the capabilities of a wide variety of investment bankers.

Economically feasible. Whereas there are hidden overhead factors to be added to the cost of an internal counsel, the expense of an external counsel can be budgeted. The external counsel is accountable for fees and expenses. This is particularly pertinent for those consultants whose fee is based on an hourly rate, where each month's bill itemizes the amount of time spent by each executive in each of the several categories in which he is functioning for the company.

- Responsible and knowledgeable in the field of SEC and other regulation as it pertains to investor relations and Rules of Disclosure. While the investor relations professional may be neither an attorney nor an accountant, qualifications must include knowledge of all significant and relevant SEC and exchange rules that pertain to an investor relations program.
- Head of a staff that includes the wide variety of skills—financial media relations, Street contact, writing, design, research, and so on—necessary for a well-rounded program.

While this would seem to weigh the argument very heavily in favor of using external investor relations counsel, the judgment is made, in many respects, no differently than is the decision to retain house legal counsel or internal auditing staff. The use of one doesn't necessarily preclude the other, and frequently they supplement one another. At the same time, it must be recognized that the nature of a particular company or of a particular investor relations problem contains factors that make the internal staff sufficiently effective to defer consideration of external counsel. On the other hand, the size of a company or the nature of a specific investor relations consideration may make the external counsel more economically feasible.

Qualifications of an Investor Relations Practitioner

In selecting either an internal or external investor relations consultant, recognize that, unlike law or accounting, there are no certifiable qualifications that define professionalism. The people in the industry are drawn from no single source that has prepared them educationally for the total investor relations counsel's role. Unlike the public relations person, however, the investor relations counsel can't subsist on merely an inventive mind, an outgoing personality, and the ability to express an idea on paper. The professional must be well grounded in financial skills, as well as communications skills, and must have experience-based knowledge of the financial world.

Qualifications for Internal Investor Relations Officer

Many investor relations professionals are themselves former investment professionals. While this is basically good, there is a peculiar problem in that a former investment professional isn't automatically qualified for investor relations. Really good security analysts can earn considerably more money practicing that craft than they can in most investor relations positions. These are the economics of both industries. An analyst who fails in his or her career as an analyst does not automatically become a good investor relations counsel. Those investment professionals who have made the successful transition to investor relations are the ones who have done so because they feel that investor relations offers them a broader scope for their total personal needs, talents and desires than does the investment world. Successful professionals are the ones who bring to investor relations a range of skills and interests that supplement their financial background. On the other hand, many excellent investment professionals have joined the ranks of investor relations successfully because they've learned the craft, to supplement their existing skills.

The qualifications for an investor relations counsel or officer, or the qualifications that should be inherent in the staff of an investor relations firm, are at least the following:

- A sound financial background. This is primary and essential. The investor relations professional should understand corporate finance, accounting, the investment banking function, and corporate structure. While not necessarily able to perform any of these tasks professionally, he or she must be able to converse easily, authoritatively, and with understanding with the chief executive officer, the vice-president of finance, the attorney, and the accountant.
- There must be an intimate knowledge of the workings of the capital markets. Not just Wall Street and the stock market, although that may be the primary area of activity, but with all the capital markets, including—and this becomes increasingly important—the foreign capital markets. The professional must understand both the mechanics and the élan of the markets in all their subtleties.
- The professional must be experienced in dealing with the entire cast of characters of Wall Street, from the registered representative to the security analyst to the money manager and portfolio manager to the trader to the investment banker.
- The investor relations professional must have both communications and marketing skills, as well as a strong sense of advocacy.
- The investor relations professional should be marketing-oriented. He or she should understand the tools and processes of marketing, and be able to apply them, within the context of an investor relations program, to meet the company's investor relations goals.
- He or she should have the breadth of experience of dealing with a great many companies, and facing a great many problems under all kinds of market conditions. It takes no great skill to function successfully for a growing and successful company in vogue in a raging bull market. The question is whether that person can function just as effectively for that company in a bear market.
- There should be an understanding of the full scope of corporate activity, including management, production, research and development, marketing and distribution, and finance.

- The investor relations professional should have a thorough experience and knowledge of the financial media, both in its mechanics and ever-changing and electronic structures, and personnel.
- The professional should be a capable and facile writer of releases, annual and interim reports, and speeches. And this means not merely the ability to repeat the clichés of what has been done before, but to approach each problem with a fresh viewpoint. The professional should, in this context, be an effective communicator.
- The investor relations professional must be confident, personally successful, and have the courage to take strong positions in telling the company story.
- An investor relations firm should have the mechanical structure and the manpower to deal effectively with all facets of the investor relations program. This includes the equipment to disseminate information at appropriate speed and with professional quality to the entire financial community and financial press. Manpower should be sufficient to allocate an appropriate amount of time to each client to effectively fulfill a program. An account executive with sole responsibility for twelve clients cannot possibly serve any one of those clients effectively.
- The professional should be familiar with the financial community nationally as well as locally in most major financial centers of the United States. This means being knowledgeable about the various financial centers, and physically capable of dealing effectively with each of them.
- An investor relations firm's manager should be a sound businessperson running a sound business. While the individual practitioner is sometimes useful for his experience and wisdom, to serve solely as a consultant he or she should still function in as businesslike a way as does the largest investor relations firm.
- The investor relations firm's people who work on any account should each be intelligent, knowledgeable, and personable. The effective investor relations counsel, as an advocate, should be capable of speaking for the company and its executives in clearly defined circumstances. Rarely does any segment of the financial community write off an inept investor relations counsel and then accept as wise and capable the management he represents. The investor relations counsel is also exactly that, a counsel. He or she may have all the skills, mechanical capabilities, and experience in the world, but would still be useless to a company if his or her judgment cannot be respected and utilized with confidence.
- While there are several general-purpose public relations firms with excellent investor relations staffs, there is a danger in that the smaller investor

relations staff of a general firm doesn't have full and autonomous capability or support. The situation would be comparable to using an auditor who is on the staff of a firm of attorneys. The chances are that his or her role is secondary to the company's primary business, leaving the auditor without facility and sometimes without portfolio. For the company seriously competing in the capital markets, investor relations is primary—not an auxiliary. And so there is greater likelihood of finding more effectiveness in a specialized rather than a generalized firm. Moreover, as has been noted before, investor relations is not public relations to the financial community. It is a highly specialized financial function.

Selecting a Firm

Selecting an investor relations firm from among the many that now specialize is in a sense no different from selecting an auditor or an attorney. Qualifications must be clearly established. Reputation is important. A Dun & Bradstreet rating is essential.

In choosing a firm, a preliminary interview should demonstrate not only qualifications, but also an understanding of the description of the company, its problems, and its opportunities. There is probably no better rule for judging a prospective investor relations counsel than to interview the individual as if he or she were being hired as an executive vice-president. Assuming the proper qualifications, you should be as personally impressed with the firm's representative as you would expect yourself to be with any candidate for a high managerial position. That is, after all, a function the investor relations professional serves.

References should be checked very carefully. These should include a broad spectrum drawn from clients, the financial press, and the financial community itself. A great deal of trust is placed in an investor relations counsel, and the responsibility in serving the company is great. No chief executive officer should retain any investor relations counsel with whom he or she is not totally impressed and upon whose judgment he feels he cannot rely.

Judging the Program

The results of an advertising campaign can be judged by sales. The results of a public relations campaign can be judged by favorable clippings, although ultimately the larger result is usually also sales, and certainly a more favorable product or service environment. An investor relations program, although it should ultimately result in achieving specific and clearly defined objectives, such as an increase in shareholder value, the price/earnings ratio or price/cash flow ratio, or volume or higher turnover, is judged in terms of continuous effectiveness.

The nature of the capital markets, and particularly the stock market, is such that there are rarely immediate reflected results in stock price, from even the most effective investor relations program. The program should, however, ultimately bring a stock's price to a market valuation that's at least appropriate to the stock's actual value (in terms of the company behind it). A company undervalued by the market should gain in share price and p/e ratio from an effective investor relations program sooner rather than later—six months rather than two years.

But there are other values in investor relations as well. An investor relations program will be effective in fulfilling its objectives if it successfully communicates your story to a broad and appropriate financial community. Over a period of time, an infinitely larger segment of the financial community should know, know about, and understand your company in all its aspects. There should be a clear and discernible interest in your company as a result of the investor relations program. This is sometimes measurable by surveys, but only if two surveys taken over a period of time are compared. There should be perceptively shareholder loyalty, as seen in the stock's buying and selling patterns.

There should be a marked increase in the company's following on the Street. More brokers, analysts and other investment professionals should be following the stock, and recommending it to their clients.

Business press coverage should increase, particularly in the financial press. If you are eligible, you should have regular Dow Jonesers and other interviews.

The ultimate results of such an interest can be, over the long run, improved market values, active sponsorship of your stock, an increased number of market makers (for an over-the-counter company), discernibly greater liquidity, and increased trading volume. However, a direct one-to-one relationship between any activity or group of activities in an investor relations program and any result is neither automatic nor timely—it's precious. The result of the investor relations effort should be sustaining, and not merely achieved by a short term promotional effort that's based on unrealistic factors.

This is one reason why, in order to be effective, a financial relations program must be assiduously pursued over a reasonable period of time before any judgment is made about its performance.

Ultimately, the best judgment of the investor relations program is the judgment of management that the various facets of the program are being intelligently and actively performed, and that the receptiveness of the financial community is evident in any of several manifestations.

There must also be consistency. Since the market, the economy, and the company are all in a constant state of flux, and since the competition for capital is exceptionally intense, the cumulative effects of a program stopped at midpoint are very quickly lost. There is very little residual value. In order to be effective, the once discontinued program must start up again, sometimes virtually from scratch.

What an investor relations program *can't* do—at least for any sustained time—is get a stock price higher than the stock is substantially worth. This can be accomplished only by the kind of market manipulation that's probably not legal. Be cautious of any practitioner who promises that kind of instant result. Promoters seem to proliferate.

In the final analysis, investor relations is a function of people—their intelligence, their skills, their eagerness, and their dedication. The final judgment of the success of an investor relations program is a judgment of these elements and their application.

Chapter 13

Competing for Capital

In the middle of a vortex, it's somewhat difficult to get one's perspective, much less a profound sense of stability.

So it is with an economic environment that not only develops and moves with great rapidity, but that seems to defy historical configurations or performance. And that's the economic environment in which we find ourselves in the last few years of the 20th century. It is this unusual economic environment in which companies must raise capital, and in doing so, pursue productive relationships with investors and those who advise them. Simply put, it's investor relations in a not entirely familiar context. But it's a context which must, somehow, be fathomed, simply because the investor relations process is more profoundly needed than ever.

We've had economic anomalies before. Remember stagflation a decade or so ago? Despite the textbook fiat that economic stagnation and inflation at the same time was not possible, we had exactly that.

We are certainly, at this time, in a salutary economic environment. Allen Sinai, chief global economist for Primark Decision Economics, sums it up. "Everything is working right," he says. "We've got low inflation, low interest rates, good business profits, a strong competitive position internationally, no systemic imbalances, and sound fiscal and monetary policies." Bruce Steinberg, a Merrill Lynch economist, says, "Never, never, never has inflation been so low at such an advanced stage of a business cycle."

The popular and astute economic writer, Jane Bryant Quinn, adds,

"Business investment has been on the rise since the middle 1980s. A high percentage of people are working today. Creeping improvements in productivity have helped hold inflation down, even though wages are edging up. Personal savings rates are rising toward 6 percent, as baby boomers now focus on retirement, and stocks are their investment of choice. Foreign money is flooding into the American market. Internationally, the United States is the place to invest."

And on February 13, 1997, the Dow hit 7,000—only four months after it hit 6,000—and then quickly headed to 8,000.

In the midst of all this startlingly good news, economic analysts, especially the Wall Street prophets, can think only in cycles. "The downturn will come," they say. "Stock prices are too high." Never mind that they've been saying it for three years now, and it hasn't happened. Never mind asking the tough questions about what's different about this economy, and what it may mean. What they really seem to be saying is, "This is how it was in my grandfather's day, and this is how it will be in my children's' day."

With the growth of international markets, the fall of communism as a viable form of economy and government, and technology, the texture of the economic world changes profoundly. Technology, for example, has changed the nature of work, and following the dislocations caused by replacing people with machines, the emerging work force is both service oriented and knowledge oriented. We are in the midst of a retraining revolution. Under such rubrics as *downsizing* and *reengineering the corporation,* the relationship between the worker and management has begun to change more drastically than it did under the labor movement of the first half of the twentieth century. Skilled workers, working in new companies in new industries with new skills, are no longer classic employees—they are virtually contractors, In some parts of the country, the outsourced "consultant"—the former employee rehired as an independent (without the perks of pension funds and medical insurance and withheld taxes)—is becoming an integral part of the business culture. It's causing the Internal Revenue Service paroxysms of anxiety. This is not a classic environment, nor even a linear extension of the past. This is not, obviously, your grandfather's, or even your father's, day.

The trouble with looking at the future, on such a short term foundation, is that we can only suspect the meaning of the situation. The naysayers may well be right. But they would be right in the face of some interesting considerations.

For example, we have had such economic strength before, particularly as we recovered from World War II, and that didn't sustain. But we didn't have the consumer purchasing power we have now, which leads to greater production, which leads to more employment, and on and on.

We didn't have the popular investment base we have now, with so large a segment of the population invested in the market, both as individuals and through institutions. When Charlie Merrill started his company, following World War I and in the 1920s, and pioneered in selling stock to a middle class market, it was virtually blasphemous in old line, white shoe Wall Street. Never mind that he built Merrill Lynch on that foundation. Investing was for the upper economic classes. You know—the ones that lost everything in 1929. Now we have blue collar workers investing in the stock market. And not always through such devices as 401(k)s and mutual funds. Just look at the growth of the investor media. Not just *The Wall Street Journal* as a national newspaper. The big city dailies. The *Investor's News*. CNN and CNBC. Bloomberg. On-line stock quotes and business news. Somebody is reading and listening and supporting all of that.

If that isn't a new investing community, then what is.

And the record breaking number of initial public offerings. And the rise, almost overnight, of a major industry—computers—that went from 0 to 1000 miles an hour in merely a moment, employing thousands of people.

What about those institutions? Mutual funds—more than 6,000 of them now. Pension funds. Derivative funds. Massive repositories of investment capital, never before seen in the history of any country, fueling the economy. Record flows of foreign capital, with the United States now the investment nation of choice. Absolutely a new phenomenon.

There is a new regulatory environment that seems to be unshackled from the one we've lived in since the 1930s, when the nation was victim to investment excess that fed the flames of depression. Few are alive today to remember those days, and so the regulators allow the erosion of those once necessary protective measures. Glass Steagall, which kept the banks out of investment, is now more quaint than valid, as business demands more sources of investment, and the public demands more investment opportunity. With the one-stop financial shopping center, pioneered by Merrill Lynch in 1970 and now ingrained in our economic culture, the lines blur between financial service organizations. Banks are brokers and brokers are banks and insurance salesmen are financial planners and there's an investment station on every corner. The classic commercial bank may become exactly that—classic and obsolete.

Is this the good old economic world—the one that gave us booms and busts and depressions and stock market crashes?

Obviously not. Where it's going nobody knows yet, but it's going where nobody's been before.

This is the world, then, in which investor relations must function. This is the new environment for investor relations practice, and the new pace at which it must function.

Fortunately, there are new tools to facilitate the function. Computers not only calculate faster, but communicate faster. Communication has gone from the telegraph of the 1930s to the e-mail and fax and on-line transmission of the 1990s and the twenty-first century. There is more about most companies on the Web pages of those companies than appeared in all publicly distributed information about a company two decades ago. And it's all accessible to more people, and faster than ever before. The on-line and CD-ROM annual report are two examples of information tools with more power than has ever existed before—power that leaves the old printed report in the dust. Not only for the abundance of the information, and the timeliness, but the sheer excitement of the medium itself.

There's a curious element to this rapid and fulsome information flow. Information about a company, it seems, alters that company, even as the information is dispersed. Information breeds expectation, and expectation brings fulfillment. The more that's known the more that's wanted to be known.

Thus, the competition for capital heats up. There may be more capital available, but there are more companies chasing after it. An economy that's growing as is this economy is voracious in its need for fuel, and capital is nothing to a company if not fuel. The chase, too, is not just for capital now, but for capital at a *cost*—and that's a role for investor relations. Defining differentiation. And reducing the cost of capital.

The history of investor relations as a technique for competing for capital is short, but kinetic. It started as a minor public relations function, in which the same public relations person who sent out your product press release sent out your dividend or earnings release. Then, as companies became aware of the competitive nature of the capital markets, investor relations campaigns began to take on more substance, and investor relations began to build a body of techniques all its own.

It took very little time for company management to realize that the more successful investor relations programs were those that had a strong base of financial sophistication, as well as communication skills. The emphasis of investor relations practice shifted, then, from public relations to a financial function. Investor relations practitioners began to be drawn from financial, rather than public relations, ranks.

In the 1980s, as the world economy grew and the competition for capital heated up, the element of marketing entered the picture. Marketing techniques began to be applied to financial and communications techniques, to shape investor relations as a new and singular profession. Today, the need for sophisticated marketing skills is on a par with the need for financial skills. The competition for capital is as keen in communications and persuasion as it is in Street smarts. It will be even tougher to compete in the twenty-first century.

As investor relations once split off from public relations, we now find the several specialties in investor relations splitting off, with some firms specializing in only one aspect of the investor relations practice.

While most companies are more than adequately served by a single investor relations officer or firm, the magnitude of the capital markets, and the companies competing in those markets, warrants specialization.

For example, if the basic tenet of marketing begins with research, it's understandable that one of the more important aspects of investor relations becomes developing techniques for better understanding the needs of the target audience—the investor, the potential investor, and those who advise them. It's understandable, as well, that we should use research to measure the results of investor relations activities. We are seeing now, appropriately, the growth of the sophisticated investor relations research function as a specialty.

The technology now involved in both analysis and communication is yet another specialty, and becomes more so as the body of knowledge increases, and the demand for these services becomes more pressing. We go into the twenty-first century with the computer technician as high priest.

Multimedia techniques now open new vistas in presentation to shareholders and analysts. Using computers and video and audio techniques, as well as teleconferencing, more people see more exciting information than ever before. Today's due diligence meeting can be almost as exciting, visually, as a Disney movie.

The distinctive nature of proxy solicitation, and the sheer weight of labor involved in it, have long warranted the proxy solicitation firm as a single entity. But the increasing complexity of the marketplace has made those firms even more viable. Gearing up for a proxy solicitation, particularly on a contested issue, requires many more hands, machinery, computers and experts than are likely to be found in the average investor relations company or department. And so the proxy firm thrives.

Annual reports are another case in point. Normally the province of the investor relations firm or department, firms that specialize in annual reports have evolved that, for the most part, do a superb job. They understand the specific requirements of an annual report, and they have the experience and capability to fulfill those requirements. The increasing use of the multimedia annual report requires another new breed of specialists. There is some weakness when the specialist is a designer rather than an investor relations expert, and the report is driven not by the needs of the capital markets but by design considerations. But the annual report is too important a document to be done casually, and so the specialist thrives.

Mailing list management is another growing specialty, refined and enhanced by computers and electronics. Mailing list management is an arcane craft, frequently equated to witchcraft. Those with a turn of mind to do it have built it into an art form, as well as a specialty. Inherent in this is not only the output—using the mailing list house to move material to investors and shareholders—but the research aspect as well. All those names, intelligently and professionally analyzed, tell a story that makes marketing both possible and sophisticated.

There are other aspects of specialization that are springing up. Some firms are specializing in just the public relations and communications aspects of investor relations, or dealing with just press relations. Others are specializing by industry, such as computers or hi-tech, on the basis of understanding and being able to communicate the unique aspects of a particular industry to those who specialize in analyzing or investing in that industry.

The Street Work Specialist

Perhaps the most interesting kind of specialized firm that continues to evolve is the specialist in Street contact— dealing directly with brokers, analysts and others. While this area is not the first or most common to emerge in investor relations, it's the most interesting, because it offers an enhanced channel for investor relations practice.

As you saw in Chapter 5, one form of dealing with the financial community is to work directly with brokers and other investment professionals to place large blocks of stock with them to resell to their customers. Some of these customers may be individuals, and others may be small institutions. It requires a keen understanding of how Wall Street works and of the company behind the stock, as well as a large measure of selling skill. This is particularly useful in representing a smaller company, usually in the over-the-counter market, with a smaller float and a stock price of under $10 a share. While every good investor relations practitioner representing larger companies has a network of such contacts, or knows how to approach institutions and industry analysts on behalf of larger companies, few investor relations professionals are equipped to reach major long-term investors on behalf of smaller companies. The approach for smaller companies requires the ability to reach many brokers quickly and efficiently.

Which is why investor relations firms specializing in broker networks that place stock are springing up. They don't do press relations, or analyst meetings, or corporate communications, or shareholder relations—just Street work.

These firms can, in proper context, be useful. But there's also a double danger, first in assuming that a segment of an investor relations program is a whole program that will achieve sustaining goals, and second in the concentration and pressure to sell stock in the short term that can, in the long run, hurt the company. So far, many of these firms, still young, seem not to have learned to resist the pressure to push stock regardless of the company behind it, or the relationship between company maturity and stock price and total market value.

The Future of Investor Relations

There's a vast difference between flying a small single engine airplane and flying a jet fighter plane. It's not just the speed, it's the kind of reflexes needed to use the speed in support of the flying effort. It's the new dimension and facility of speed, and the ability to function in many more axes, with more facility.

This difference is what the twenty-first century brings to investor relations, as well as to much of the world. New dimensions in relating to vast new pools of capital, in ways that never were possible before. New ways to understand the needs and desires of the investor, be it the individual shareholder with 100 shares or the vast money manager controlling billions of dollars in assets.

The difference, also, is in the rapidity with which information flows, and how it changes the nature of the information itself. If everybody knows everything about a stock at the same time, how does the investor act on it?

Or more to the point, what is the role of the investor relations professional in finding a basis to differentiate information in ways that persuade the investor that a dollar invested in company A is going to do better than a dollar invested in company B?

The answer lies, of course, in marketing skills—the skills of understanding needs and desires, and the skills of communicating the ability to meet those needs and desires.

Certainly, investor relations specialists are going to have to be as conversant with marketing skills as they are with financial and economic skills. And in this new world, the professional will also have to be even more Street wise than ever before.

In the need for greater sophistication of a practice such as investor relations, and in competing in the capital markets, it's inevitable that growing complexity and magnitude should breed firms specializing in one aspect or another of the practice. An industry shapes itself to meet the needs of the market it serves, and if that market changes, then so will the industry serving it change. And as we've seen historically, the capital markets have changed substantially in the last decade, but no one can predict the ways in which the capital markets will change in the next century.

But there should be cautious consideration of the difference between focus and specialization. It's one thing to focus an investor relations program on one aspect or another of the program—meetings, mailings, shareholder relations, etc. As the demands of the program change, so then should the program. Specialization, on the other hand, too often freezes the program in that specialty. There are times when a broker network is a poor answer to the needs of a company competing in the capital markets; there are times when it's the best place to focus. To substitute specialization for focus can sometimes make for a poor program. To focus on the narrow area of techniques makes it too easy to lose the larger perspective—and the larger perspective is really the dynamic.

If there is one major difference in investor relations between then and now—the difference that really matters—it's that investor relations can no longer deal with just the day-by-day functions of the investor relations program. What matters now is the dynamic—the motion of the environment. The static days are gone. Reality now resides not in static solution, but in the dynamic flow. It's the difference between flying the small propeller plane and the giant jet aircraft.

It's now a given that there are dynamic, swirling changes in the capital markets, both domestically and internationally. But the very nature of competing successfully is to function from the strength of the change, and not the static; to lead the future wherever possible, and to bend with change as it occurs if it's not. To do anything mindlessly in today's world because that's the way it was done yesterday is to deprive oneself of opportunity.

There will undoubtedly be many other ways in which investor relations practice will change, in both the near and far term, but to predict beyond evidence is foolhardy. The evidence of change is always with us, as is sometimes the nature of change. But the ultimate essence of the future eludes us, as it should. Besides, if somebody told you tomorrow's stock market closing prices, would you believe it?

Competing in the new capital markets of the twenty-first century is not only going to be different, and in ways we can't yet know, but it's clearly going to be more arduous and more demanding.

The chances are that it's also going to be more profitable for everybody involved—and more exciting.

Appendix A

Costs and Budgets

In a well-run investor relations program, there is no question that the greater and more extensive the effort, the greater the effectiveness. Nevertheless, the cost of an investor relations program is not a measure of its potential success. Programs that cost a great deal may be no more effective than programs that are moderately priced. The measure is the program—not the cost. Virtually every cost factor may be foreseen. And at least, a program should be budgetable.

Essentially, the fee and expense elements of an investor relations program are the following:

- Consulting fees
- Shareholder and Street research
- Design and printing
- Mailing
- Broadcast fax
- Investor meetings
- Teleconferencing
- Web site
- Fax on demand
- Travel costs to meetings, major press interviews, and so forth
- Out-of-pocket and miscellaneous expenses, including phones, teletype, Dow Jones and Reuters, entertainment, and so on
- Contingencies

Fees

For companies using outside consultants, the fee structure is determined at the outset.

Fee structures vary from one consulting firm to another, although basically there are only two types used by most consultants—straight fee and hourly rate. Fees for an effective full program are usually in the range of $60,000 to $96,000 a year for smaller consultants, and $72,000 to $150,000 for larger consultants. This is predicated on the assumption, of course, that the larger firm offers more extensive programs and services—which is indeed an assumption. Talent, which is what you're really buying, doesn't necessarily reside solely in the larger, higher-priced firm, although many large firms have some extraordinarily good people. But then, so do many of the smaller firms. Although some programs can exceed these amounts, it's unlikely that an effective and well-rounded program can be performed professionally for less than $60,000. However, there are good consultants who might give you appropriate segments of a total program, which may well serve your needs, for $30,000 to $54,000 annually.

The straight fee basis is usually a simple fixed amount, paid monthly. This has the advantage of simpler budgeting.

The hourly rate functions much the same as with accountants and attorneys. Usually a basic minimum fee is agreed upon, with hours charged against that fee, also as agreed upon. The hourly basis functions best if there is a clear understanding beforehand of the hourly rate of each person who is to work on the account. Each month, the client is billed on a printout which indicates each person who worked on the account, that person's hourly rate, and the time he or she put in. Each person's time is broken down in each of one to two dozen major categories by the quarter hour. This allows the client the added advantage of seeing how the time was spent in each of the categories. Many firms also use the hourly rate to advantage by budgeting allotted time for specific tasks to each executive and each of several offices. The interoffice allocation makes it possible for the firm to function more effectively on a national basis by virtue of clearcut, time-budgeted assignments from office to office. It also helps the client to know what he is getting for his money.

There are investor relations consultants who are willing to accept warrants or stock as payment, but they are out of the mainstream, and should be considered cautiously.

Most firms bill a month in advance. Those firms that use the hourly rate usually bill about half the agreed-upon minimum in advance. Because it generally takes at least six months to measure the effects of a program, most contracts are for that period, although some of the better firms can be flexible.

Considering the complexities of evaluating the effectiveness of a program, any fee structure, whether it be a monthly flat fee or the hourly rate, depends for its success on some kind of detailed annual plan and reporting system. Since much of the investor relations effort is done in the consultant's rather than the company's offices, only a sound plan and reporting system allows the client to know that the fee is actually going to effective effort.

Research

While research on both shareholder lists and professional investors is an inherent part of any sound program, and is usually included in the fee, there are times when more extensive research is warranted. Outside research firms will analyze lists, do research on shareholder attitudes, and so forth. These firms charge separate fees, which must be negotiated.

Design and Printing Costs

Printing, in investor relations, is primarily for annual and interim reports, corporate profiles, reprints of speeches or articles, brochures, and postmeeting reports.

The design of an annual report, the most expensive printing item in an investor relations budget, ranges from $200 a page to a total of $30,000 or more for a more extensive report. Layout, typography, galley proofs, and camera ready mechanicals may add another $5,000 to $25,000. Photography and other expenses attendant to the report, such as travel and research, are extra. Photographers generally charge $300 to $2,500 a day for their services, plus expenses. The cost of printing the report depends, of course, on its size, the number of copies, the quality of paper, and so on. It's a good idea to get three or more bids from printers, selecting only those whose quality of work has been judged on the basis of samples. Printing costs vary from one locale to another, and price is not necessarily a key to quality. Printing costs in New York, for example, are likely to be higher than in Cincinnati, despite the fact that Cincinnati is one of several major cities with excellent printers. It can cost $2 to $4 per copy for printing a small-quantity report and $1 to $3 per copy on reports in larger quantities.

An element of cost enters into selecting the designer for a company located in a different city than its consultant. If there is sound reason for a New York consultant to use a New York designer, even if the report is to be printed elsewhere, then expenses for the consultant to deal with the designer are lower. Sometimes, however, a company will find it more convenient to use a local designer, in which case the consultant will have to visit with him at least once or twice to supervise the production of the report. Experience in multi-city operations can do wonders to rationalize costs.

Design costs for interim reports and other material are usually considerably lower, not only because of the size, but because of the simplicity of the format. Interim reports sometimes follow the same format from one to the other, at least during the course of any one year, which can reduce design costs. Speeches and similar printed matter, while usually just straight text, still require a measure of design and production expense, since they must be attractive in their appearance no matter how simple the makeup. Corporate profiles generally follow a predetermined format with very little design factor involved, although, in the face of competition for attention, this is changing rapidly. While they are usually offset from typed copy, there's frequently a measure of professional paste-up to be done, usually at negligible cost. Reprints are usually photo offset from paste-ups of the original copy. Here, too, while the paste-up cost is negligible, it's still a factor. Offset printing costs vary, but are easily determined. Brochures that may occasionally be part of an investor relations program are designed and produced in essentially the same way, and at essentially the same cost, as annual reports.

Mailing

The elements to be calculated in mailings to shareholders and the financial community include:

- Mailing lists
- Envelopes
- Paper
- Postage
- Labor for sorting, sealing, collating, stapling, inserting, stamping and post office delivery
- Printing
- Return postage paid postcards, fax-back sheets

Mailing lists, it has been noted, are very difficult to maintain, and therefore, consume a measure of time—whether it be internal or external. In mailings to the ever-mobile financial community, what often may seem to be an undue amount of time and attention go into a constant updating, checking, and changing mailing lists, including the return postcard technique.

When an outside mailing house is used, these costs are incorporated into the basic price of mailing, since it is assumed that the mailing house keeps its lists updated for all its clients. Mailing lists today are maintained on computer, and each computer listing changed is an expense. It's less of an expense, however, than the very high cost of mailing material to the wrong address.

The cost of envelopes must be considered as an additional expense of any mailing. Most consulting firms use their own envelopes for releases and may charge clients for exact cost or with a normal markup. Annual reports are usually mailed in nine-by-twelve-inch envelopes, most often custom printed for the purpose. In the design of any printed material unusual sizes mean special and expensive envelopes. It's infinitely cheaper to design for a standard size envelope.

There's really nothing to be said about postage, except that it keeps going up. Pre-sorted bulk mailing can help control costs, although there are no returns of undelivered mailings.

As in any corporate effort, labor is an element that must be calculated in any budget, from stuffing envelopes to maintaining mailing lists. Except if it's broken out separately for mailing list maintenance, it's usually incorporated in the total cost of mailing.

Most investor relations consultants, whether they use an outside mailing house or their own internal structure, are able to supply a rate schedule for reproducing and mailing material. It's best billed as a separate expense item. More and more, rising costs have forced investor relations consultants to adopt advertising and PR expense billing practices, and they now add a fixed percentage charge to many costs. That charge is creeping up from the traditional 17.5 percent to 20 percent or more. Faxes, for example, are now charged at $1 to $3 a page. Fewer consultants now rebill such expenses at exact cost.

Analyst and Broker Meetings

Large luncheon meetings can be the largest expense in dealing with professional investors in an investor relations program. It's simply the cost of lunch for any group of people. Most investor relations consultants hold meetings in good restaurants and private clubs that are normally familiar with serving group meetings, and their costs are readily predetermined. All reputable firms should merely pass on the cost of these affairs, with no markup.

A conference of investors can cost $8,000 to $10,000, and large video conferences can cost even more. Video taping can cost as much as $14,000 and up.

Expenses beyond the cost of meals and drinks are negligible, although they may include sound system and audiovisual equipment rental. Displays specially designed for meetings are usually arranged for with display firms, and are a separate expense.

The program may include visits by analysts, press, and others to the company's office, plant or other facilities. Normally, for an IR consultant to be present, the expenses involved are travel costs, housing, meals, and local transportation.

Major Travel Costs to Meetings

The cost of travel by executives to meetings held in other than their own cities must be calculated. A normal investor relations practice, designed to save expenses, is to arrange meetings to coincide with executive travel for other reasons. Thus it's sound practice to keep the investor relations consultant advised of out-of-town travel by management.

Out-of-Pocket and Miscellaneous Expenses

Normally, out-of-pocket and routine expenses include:

- Photography and art work
- Telephone, fax, electronic transmission
- Wire services such as PR Newswire and Business Wire
- News bulletins and other lettershop charges for stationery, printing, collating, postage (including return postage), and mailing
- Transportation
- Entertainment expenses for meetings with press, analysts, and so on
- Postage (including return postage)
- Messenger services, including air messenger services (Fedex, UPS, Purolator, etc.)
- Photocopier and supplies
- Subscriptions to trade publications
- Dow Jones and Reuters newswires
- Travel expenses, local and out of town
- Secretarial overtime on special projects
- Clipping services
- Miscellaneous minor expenses

Telephones, facsimile, and other means of communications are sometimes billed at exact cost, determined from both records and bills. The larger the firm the more readily available these records should be through effective use of easily available technology and accounting codes.

PR Newswire and local, state, and city news services usually charge an annual membership fee, and then a use fee, predicated on the distribution and the length of the material. For example, PR Newswire charges $100 for a 12-month membership, and for distribution to its entire U.S. list, $375 for up to 400 words, and $95 for each additional 100 words. It breaks down its list by states and some major cities, and charges accordingly. It now has a PRN Facsimile Service, which can distribute your release by fax to a pre-determined list at a very reasonable price.

Transportation expenses usually include transportation within a city, such as cabs, and so on, car rental, or use of one's own car. Travel transportation and expenses should be broken out and listed separately, especially air fare.

During the course of an investor relations program, it's frequently necessary to conduct business with members of the press and the financial community over lunch, dinner, or cocktails. These expenses are usually documented by receipts.

In addition to postage for regular mailings, there is postage normally used in mailing letters, fulfilling analysts' information requests, packaging and shipping quantities of background material, including Federal Express, UPS, and so forth.

Costs for messenger service are usually incurred within one city, although occasionally messengers must be used to transmit important material between cities. These expenses are supported by copies of bills from the messenger service.

Photocopying and faxing are usually calculated on a predetermined rate based on costs and personnel time. Broadcast faxing charges can add up quickly. There are now services that can perform that service at a small service charge.

In order for an investor relations firm to function, it must keep abreast of the industry of which its client is a part, as well as the trade press for that industry. Subscriptions to publications necessary for that purpose are normally billed to the client, at cost.

Larger investor relations consultants usually maintain Dow Jones and Reuters tickers, or Bloomberg services, to monitor news releases and other material of importance to the client. The cost of this service is usually apportioned to each of the consultant's clients. Ticker services are less necessary now, because Internet gives quick and easy access to the information.

The costs of travel—indeed all expenses in behalf of a client—are usually allocated on the same basis as determined by the Internal Revenue Service. This includes transportation, meals, hotel expenses, transportation within a city, auto mileage, tips, and miscellaneous out-of-pocket expenses, and so forth.

While normal secretarial and office services are considered part of a consultant's or company's own internal operating expenses, special projects frequently require additional expense, such as secretarial overtime or the use of temporary office help. Consulting firms normally include these costs in expense billings.

Clipping services charge a monthly fee plus a cost for each clipping. Clipping services are necessary to determine the extent to which any publicity issued by the company is printed. Unfortunately, no low-cost method has yet been devised to mechanize what is essentially a human job—scanning thousands of publications. As a result, the number of clippings received is usually a small representation of any material that appears.

In the normal course of a program, miscellaneous minor expenses are sometimes incurred. These include additional copies of publications, tips, phone calls made away from the office, and so on.

Contingencies

Even in the best planned program, circumstances frequently arise, often in the form of opportunities for special projects or activities. This may include an opportunity to participate as a panelist in a seminar, the need for a special brochure or pamphlet, and so forth.

While these occasions are normally unexpected, their value can sometimes be measured in terms of cost, and may be perfectly valid as additional expenses. It's a good idea to add 10 percent to the expense budget for contingencies.

Out-of-pocket expenses, for most programs, generally run from $1,00 to $2,500 a month, when the client and investor relations consultant are in different cities, and less when they are in the same city. The expense charges should adequately support the fee, in the sense that there are no savings in a large fee, if the expenses are stinted.

Granted the flexibility of expenses that tend to be variable, it's still possible to review a program well in advance and generally estimate what the expenses relative to that program are likely to be. This should make it possible for any company or experienced investor relations consultant to budget appropriately for the cost of the program. By frankly discussing expenses and expense billing policies with an agency during an initial interview period, budget shocks can usually be avoided. And in checking references, expenses should be one of the items to be queried.

The Public Offering

The investor relations process in a public offering is, to a large degree, a function of following SEC rules. Essentially, the rules are designed to preclude any preselling of the issue until the issue is out of registration. There are still a great many activities to be undertaken. The following is a checklist of the investor relations process for a public offering.

The success of a strategic investor relations program for an initial public offering depends to a substantial degree upon a meticulous process that begins well before registration. The pre-registration activities serve as a foundation for the first stages of the offering, and can frequently make the difference between successful and mediocre investor relations. This strategy is dictated by both competitive demands and the legal constraints in marketing a new issue, in which there are periods during which certain communications activities are restricted. To overcome this, a number of activities are necessary to build name recognition by the target audiences in the financial community, to make them more receptive to the financial message. It's also the time to start building databases and preliminary contacts that will be used following the registration. This is best done in advance, because it's an intensive and sensitive job.

Pre-Registration

As far in advance of the registration as possible, the foundation must be established for company recognition within the financial community, and the mechanism must be established for communicating with shareholders and the target investment audience. Name recognition by registration time can favorably affect the issuing price and facilitate syndicate enthusiasm, and enhance post-registration acceptance of the issue.

However, the target audience in the financial community—the analysts, institutions, and so forth—may not yet be aware of the company. To the extent that the investor relations program can accomplish this during the months prior to registration, an all-out effort should be made. This would consist of:

- *Developing a position*—a single objective and focal point that serves as the thrust of the investor relations marketing effort. It is a focused message that encompasses what you most want the target financial audiences to know, think or feel as a result of the investor relations campaign. It serves as the foundation for all marketing activities during the pre-registration period, and possibly beyond. And most significantly, it is drawn from an understanding of the target audience itself, and how it can best process the information in your favor.

  The most effective position is one that stems from understanding the needs of the market—in this case, the investment community—as they relate to your company, and then telling your story in terms of that market need.

- *Establishing name recognition* within the target audiences, using the position as the foundation for the message. This can be accomplished by:
  - A direct mail campaign to selected individuals and institutions, with company literature and reprints of business press articles.
  - Issuing material that includes limited but informative financial information. This could include a form of annual report.
  - Corporate advertising in the financial press.
  - Increased financial and business press coverage about the company and the industry, including case histories .
  - Press material on the industry itself, to show a context for potential growth of the industry, and by the same token, for the leading company in the industry. (This includes not only the jet time-share industry—which consists of only two major companies—but the entire private and corporate jet industry, and jet leasing.) The greater the understanding that the financial community has of the industry, the greater the likelihood that they will understand and appreciate the values of Executive Jet.

- *Establish a Web site* and electronic system. The sooner a Web site is established the better. If it is established too closely in time to the registration, the SEC might misconstrue its purpose. If it is established early, then it becomes a pre-existing communications factor, which is allowable even during the quiet period. The Web site must be maintained and promoted. Establishing the communications system—e-mail, teleconferencing capability, etc.—at this stage has the advantage of a training and break-in period, so that when it becomes a crucial means of communication, it's ready. This includes communication to not only the financial community, but ultimately, shareholders themselves.

- *Identify target audiences in the financial community.* This is the major first step, and a significant research effort. Based on the configuration of the offering, the nature of the company, the size and geographic distribution of the float, and other similar factors, appropriate targets must be identified and logged from a vast and rapidly growing universe of potential investors and investor advisors. There is a vast array of potential targets, from which must be gleaned those who are most likely to be interested in the issue, in such segments as:
  - Retail brokers
  - Analysts
  - Industry specialists
  - Institutions
  - Money managers
  - Traders and potential market makers
  - High asset individuals

Three Months Prior to Registration

This is a sensitive period, during which new publicity, advertising programs, and other activities that the SEC might construe as promotional for the issue, may not be undertaken. Nothing may be done that appears to be pre-selling the stock.

However, the company may maintain a level profile, in which any preexisting publicity and advertising activities may be continued. This is why the earlier activities are so important. For example, establishing a Web site at this point would be frowned upon by the SEC, while maintaining an existing Web site would not be amiss. All this assumes, however, that nothing be done to appear to be pre-selling the stock.

Sixty Days Before the Registration

Sixty days before the registration you are allowed to issue a press release announcing your intent to file, but you are otherwise in a period of virtual dormancy, in terms of promotional activity that might be construed as pre-selling the stock You can maintain existing marketing, sales, financial, and business communication. And while the announcement may engender press inquiries, responses must be factual and straightforward, with no discussion that might be considered promotional in pre-selling the stock.

The Registration Period

When the registration of the offering is official, a new quiet period of 25 days begins. And while public or financial outreach is precluded, there is an intensive amount of preparatory activity that must be undertaken. This includes:

- Issuing a press release at filing
- Preparing printed material and company report for brokers, analysts, and others, based on the prospectus
- Preparing for the road show, which, in the first instance, is set up by the underwriter, including:
  - Fact sheets
  - Multimedia presentation
  - Basic press material
  - Preparing management for presentations, including scripting and training (if necessary) and questions to be anticipated
- The basic investor relations program structure and materials must be prepared or upgraded, including:
  - Refining media and analyst list
  - Preparing disclosure guidelines
  - Coach internal team on disclosure (in conjunction with lawyers), analysts' needs
  - Create press kit
  - Write fact book
  - Review advertising options needs
  - Develop internal communications guidelines
  - Review release procedure, schedule
  - Prepare shareholder welcome letter, survey, guide
  - Design first quarterly report
  - Prepare strategy for using Web site and other electronic systems
- Develop strategic action plan and schedule.

The Strategic Plan

Essentially, strategy consists of choices and timing.

In the vast and growing array of prospective investors and investment advisors, there is a broad spectrum of individual and institutional preferences. Different institutions and managers, for example, have different investment approaches. There are hedge funds and index funds; funds specializing in blue chip stocks and funds that buy only emerging or low cap companies; funds that focus on industries and funds that focus on risk parameters. There are retail analysts and brokers, and special situation analysts and generalists. And as more and more money enters the market, not only do the numbers of investors proliferate, but so too, do the kinds of specialists increase.

Strategy, in investor relations, consists of determining the best array of institutions, analysts, brokers, and money managers that will benefit your stock, and then focusing the program to address their needs. Moreover, good strategic planning recognizes that needs and concerns change, and that feedback is important so that the strategy may be adjusted on virtually a real-time basis. Marketing's first tenet is to know your market.

And strategy includes knowing when to do what with whom. Timing, in reaching out to the financial and investment community, is crucial. It's dictated by a number of factors, including the needs of the company, the needs of the target group, and the exigencies of both the economy and the market itself.

There are times when a discussion with the manager of a hedge fund is appropriate, and times when that time is better spent with an analyst for a wire house. Strategy is knowing who, what, and when.

To that end, there's a great deal that can be done to identify and target prospective investors. Lead generation programs, advertising, market research, purchased lists—all contribute to focusing the investor relations effort to be more effective, and cost-effective, in identifying the most likely buyers of the company's stock. The more that's known about the market, the greater the likelihood of successful targeting.

Another aspect of strategy deals with a growing trend for institutional holders to vote their stock in the context of corporate governance. This means that the investor relations program must establish strong relationships with large holders who might be participants in shareholder actions. This is a function of intensive communications, and management's personal contact with large institutional holders.

Inherent in strategic planning in investor relations is to understand that the focal point is always the company's management. The company's numbers, and the company's plans, are relatively simple to communicate. The ultimate judgment of a company's potential success resides in the perception of management—its strengths, credibility, and skills. At the heart of all investor relations strategy, then, is to project these management qualities. This process must be carefully managed.

First Year Public

In the first year following the public offering, a great deal of activity is designed to keep the target audiences, including shareholders, informed and enthusiastic about the company's progress and the factors underlying the value of the stock. All segments of the target audience must be constantly informed, and constantly enthused, about the values and prospects of the company, in order for share value to continue to appreciate.

If the first part of any marketing effort is to understand your market, and then to understand your company in terms of the needs and opportunities of the market, then the second part of marketing is to choose your marketing tools, and then to manage them.

In investor relations, and particularly for an initial public offering, those tools consist of:

- Preparing and distributing appropriate information. This includes:
  - A basic fact book for the financial community and the press
  - Maintaining the Web site and other electronic media
  - Developing and distributing an analytical financial fact sheet
- Direct outreach to the financial community targets in major cities and throughout the nation, including:
  - Analyst group meetings
  - Individual meetings with major institutional buyers
  - Meetings with sell side analysts and key stock brokers
  - Teleconferencing
  - Distribution of printed and audiovisual material
  - Follow-up with analysts on a continuous basis
  - Meetings with market makers
  - Mailing information to regional firms
  - Planning meetings with buy side
- Publicity support, including:
  - Preparing press kits and other material
  - Seeking regional newspaper listings
  - Ongoing release of appropriate news
  - Major press interviews, including with wire services (Dow Jones, Bloomberg, Reuters, AP, etc.) and key business and financial press
- Develop and execute a program of shareholder communications, including Web site maintenance, interim reports, shareholder response mechanism, and informational mailings
- Begin annual report, depending upon timing of annual meeting, which dictates mailing lead time, which dictates design, writing, and preparation lead time
- Prepare for annual meeting, including writing speeches, preparing questions, preparing and distributing follow-up meeting report
- Consider Stock Watch program to monitor action of stock trading
- Measure program impact through market research

Appendix C

Private Securities Litigation Reform Act of 1995

While there are many laws and regulations governing the activities of public companies, the Private Securities Litigation Reform Act of 1995 and the Safe Harbor Act particularly affect the practice of public relations. The following memos, issued as EXECUTIVE ALERT bulletins by The National Investor Relations Institute (NIRI), and written by its president and chief executive officer, Louis M. Thompson, Jr., are particularly cogent discussions of these laws and how investor relations professionals can best function under them. The National Investor Relations Institute is a professional association of corporate officers and investor relations consultants responsible for communication between corporate management, shareholders, security analysts and other financial publics. NIRI is dedicated to meeting the growing professional development needs of the investor relations practitioner. Those who wish to have a copy of the complete law and the Conference Committee Report (which provides the rationale behind the legislation) may order directly from NIRI at 8045 Leesburg Pike, Suite 600, Vienna, VA 22182.(703) 506-3570. A moderate fee will be charged to cover reproduction and mailing costs.

December 29,1995

PRIVATE SECURITIES LITIGATION REFORM ACT OF 1995—AN
EXPLANATION OF THE NEW LAW
by
Louis M. Thompson, Jr.
President & CEO
National Investor Relations Institute

The Private Securities Litigation Reform Act of 1995 became law when Congress overrode the president's veto of the legislation during the week of December 18–22, 1995. Strong bipartisan support for the bill resulted in the first veto override in President Clinton's administration. Democratic National Committee Chairman and Senator Christopher Dodd of Connecticut, co-author of the original shareholder litigation reform legislation—along with Republican Senator Pete Domenici of New Mexico—held democratic senators in line for the veto vote—two votes more than the necessary two-thirds. The vote in the House was an overwhelming 319 to 100—29 votes more than needed for the override. Republican Congressman Christopher Cox of California authored the House bill.

The new law is designed to deal with the abusive practices committed in private securities litigation, including (1) the routine filing of class action lawsuits against public companies with no more evidence than a sharp drop in stock price; (2) the targeting of defendants with deep pockets who may be covered by insurance, without regard to their culpability; (3) the abuse of the discovery process by plaintiffs' attorneys who extort multi-million dollar settlements from targeted companies that want to avoid even more costly litigation; and (4) the use of "professional plaintiffs" by class action lawyers to facilitate their race to the courthouse in order to be the lead plaintiff's attorney and receive the largest portion of the lawyers' fees in the event of the settlement.

Additionally, the law provides a new Safe Harbor for Forward-Looking Statements to encourage companies to provide prospective information about their companies without fear of litigation so long as those oral or written statements are (1) identified as forward-looking statements and (2) are accompanied by meaningful cautionary statements identifying important factors that could cause actual results to differ materially from those projected in the statement. Obviously, those statements should be based on reasonable information and assumptions.

Reforms of the Securities Act of 1933 and the Securities Exchange Act of 1934

Section 101 amends the Securities Act of 1933 (33 Act) by adding a new section 27 and the Securities Exchange Act of 1934 (34 Act) by adding a new section 21D. These provisions are intended to return control of litigation to the investor plaintiffs who are most capable of representing the plaintiff class and to provide supervision and control of the lawyers for the class. Additionally, the legislation provides that all discovery is stayed while any motions to dismiss or for summary judgment are pending. This is intended to avoid the imposition of unnecessary discovery costs on the defendants until such a judgment is made.

Plaintiff Certification

The lead plaintiff must file a certified statement with the complaint showing that he or she (1) has reviewed and authorized the filing of the complaints (2) did not purchase the securities at the direction of counsel or in order to participate in a lawsuit, (3) is willing to serve as lead plaintiff on behalf of the class, and (4) will not receive a fee or "bounty" for serving as lead plaintiff.

Determining the "Most Adequate Plaintiff"

The new law is intended to stop the "race to the courthouse" whereby the lead plaintiff's attorney is determined on a "first come, first serve" basis. Now, the plaintiff filing the class action must, within 20 days, provide notice to the purported class through a widely circulated notice which must identify (1) the claims in the lawsuit, (2) the class period of the suit and (3) inform class members that within 60 days, the plaintiff filing may move to serve as class plaintiff.

The court, within 90 days after the published notice, must appoint the lead plaintiff. The House-Senate Conference Committee in its report to Congress stated the belief that increasing the role of institutional investors—who often have the largest stake in the company—in determining the lead plaintiff will benefit all shareholders and assist the courts in "improving the quality of representation in securities class actions." NIRI, in its work on the legislation, supported this concept. Obviously, it will behoove companies to maintain good relations with those investors.

SEC Chairman Arthur Levitt, in a speech two years ago in San Diego to securities lawyers, made the point that in the settlement of most securities class action suits, the majority of investors—including the institutional investors—do not participate in the class suing the company and, therefore, see their shareholder wealth being transferred to the small group of investors involved in the class.

Improvements to the Settlement Process

The section 27(a)(5) of the '33 Act and section 21 D(a)(5) of the '34 Act generally bar the filing of settlement agreements under seal. However the law provides that if either party shows "good cause" that publication of portions of the agreement could result in substantial harm to any party, those portions can be sealed.

Previously, plaintiffs' attorneys were taking as much as 35 percent of the settlement. Under the new law, attorneys' fees will be fixed by the court to a "reasonable percentage of the amount of recovery awarded the class." Moreover, the amount of the fees will be fully disclosed.

Requirements for Securities Fraud Actions

The new law adopts the requirement that plaintiffs must plead allegations of fraud with "particularity" (a standard adopted by the Second Circuit). No longer can plaintiffs' attorneys target companies which experience a sharp drop in stock price, file suit with vague allegations of fraud under Rule 10b-5 with the hope that companies will quickly settle to avoid additional litigation costs or, if not, that they can prove their case through a "fishing expedition" during discovery.

Now, the plaintiff must demonstrate that the omission of a material fact caused a statement to be misleading. "The complaint must state in particularity all of the facts on which that belief is formed." (Sec. 21D(b)(1)).

Safe Harbor for Forward-Looking Statements

In January 1994, NIRI was the first organization to conduct a survey of its corporate members to determine the extent to which frivolous litigation was affecting voluntary corporate disclosure. Our survey showed that half of our members said they were under increased pressure from senior management or legal counsel to reduce their level of voluntary disclosure and more than one third said they had bowed to that pressure.

Subsequent surveys by the American Stock Exchange of its listed company CEOs and the National Venture Capital Association, both of which represent a larger percentage of small to mid-size companies than NIRI, showed much more dramatic evidence of the effects of shareholder litigation on voluntary disclosure.

The difference between NIRI and the other organizations is that all the companies surveyed by NIRI have an investor relations person who would more likely be an advocate for more open disclosure. Moreover, NIRI members represent a higher percentage of large-cap companies with a long track record of open disclosure, in spite of the litigation threat. In either case, however, there was a clear need for a new safe harbor to provide legal protection for companies to be more forthcoming with forward-looking information so analysts and investors could better determine the future value of those companies.

The Statutory Safe Harbor

This provision adds a new section 27A to the 33 Act and a new section 21E to the 34 Act which protects certain forward-looking statements made by specified persons from liability in private securities lawsuits.

Definition of a Forward-Looking Statement

The following definitions are quoted directly from the new law:

"(A)   a statement containing a projection of revenues, income (including income loss), earnings (including earnings loss) per share, capital expenditures, dividends, capital structure, or other financial items;

(B)   a statement of the plans and objectives of management for future operations, including plans or objectives relating to the products or services of the issuer;

(C)   a statement of future economic performance, including any such statement contained in a discussion and analysis of financial condition by management or in the results of operations included pursuant to the rules and regulations of the Commission;

(D)   any statement of the assumptions underlying or relating to any statement described in subparagraph (A), (B), or (C);

(E)   any report issued by an outside reviewer retained by an issuer, to the extent that the report assesses a forward-looking statement made by the issuer; or

(F)   a statement containing a projection or estimate of such other items as may be specified by rule or regulation of the Commission."

To Whom or What Does the Safe Harbor Pertain

The Safe Harbor pertains to the following individuals or business entities:

(A)   issuer that, at the time the statement is made, is subject to the reporting requirements of section 13(a) or section 15(d) of the Securities Exchange Act of 1934;

(B)   a person acting on behalf of such issuer;

(C)   an outside reviewer retained by such issuer making a statement on behalf of the issuer; or

(D)   an underwriter, with respect to information provided by the issuer or information derived from information provided by the issuer.

NOTE: *The Safe Harbor does not apply to penny stock companies, forward-looking statements made in connection with a rollup transaction or made in connection* *with a "going private" transaction. Moreover, it does not apply to information included in financial statements prepared in accordance with GAAP; that contained in a registration statement of or issued by an investment company, that made in connection with a tender offer or an initial public offering; that made in connection with an offering by or relating to the operations of a partnership, limited liability company or a direct participation investment program; or that made in a disclosure of beneficial ownership in a report required by the SEC pursuant to section 13(d) of the Securities Exchange Act of 1934.*

Moreover, the Safe Harbor does <u>not</u> apply to a cautionary statement that misstates <u>historical facts.</u>

To Avoid Liability for Forward-Looking Statements

The concept of the Safe Harbor is based on aspects of SEC Rule 175 and the judicially created "bespeaks caution" doctrine. It applies to <u>both</u> written and oral statements. Both written and oral statements must be: (1) identified as forward-looking, and (2) accompanied by meaningful cautionary statements identifying important factors that could cause actual results to differ materially from those projected in the statement.

According to the Conference Committee report, "boilerplate warnings will not suffice as meaningful cautionary statements identifying important factors that could cause results to differ materially from those projected in the statement. The cautionary statements must convey substantive information about factors that realistically could cause results to differ materially from those projected in the forward-looking statement, such as, for example, information about an issuer's business.

"'Important' factors means the stated factors identified in the cautionary statement must be relevant to the projection and must be of a nature that the factor or factors could actually affect whether the forward-looking statement is realized."

The Conference Committee expects the cautionary statements will identify <u>the important</u> factors—not all of the factors that could cause results to differ <u>materially.</u>

An Alternative Analysis for Liability

The Safe Harbor provides an alternative means to analyze liability for a false or misleading forward-looking statement. A plaintiff may seek to prove that (1) the statement was made by a person with <u>actual knowledge</u> that the statement was false or misleading, or (2) that it was made by a business entity with the approval of an executive officer of that entity who had <u>actual knowledge</u> that the statement was false or misleading.

Oral Forward-Looking Statements

The Conference Committee recognized that it might be unwieldy to make oral forward-looking statements with all of the cautionary language. Instead, the **spokesperson may refer to "readily available" written information that contains the factors that could cause the results to differ materially.**

Duty to Update Forward-Looking Statements

The new law states that <u>"Nothing in this section shall impose upon any person a duty to update a forward-looking statement,"</u> This language was adopted so there was not a <u>legal</u> obligation to update <u>every</u> forward-looking statement that changed in some material way (such as, information in periodic reports to shareholders, management speeches, press releases, or forward-looking information displayed on corporate home pages on the Internet, etc.). The process of ensuring, based on a legal liability, that every forward-looking statement is updated could become a nightmare for companies and would probably have a diminutive effect on voluntary disclosure of such statements. In other words, we would be back where we started.

Yet, <u>we know that a company's credibility or that of a spokesperson can be severely damaged by the failure to update forward-looking statements that change in a material way, thereby leaving analysts and investors the impression that nothing materially has changed</u>.

Therefore, it is the position of the National Investor Relations Institute that while companies may not have a <u>legal</u> obligation to update material changes in forward-looking statements, <u>publicly-held corporations would be well advised, as a matter of good business and credible investor relations, to consider updating forward-looking statements to reflect material changes, to the extent possible</u>.

NOTE: *The courts have been somewhat ambivalent with respect to a "duty to update." However, the case law has been much less ambivalent when it comes to a "duty to correct." A "duty to update" presumes that a statement was correct or* *based on reasonable information or assumptions at the time it was made, but changes have occurred in the meantime that make the statement materially different, and, therefore, one incurs a "duty to update." A "duty to correct" presumes that at some point in time after a statement was made, a company discovers that the statement was materially incorrect. Therefore, it incurs an obligation, as soon as the error is discovered, to issue a public statement "correcting" the misstatement.*

Should companies "stand on the law" that there is no legal obligation to update and leave forward-looking statements hanging when material changes have occurred, the credibility of the "Safe Harbor" we have fought so hard to create will suffer greatly in the eyes of investors and could spawn new efforts to change this creation designed to provide more open disclosure to the marketplace.

Other Provisions in the New Law

There are other provisions in the law, such as improvements to the settlement process, "fair share" rule of proportionate liability, which affect mostly accountants and underwriters, auditor disclosure of corporate fraud and the inapplicability of Racketeer Influenced and Corrupt Organizations Act (RICO) to private securities actions.

Conclusion

The Private Securities Litigation Reform Act of 1995 represents the most substantive changes to the nation's securities laws since President Roosevelt, in his version of "A Contract With America," called for the creation of federal securities laws in the aftermath of the stock market crash in 1929. This resulted in passage of the Securities Act of 1933 and the Securities Act of 1934, creating the Securities and Exchange Commission.

While the new law will in some ways change the litigation landscape dramatically, it will not mean an end to private securities litigation, by any means. Plaintiffs' attorneys will have to bring more evidence to the table when filing suit. As legislative author Chris Dodd said in introducing his first bill in 1994, this legislation will place "speed bumps" in the path of attorneys racing to the courthouse to be the first to file. It gives judges means to return more control to the investors involved in such litigation and takes away the initiation of such suits by the lawyers.

The safe harbor for forward-looking statements will offer, particularly the small to mid-size companies in industries where stock prices are more volatile, a means for more open disclosure to the investment community. For those companies with established track records for open disclosure and strong relations with the investment community, the safe harbor probably will not change their lives that significantly.

Yet, whatever a company's style has been with respect to disclosure, <u>the new law and other disclosure issues</u>, particularly those related to a company's relations with analysts and portfolio managers, <u>cry out for companies to establish written disclosure policies where they do not exist today.</u>

Guidance for Using the "Safe Harbor" for Forward-Looking Statements Under the Private Securities Litigation Reform Law

by
Louis M. Thompson, Jr.
President & CEO
National Investor Relations Institute

PURPOSE: To assist companies in using the Safe Harbor provisions under the recently passed Private Securities Litigation Reform Law of 1995.

BACKGROUND: The Private Securities Litigation Reform Act became law on December 22, 1995 when Congress overrode President Clinton's veto of the bill. Corporations had only a few weeks before they were facing preparation of their earnings releases for the quarter ending December 31 and were trying to understand what the law called for. While NIRI, other organizations and some law firms issued explanations of the new law, there was virtually no guidance coming from any source for companies to use in interpreting what the new law called for under the safe harbor provisions nor a model demonstrating use of the safe harbor. Consequently, we have seen a wide variety of interpretations in the use of the safe harbor in earnings releases, annual reports and analyst conference calls.

The Safe Harbor for Forward-Looking Statements

This provision in the new law provides a "safe harbor" from civil litigation for companies that make prospective statements so long as those statements comply with certain requirements. While neither the courts nor the SEC have found in the federal securities laws a general disclosure obligation, beyond the filing requirements with the SEC, corporations often need to discuss prospects for corporate performance with financial analysts and investors to achieve a fair valuation of the companies' securities. This safe harbor should also encourage companies to put the kind of forward-looking information that they may feel comfortable in discussing with analysts and portfolio managers in public releases and SEC filings which are available to all investors.

The safe harbor is based on the court-developed "bespeaks caution doctrine," which in essence, holds that so long as a forward-looking statement is accompanied by sufficient cautionary language, even if the projection misses the mark, it would not violate the anti-fraud provisions of the federal securities laws.

In order to meet the safe harbor requirements under the new law, a forward-looking statement must be identified as such and must be accompanied by meaningful cautionary language identifying the important factors that could cause actual results to differ materially from those projected in the forward-looking statement. Statements that are immaterial or statements which the plaintiff fails to prove were made with actual knowledge that they were false are also covered under the safe harbor.

(1) The use of the Safe Harbor for Forward-Looking Statements should be viewed in terms of the "total mix of information." In other words, using the concept of the "bespeaks caution," the investor should be given adequate warning that the forward-looking statement involves certain risks that might cause it not to come to pass. Therefore, every possible contingency which could cause a projection to miss its mark need not be listed or stated.

(2) Even if the factor which causes the forward-looking statement to miss its mark is not among the risk factors cited, so long as there is sufficient cautionary language in the "total mix of information" to warn an investor that there are risks involved, the company could still be protected by the safe harbor.

(3) Boiler-plate warnings which cite a list of industry or economic factors that are not specifically related to the forward-looking statement will not suffice as meaningful cautionary language. **NOTE:** The SEC has seen numerous releases containing boiler-plate language with little or no direct relevance to the forward-looking statements. At this time, the SEC is not commenting on whether individual companies are in compliance with the safe harbor or not.

How Can Companies Best Use the Safe Harbor in Written Communications?

Most individual investors get their information from written corporate documents, e.g. press releases, quarterly and annual reports, management letters to stockholders, etc. On the other hand, financial analysts and professional investors not only get their information about companies from written corporate documents, but a substantial amount of information is disclosed orally in telephone calls and meetings by investor relations officers, and/or other company leaders with analysts and portfolio managers Therefore, the safe harbor has certain provisions for written statements and some different provisions for oral statements.

While technology, such as the Internet, is bringing various forms of corporate information, including SEC filings, within easy reach for individual investors, many do not have access to the Internet at this time. Most shareholder suits in the past were filed on behalf of individual investors, even though under the new law, a judge may determine the "most adequate" plaintiff to be an institutional investor. Therefore companies might be well served by making it easy for individual investors, in particular, to identify and understand the risk factors associated with forward-looking statements.

(1) Identification of Forward-Looking Information. Consider identifying the specific statements as forward-looking or placing them in a special section of the release, annual report or other written documents so they are clearly identified as such. Generalized statements in releases, annual reports or other forms of communication, such as, "Information contained in this release, other than historical information, should be considered forward-looking and may be subject to the following risk factors...." in essence say to an investor or analyst, there may be forward-looking information in this release, but you have to find it. There are releases in which this kind of language has been used which do not even contain forward-looking information! This is not what is meant by "clearly identifying" prospective information.

(2) Accompany Forward-Looking Statements with Meaningful Cautionary Language. The ideal would be a prospective statement directly accompanied by one, two or three of the most relevant points that the company believes could alter the statement. A "laundry list" of cautionary statements usually becomes "boiler-plate" information. Simply state the most important specific, meaningful factors the company.

(3) Be Careful When Preparing Written Statements in Relying Primarily on References to Documents Filed with the SEC for the Cautionary Statements. The PSLR law does not specifically provide for "reference to readily available" documents (those released by the company through broad means of distribution to the public or those filed with the SEC) in written statements. The law does provide this in oral statements, as discussed below. Remember that most individual investors get their information from corporations through written sources.

In either case investors or analysts should be able to read a corporate document containing forward-looking information and (1) clearly see that it is forward-looking, and (2) immediately see the cautionary statements regarding the factors that could cause the statement to change from what was projected. They should not have to refer to SEC filed documents to relate a specific statement in an earnings release, for example, with cautionary language filed in the MD&A in a 10-K, 8-K or 10-Q. While some may argue these constitute "readily available" documents, one may question whether these are "readily available" to the individual investor without a means for quick access in order to interpret a forward-looking statement.

Why not provide your company with greater protection and accompany a prospective statement with relevant, meaningful cautionary language? While there may be no harm in referring to documents filed with the SEC, there is nothing to suggest, so far, that this will provide much protection for companies. (Companies should, however, include important cautionary language relevant to projections or trend information contained in the Management's Discussion and Analysis (MD&A) in Forms 10-K and 10-Q or 8-K's filed with the SEC.) **In a nutshell, we are talking about communicating clearly with investors, not making them search for information or clarification about what companies are saying.**

Using the Safe Harbor in Oral Communications

The safe harbor for oral communications was developed in recognition that much of what companies communicate with analysts and professional investors is done orally—through one-on-one meetings, telephone calls, small or large group analyst meetings, conference calls with analysts and portfolio managers, etc. Therefore, one may assume that most analysts and institutional investors have ready access to press releases, earnings releases, and documents filed with the SEC (10K annual reports, 10Q quarterly reports and 8K current reports).

For example, in the case of a conference call with analysts, following the issuance of an earnings release that contains forward-looking information accompanied by meaningful cautionary language, the person conducting the conference call could merely refer to the newly issued earnings release for the caution language when expounding on the forward-looking statement or statements in the release. However, new information is discussed that is forward looking and considered material, that new information should be identified as such and the cautionary language relevant to that statement should follow. Moreover, if it is new, material information, the company should prepare a news release on that information and issue it immediately upon conclusion of the conference call.

In discussions with analysts and portfolio managers in one-on-one or small-group situations, when you get into projections of forward-looking information that is fairly obvious, a statement like, "We predict . . ." or "We project . . ." or "We expect . . ." should suffice as identification of forward-looking information. And most company spokespersons, when making those statements, will qualify them with those factors the company considers most relevant that could alter the results. While this process has gone on for years, what is new is that companies now have to pay more attention to the format of how they make statements.

Conference calls have become one of the primary means of communication with analysts and professional investors. While companies may think that the only people listening to the call are the invitees, think again. Reporters, for example, may be sitting in analysts' offices listening to the calls. On the other hand, some companies open the calls to individual investors and reporters using a "listen only" mode while allowing dialog only with specific invitees. In any case, companies should be realistic and view the conference call as a fairly open forum. Therefore, rehearsing the call is very important. The person conducting the call should be knowledgeable about what material information is in the public domain and what is not. They should know when they are breaking new ground with material information that will require the company to issue a news release immediately after the call.

Duty to Update

While the new law does not impose an obligation to update forward-looking statements, this does not mean that existing case law with respect to a duty to update has been superseded. In fact, the National Investor Relations Institute strongly believes that it is a matter of good business and good investor relations to update forward-looking statements that change in a material way. We believe that the credibility of the safe harbor rests on the willingness of companies to keep their material forward-looking statements updated to the extent possible.

Conclusion

One cannot expect corporate cultures with respect to voluntary disclosure to change overnight. The process of implementing the safe harbor will take time. Development of case law which will aid in interpreting the new law will also take time. Meanwhile, if your company makes forward-looking statements publicly, there is no protection in delaying use of the safe harbor. Some companies are in industries where the future is very uncertain, and they will tend to be conservative in making financial quantitative projections or may refrain from making

Developing a Corporate Disclosure Policy

by
Louis M. Thompson, Jr.
President & CEO
National Investor Relations Institute

Navigating the sea of voluntary corporate disclosure for many can be like sailing through uncharted waters. To get a better handle on the issues related to disclosure that confront companies, the National Investor Relations Institute (NIRI) conducted a survey in 1995 of corporate disclosure and communication practices.

The survey revealed a clear need for better guidance in a number of areas. Included was what needs to be disclosed, how and when information should be disclosed, avoiding the pitfalls of selective disclosure in providing information and guidance to analysts, and understanding the roles of the analyst, professional investors, individual investors and reporters in the disclosure process.

To meet this need, NIRI formed a task force on corporate disclosure issues with the able support and advice from an Association for Investment Management and Research (AIMR) advisory committee representing the analysts and portfolio managers. The task force developed the newly issued *Standards and Guidance for Disclosure*.

The NIRI survey also indicated that only half of the companies had written corporate disclosure policies. Yet, following passage of the Private Securities Litigation Reform Act and publication of the NIRI survey and the new *Standards and Guidance for Disclosure,* we have had numerous requests for examples of a written corporate disclosure policy.

While some legal counsel resist the idea of putting a company's disclosure policy in writing, others believe it brings structure and discipline to the disclosure process. Moreover, it provides all of those who have a direct or indirect role in the process, clear policies with respect to various disclosure issues. Generally, companies do not wish to share their written policies publicly. Therefore, NIRI has developed a generic, sample disclosure policy from which companies can draw ideas in developing their own. But, first, there are some general propositions companies may want to consider in developing a disclosure policy. They are as follows:

1. MAINTAIN INVESTOR EXPECTATIONS AT A REASONABLE LEVEL AS BEST YOU CAN. Tell the truth consistently even when it may seem easier to down-play bad news. Analysts and investors will develop a certain comfort level with top management as they come to rely on a company to adjust their expectations when there is reason to do so. Be sure, however, to make these disclosures on a broadly disseminated basis—not selectively. Avoid being overly optimistic on prospects for company performance. While there is generally no duty to update earlier information which was correct when disclosed, when events occur that cause the previously disclosed information to be potentially misleading, it is usually sensible to update the information.

2. KEEP THE MESSAGE SIMPLE AND CONSISTENT. Make sure all of those speaking for the company understand the information you want to disclose. It is important to be consistent in your disclosures. This applies to analyst meetings and other oral disclosures along with written disclosures such as annual and quarterly reports and press releases.

3. LIMIT THE NUMBER OF MESSENGERS. By limiting the number of authorized spokespersons, you are better able to maintain a consistent message and have more control over what is disclosed. Employees who are not authorized spokespersons for the company must know how vulnerable they make the company when they agree to talk only about what they know, but do not have the "big picture," or when they take comfort in talking on a non-attribution basis.

4. BRIEF THOSE HOLDING INDIVIDUAL OR GROUP ANALYST MEETINGS OR SESSIONS WITH PORTFOLIO MANAGERS. No matter how familiar the CEO or CFO may be with the company numbers and soft information, a briefing before such meetings will help ensure consistency in the message. Reviewing what the person plans to say may help avoid selective disclosure of material, non-public information.

5. DEBRIEF PEOPLE FOLLOWING DISCUSSIONS WITH MEMBERS OF THE INVESTMENT COMMUNITY OR REPORTERS. The Investor Relations Officer should be present at all company meetings or discussions with members in the investment community or with reporters. The IRO should be the person most knowledgeable of the company's disclosure record, i.e. the material information which has been publicly disclosed and that which has not. Therefore, if new material information is disclosed in such a meeting, the IRO can immediately issue a press release containing that information for full dissemination to the investment community. *If for some reason someone other than the IRO should hold a one-on-one meeting, the IRO should immediately debrief that person to determine if any new material information was disclosed during the discussion. If so, that information must be publicly released immediately.*

6. KEEP A RECORD OF DISCLOSURES. Maintaining a file of disclosure documents—SEC filings, press releases, management speeches, and analyst presentations—is fairly standard. However, some companies go beyond this and keep a file of brief memos-for-the-record of key questions and answers from oral discussions such as analyst calls or meetings. At a minimum, you should keep a log of analyst calls. Sometimes this record can be useful when reconstructing a situation in response to an inquiry by the SEC or the listing exchange or stock market. Some counsel say that these files are just one more item for a plaintiff's attorney to subpoena and, therefore, advise against them. This is a situation in which there are risks either way you do it. You should consult your attorney concerning your policy in this regard.

7. PAY ATTENTION TO THE SEC'S EMPHASIS ON DISCLOSURES IN THE MD&A (Management's Discussion and Analysis). In essence, the SEC has said that when management has determined that a material trend or development is significant enough to bring to the board's attention, it should probably be disclosed in the next quarterly MD&A. A list should be made in the MD&A of trends or developments that are "reasonably likely to have a material effect on the company's financial condition or results of operation." (SEC Release No. 30532, re Caterpillar, Inc.)

8. PROVIDING GUIDANCE ON EARNINGS ESTIMATES. The NIRI survey indicated that 69 percent of the companies always or usually review and comment on analysts' earnings projections or models before they are published. Another 21 percent say they do it occasionally. The NIRI *Standards and Guidance for Disclosure* discusses this subject in detail.

9. REVIEWING AND CORRECTING DRAFT ANALYST REPORTS. The NIRI survey indicates that 78 percent of companies always or usually review and correct draft analyst reports. Another 18 percent do so occasionally. If you do this, *review them only for factual information or the underlying assumptions. Do not embrace the soft information or conclusions.* Securities lawyers are not comfortable with this practice, saying they would have trouble demonstrating that a client company only reviewed a report for factual error and did not implicitly embrace the whole report. One called it "a slippery path downward." On the other hand, most companies believe that the legal liabilities are outweighed by the opportunity to correct factual errors before they become public and then have to deal with damage control in the aftermath. Moreover, in the view of most companies, this process enhances relationship-building between the company and the analysts and gives the company the opportunity to prepare to react to the contents of the report once it is published.

10. CORRECTING MISSTATEMENTS. A company generally has a duty to correct a misstatement or misleading statement it has made, but it does not have such a duty with regard to misstatements or misleading statements made by others unless the company was in some fashion involved in the misstatement or misleading statement, e.g., someone in the company had provided the information to the other person or in some way, directly or indirectly, led that person to believe the statement was true.

Suggested Contents for a Disclosure Policy

Based on the above propositions, NIRI recommends that a corporation develop a disclosure policy with the following key elements:

a. Prepare a generalized statement of commitment to a consistent disclosure policy during good times and bad.

b. Designate the authorized company spokespersons (their number should be limited) and their responsibilities. Those who are authorized to speak on behalf of the company should be in positions where they will at all times be fully apprised of company developments, e.g. if there are merger negotiations underway, they should be in a position to be constantly aware of their status.

c. Designate a Disclosure Policy Committee and a Disclosure Officer from that committee. The committee should consist of the chief investor relations officer, the chief financial officer, the general counsel and the chief corporate communications executive (if the latter is separate from the IR function). This Committee should be kept small so it can react quickly to developments requiring a material disclosure decision. It can also recommend to the CEO whether the company should respond to market rumors, what the various disclosure policies should be and what records of disclosure should be kept.

d. Instruct employees who are not authorized spokespersons that when analysts or reporters call, to refer them to persons who are authorized to speak on behalf of the corporation.

e. Prepare a policy with respect to the company's desired response to analyst projections and reports (See NIRI *Standards and Guidance for Disclosure*).

f. Prepare a policy on reviewing analyst reports when requested to do so.

g. Prepare a policy with respect to commenting on market rumors *(See NIRI Standards and Guidance for Disclosure and the disclosure section of your listed company handbook published by your exchange or NASDAQ)*.

h. Prepare policies with respect to providing guidance to analysts (*See NIRI Standards and Guidance for Disclosure*).

i. Prepare a policy regarding the provision of forward-looking information under the Safe Harbor contained in the Private Securities Litigation Reform Act (See NIRI Executive Alert, "Guidance for using the Safe Harbor for Forward-Looking Statements under the Private Securities Litigation Reform Law").

j. State how often the disclosure policy should be reviewed. As a minimum, it should be reviewed on an annual basis or if the company experiences a disclosure problem that necessitates a revision in the policy.

SAMPLE

COMPANY X DISCLOSURE POLICY

(Prepare a generalized statement of commitment to a consistent disclosure policy.)

Company X continues to be committed to providing timely, orderly, consistent and credible information, consistent with legal and regulatory requirements, to enable orderly behavior in the market. It is imperative that this continues to be accomplished evenly during both good times and bad and that all parties in the investment community have fair access to this information.

This disclosure policy confirms in writing our existing policy. Its goal is to develop and maintain realistic investor expectations by making all required disclosures on a broadly disseminated basis and without being unduly optimistic on prospects for future company performance.

(Designate a Disclosure Policy Committee.)

1.   The Disclosure Policy Committee shall consist of the general counsel, chief financial officer, chief investor relations officers, chief corporate communications officer (if separate from the IR function), corporate secretary and treasurer.

(Designate the authorized company spokespersons' responsibilities.)

2.   The Company X Disclosure Policy Committee must react quickly to material developments and make recommendations to the chief executive officer and meet as conditions dictate. The Disclosure Policy Committee will systematically review the Company's prior disclosures, SEC filings and other public information to determine whether any updating or correcting is appropriate.

(Those who are authorized to speak on behalf of the company should be in positions where they will at all times be fully apprised of company developments.)

3.   The investor relations officer and chief corporate communications officer is/are designated as the primary company spokesperson(s). Others within Company X or its operating units may from time to time be designated by the spokesperson(s) or the CEO to respond to specific inquiries as necessary or appropriate. It is essential that the spokesperson(s) as well as corporate counsel continue to be fully apprised of all company developments in order that they be in a position to evaluate and discuss those events that may impact the disclosure process, e.g. the status of any merger activities, material operational developments, extraordinary transactions, major management changes, etc. Company X spokesperson(s) shall continue to be integrally involved in scheduling and developing presentations for all meetings and other communications with analysts, institutional investors and shareholder, arranging appropriate interviews with

the Company management and responding to all inquiries from the public for additional information. After public dissemination, all of the Company's disclosures will be monitored by the Company spokesperson(s) to ensure accurate reporting and to take corrective measures, if and when necessary.

(Instruct employees who are not authorized spokespersons to refer calls to authorized spokesperson.)

4.   Employees who are not authorized spokespersons shall continue to be instructed to refer all calls from the financial community, shareholders and media to the persons authorized to speak on behalf of the corporation. (Existing relationships with the local press in areas where the company has subsidiary operations may be exempted from this referral requirement under written guidelines.)

(Prepare a policy on reviewing analyst reports.)

5.   With regard to responding to financial models or drafts of analysts' research reports, it will be Company X's policy to review for factual content only (not soft information) and to give guidance when <u>assumptions</u> have been made on the basis of incorrect data that render unrealistic conclusions. This review process will be conducted orally with the analyst and the draft report or model will <u>not</u> be retained if provided to the company. It is imperative that the control of this process continue to be centralized through the investor relations officer.

(Prepare a policy on responding to rumors.)

6.   So long as it is clear that the company is not the source of the market rumor, it shall be the policy of Company X to respond consistently to market rumors in the following manner, "It is our policy not to comment on market rumors or speculation." Should the (exchange or NASDAQ Stock Market) request us to make a more definitive statement, the determination to do so will be made by the Disclosure Policy Committee.

(Prepare a policy on commenting on analysts' earnings estimates.)

7.   It shall be a policy of Company X when analysts inquire with respect to their earnings estimates for the Company <u>(1) to acknowledge what the range of street estimates is and (2) question an analyst's assumptions if his/her estimate is out of line with current "Street" estimates or point out an error or errors in historical fact that the analyst used in making such an estimate,</u>

Should the Company determine during the quarter that earnings will likely be out of the range of the current estimates (particularly if earnings will likely be below the range), the Company may consider issuing a broadly disseminated press release, <u>followed by</u> individual or group calls to analysts and significant investors, explaining this and possibly the reason or reasons why. This would be done to avoid "earnings surprises" to the extent possible.

It shall also be the policy of the Company to observe a "Quiet period" two weeks prior to normal Quarterly earnings announcements, during which time there will be no comment-on analysts' earnings estimates.

(NOTE: A company may instead choose a policy of not commenting on analysts' earnings estimates at all. However, a 1995 NIRI survey indicates that only 8 percent of the companies represented in its membership have such a policy. Another alternative is to acknowledge what the range of estimates is but not comment further, i.e. Saying whether the company is comfortable with that range or challenging an analyst's assumptions as in the example above. A policy of simply acknowledging what the range is but making no further comment generally does not obligate the company to issue a preemptive press release should it realize that earnings will be out of the range of "Street" estimates.

(Policy on projections or estimates that are identified as forward-looking statements)

8.   It is Company X's policy to provide forward-looking information to enable the investment community to better evaluate the company and its prospects. The Company will make statements and respond to inquiries with respect to: (examples) revenue projections, income or income loss projections, pricing and profit margin trends, significant new product developments, projected demand or market potential for products or services.

If there is any question regarding the audience's or potential audience's understanding that these are forward-looking/prospective statements, the company will ensure that such statements are identified as forward-looking. Moreover, all statements will be accompanied by meaningful cautionary statements identifying important factors that could cause actual results to differ **materially** from those projected in the statement.

Company X will endeavor to update forward-looking statements which change materially to the extent possible.

9.   The Board of Directors should continue to be kept aware of all material developments and significant information disseminated to the public. Moreover, Board members and other insiders will be apprised of material developments which the company is not ready to announce publicly in order to avoid premature or selective disclosure or inadvertent insider trading.

10.   Company X has developed and intends to maintain a routine procedure for all corporate communications. The procedure consists of drafting a press release, circulating it for review to the members of the Disclosure Policy Committee, the chief executive officer and other officers as appropriate, alerting the appropriate stock exchange and disseminating the release through a national wire service and other distribution channels so as to effect broad dissemination to all public entities.

11. This disclosure policy will be reviewed annually by the Disclosure Policy Committee or as the need arises.

The execution of this disclosure policy will help to ensure compliance with the rules and regulations applicable to public companies and will help reduce volatility, improve market valuation, increase liquidity, increase Company X's credibility and enhance shareholder value.

ACKNOWLEDGMENT: *I wish to thank* **A. A. Sommer, Jr.,** *of Counsel with Morgan, Lewis & Bockius and former SEC Commissioner and* **Harvey Pitt,** *Partner with Fried, Frank, Harris, Shriver and Jacobsen and former SEC General Counsel, for their input in preparing this NIRI Executive Alert.*

Federal Securities Law and the Internet

When Spring Street Brewing went on the Internet to raise capital—to go public on-line—it opened up a new line of legal ramifications. Add to that problem the burgeoning use of the Internet to communicate financial information to shareholders and others, and there arises virtually a new branch of law—Internet practices under the Securities Act of 1933 and the Securities Exchange Act of 1934. These are the two major laws that govern securities and the rights of shareholders.

The SEC recently issued guidelines that reflect the growing use of the Internet and electronic communication. In its guidelines, the SEC recognized the growing significance of the Internet: "given the numerous benefits of electronic distribution of information and the fact that in many respects it may be more useful to investors than paper, its use should not be disfavored." The SEC considered electronic communication valuable because it "permits small investors to communicate quickly and efficiently with companies as well as with each other." Moreover, the SEC stated, electronic communication "enhances the efficiency of the securities markets by allowing for the rapid dissemination of information to investors and financial markets in a more cost-efficient, widespread, and equitable manner than traditional paper-based methods."

And as an overriding factor, the SEC further said that "information that can be delivered in paper under the federal securities laws may be delivered in electronic format."

As a practical matter, how do these guidelines translate into action for investor relations professionals? In an article written by attorneys Boris Feldman and David Priebe (© Feldman and Priebe), lawyers with Wilson Sonsini Goodrich & Rosati in Palo Alto, California (http//www.wsgr.com), the authors addressed ten key questions pertaining to securities law and the Internet. The article appeared in Vol.1 No. 4 of *Cyberspace Lawyer*. These questions and abstracts and summaries of their answers appear with permission of the authors. (*It should be noted that the following is not a legal document. It is for information only. For footnotes and clarification, contact the authors or discuss with your own lawyer.)*

1.   *Can my company sell stock to the public over the Internet without going through the public offering process using underwriters?*

The public offering process usually involves investment banking firms acting as underwriters. The underwriters solicit potential investors and determine the price at which shares can be sold. On the effective date, the underwriters commit to buy the shares from the company at the offering price (minus an underwriters' discount). The underwriters participate in drafting the prospectus to ensure that investment risks are adequately disclosed.

Private placements are exempt from SEC registration requirements under Section 4(2). The October 1995 Interpretation states that a public company may not include on its Web site offering materials for a private placement, where the investors have not already been located without a general solicitation. The SEC reasoned that such publication would be inconsistent with the rule against general solicitation or advertising in a private placement. Thus, a common type of stock offering that companies may conduct without registering the stock with the SEC may not be done over the Internet.

The Spring Street Brewing IPO made clear, however, that a company may conduct a public stock offering on the Internet, rather than through an underwriter. Spring Street Brewing also illustrated the use of Regulation A to streamline the public offering process. The October 1995 Interpretation explicitly states that an issuer may structure its offering "as one that will be made only through electronic documents." Nevertheless, a company should consider whether the assistance of an underwriter is desirable—for example, to help raise the desired amount of capital, to validate the company as one taken public by an investment banking firm experienced in the particular industry, and to help price the stock.

A company considering selling shares directly to the public over the Internet should be aware of potential liability from a statute that may not apply to the Company in an underwritten offering: Section 12(2) of the 1933 Act. Section 12(2) liability is not so restricted; it prohibits any materially false or misleading oral or written statement in connection with a solicitation to sell stock. In a typical "firm commitment" underwriting, investors purchase their shares from the underwriter, not the company. Several courts have ruled that lack of privity between the company and the investor precludes a claim that statements in the prospectus constitute a "solicitation" for Section 12(2) purposes. Such privity would exist however, if a company sold its shares directly to the public on the Internet. Thus, if a company conducts an Internet public offering through a prospectus posted on a Web page, and the Web page contains direct links to other information about the company, a disgruntled shareholder may attempt to hold the company liable under Section 12(2) for material errors in that information.

2. *Could our Web page be construed as "gun jumping" at the time of a public offering?*

The SEC imposes restrictions on publicity about a company during various stages of the public offering process. Prior to filing the registration statement, a company cannot offer to sell securities at all, absent an applicable exemption to the registration requirement. If a company makes public statements that condition the public to expect an offering or that arouse investor interest in the company, the SEC may construe the activity as "gun jumping" and delay the effectiveness of the registration statement. Once the registration statement (containing the preliminary prospectus) is filed, written offers to sell must be made using the prospectus; a company may not disseminate any other written information that could be construed as offering material. This is designed to ensure that investors make decisions based on the full disclosure of risks in a prospectus. After the offering has become effective, the sale of the security must be accompanied or preceded by a prospectus. For simplicity's sake, we will refer to these various types of prohibited offering-related publicity as "gun-jumping."

There is a danger that a company will be found to have engaged in gun-jumping because of information accessible on its Web page. The SEC's October 1995 Interpretation presented a hypothetical in which a company places on its Web page a copy of its preliminary prospectus, as well as a link to a research report on the Company located on a brokerage firm's Web site. The SEC concluded that such linkage would not be permissible: the link would violate the rule against gun-jumping by "provid(ing) the ability to access information located on another Web site almost instantaneously."

In another hypothetical, a company places its final prospectus and "supplemental sales literature" on its Web site; "both could be accessed from the same menu, are clearly identified on, and appear in close proximity to each other." The SEC said that the sales literature must be preceded or accompanied by the final prospectus, as would be required in the case of a paper prospectus. The SEC said that this hypothetical would satisfy that requirement, so long as the prospectus and the literature were in 'close proximity to each other on the menu": "[for] example, the sales literature should not be presented on the first page of a menu while the final prospectus is buried within the menu." This requirement would also be satisfied if the sales literature contained a link providing "direct access" to the final prospectus, enabling the latter "to be viewed directly as if they were packaged in the same envelope as the sales literature."

Based on those examples, other information on a Web page to which investors have "direct access" might be said to constitute a communication to investors during the quiet period, in violation of the rule on gun-jumping. The concern over gun-jumping should not be taken to extremes. Some companies use their Web sites for customer inquiries and service calls. Such companies should not be required to turn off those portions of their Web sites during a quiet period, any more than they would be required to ignore paper documents sent for the same purposes.

3. *Can our company's stock trade on the Internet alone, instead of on an exchange?*

For most people, public stock trading means trading through an exchange, such as the New York Stock Exchange or NASDAQ. In order to trade on an exchange, a company must meet minimum capitalization and other requirements, and agree to various corporate governance provisions.

Some companies may wish to avoid the costs of trading on an exchange by trading directly on the Internet. Even before the Internet, the SEC did not require companies to trade on exchanges. More recently, the SEC has given qualified approval to Spring Street Brewing to operate an Internet trading mechanism called "Wit-Trade". Wit-Trade is the only system on which Spring Street Brewing shares will be traded in the secondary market. According to a recent press release, Wit-Trade expects the system to be given final approval upon implementation of four steps suggested by the SEC to potential investors: the company will use an independent agent to receive checks from purchasers of the securities; the company will publish certain warnings on its Web materials; the company will disclose through Wit-Trade a complete transaction history showing the price and number of shares for each recent transaction, and the company will subject financial information provided through Wit-Trade "to certain SEC oversight."

Companies should be aware that there may be significant costs associated with trading outside the existing exchanges. The exchanges attempt to promote orderly trading of a company's shares. They also attempt to provide investors with a fair price for shares in listed stocks. On-line trading may be unable to provide those benefits. The exchanges also receive wide dissemination of stock prices in daily newspapers, which may be of value to investors not comfortable with the Net.

Deciding not to trade on an exchange may require registering with numerous state securities commissions. Most states have their own securities regulations, commonly known as "blue sky laws." Those laws typically require companies to register their stock in order to offer or sell shares in that state. Most states have an exemption from this requirement if a company's stock is traded on a national exchange or is listed on the NASDAQ National Market System. If a company decides to trade on the Net, it may not be able to trade in a particular state unless it registers its shares there.

4. *Do I need to file with the SEC information placed on our Web page?*

The answer to this question is no, unless the information on the Web page is also the type of information that must be filed with the SEC.

Public companies are required to file certain reports, such as quarterly reports on Form 10-Q, with the SEC. There is no general requirement that a company submit all of its investor communication materials to the SEC. For example, companies do not typically submit press releases to the SEC. SEC Regulation 8-K requires companies to file interim reports upon the occurrence of extraordinary events. Companies may benefit from filing such interim reports, because they provide constructive notice to investors of the information disclosed in them.

Even though companies need not file press releases or other non-mandated investor communications with the SEC, this does not mean that the SEC—or private litigants—will ignore those materials. The SEC has brought several enforcement actions against individuals alleged to have committed securities fraud by posting false or misleading investment information on the Internet.

5. *Is marketing material that I post on our Web page subject to the same standards as investor relations material?*

Investor communications are governed by the antifraud provisions of Section 10(b) of the 1934 Act and SEC Rule 10b-5. Rule 10b-5 imposes liability for materially false or misleading statements made with intent to deceive investors or with reckless disregard of the truth. Most shareholder lawsuits are brought under Rule 10b-5. The plaintiff asserts that the company and its officers issued false statements in order to entice investors to purchase the company's stock at an artificially inflated price. If the plaintiff can prove those allegations (and satisfy various other requirements), shareholders can recover the difference between the price they paid for the stock and what they would have paid had the truth been disclosed to the market In many cases, the damage claims amount to hundreds of millions of dollars.

The fact that a company posts a statement on a Web page, rather than issuing it in a press release, does not insulate the statement from securities liability. In the October 1995 Interpretation, the SEC stated that: "the liability provisions of the federal securities laws apply equally to electronic and paper-based media. For instance, the antifraud provisions of the federal securities laws as set forth in Section 10(b) . . . and Rule 10b-5 . . . thereunder would apply to any information delivered electronically, as it does to information delivered in paper." The SEC Interpretation appears to apply the same legal standards to Web pages as it does to other corporate communications:

> Electronically delivered documents must be prepared, updated, and delivered consistent with the provisions of the federal securities laws in the same manner as paper documents. Regardless of whether information is delivered through paper or electronic means, it should, of course, convey all material and required information.

6. *Does posting information to our Web page satisfy our disclosure obligations?*

The SEC has taken the position that posting information to a Web page does not satisfy a company's disclosure obligations, in those circumstances where a company is required to deliver information to prospective investors or shareholders.

In the October 1995 Interpretation, the SEC stated that "delivery of information through an electronic medium generally could satisfy delivery or transmission obligations under the federal securities laws." But where the 1933 Act or 1934 Act require delivery of a particular document to investors, the SEC has stated that a company does not satisfy its delivery obligation simply by posting the document on its Web site, because it is not proper to presume that everyone has access to the Internet. The SEC's test is whether :such distribution results in the delivery to the intended recipients of "substantially equivalent information" to investors as they "would have had if the information were delivered to them in paper form." The SEC looks to three factors. The first factor is notice: "the extent to which the electronic communication provides timely and adequate notice to investors that information for them is available." The SEC explained that if necessary a company should "consider supplementing the electronic communication with another communication that would provide the notice similar to that provided by delivery by paper." Thus, if an investor document "is provided on an Internet Website . . . separate notice would be necessary to satisfy the delivery requirements unless the issuer can otherwise evidence that delivery to the investor has been satisfied or the document is not required to be delivered under the federal securities laws."

The second factor is access. The SEC stated that "the use of a particular medium" to deliver an investor communication "should not be so burdensome that intended recipients cannot effectively access the information provided." The investor "should have the opportunity to retain the information or have ongoing access equivalent to personal retention." The SEC stated that if a disclosure is made available by posting on the Internet or on-line services, "the document should be accessible for as long as the delivery requirement applies." The SEC also noted that investors should be able to make paper versions of electronically delivered documents.

The third factor is proof of delivery. The SEC stated that companies delivering information electronically should "have reason to believe that any electronic means so selected will result in the satisfaction of the delivery requirements." The SEC suggested several means by which this proof requirement could be satisfied: obtaining prior informed consent to deliver a communication electronically; obtaining evidence of actual receipt by the investor, disseminating information through a facsimile; hyperlinking; and providing proof that an investor had used forms or other material available only if the investor had received the electronically transmitted information.

The October 1995 Interpretation presented several scenarios in which posting information on a Web page would not satisfy those requirements for mandated investor communications. Several principles can be inferred from those examples. First, "if consent (to electronic dissemination of information to a particular investor) is to be relied upon, the consent should indicate the specific electronic medium or media that may be used for delivery." Second, if an investor requests delivery by a particular form of electronic transmission, delivery by that form is effective. Third, any notice of an investor communication must, among things, make investors "aware of the availability and location of the electronic document." If a company decides to use an underwriter to conduct a public offering, the October 1995 Interpretation states that the underwriter may rely on a consent to electronic delivery of information supplied to the company by an investor.

For required post-offering disclosures, such as quarterly reports, the SEC has promoted electronic filing. Companies may now file documents with the SEC via an electronic database called EDGAR. The SEC has not, however, allowed companies to file required reports solely through posting on Web sites. Moreover, as of May 1996, EDGAR does not allow filing of audio, video, or graphic presentations. To ensure that the EDGAR version of a disclosure document does not vary from versions disseminated by other electronic means, the May 1996 Rules provide that where "documents delivered to investors or others contain material that cannot be reproduced in an EDGAR filing," the EDGAR filing must include a fair and accurate narrative description, tabular presentation or transcript of the omitted material.

7. *Does posting material information on our Web page constitute selective disclosure?*

When a company issues material information about its business, it must disclose that information to the market as a whole, not just selectively to favored investors. Tipping off some persons but not others about a major corporate development invites an SEC prosecution for insider trading, if it can be proven that the person doing the "tipping" had reason to believe that the person receiving the tip would use it to buy or sell the company's stock.

The SEC's use of the phrase "enhances the efficiency of the securities markets" invokes a central doctrine of securities law: the efficient market hypothesis. Under this principle, all publicly available information about a company is absorbed by the market and reflected in the company's stock price. In deciding whether a company adequately disclosed particular information, the test is whether the disclosure occurred by means that ensured that the information "credibly entered the market." If the statement "received only brief mention in a few poorly circulated or lightly-regarded publications," this requirement might not be met.

Given the SEC's position that the Internet is so widely used that it "enhances the efficiency of the securities markets"—indeed, that it offers a more equitable means of dissemination of information than "traditional paper-based methods"—a disclosure on the Web should satisfy the standard of the efficient market hypothesis and hence be regarded as disclosure to the market as a whole. This issue certainly will be tested in future lawsuits, as plaintiffs claim that information posted on a particular Web location was not disclosed to a place with sufficient circulation to ensure that it "credibly entered the market." Until the issue is resolved definitively, a prudent company should avoid posting material information only to its Web site without also issuing it in a press release or SEC filing.

8.   *Do I have any duty to update information on our Web page?*

Few securities law issues are as controversial as the duty to update. Many shareholder lawsuits are filed when a company's stock price drops following the disclosure of disappointing financial results. In such cases, plaintiffs allege that the company should have updated its prior forecasts publicly as soon as it knew that they would not be achieved. While this position has often been accepted by courts, it is not conclusively settled. The alternative view is that if a company chooses to issue a public forecast of expected financial results, the forecast speaks only as of the date it was issued. Under this view, there is no duty to issue a new forecast, based on new information, when the circumstances of the old forecast have changed.

The duty to update is particularly important in the Web context. The Web allows a company to post a great deal of information about the company and its products. If all that information must be constantly updated, companies will have to spend a great deal of time and effort policing their Web sites.

The SEC appears to have taken the position that the duty to update applies to information posted on the Net. The October 1995 Interpretation states that "electronically delivered documents must be prepared, updated, and delivered consistent with the provisions of the federal securities laws in the same manner as paper documents." The SEC further noted that "if an issuer posts electronically a preliminary prospectus on its Web site, the prospectus should be updated to the same degree as paper . . ."

These statements should not be read too broadly. They do not affirmatively create a duty to update; rather, they state that any such duty, where it exists, also applies to Web-posted documents. Moreover, the comments occurred in the context of discussing a document that requires updating in the normal course: a preliminary prospectus. The SEC's view, however, is likely to be given some weight by courts. To the extent that case law presently imposes a duty to update, a company should assume that the duty applies to information posted on the Web, until a substantial body of law develops to the contrary. A company may attempt to disclaim any duty to update information posted on its Web page; to date, the effectiveness of such a disclaimer has not been tested in court.

9.   *Do I incur any liability by providing links to other Web pages?*

Generally, persons can be liable under the securities laws only for statements that they make. In limited circumstances, a company may be liable for statements that appear under the name of others. This arises most often in 'the context of analyst reports. In many shareholder lawsuits, the only persons who had issued public forecasts about a company's expected earnings were securities analysts. To establish that a company owed a duty to disclose the earnings shortfall prior to its actual disclosure, plaintiffs typically allege that the company should be held responsible for forecasts in analyst reports. Plaintiffs attempt to prove that the company adopted or endorsed the analyst's reports.

The October 1995 Interpretation takes the position that a link allowing "direct access" from one Web site to another Web site, "provid[ing] the ability to access information located on another web site almost instantaneously," associates the two Web pages as one electronic document. In determining whether a company can be liable for providing a link to any particular piece of information on another Web site, the threshold issue is whether the manner in which the information from one Web site to another is linked provides "direct access."

One rule suggested by the October 1995 Interpretation is that direct access exists if the two pieces of information are accessible from the same menu or from an uncomplicated menu structure. In discussing access, the SEC noted that "if an investor must proceed through a confusing series of ever-changing menus to access a required document so that it is not reasonable to expect that access would generally occur, this procedure would likely be viewed as unduly burdensome." In a contrasting hypothetical, in which links to a prospectus and to supplemental sales literature were "accessible on the same menu," the SEC noted that "the existence of the prospectus and its location [were] readily ascertainable by the investor viewing the sales literature."

Two other hypotheticals suggest that the existence of direct access depends on the burdensomeness of accessing linked information. One hypothetical involved a mutual fund posting on the Internet supplemental sales literature and a prospectus. In that situation, the SEC stated that delivery of the prospectus could be inferred where an investor "would not need any additional software or need to take burdensome steps to access the prospectus and thus has reasonable comparable access to both documents." In a contrasting hypothetical, the SEC said that delivery could not be inferred where "Logistically it is significantly more burdensome to access" a document, "e.g., the investor needs to download special software before accessing the prospectus." Thus, one might read the SEC's position as holding that a company can be liable for providing links to information available on another Web site. This is an important factor that companies should consider in structuring their Web sites—especially if a duty to update exists, which would be hard to discharge for information on another person's Web site.

10. *How can I use our Web page to protect against a shareholder suit if our stock price drops?*

Instead of just worrying about incurring liability through a Web page, a company may use the Web proactively to protect against a shareholder suit if its stock price falls. First and foremost, a company should post its cautionary disclosures (whether made in SEC filings, press releases, or letters to shareholders) on its Web page. Shareholder lawsuits, after all, are about concealing adverse information. If a company has fully laid out on the Internet the risks and challenges facing its business, a claim of concealment will ring hollow.

Second, if a company decides to disclose forward-looking information—i.e., statements or forecasts about its future prospects—it should structure its Web site to take advantage of the "safe harbor" provisions of the Private Securities Litigation Reform Act of 1995 (the "Reform Act"). According to the legislative history of the statute, Congress created a statutory safe harbor "to provide certainty that forward-looking statements will not be actionable . . . if they are accompanied by a meaningful cautionary statement." If a company accompanies its forward-looking statement with a list of the risk factors that could cause actual results to vary, a plaintiff challenging the forward-looking statement "must plead with particularity all facts giving rise to a strong inference of a material misstatement in the cautionary statement to survive a motion to dismiss." The plaintiff also must plead the facts giving rise to a strong inference that the speaker of the statement had "actual knowledge . . . that the statement was false or misleading."

In the months since the Reform Act took effect, companies have experimented with a variety of ways to accompany forward-looking information with cautionary disclosures. The October 1995 Interpretation suggests that companies can use Web links to achieve this end, as long as the links provide direct access from the forward-looking statement to the cautionary disclosures, along with notice of the location of those disclosures. In explaining the requirement that notice of the Web location of a final prospectus must be prominent in any accompanying sales literature, the SEC said that such notice "should be in the forepart of the literature and clearly highlighted to make investors aware of the availability and location of the final prospectus." Based on this principle, a company should consider placing a notice of the availability and location of a link to cautionary disclosures in the forepart of any portion of the Web site containing forward-looking information.

An alternative approach is to place the cautionary language about investment risks in the forepart of the menu structure of the Web site itself. Spring Street Brewing has partially implemented this approach. The main menu for its Web site contains a table of contents posting links to topics about the company and its products. To enter the Wit-Trade mechanism on which the company's stock is traded, a user clicks on a page that bears the following disclaimers:

> Investing in Spring Street Brewing Company's common stock is speculative, involves substantial risks and should be considered only by persons able to bear the economic risk of the investment for an indefinite period of time.

> Spring Street Brewing Company developed and operates this stock market mechanism for the benefit of its shareholders. The Company's role in this mechanism is limited to facilitating transactions between parties that have agreed through direct correspondence to enter into a trade. The company does not

trade directly or indirectly in its common stock and nothing herein should be construed to mean that the Company offers to buy or sell, or guarantees any purchase or sale, of common stock.

This approach is consistent with the SEC's admonition that, where a prospectus must accompany supplemental sales material sent to an investor through the Internet "the sales literature should not be presented on the first page of a menu while the final prospectus is buried within the menu."

Third, a company should use multiple links to invoke the protection of the "bespeaks caution" doctrine. Under this doctrine, if a document contains sufficiently specific disclosures of investment risks to "warn potential investors [of the risks] in a meaningful way," a securities fraud claim cannot be based on the assertion that other positive statements made by the company ultimately proved to be inaccurate. A few courts have erroneously assumed that the bespeaks caution doctrine applies only to statements contained in a single document. Under that view, even if a company disclosed its risks in a recent prospectus or quarterly report, it would not be able to invoke those risks if a plaintiff challenged forward-looking statements made in a subsequent press release. The SEC's endorsement of links provides a powerful mechanism by which a company can use forward-looking statements posted on its Web site to accompany all of the risk disclosures accessible on the Web site. This would increase the probability that a court would find that a company's disclosures sufficiently apprised investors of those risks.

Finally, as a precautionary measure, a company should avoid linking its Web site to information from stock market analysts. If a company decides to issue forward-looking statements, such as earnings projections, it should do so in its own name and follow the guidelines of the Reform Act's safe harbor. If a company decides that it does not want to provide such information, it should avoid the potential liability that may result from linking to the same type of information from stock market analysts.

Appendix G

Computers

The rush in technology in these past few years has made it impossible to stay abreast of it all. The range of software for the average user alone is breathtaking, and never mind the breakthroughs in communication, the Internet, transfer of data, and the facility with which data can be interpreted and integrated with virtually any aspect of the decision making process.

One thing is sure—the option to ignore technology, to attempt to function in any business capacity without staying abreast of it, no longer exists.

At the same time that technology moves forward in communications and data processing, advancements in personal computer software seem to have slowed down. New versions of software in recent years have been either cosmetic—to pick up and correct flaws and bugs of earlier versions—or the result of business mergers. In application software, the winners seem to have evolved to just a few companies, although every so often a new product emerges to challenge the leaders. The market has matured to the point that there is no more easy entry to challenge the leaders. It may be easier, today, to start a new auto manufacturing company than a new consumer application software company. The advantage to the user is that obsolescence seems to be diminishing—little fear that the package you buy today will be obsolete by tomorrow. On the other hand, there is little innovation worth bothering with in the standard application programs, which really poses no hardship. There's not much more that you might want from the standard word processing or spreadsheet program than you already have. (This is not necessarily the case in heavy corporate programs.) There has been progress, though, in integrating applications, so that they work seamlessly with one another. Today, for example, you can buy a separate word processor, database program, spreadsheet, and personal organizer. But you are more likely to buy these products in a suite that contains all four or more, plus graphics capability. They then work either separately or together, so that, for example, you can transfer your database to your spreadsheet, or enter data from your personal organizer into your word processing document. This kind of facility is where the current software action is.

The raging breakthroughs, though, continue to come in the realm of the Internet and the Intranet. The growing use of the Internet is phenomenal. Virtually every business has its e-mail address and, increasing explosively, its Web page. E-mail and Web pages are almost as ubiquitous today as telephones, and will continue to proliferate. It's in this area that new software is emerging— programs that help design Web pages, that facilitate access to the Internet, and so forth. There's no doubt that the novelty—and there's still a great deal of novelty in the Internet—will wear off. Usage may or may not decline, but it will settle down, as the novelty wears off, to the same kind of usefulness that resides in other standard forms of communication, and the Internet will be an integral part of business and daily life.

The most fascinating growth, however, is in the *Intranet.* This is a variation of the Internet in which the connection is either internal—a dedicated net for a large company—or to specified partners, such as customers, brokers, and so forth. A company with customers on the Intranet, for example, may have an automated inventory ordering program, or some other kind of automated feed-back. This is where the pioneering work is being done in computers today.

It would be as easy as it would be foolish to predict what the computerized world of the twenty-first century will be. It will, indeed, be different. But pre-dicting its shape and texture at this point would be, as the English say, a mug's game.

Following are the leading PC software applications in use at this point. The list is by no means complete —that would be impossible. Nor does absence from the list imply inferiority. It just means that space is not infinite.

The choice of software is often as much a matter of experience as it is su-periority. Weaning oneself from the word processing program on which you learned, even if it's to a superior one, is like getting someone to depart from using a native language. Those of us who started with WordStar agonized when we switched to a WordPerfect, an AmiPro, or a Microsoft Word. But reticence is inherent in progress, isn't it?

No matter what program you use, look at the others, particularly if they have features that might serve you better. Try it. You may like it.

Applications

Microsoft Office 97 (Professional Edition). This is the ultimate automated infor-mation processing tool, of which Microsoft Word is merely one part. It inte-grates a database (Microsoft Access) a spreadsheet (Microsoft Excel), a table drawing tool, and immediate access to a bookshelf of literary tools. Its auto-mated features are overwhelming, from auto formatting to automatic spelling and grammar correction. It can automatically connect you to the Internet, send faxes and e-mail. It has a vast library of clip art built in. It is a total computing solution for the individual worker. Made for Windows 95 only, it is expected to be even more convenient to use in the forthcoming Windows 97. Lotus Organizer 97, either standalone or as part of Smartsuite, is probably the most versatile and comprehensive personal information manager on the market. More than just a calendar, it allows you to link to special anniversary, note, or address sections, and to autodial. It also has a dual calendar feature that allows you to keep both a personal schedule and a group schedule simultaneously.

Lotus Smartsuite 97 is in many ways as rich in capability as is Microsoft Office 97. At its core are WordPro 97, a successor to AmiPro but with different structures and capabilities; the spreadsheet Lotus 1-2-3, the database program Lotus Approach; Lotus Freelance Graphics, Lotus Organizer, and ScreenCam 97, which can record every on-screen click to reprint all screen activities. WordPro allows several people to work on the same document as group work, so that each can see what the others have done. It, too, allows rapid access to the Internet with all of its programs. It's a full service application.

Corel WordPerfect Suite 8 includes the latest version of the classic WordPerfect, plus the spreadsheet Quattro Pro 8 and Corel Presentations 8. It is full featured and integrated, and includes Internet access.

Lotus Notes remains the leading groupware program now used by thousands of companies. It brings all users in a company together to work as if they were in the same room. It communicates within the company, and sends and receives e-mail both within and outside the company. It is a mutual tool that brings a new work dimension into play—one that has never before been possible —one that allows people to work together on documents, plans, schedules, no matter how each is geographically removed from the others. More than almost any other application, Lotus Notes may be what the computer is about.

Symantec, another major software producer, specializes in service applications, with superior products. Symantec's Norton products are the leading—and most reliable—utilities in the field. Its AntiVirus program is one of the most effective available, and can be automatically updated on-line periodically. Norton Navigator simplifies functioning in an increasingly complex Windows environment, with sophisticated file management functions. The Norton Utilities are an absolute must for every computer. They completely tune up the computer, save accidentally removed files, and help recover data from damaged disks. Norton Your Eyes Only is a data protection program that includes automatic encryption technology that decrypts as the authorized user opens the file. Norton Healthy PC is a one-button PC checkup that pinpoints problems before they get out of hand. In the communications field, Symantec's pcAnywhere allows running a computer from a remote source. Two relatively recent Symantec acquisitions are ACT and WinFax. WinFax now includes speakerphone and voice mail capabilities. Act is the leading contact manager. Each contact is entered, including information about the individual or company. An autodialer is included, and followup directions can be programmed. It's invaluable for salespeople and professionals. WinFax is the leading faxing and communications software, with extensive features that cover and enhance every aspect of faxing, both sending and receiving. WinFax now includes speakerphone and voice mail capabilities. Internet FastFind uses all the Internet search engines to quickly access anything you're looking for on the Web.

Quarterdeck, which makes the excellent memory manager, QEMM 97, is also a leader in Internet tools, including WebStar, to set up multiple servers on the Internet; Internet Suite, which is a full range of Internet utilities; Web Compass, which facilitates navigating the Internet; and WinProbe, an excellent Windows 95 trouble shooter. Quarterdeck's CleanSweep is a remarkable program that analyses all your files, indicating which are redundant, which are no longer attached to an application, and which can be safely removed. It uninstalls entire applications. Quarterdeck's Fix-It attacks software conflicts and offers crash protection.

Micro Logic, which makes Info Select, the note taker and autodialer that's so useful and effective, has a new program called Disk Mapper, which shows you visually how your hard disk is being used. This allows you to consolidate and clean up programs, giving you more disk space.

McAfee, a pioneer in virus protection, now has a program called the VirusScan Security Suite, which combines every security component needed for complete desktop protection. It detects and eradicates viruses, encrypts and authenticates sensitive data, automatically backs up data, and downloads antivirus updates.

Touchstone Software produces a number of programs to keep the PC functioning at peak capacity. WINcheckit analyzes and optimizes performance and condenses unneeded files to free up disk space. PC-cillin 95 is a comprehensive anti-virus scanner that checks e-mail from the Internet. FastMove cleans files and transfers them to other computers.

Cybermedia has First Aid 97—an excellent computer protection program. First Aid warns in advance of any potential hard drive failures, and corrects a vast number of computer problems automatically. It will even search the Internet to find answers to computer problems, and to update itself automatically. Its Oil Change program updates software automatically, via the Internet, which is an extremely valuable utility.

Goldmine is an excellent contact manager that helps track contacts, with followup instructions and information. It has a built-in report writer, and offers direct access to the Internet.

Turbo Browser for Windows 95 manages files quickly and efficiently, and previews files for better management. It facilitates managing, archiving and cleaning up data.

Desktop publishing and Web page design become simpler, with three new programs from three different sources.

Microsoft Publisher 97 by Design is particularly useful for the non-professional designer. It performs a full spectrum of design functions simply and efficiently, producing everything from Web pages to logos and posters.

Corel Ventura 7 is the most professional of the three. It is capable of producing elaborate newsletters, and even books, as well as Web pages, logos, books, and brochures. Coreldraw is a separate graphics program that's probably the most useful and sophisticated now on the market. With this program, there is virtually no computer artwork that can't be designed and produced.

Adobe PageMaker is also a professional program for page layout. PageMaker is one of the earlier desktop publishing program, and is possibly the simplest of the professional programs to use.

Adobe, which is the leading name in typography, makes a number of useful graphics and imaging products. Adobe Acrobat makes it possible to read graphics files generated from other software platforms. Adobe Photoshop is a photo design and production tool to design and edit artwork. Adobe Type Manager supplies and manages a broad spectrum of typefaces and fonts.

Phone Disc puts more than a million residential and business names and address on CD-ROM, making access particularly useful. The information can be downloaded and used as mailing lists.

Timeslips Deluxe is a powerful time billing and income management program that's particularly useful for professionals and others who bill by the hour.

Win What Where is a time and usage monitor that keeps track of all aspects of the use of individual PCs.

Luckman's Net Commander includes more than 25 Internet applications, including a browser, document readers, utilities, and communications. Luckman's WWW Yellow Pages accesses more than 10,000 Web sites.

Intuit is noted for the most popular personal finance program now in use —*Quicken 7*—which is the standard in checking account, stock holdings, and other personal asset management. It now produces a finance program for small businesses called Quickbooks, which brings small business accounting within the realm of the nonaccountant. Quicken Financial Planner is a sophisticated financial planning program that, through simple interfaces, makes the process particularly accessible.

Netcom Netcruiser Plus is an Internet access kit that facilitates Internet access, with simple interface and effective Web browsers.

Softquad Hot Metal Pro 3.0 is a Web page creator that takes the user step by step through the design of a personal or business Web page. Its point and click interfaces make the process relatively simple.

Caere Omnipage Pro is the leader in the relatively new field of scanner software and optical reading of text. Scanners are now selling at reasonable prices, and text can now be scanned, entered into a computer, and edited. Saves a lot of typing.

Jian Marketing Builder is an interesting approach to marketing planning for the nonprofessional. It includes complete sales and marketing planning, implementation and analysis.

Forman Interactive Internet Creator is a Web site builder that uses point and click technology and other shortcuts to make Web site building simpler.

On-line Internet Providers

There are two approaches to getting on-line—the general network provider, and the dedicated on-line Internet provider.

The general providers include CompuServe, Microsoft Network, Prodigy, and America Online. They have a number of services in addition to the Internet, and are popular with both businesses and individuals. They all have e-mail. The choice should be based on the quality of software provided, the level of the services, and the accessibility by local phones.

Dedicated providers are too numerous to list. Choice should be on accessibility, outreach, and cost. Popular services sometimes get jammed with limited phone lines, causing long delays.

Publications

One would think that after several decades of the personal computer, instruction manuals would be simple and clear. Unfortunately, this is not always true—which is why the books produced to simplify using computer applications proliferate.

Most come from just a few good publishers, and some of their recent works are included here.

Special mention must be given to the work done by The American Association of Individual Investors, (625 North Michigan Avenue, Chicago IL 60611) which publishes an excellent newsletter, *Computerized Investing*, and the annual *The Individual Investor's Guide to Computerized Investing*, both of which are edited by John Bajkowski. The Association also issues the Guide on CD-ROM, as well as a CD-ROM of investment shareware, and a spreadsheet collection.

Among the more recent and useful computer books are.:

Office 97 Secrets. Steve Cummings & Robert Cowart. IDG Books Worldwide, Foster City CA 94404.

Word 97 Simplified. IDG Books Worldwide, Foster City CA 94404.

Discover Word 97. Shelley O'Hara. IDG Books Worldwide, Foster City CA 94404.

Microsoft FrontPage 97. Kerry A. Lehto & W.Brett Polonsky. Microsoft Press, Redmond, WA 98052-6399.

Excel 97 Secrets. Patrick J. Burns & Alison Barrows. IDG Books Worldwide, Foster City CA 94404.

Excel 97 Simplified. The Maran Family. IDG Books Worldwide, Foster City CA 94404.

Windows For Dummies. Andy Rathbone. IDG Books Worldwide, Foster City CA 94404.

Teach Yourself Windows 95 Visually from Marangraphics. IDG Books Worldwide, Foster City CA 94404.

More Windows 95 Simplified. IDG Books Worldwide, Foster City CA 94404.

Windows 95 Uncut. Alan Simpson. IDG Books Worldwide, Foster City CA 94404.

Windows 95 Secrets, 4th Edition. Brian Livingston & Davis Straub. IDG Books Worldwide, Foster City CA 94404.

Discover the World Wide Web. John Ross. IDG Books Worldwide, Foster City CA 94404.

The Internet for Dummies. John R. Levine & Carol Baroudi. IDG Books Worldwide, Foster City CA 94404.

The Web After Work for Dummies. Jill Ellsworth, Ph.D. & Matthew V. Ellsworth. IDG Books Worldwide, Foster City CA 94404.

Creating Cool Interactive Web Sites. Paul M. Summitt & Mary J. Summitt. IDG Books Worldwide, Foster City CA 94404.

HTML & Web Publishing Secrets. Jim Heid. IDG Books Worldwide, Foster City CA 94404.

Looking into Intranets & the Internet. Anita Rosen. AMACOM, 1601 Broadway, New York, NY 10019.

The Internet Roadmap. Bennett Falk. Sybex, 2021 Challenger Drive, Alameda CA 94501.

60 Minute Guide to Internet Explorer 3. J. W. Olsen & David D. Busch. IDG Books Worldwide, Foster City CA 94404.

Producing Web Hits. David Elderbrock, Jonathan Ezor, Laura Dalton, & Jed Weissberg. IDG Books Worldwide, Foster City CA 94404.

Excel for Windows 95 Secrets. Pat J. Burns & John R. Nicholson. IDG Books Worldwide, Foster City CA 94404.

60 Minute Guide to Netscape 2. Dennis Hamilton, Craig & Coletta Witherspoon. IDG Books Worldwide, Foster City CA 94404.

Netscape 2 Simplified. IDG Books Worldwide, Foster City CA 94404.

Compuserve For Dummies. Wallace Wang. IDG Books Worldwide, Foster City CA 94404.

MS-DOS 6.2 Upgrade for Dummies. Dan Gookin. IDG Books Worldwide, Foster City CA 94404.

DOS 6.2, Second Edition. Robert M. Thomas. Sybex, 2021 Challenger Drive, Alameda CA 94501

Word 6 for Windows Simplified. IDG Books Worldwide, Foster City CA 94404.

Discover Quicken 6 for Windows. Kathy Ivens & Stephen I. Bush. IDG Books Worldwide, Foster City CA 94404.

Corel Draw 7 Bible. Deborah Miller. IDG Books Worldwide, Foster City CA 94404.

Appendix H

Resources

Effective investor relations requires using a great many different resources for a variety of specialized purposes, ranging from the business and financial press, to financial information distribution services. It would be impossible to list here all of the resources available to the investor relations practitioner—the list is too long, and there are better sources of information and directories (most of which are listed here). Following is a broad sampling of the key resources essential to any investor relations activity.

Wire Services

Dow Jones News Service, 200 Liberty Street, New York, NY. (212) 416-2471. News phone: (212) 416-4008. **The Wall Street Journal Interactive Journal** (http://wsj.com) provides the latest stories in business, technology and more updated continuously on the Web. You can access the **Dow Jones News/Retrieval Publications Library**, and search more than a million articles from more than 3,600 business publications. Sign up on-line at http://wsj.com or call 800/369-2834. **Journalphone** (1-900-JOURNAL/ 1-800-4WSJ) uses a touch-tone phone to get current stock quotes and a stock market update. **The Wall Street Journal Guides** 1-800-581-9884— Easy-to-use primers that help take the mystery out of investing, taxes and retirement. **Dow Jones News/Retrieval Private Investor Edition** 1-800-522-3567 ext. 207. New, easy-to-use software.

Bloomberg Business News, Bloomberg Business Park 100 Business Park Drive Skillman, NJ 08558. (609) 279-4000. Fax: (609) 497-6577. Bloomberg Business News reaches the international investment community instantaneously via the Bloomberg interactive terminal. Major stock exchanges, including the New York Stock Exchange, the American Stock Exchange and

NASDAQ, all recognize Bloomberg as an acceptable disclosure medium under the SEC Rules of Disclosure.

Business Wire, 44 Montgomery Street, 39th Floor, San Francisco, CA 94104. (415) 986-4422. (800) 227-0845. Fax: (415) 788-5335. 1185 Avenue of the Americas, 3rd Fl,. New York, NY 10036. (212) 575-8822. (800) 221-2462. Fax: (212) 575-1854. Business Wire is a leading distributor of press releases and other news to the financial community, both domestically and internationally, including both press and brokerage firms. A timely news release on Business Wire is considered to be appropriate disclosure under the SEC Rules of Disclosure.

PR Newswire, 810 Seventh Avenue, New York, NY 10019. (212) 569-1500/ (800) 832-5522. Fax: (800) 793-9313. Computer: (800) 597-9701. PR Newswire distributes press releases to virtually every major news publication in the United States. A timely news release on PR Newswire is considered to be appropriate disclosure under the SEC Rules of Disclosure.

Reuters, 1700 Broadway, New York, NY 10022. (212) 859-1600. Home page: http://www.reuters.com.

Directories

All-In-One Media Directory, Gebbie Press, Box 1000, New Paltz, NY 12561.

Bacon's Information Inc., (Newspaper/Magazine Directory; Radio/TV/Cable Directory; Media Calendar Directory; Business Media Directory; Int'l Media Directory (W. Europe); MediaSource media software; New York Media Directory; California Media Directory). 332 S. Michigan Ave., Chicago, IL 60604.

Directory of Management Consultants, Kennedy Publications, Templeton Rd., Fitzwilliam, NH 03447.

Directory of News Sources, National Press Club, 529 14th St., N.W., Washington, DC 20045.

Editor & Publisher International Year Book, 11 West 19th St., New York, NY 10011-4234.

Executive's Handbook of Trade and Business Associations, Greenwood Publishing, 88 Post Rd. West, Box 5007, Westport, CT 06881.

MediaPRO Electronic Pitching Directory, Infocom Group, 1250 45th St., Emeryville, CA 94608-2924.

National PR Pitch Book, Infocom Group, 1250 45th St., Emeryville, CA 94608-2924.

New York Publicity Outlets, Public Relations Plus, P.O. Box 1197, New Milford, CT 06776.

O'Dwyer's Directory of Corporate Communications; Directory of PR Executives; Directory of PR Firms; New York PR Directory and *Washington, D.C. PR Directory,* 271 Madison Ave., New York, NY 10016.

Publicity Club of Chicago Directory and Media List, 11 E. Hubbard, #200, Chicago, IL 60611.

Radio-TV Contacts, The Ross Reports, 1515 Broadway, New York, NY 10036-8986.

Securities Industry Yearbook, SIA, 120 Broadway, New York, NY 10271.

Ulrich's International Directory, Reed Elsevier, New Providence, NJ 07974.

Washington Directory: A Guide to Public and Private Institutions in the Capitol Area, Columbia Books, 1212 New York Ave. NW, #330, Washington, DC 20005.

Washington Information Directory, Congressional Quarterly Books, 1414 22nd St., N.W., Washington, DC 20037.

Webster's New World Dictionary of Media and Communications, Richard Weiner, Simon & Schuster-Prentice Hall, PO Box 11071, Des Moines, IA 50336-1071.

Who's Who in Public Relations, PR Publishing, P.O. Box 600, Exeter, NH 03833.

Books

The Active Shareholder. William F. Mahoney. John Wiley & Sons, Inc., New York, NY.

Against The Gods. Peter L. Bernstein. John Wiley & Sons, Inc., New York, NY.

Business, Media, and the Law. Robert Lamb. N.Y.U. Press, 70 Washington Square South, New York, NY 10012.

Competing for Clients in the '90s, Bruce W. Marcus. Probus Publishing Co., 1925 N. Clybourn, Chicago, IL 60614.

Creating Shareholder Value. Alfred Rappaport. The Free Press, New York, NY.

Cyber Investing, Second Edition. David L. Brown & Kassandra Bentley. John Wiley & Sons, Inc., New York, NY.

Graham and Dodd's Security Analysis, 5th Edition. Sidney Cottle, Roger F. Murray & Frank E. Block. McGraw-Hill Book Co., New York, NY.

Handbook of Communications in Corporate Restructuring and Takeovers, Clarke L. Caywood, editor. Simon & Schuster, P.O. Box 11071, Des Moines, IA 50336-1071.

Individual Investor's Guide to Computerized Investing. 13th Ed. 1996. American Association of Individual Investors. 625 North Michigan Ave., Chicago IL 60611.

Investor Relations: Professional's Guide to Financial Marketing and Communications. William F. Mahoney. New York Institute of Finance, New York, NY.

The Investor's Anthology. Charles D. Ellis. John Wiley & Sons, Inc., New York, NY.

Jenrette—The Contrarian Manager. Richard H. Jenrette. McGraw-Hill, New York, NY.

Managing the Professional Service Firm, David H. Maister. The Free Press, 866 Third Ave., New York, NY 10022.

Modern Portfolio Theory. Andrew Rudd & Henry K. Clasing, Jr. Dow Jones-Irwin, Homewood, IL 60430.

The New Stock Market. Diana R. Harrington, Frank J. Fabozzi & H. Russell Fogler. Probus Publishing Co., Chicago, IL.

Professional's Guide to Publicity. Richard Weiner. Public Relations Pub., 437 Madison Ave., New York, NY 10022.

The Stock Market, 6th Edition. Richard J. Teweles, Edward S. Bradley & Ted M. Teweles. John Wiley & Sons, Inc., New York, NY.

Value Investing Made Easy. Janet Lowe. McGraw-Hill, New York, NY.

The Warren Buffett Way. Robert G. Hagstrom, Jr. John Wiley & Sons, Inc., New York, NY.

Webster's New World Dictionary of Media and Communications. Richard Weiner. Public Relations Pub., 437 Madison Ave., New York, NY 10022.

Writing with Style: The News Story and the Feature, Peter Jacobi. Ragan Communications, 212 W. Superior, #200, Chicago, IL 60610.

Periodicals

Better Investing, National Association of Investors Corporation (NAIC), 711 West Thirteen Mile Road, Madison Heights, MI 48071. (810) 583-6242 Ext. 304. Fax: (810) 583-4880.

Bloomberg Magazine, P. O. Box 888 Princeton NJ; P.O. Box 888, 100 Business Park Drive, Skillman, NJ 08558-2601. (609) 279-3000. Fax: (609) 2279-5967. Home Page: http://www.bloomberg.com

The Bond Buyer, One State St. Plaza, 26th Floor, New York, NY 10004-1505. (212) 803-8205. Fax: (212) 843-9614. Home Page: http://www.bondbuyer.com

Bondweek, 488 Madison Ave., 15th Floor, New York, NY 10022-5702, (212) 303-3300. Fax: (212) 421-7038. e-mail: lgoldbaum@aol.com

Business Week, 1221 Ave. of the Americas, 39th Fl., New York, NY 10020-1093. (212) 512-2511. Fax: (212) 512-4938. Home Page: http://www.mcgraw-hill.com   e-mail: morrisonbw@aol.com

Buyside Magazine, P.O. Box 1329, Sonoma, CA 95476-1329, 1055 Broadway, Sonoma CA. 95476-7404. *(707)* 935-9200. Home Page: http://www.streetnet.com e-mail: editinfo@buyside.com

CFO, 258 Summer Street, Boston, MA 02110.

Crain's Chicago Business, 740 N. Rush Street, Chicago IL 60611-2535. (312) 649-5411. Fax: (312) 649-5415. Home Page: ccbnews@aol.com

Crain's Cleveland Business, 700 W. St. Clair Ave., #310, Cleveland, OH 44113-1230. (216) 522-1383. Fax: (216) 522-0625.

Crain's Detroit Business, 1400 Woodbridge, Detroit, MI 48207-3110. (313) 446-6000. Fax: (313) 446-1687. Home Page: http://www. crainsdetroit. com e-mail: pnussel@crain.com

Crain's New York Business, 220 E. 42nd St., New York, NY 10017-5846. (212) 210-0277. Fax: (212) 210-0799. Home Page: http://bizserve.com/crains/ e-mail: 76135.3515@compuserve.com

Dow Jones Investment Advisor, P.O. Box 7930, Shrewsbury, NJ 07702-7930; 179 Avenue at the Common, 2nd Floor, Shrewsbury, NJ 07702-4804. (908) 389-8700. Fax: (908) 389-8701. e-mail: 75054.1777@compuserve.com

Dowline, P.O. Box 300, Princeton, NJ 08543-0300. (609)520-4000. Fax: (609) 520-4655. Home Page: httpp://bis.dowjones com

Equities, 160 Madison Ave., 3rd Floor, New York, NY 10016-5412. (212) 213-1300. Fax: (212) 213-5031.

Financial Analysts Journal, P.O. Box 3668, Charlottesville, VA 22903-0668. (804) 980-9775. Fax: (804) 980-3634. Home Page: http://www.aimr.com/ aimr.html e-mail: faj@aimr.com

Financial Executive, P.O. Box 1938, Morristown, NJ 07960-1938.10 Madison Ave., Morristown, NJ 07960-6096. (201) 898-4621. Fax: (201) 538-6144. e-mail: rcc@fei.org

The Financial Post, 14 E. 60th St., Penthouse, New York, NY 10022-1087. (212) 371-3088. Fax: (212) 753-4814

The Financial Times, 1 Southwark Bridge, London, England SE1 9H2, 011 44 171 873-3000. 14 E. 60th Street, New York, NY 10022-1087. (212) 752-7400. Fax: (212) 753-4814.

Financial Trader, One Penn Plaza, New York, NY 10119-0002. (212) 714-1300. Fax: (212) 279-3958. e-mail: Imontgomery@mfi.com

Financial World, 1328 Broadway, 3rd Floor, New York, NY 10001-2198. (212) 594-5030. Fax: (212) 629-0026. Home Page: http://www.financialworld. com e-mail: letters@aol.com

Forbes, 60 Fifth Avenue, New York, NY 10011-8802. (212) 620-2200. Fax: (212) 620-2417. Home Page: http://www.forbes com e-mail: 5096930@ mcimail.com

Fortune, Time/Life Bldg., Rockefeller Center, New York, NY 10020-1393. (212) 522-1212. Fax: (212) 246-3375. Home Page: http://www.pathfinder.com/fortune   e-mail: fortune@cis.compuserve.com

Going Public: The I P O Reporter, 2 World Trade Center, 18th Floor, New York, NY 10048-0203. (212) 432-0045. Fax: (212) 321-3805. e-mail: ipo@iddis.com

Inc., 38 Commercial Wharf, Boston, MA 02110-3883. (617) 248-8000. Fax: (617) 248-8090. Home Page: http://www.inc.com e-mail: editors@inc.mag.com

Individual Investor, 1633 Broadway, 38th Floor, New York, NY 10019-6708. (212) 843-2777. Fax: (212) 843-2789.

Institutional Investor, 488 Madison Ave., 12th Floor, New York, NY 10022-5782. (212) 224-3300. Fax: (212) 224-3171.

Investment Dealers' Digest, 2 World Trade Center, 18th Floor, New York, NY 10048-0179. (212) 227-1200. Fax: (212) 321-3805. Home Page: http://www.iddis.com   e-mail: idd@iddis.com

Investor Relations Magazine, 17 Battery Place, 18th Floor, New York, NY 10004. (212) 425-9649. Fax: (212) 425-7589.

Investor Relations Update , P.O. Box 2365, West Chester, PA 19380-0112. 716 S. Brandywine St., West Chester, PA 19382-3511. (610) 430-7057. Fax: (610) 430-0515. e-mail: 104135,351@compuserve.com

Investor's Business Daily, 12655 Beatrice St., Los Angeles, CA 90066-7303. (310) 448-6000. Fax: (310) 577-7350. News Phone: (310) 448-6373. Home Page: http.//www.ibd.ensemble com   e-mail: ibdnews@aol.com

Journal of Commerce, 2 World Trade Center, 27th Floor, New York, NY 10048-0298. (212) 837-7000. Fax: (212) 837-7130.

Nation's Business, 1615 H St., NW, Washington, DC 20062-0001. (202) 463-5650. Fax: (202) 887-3437.

The New York Times, 229 W. 43rd., St. New York, NY 10036-3959. (212) 556-1234. Fax: (212) 556-3815. News Phone: (212) 556-1726. News Fax: (212) 556-3690. Home Page: http://www.nytimes.com   e-mail: natnews@ nyt.com

Registered Representative Magazine, 18818 Teller Ave., Suite 280, Irvine, CA 92715. (714) 851-2220. Fax: (714) 851-1636.

Securities Industry News, 1 State Street Plaza, New York, NY 10004-1505. (212) 803-8200. Fax: (212) 344-0062. e-mail: editor@secdaily.com

Security Traders Handbook, 440 Route 198, Woodstock Valley, CT 06282-2427. (860) 974-2223. Fax: (860) 974-2229.

Securities Week, McGraw-Hill Inc., 1221 Ave. of the Americas, 36th Fl., New York, NY 10020-1001. (212) 5126-6148. Fax: (212) 512-3435.

Wall Street Letter, 488 Madison Ave., 12th Floor, New York, NY 10022-5702. (212) 224-3245. Fax: (212) 421-7038.

Wall Street Reports, 100 Wall St., 9th Floor, New York, NY 10005-3701. (212) 747-9500. Fax: (212) 668-9842.

The Wall Street Transcript, 100 Wall St., 9th Floor, New York, NY 10005-3701. (212) 747-9500. Fax: (212) 668-9842.

World Business, 65 E. 55th St., 35th Floor, New York, NY 10022-3219. (212) 909-5100. Fax: (212) 909-5087. e-mail: kpmgwbiz@kpmg.com

Worth, 575 Lexington Avenue, New York, NY 10022.

Newsletters

Bulldog Reporter, Infocom Group, 1250 45th St., Emeryville, CA 94608-2924.

Consultants News, Kennedy Publishing, Templeton Rd., Fitzwilliam, NH 03447.

PR News, 1201 Seven Locks Rd., #300, Potomac, MD 20854. (301) 424-3338.

PR Reporter, P.O. Box 600, Exeter, NH 03833. (603) 778-0514.

The Ragan Report, Ragan Communications., 212 W. Superior St., #200, Chicago, IL 60610. (800) 878-5331.

Ragan's Interactive Public Relations, Ragan Communications., 212 W. Superior St., #200, Chicago, IL 60610. (800) 878-5331.

Sid Cato's Newsletter on Annual Reports, Cato Communications, Inc., P.O. Box 19850, Kalamazoo, MI 49019-0850. (616) 344-2286. Fax (616) 344-4145.

Media Distribution Services

Media Distribution Services, 307 West 36th St., New York, NY 10018-6496. (800) MDS3282. Fax: (212) 714-9092.

Press Access, Inc., 120 Boylston St., Boston, MA 02116. (617) 542-6670. Fax: (617) 542-6671.

Financial Information Services

First Call Corporate Services, 22 Pittsburgh Street, Boston, MA 02210 (617) 345-2100. Fax: (617) 261-5627. A real-time electronic information system that transmits full text corporate news over the First Call network. Reaches First Call's 1,000 institutional subscribers. Service includes direct access to

First Call analysis comments, earnings estimates, and company fundamentals via a fully dedicated terminal dial-up system, or direct Fax.

The Bloomberg Terminal, 499 Park Avenue, 15th Floor, New York, NY 10022, (212) 318-2200, (800)448-5678. Fax: (212) 318-2080. Provides real-time pricing and data, history, news, analytics and electronic communications 24 hours a day through 50,000 terminals used by over 250,000 financial professionals in 80 countries worldwide.

Disclosure, A Primark Company. 5161 River Road, Bethesda, MD 20816. (800) 754-9690. Fax: (301) 951-1753. Home page: http://www.disclosure.com A full service financial research service and SEC data base, with access to up-to-date data on more than 50,000 U.S. and international companies.

Carson Group, 1790 Broadway, New York, NY 10019, (212) 581-4000. Fax: (212) 765-0808. *Capital markets surveillance:* Tracks ownership changes on a real-time basis, analyzing and interpreting security holder trends and developments as they happen, security holder information/task management system.

CDA/Bullseye, 40 West 57th Street, New York, NY 10019, (212) 484-3702. Focusing on ownership in street name, Bullseye's identification process provides an up-to-date snapshot of current institutional and beneficial owners, including share amounts and the custodian where shares are actually held.

Georgeson & Co. Inc., Wall Street Plaza, New York, NY 10005, (212) 440-9800. Fax: (212) 440-9013. A database system to integrate all the information describing institutional investors, including qualitative and quantitative information on institutional investors and insight into their governance voting policies.

Technimetrics Inc., 80 South Street, New York, NY 10038, (212) 509-5100. Fax: (212) 363-3971. International (Tel: 44-171-580-6462). Automates and simplifies IR communication programs. Segments and targets investor audiences, retrieves detailed information about investors, produces analytical reports, maintains extensive contact logs, manages mailing lists, and generates personalized letter and mailing labels.

Proxy Solicitation

Allen Nelson & Co., P.O. Box 16157, 1906 California Ave., SW, Seattle, WA 98116. (206) 938-5783. Fax: (206) 938-2072.

Corporate Investor Communications Inc., 111 Commerce Road Carlstadt, NJ 07072-2586, (201) 896-1900. Fax: (201) 804-8017

Georgeson & Co. Inc., Wall Street Plaza, New York, NY 10005, (212) 440-9800. Fax: (212) 440-9013.

D. F. King & Co. Inc., 77 Water Street New York, NY 10005, (212) 269-5550.

Kissel-Blake Inc., 25 Broadway, New York, NY 10004, (212) 344-6733.

Mackenzie Partners Inc., 156 Fifth Avenue, New York, NY 10010, (212) 929-5500. Fax: (212) 929-0308.

Morrow & Co. Inc., 909 Third Avenue, New York, NY 10022, (212)754-8000.

The Proxy Solicitation Company Ltd., 55 University Ave., Suite 1705, Toronto, Ontario M5S 2H7, (416) 862-8088.

Regan & Associates Inc., 15 Park Row, Suite 800, New York, NY 10038, (212) 587-3005. Fax: (212) 587-3006.

Index